Good Governance for Pension Schemes

Regulatory and market developments have transformed the way in which UK private sector pension schemes operate. This has increased demands on trustees and advisers and the trusteeship governance model must evolve in order to remain fit for purpose.

This volume brings together leading practitioners to provide an overview of what today constitutes good governance for pension schemes, from both a legal and a practical perspective. It provides the reader with an appreciation of the distinctive characteristics of UK occupational pension schemes, how they sit within the capital markets and their social and fiduciary responsibilities.

Providing a holistic analysis of pension risk, both from the trustee and the corporate perspective, the essays cover the crucial role of the employer covenant, financing and investment risk, developments in longevity risk hedging and insurance de-risking, and best practice scheme administration.

PAUL THORNTON is responsible for the Pensions Advisory team at Gazelle Corporate Finance Ltd. He was the Senior Partner of Watson Wyatt LLP and is a Past President of the Institute of Actuaries and of the International Actuarial Association. In 2007, he led an independent Review of Pensions Institutions for the Department of Work and Pensions.

DONALD FLEMING joined Gazelle Corporate Finance Ltd in 2005 to launch its Pensions Advisory business. He has also worked as a corporate financier at Cazenove & Co. (latterly JPMorgan Cazenove) and practised as a banking lawyer with Clifford Chance, specialising in securitisation.

Law Practitioner Series

The *Law Practitioner Series* offers practical guidance in corporate and commercial law for the practitioner. It offers high-quality comment and analysis rather than simply restating the legislation, providing a critical framework as well as exploring the fundamental concepts which shape the law. Books in the series cover carefully chosen subjects of direct relevance and use to the practitioner.

The series will appeal to experienced specialists in each field, but is also accessible to more junior practitioners looking to develop their understanding of particular fields of practice.

The Consultant Editors and Editorial Board have outstanding expertise in the UK corporate and commercial arena, ensuring academic rigour with a practical approach.

Consultant editors
Andrew Peck, retired partner of Linklaters
Mr Justice David Richards, Judge of the High Court of Justice, Chancery Division

Editors
Chris Ashworth – Knight Vinke Asset Management
Judith Hanratty – BP Corporate Lawyer, retired
Sally James – UBS Investment Bank
Vanessa Knapp – Freshfields Bruckhaus Deringer LLP
Richard Lee – Addleshaw Goddard LLP
Charles Mayo – Simmons & Simmons LLP
Gary Milner-Moore – Herbert Smith LLP
Tim Plews – Clifford Chance LLP
Timothy Polglase – Allen & Overy LLP
Laurence Rabinowitz QC – One Essex Court
Dr Pippa Rogerson – University of Cambridge
Richard Snowden QC – Erskine Chambers
Mark Stamp – Linklaters LLP
William Underhill – Slaughter and May
Dirk Van Gerven – NautaDutilh, Brussels
Sandra Walker – Rio Tinto

Other books in the Series

A Practical Guide to Private Equity Transactions
Geoff Yates and Mike Hinchliffe

Stamp Duty Land Tax
Michael Thomas, with contributions from KPMG Stamp Taxes Group; Consultant Editor David Goy QC

Accounting Principles for Lawyers
Peter Holgate

The European Company: Volume 1
General Editors: Dirk van Gerven and Paul Storm

The European Company: Volume 2
General Editors: Dirk van Gerven and Paul Storm

Capital Markets Law and Compliance: The Implications of MiFID
Paul Nelson

Reward Governance for Senior Executives
Edited by Carol Arrowsmith, Rupert McNeil

Prospectus for the Public Offering of Securities in Europe Volume 1: European and National Legislation in the Member States of the European Economic Area
General Editor: Dirk van Gerven

Prospectus for the Public Offering of Securities in Europe: Volume 2: European and National Legislation in the Member States of the European Economic Area
General Editor: Dirk van Gerven

Common Legal Framework for Takeover Bids in Europe: Volume 1
General Editor: Dirk van Gerven

Common Legal Framework for Takeover Bids in Europe: Volume 2
General Editor: Dirk van Gerven

Accounting Principles for Non-Executive Directors
Peter A. Holgate and Elizabeth Buckley

The Law of Charitable Status
Robert Meakin

The Business Case for Corporate Governance
Ken Rushton

Cross-Border Mergers in Europe: Volume 1
Edited by Dirk Van Gerven

Good Governance for Pension Schemes

PAUL THORNTON
and
DONALD FLEMING

CAMBRIDGE UNIVERSITY PRESS
Cambridge, New York, Melbourne, Madrid, Cape Town,
Singapore, São Paulo, Delhi, Tokyo, Mexico City

Cambridge University Press
The Edinburgh Building, Cambridge CB2 8RU, UK

Published in the United States of America by Cambridge University Press, New York

www.cambridge.org
Information on this title: www.cambridge.org/9780521761611

© Cambridge University Press 2011

First published 2011

Printed in the United Kingdom at the University Press, Cambridge

A catalogue record for this publication is available from the British Library

Library of Congress Cataloguing in Publication data
Thornton, Paul, FIA
    Good governance for pension schemes / Paul Thornton, Donald Fleming.
        p.   cm. – (Law practitioner series)
    Includes bibliographical references and index.
    ISBN 978-0-521-76161-1 (hardback)
    1. Pension trusts–Law and legislation–Great Britain.   I. Fleming, Donald.   II. Title.
    KD3132.T46   2011
    344.4101'252–dc22
    2011015790

ISBN 978-0-521-76161-1 Hardback

Contents

List of figures   *page* vii

List of tables   viii

List of contributors   ix

List of abbreviations   x

1 Introduction   1
   Paul Thornton and Donald Fleming

2 Regulatory and supervisory context for occupational
   pension provision   3
   John Ashcroft, Juan Yermo and Fiona Stewart

3 Pension funds and the capital markets   28
   Barry Riley

4 Social responsibility and fiduciary duties of trustees   48
   Paul Watchman

5 Good trusteeship   67
   Eddie Thomas

6 Conflicts of interest   85
   Ian Gault, Samantha Brown and Susanne Wilkins

7 The pension scheme in the employment package   104
   Wyn Derbyshire, Stephen Hardy and David Wilman

8 Employer support and the development of the sponsor
   covenant concept   119
   Paul Thornton and Donald Fleming

9 Establishing the funding requirements of pension schemes   134
   Martin Slack

10 Effective oversight of pension administration   151
    Avgi Gregory

11 Investment governance of defined benefit pension funds   173
    Roger Urwin

12 Hedging investment risk   187
    Dawid Konotey-Ahulu

13 Managing longevity risk   207
    Chinu Patel

14 The role of insurance in the occupational pensions market 224
    David Collinson

15 Pensions – a corporate perspective   246
    David Blackwood

16 A note on the investment management of defined
    contribution schemes   265
    Paul Thornton

17 Effective investment governance in defined contribution
    schemes   267
    Dietrich Hauptmeier and Graham Mannion

18 Inside pension scheme governance   289
    Simon Deakin

    Index   297

Figures

2.1	Perceived impact of key aspects on raising standards of governance	*page* 25
8.1	Key pension scheme relationships	120
11.1	Trustees' investment functions	175
11.2	Summary of the risk-budgeting method	177
12.1	Delta ladder – example	189
12.2	Deterministic liability rate analysis (un-hedged)	190
12.3	Deterministic liability rate analysis (hedged)	190
12.4	Liability profiles with inflation expectations (£ million)	191
12.5	Decay factor	193
12.6	Risk attribution report	197
12.7	Portfolio stress test	198
12.8	Rates and inflation – 2001–10	200
12.9	Real yield December 2003 – September 2006	202
12.10	Credit default swaps through the credit crunch	203
12.11	Inflation risk hedged	204
13.1	FTSE 100: attribution of pension risk	208
13.2	Longevity swap	218
14.1	Transaction volumes in the pension insurance market	227
14.2	What is a buy-in?	229
14.3	What is a buy-out?	231
14.4	Pension fund: risk breakdown	234
14.5	Insurance company: risk breakdown	234
14.6	Typical insurance quotation process	241
14.7	Typical sequence of events: policy signing to issuing individual policies	244
15.1	Representation of the 'economic' balance sheet (I)	247
15.2	Representation of the 'economic' balance sheet (II)	251
15.3	Pension scheme projected nominal cash flows by year	254
15.4	Asset/liability planned migration	257
15.5	Example VaR analysis	258

Tables

2.1   TPR 2009 Scheme Governance Survey   *page* 26
3.1   Beneficial ownership of UK equities 1963–2008 (%)   30
3.2   Average UK pension fund investment strategy across major
     asset classes   35
3.3   UK self-administered pension funds net investment in equities
     (£ billion)   40
3.4   Yale Endowment Fund annual return on assets (%)   43
3.5   Yale Endowment Fund asset allocation at the peak value of
     $22.8 billion in June 2008 (%)   44
10.1 Advantages and disadvantages of in-house and outsourced
     administration   157
10.2 Example of a complaints log   168
10.3 Risks related to administration matters   169
12.1 Sample asset and liability breakdown report (analysis of VaR
     stemming from each area of the scheme's assets and liabilities)   195
12.2 Sample asset and liability breakdown report (different types of
     VaR within a pension scheme's portfolio)   196
15.1 Basic facts – closed scheme   251
17.1 Categories of target consumer characteristics relevant for DC
     investment governance   271
17.2 Key activities and parties involved in trust-based and
     contract-based plans   288

Contributors

PAUL THORNTON OBE, Chairman, and Donald Fleming, Managing Director, Pensions Advisory, Gazelle Corporate Finance

JOHN ASHCROFT, formerly Director of Strategy at The Pensions Regulator and past Chairman of the International Organisation of Pension Supervisors, Juan Yermo, Head of the Private Pensions Unit, OECD, Fiona Stewart, Secretariat, International Organisation of Pension Supervisors

BARRY RILEY, former *Financial Times* columnist

PAUL WATCHMAN, formerly Freshfields Bruckhaus Deringer LLP

EDDIE THOMAS, Director, Law Debenture Pension Trust Corporation plc

IAN GAULT, Head of the Pensions Group, Samantha Brown, Senior Associate and Susanne Wilkins, Professional Support Lawyer, Herbert Smith LLP

WYN DERBYSHIRE, Partner, Stephen Hardy, Barrister specialising in employment law, and David Wilman, Associate, SJ Berwin LLP

MARTIN SLACK, Partner, Lane Clark & Peacock LLP

AVGI GREGORY, Director, Muse Advisory

ROGER URWIN, Global Head of Investment Content, Towers Watson

DAWID KONOTEY-AHULU, Co-Chief Executive, Redington

CHINU PATEL, formerly Senior Consultant, Watson Wyatt

DAVID COLLINSON, Co-Head of Business Origination, Pension Corporation

DAVID BLACKWOOD, Group Finance Director, Yule Catto & Co plc

DIETRICH HAUPTMEIER, Associate Principal Palamon Capital, and Graham Mannion, Managing Director, DCisions, formerly PensionDCisions

PROFESSOR SIMON DEAKIN, Professor of Law, Faculty of Law and Centre for Business Research, University of Cambridge

Abbreviations

ABO	Accrued Benefit Obligation
ACAS	Advisory, Conciliation and Arbitration Service
ALM	asset liability modelling
AMWG	Asset Management Working Group
bp	basis point
CAGR	compound average growth rate
CEIOPS	Committee for European Insurance and Occupational Pensions Supervisors
CEO	Chief Executive Officer
CIO	Chief Investment Officer
CMI	Continuous Mortality Investigation
CND	Company Nominated Director
CSA	Credit Support Annex
DB	defined benefit
DC	defined contribution
DWP	Department of Work and Pensions
EBITDA	Earnings Before Interest, Tax, Depreciation and Amortisation
EDM	electronic document management
EHTV	Enhanced Transfer Value
EIOPA	European Insurance and Occupational Pensions Authority
ERISA	Employee Retirement Income Security Act 1974
ESG	Environmental, Social and Governance
EU	European Union
EV	enterprise value
FRC	Financial Review Council
FRS	Financial Reporting Standard
FSA	Financial Services Authority
FSCS	Financial Services Compensation Scheme
FTSE	Financial Times and London Stock Exchange
GLM	generalised linear model
GMP	Guaranteed Minimum Pension
HMRC	HM Revenue & Customs

HR	human resources
IAS	International Accounting Standard
IFSL	International Finance Services London
IGG	Investment Governance Group
IMF	International Monetary Fund
IMSDG	Investment Management STP Development Group
IOPS	International Organisation of Pension Supervisors
IORP	institutions for occupational retirement provision
IR	interest rate
ISDA	International Swaps and Derivatives Association
IT	information technology
ITT	invitation to tender
LDI	Liability Driven Investing
LPI	limited price indexation
M&A	mergers and acquisitions
MFR	Minimum Funding Requirement
MND	Member Nominated Director
NEST	National Employment Savings Trust
NHS	National Health Service
NPD	normal pension date
OECD	Organisation for Economic Cooperation and Development
OM	operating model
OPRA	Occupational Pensions Regulatory Authority
PBO	Project Benefit Obligation
PMI	Pensions Management Institute
PPF	Pension Protection Fund
PR	public relations
PRI	Principles of Responsible Investment
QPA	Qualification in Pension Administration
RFI	request for information
RPI	Retail Price Index
SAPS	self-administered pension scheme
SEC	Securities Exchange Commission
SIP	statement of investment principles
SLA	service level agreement
SPV	special purpose vehicle
SSAP	Statement of Standard Accountancy Practice
STP	straight through processing
SWIFT	Society for Worldwide Interbank Financial Telecommunication
TKU	trustee knowledge and understanding
TPA	third-party administrator
TPAS	The Pensions Advisory Service
TPR	The Pensions Regulator
TUPE	Transfer of Undertakings Protection of Employment

UK	United Kingdom
UN	United Nations
US DOL	US Department of Labor
VaR	Value-at-Risk

1
Introduction

PAUL THORNTON AND DONALD FLEMING

This book has been written to bring together the thinking of leading practitioners in the field of pensions in order to provide an overview of what constitutes
good governance for pension schemes. As the closing chapter indicates, the
concept of pension scheme governance is something that has been changing
considerably in recent years and will no doubt continue to evolve in the future.
The aim of this book is to set out what is current best practice at the time of
writing, in late 2010.

The book begins by setting the subject in context in Chapter 2. Whilst
pension schemes in the United Kingdom have evolved in a particular way, the
underlying issues of sound provision of private sector pensions are not unique
to one country, and governments around the world are concerned with effective regulation and supervision of schemes.

Chapter 3 explains how pension schemes are inextricably involved in the
capital markets and both affect and are affected by market trends.

This leads on, in Chapter 4, to the question of what social and fiduciary
responsibilities are owed by the trustees of pension schemes.

The book moves on in Chapter 5 to the practicalities of good trusteeship,
and then the issue of conflict of interest in Chapter 6, which has become of
significant concern.

Pension schemes are undertaken by employers as part of a remuneration
package, and Chapter 7 explores the tri-angular relationship between the
pension scheme itself, the members and their employer, who is also the sponsor of the scheme.

Chapter 8 explores changing relationships with other parties and the nature
of the employer support for the scheme, or employer covenant as it has become
known. This leads on to the financing requirements of schemes and how they
are set in Chapter 9.

Effective administration of the scheme is vital and Chapter 10 sets out best
practice.

Risk manifests itself in many forms, and the Chapters 11 to 14 deal with
how investment risk is managed and hedged, how longevity risk can be hedged
and how the insurance market can be used for de-risking.

All of this is viewed from the perspective of the pension scheme itself, so Chapter 15 examines pension risk from the employer's end of the telescope.

Much of the book's emphasis is on defined benefit schemes, but as such schemes are being progressively closed to future entrants, and then to future accrual, it is necessary to consider the governance issues in the defined contribution schemes which typically replace them, and this is covered in Chapters 16 and 17.

Finally, Chapter 18 draws some threads together.

Our hope is that by bringing together the combined wisdom and experience of leading practitioners across a range of relevant topics, we will enable the reader to see pension scheme governance in the round and will enable them to play whatever part they may have in fulfilment of the best principles of good governance.

2
Regulatory and supervisory context for occupational pension provision

JOHN ASHCROFT, JUAN YERMO AND FIONA STEWART

Fundamental concepts

This chapter aims to place the discussions that follow within the context of the regulation and supervision of pension scheme governance. It starts with a brief overview of the development of and fundamental differences between private pension systems and their regulation and supervision across the world, including the development of risk-based regulation and supervision. The chapter then considers what constitutes good pension scheme governance and the main weaknesses and challenges relating to it. The chapter goes on, drawing on Organisation for Economic Cooperation and Development (OECD) and International Organisation of Pension Supervisors (IOPS) guidance, to highlight ways in which regulation can promote better governance and how supervisory authorities undertake their oversight of governance arrangements. Finally, the chapter outlines the United Kingdom's regulatory and supervisory framework and its application to governance.

It is first worth clarifying terminology. In the OECD's taxonomy, a *pension plan* comprises the promise of benefits to the members, while a *pension fund* comprises the portfolio of assets held to finance the promised benefits. The entity responsible for the governance of the assets and administration of the fund is also referred to as a pension fund, although this may be a part of or supplied by a larger organisation, the *pension provider*. In the United Kingdom, however, the plan and fund taken together are commonly referred to as a *pension scheme*.

This chapter covers pension *regulation*, the legal framework and rules that govern the design of pension plans and management of pension funds, and pension *supervision*, the enforcement by one or more authorities of such regulation.

The development of private pensions, their regulation and supervision

For over 100 years employers in developed countries have established and funded pension plans for their employees, to improve financial security in old age and as a means of deferring employee compensation. Governments have increasingly valued occupational pensions as a means of complementing state-financed retirement benefits and have provided tax incentives. These incentives commonly extend to private pension products sold to individuals by commercial financial services companies – a market that has grown rapidly over the last few decades. Hence we see the OECD (and EU) three-pillar model: (1) state-financed benefits complemented by (2) occupational pensions and (3) personal pensions.[1]

Occupational pensions were originally regulated through trust law in countries in the Anglo-Saxon legal tradition. In other countries, contract law, company law and employment law were applied at different times. The legal form of pension fund also varies across continental European countries – foundations and associations being the two most common forms. Occupational pension schemes can also be provided from (book) reserves in the employer's accounts, as for instance in Germany, Austria and Sweden. The potential negative impact on government tax revenues, and the cost of state provision should private pension arrangements be abused or fail, has resulted in specific government regulation of occupational pensions, spurred on by particular crises such as Robert Maxwell's looting of his UK company pension funds.

The OECD and other international organisations recommend that governments should actively promote the second and third pillars of retirement provision so as to provide financial security in retirement for populations that, worldwide, include higher proportions of older people, without unsustainable calls on public expenditure. This is particularly the case where (as in most countries) the proportion of citizens above retirement age is growing rapidly.

An increasing number of countries' governments have gone beyond reactive regulation of pre-existing pension funds and encouraged or mandated membership of private pension plans as a matter of public (welfare) policy, to help supplement pillar I provision. In the United Kingdom and Ireland, this has meant requiring employers to make pension plans available to their employees, but with no requirement to make contributions.[2] Australia has since 1992 required contributions to a licensed pension plan (currently of at least 9 per cent of salary) and New Zealand has since 2007 required contributions unless employees opt out.[3] Other Western European countries with mandatory private schemes include Iceland, Norway, Sweden and Switzerland. As a result of industry-wide collective bargaining, occupational pension schemes also achieve quasi-mandatory levels of coverage (over 80 per cent of the workforce) in countries like Denmark and the Netherlands.

---

1 The three-pillar models used by the OECD and the EU differ in so far as benefits financed from employer or employee payments to the state but administered by private sector pension funds are treated as pillar II by the OECD, but can be pillar I in EU terminology.

2 In the UK the requirement applies only to employers with five or more employees.

3 The New Zealand system has strong similarities with the system of auto-enrolment and personal accounts to be introduced in the UK from 2012.

More radically, countries across Eastern Europe and Latin America have undertaken World Bank-recommended pension reforms and replaced part of the public pension system by private pension systems with mandatory participation.[4] The private pension systems are all based on defined contribution (DC) formulas and are administered by a relatively small number of commercial pension providers.[5] In most countries, pension providers run pension funds as legally separated contractual pools of assets without legal personality. In the absence of well-developed, pre-existing financial markets, and because of their role in pension provision, these systems are commonly heavily regulated.

It can be seen that private pensions are inextricably linked to governments' social welfare policies – distinguishing them from other financial services. This relationship has meant that governments have been reluctant to leave pension funds lightly regulated and have, over time, legislated for nearly every eventuality, albeit with differing degrees of prescription. Legislation tends to be particularly tight where contributions to a pension fund are to some extent mandatory. For example, the move to a mandatory system in Australia was followed by the introduction of stringent new licensing and risk management frameworks. Pension fund governance therefore cannot be understood in isolation from a country's regulatory framework.

Governments have established pension supervisory authorities to help to ensure that regulation is effectively enforced. In some countries the supervisory authority is also responsible for drafting some or all of the pension's regulation, either alongside the regulator or acting as regulator. In other countries the supervisory authority is operationally independent from the regulator (commonly a government department) and is very often within an 'integrated' authority responsible for supervising other types of financial services, most notably insurance. Where financial services are integrated using the 'twin peaks' model of separate authorities for prudential supervision and market conduct supervision, two supervisory authorities have complementary responsibilities in this area.[6] In some countries, most notably the United States, the tax authority also has regulatory and supervisory responsibilities.

Within the European Union, a further layer of regulation has been provided by the IORP Directive,[7] which establishes minimum standards on:

- the legal separation of the scheme from the sponsoring employer or a company providing other services;

---

4 Confusingly, the World Bank uses a three-pillar model with: (I) state-unfunded provision; (II) mandatory, privatised state provision; and (III) voluntary provision. The third pillars would therefore encompass occupational provision, a rarity in the countries adopting the World Bank model.

5 For instance, there are six providers in Chile.

6 As in Australia and the Netherlands.

7 Directive 2003/41/EC, Activities and supervision of institutions for occupational retirement provision (IORPs).

5

- minimum conditions (including fitness and propriety) for registering schemes;
- annual reports and accounts;
- information to be given to the members and beneficiaries;
- the powers and duties of supervisory authorities, including information to be provided to them;
- the calculation and funding of scheme liabilities (technical provisions);
- investment rules and statements of investment policy principles;
- freedom to appoint managers and custodians from other member states; and
- cross-border schemes.

In developing the regulatory and supervisory regime for occupational pensions, the European Commission has been advised by the Committee for European Insurance and Occupational Pensions Supervisors (CEIOPS),[8] on which the United Kingdom has been represented by the Financial Services Authority and the Pensions Regulator.

The focus of regulation and supervision

Viewing the worldwide diversity in private pension systems, a distinction can be made between:

- **Occupational provision** via closed funds established by the employer, or associations of employers (sometimes also with the participation of labour unions), to provide retirement benefits to their own employees.[9] By and large, closed funds are established as not-for-profit entities owing a primary fiduciary duty to the members. They offer defined benefit (DB), hybrid or DC benefits, with regulation as a legislative overlay across pre-existing legal frameworks; and
- **Contractual provision** via insurance arrangements or open funds established by commercially run pension providers that can be joined by any individual on a contractual basis. Open funds usually offer DC benefits. Individual members can choose the provider, and hence competition between providers is expected to place some discipline on pension fund governance. In these cases, the employer's role may be limited to paying over contributions, although it may also select the provider where the member does not exercise choice.[10]

The two types of system can exist alongside each other, as indeed is the case in the United Kingdom, where employers can either offer an occupational pension scheme or facilitate employee access to a contractual pension scheme,

---

8 CEIOPS has now been replaced by the European Insurance and Occupational Pensions Authority (EIOPA), with strengthened powers. See https://eiopa.europa.eu/.

9 As a result of the legislation introduced in Australia in 2005, closed superannuation (pension) funds have been able to open up their membership to employees of companies unrelated to original fund sponsors.

10 As in Australia and New Zealand, but not Eastern Europe or Latin America.

usually a personal pension provided by an insurer and equivalent of the open funds observed elsewhere.

In essence, regulation and supervision of occupational provision can rely to some extent on the fiduciary role of the governance entity (closed fund) with a legislative and supervisory focus on issues, such as the funding of DB plans, where such reliance has proved to be ineffective. The regulation and supervision of contractual plans (open funds), on the other hand, tends to be more prescriptive, with rigorous licensing of the entities, detailed rules for their administration and governance and extensive inspection of supervisory returns and scheme management, reflecting the risk of commercial considerations outweighing fiduciary responsibility. There is also commonly a focus on making competition more effective through disclosure to members.

Regardless of the system, however, regulators and supervisors have come to recognise that it is better to ensure that schemes are well governed than to prescribe the minutiae of what they should do, or hope that member choice will supply sufficient discipline. Hence, there has been increasing focus on improving risk management by pension funds and concentrating supervisory effort on the highest risks rather than compliance with legislation. For instance, the restrictions placed by many countries on the level of investment in riskier assets are being relaxed with the introduction of the 'prudent person principle' covering how scheme managers and fiduciaries should address investment risk.[11]

For funds which deliver guaranteed benefits,[12] the move to a risk orientation has meant a focus on solvency and investment risk, where the sponsoring employer does not underwrite the guarantee, or employer default risk where (as is the case in the United Kingdom) it does. Quantitative solvency models, as found in the banking and insurance sectors, have found favour in many of these countries.[13] Longevity risk is receiving attention everywhere.

For DC schemes, the focus tends to be on the management of investment and operational risks, to which members are directly exposed, together with the level of charges and risks arising from converting pension saving into annuities at retirement, where this is mandated.[14] There is also a strong focus in many countries on the accuracy, quality, accessibility and comparability of disclosure to current and potential scheme members, especially where they can choose their scheme.

---

11 The prudent person principle is required by the EU IORP Directive.

12 This category includes not just the defined benefit arrangements common in the UK and other developed countries, but also defined contribution plans with minimum performance guarantees as found across continental Europe and in Latin America.

13 These include the Netherlands, where a modified insurance solvency model is used, and Denmark and Germany, where EU insurance solvency rules are applied.

14 While the majority of countries with defined contribution plans require that some or all of the benefits be used to buy life annuities or regulated income draw-down products, Australia and the United States are two notable exceptions.

Risk-based regulation and supervision also encompasses the fitness of those who run the scheme (hence the UK focus on trustee knowledge and understanding mentioned later in this chapter), the scheme's governance processes and internal controls, member representation and the management of conflicts of interest.

Pension fund governance

What is good pension fund governance?

The governance of private pension plans and funds involves the managerial control of these organisations and how they are regulated, including the accountability of management and how they are supervised. The basic goal of pension fund governance regulation is to minimise the potential agency problems, or conflicts of interest, that can arise between the fund members and those responsible for the fund's management, and which can adversely affect the security of pension savings and promises.

Good governance goes beyond this basic goal, and aims to deliver high pension fund performance while keeping costs low for all stakeholders. It can have many positive side effects, such as creating trust amongst all stakeholders, reducing the need for prescriptive regulation and facilitating supervision. Good pension fund governance can also be conducive to more effective corporate governance of the companies in which they invest, as well-managed pension funds are more likely to seek value for their investments via a more active shareholder policy. Good governance also needs to be 'risk-based' – for example, the more sophisticated the investment strategy adopted by the pension fund, the stricter the governance oversight required; or the more complex the administrative arrangements of the plan, the tighter the operational oversight needs to be.

How is pension fund governance structured?

In meeting these goals, pension fund governance is structured in different ways in different countries. All autonomous pension funds have a governing body or board, which is the group of persons (or in some cases a single person) responsible for the operation and oversight of the pension fund. The governing board is the ultimate decision-maker, having overall responsibility for strategic decisions such as setting the investment policy, choosing the investment manager(s) and other service providers, and reviewing the fund's performance.

The pension fund's governing board is the equivalent of the board of directors of a corporation, which has the ultimate responsibility for protecting the shareholders' assets. The governing body may be internal or external to the pension fund, it may have a single or dual board structure and may delegate certain functions to professionals. These features of pension funds depend on the legal form of the fund and the regulation in place and are the starting point for understanding differences in the quality of pension fund governance across countries.

The structure of the governing body is determined by the legal form of the pension fund. This chapter has already referred to the distinction between occupational and contractual systems. Occupational pension funds have two types of governance structures:

- The **institutional type** of fund is an independent entity with legal personality and capacity and hence it has its own internal governing board, owing fiduciary responsibility to plan members. Examples include pension foundations and associations as they exist in countries such as Denmark, Finland, Hungary, Italy, Japan, Norway, Poland, the Netherlands and Switzerland, as well as corporations such as Pensionskasse in Austria and Germany. In most of these countries pension funds have a single governing board, the members of which are typically chosen by sponsoring employers and employees (or their representatives). In some countries, like Germany and the Netherlands, there is a dual-board structure. In Germany, a supervisory board is responsible for selecting and monitoring the management board, which in turn is responsible for all strategic decisions.
- The **trust form** is used by pension funds in countries with an Anglo-Saxon legal tradition. Under the trust form it is the trustees who legally own (have the legal title to) the pension fund assets. Trustees must administer the trust assets in the sole interest of the plan participants, who are the beneficiaries from the investment of those assets according to the trust deed. While this feature of trusts is similar to that of foundations, the trustees are not legally part of the trust. Indeed, a trustee may be of the corporate type (as is usually the case in Australia, and sometimes in the United Kingdom and Ireland).

By contrast, a **contractual type** of pension fund consists of a segregated pool of assets without legal personality and capacity that is governed by a separate entity, typically a financial institution such as a bank, insurance company or pension fund management company (which may in turn be a subsidiary of a bank or insurer). The governing body of a fund set up in the contractual form is usually the board of directors of the management entity, although in some countries (for example, Spain), some key responsibilities are shared with a separate oversight committee (*comisión de control*). In Australia, contractual providers generally have to be established under a master trust, which is intended to impose a greater fiduciary discipline (and is found in a few UK providers).

The United States has an additional feature as the governing body may be the plan sponsor, the trustee and/or some third party. The Employee Retirement Income Security Act of 1974 (ERISA) requires single company pension plans to have one or more named fiduciaries who have authority to control and manage the pension plan, including its investments. The sponsoring employer and the trustee are always named fiduciaries, but it is possible for the trustee to be devoid of any major fiduciary responsibility (directed trustee), following

9

instead another named fiduciary (for example, a plan committee). In addition, asset managers, financial advisers and other persons and entities that exercise some discretion over the fund's assets are considered to be functional fiduciaries, and have some legal responsibility for the pension fund.

Good governance is increasingly recognised as an important aspect of an efficient private pension system, enhancing investment performance and benefit security. Yet, weaknesses still persist. The regulatory control and supervisory oversight of this important area have therefore been strengthened in recent years.

The regulation of pension fund governance

The role of the OECD

The OECD has for some years taken a keen interest in the regulation of private pensions through its Working Party on Private Pensions, which is drawn from representatives of pensions regulators across the OECD and some selected non-OECD countries. The Working Party prepared a set of guidelines on pension fund governance in 2001, which were later (in 2005) approved as an OECD recommendation, namely, a non-binding agreement among OECD members reflecting a common and unanimous position on the topic. The recommendation was revised in June 2009, strengthening some regulatory aspects of pension fund governance.[15]

The OECD has been promoting these guidelines in conferences around the world and via its membership, and in 2007 carried out a review of their effectiveness in improving governance standards. The review, summarised in Stewart and Yermo,[16] revealed that thirteen countries had introduced substantial governance reforms since the first version of the guidelines was developed. The Working Party has also used the guidelines as part of its assessment of candidate countries for OECD accession.

Governance problems

Despite increased recognition of the importance of good pension fund governance, surveys still show that problems and weaknesses remain.[17] Firstly, in trust-based systems trustees and fiduciaries commonly lack suitable knowledge, experience or training, which additionally hinders them from understanding and questioning the advice they receive from outside experts. Secondly, conflicts of interest still remain, both within boards and in relation to independent, commercial trustees.

---

15 The guidelines are available at www.oecd.org/dataoecd/18/52/34799965.pdf.

16 F. Stewart and J. Yermo, 'Pension Fund Governance: Challenges and Potential Solutions', OECD Working Papers on Insurance and Private Pensions, No. 18 (Paris: OECD Publishing, 2008).

17 See Stewart and Yermo, 'Pension Fund Governance', cited above fn. 16.

Finally, the problem of how to ensure that suitable governance mechanisms are in place for contract-based DC pension plans has yet to be solved.

Many problems stem from weaknesses in the governing boards – including the responsibilities of the board not being clearly defined, board members being selected as representatives rather than for their knowledge, a lack of self-assessment – including of training needs – by boards and conflicts of interest not being effectively handled. Compounding these challenges is the problem of scale, as implementing good governance mechanisms can be a real issue for smaller pension plans.

Regulatory solutions

Policy-makers in many OECD countries have therefore stepped up efforts to address such identified weaknesses – in some cases issuing new regulations or publishing good practice guidelines. Examples of regulation used to tackle these problems include the following:[18]

- *Defining the board's responsibilities*: require plan documents to identify clearly the role and responsibilities of the board and board members to restate annually that they are aware of their governance obligations.
- *Composition of governing boards*: encourage employee-/member-nominated representatives, taking into account the need for an appropriate mix of skills, define 'fit and proper' criteria and allow the use of independent trustees.
- *Ensuring regular self-assessment and training*: encourage self-assessment by boards, allow third-party oversight and encourage ongoing training of board members.
- *Handling conflicts of interest*: require a policy, disclose conflicts – with conflicted board members refraining from voting, supervisory authorities should have the power to appoint independent trustees.
- *Governance mechanisms for DC funds*: establish independent oversight bodies, create the legal environment for sponsors/employers to monitor plans (i.e. safe harbour rules), strengthen the monitoring and oversight of the supervisory authority.

OECD Guidelines for Pension Fund Governance

In terms of regulatory guidance on governance issues, the OECD first produced a set of international governance guidelines in 2005.[19] These are structured in the following manner, highlighting key governance issues:

- Governance structure
  - Identification of responsibilities
  - Governing body

---

18 Stewart and Yermo, 'Pension Fund Governance', cited above fn. 16.
19 See www.oecd.org/dataoecd/18/52/34799965.pdf (revised guidelines published in 2009).

11

- Accountability
- Suitability
- Delegation and expert advice
- Auditor
- Actuary
- Custodian
- Governance mechanisms
  - Risk-based internal controls
  - Reporting
  - Disclosure

The OECD Guidelines for Pension Fund Governance (hereafter, OECD 2009 governance guidelines) were revised in 2009 to reflect the changing circumstances of pension fund governance. The main changes to the guidelines included imposing more stringent requirements on the suitability of the governing body, highlighting a high level of integrity, competence, experience and professionalism, whilst stressing that the necessary skills and knowledge of the board should be assessed on a collective basis. The ability to be able to understand expert advice and the need for ongoing training were added as requirements, as follows:

> The governing body should regularly review its collective skill set and consider whether it is adequate. Where relevant, it should seek to enhance its collective knowledge of pension fund matters via appropriate training, paid for by the pension entity. An annual skills inventory and training plan may be prepared for this purpose. In general, training is recommended both initially on appointment and on an on-going basis (at least every two years). Such training could be supported by pension fund regulatory or supervisory bodies (for example via free on-line courses, other material or approval of other education providers). Alternatively, the supervisory authorities may identify or approve suitable courses. More advanced training may be needed to ensure that the governing body fully understands investment in complex financial instruments.

The revised guidelines also require that the governing body pays more attention to the advice received by external experts, 'assess[ing] the advice received, including its quality and independence, and verify[ing] that all its professional staff and external service providers have adequate qualifications and experience'.

The revised guidelines now include a reference to 'risk-based' internal controls, stating that these should 'vary according to the type and size of pension plan, fund and entity and the type and extent of risks faced'. As the guidelines state: 'As good governance should be "risk-based", the division of responsibilities should reflect the nature and extent of the risks posed by the fund. For example, where funds adopt a sophisticated investment strategy, an investment sub-committee may be appropriate.' An internal control which is stressed in the new guidelines is the conflict of interest policy, which is particularly required for members of a commercial board. The members of the governing body and staff should regularly report compliance with the code, conflicts should be disclosed in the board's minutes and conflicted parties should abstain from voting.

Finally, the guidelines emphasise the necessity of putting in place governance mechanisms for DC funds:

> With DC pension funds, additional key tasks of the governing body include ensuring that: (i) suitable investment choices are offered to members (including a suitable default fund), (ii) the performance of these funds is monitored, (iii) costs charged to members are optimized and disclosed in their disaggregated form and (iv) members are offered guidance and where relevant projections of expected benefits. To enable the governing body to undertake its role effectively, safe-habour rules may be appropriate.

Supervising pension fund governance

The development and dissemination of guidelines and good practice experience in relation to pension supervision is the responsibility of a separate body: the IOPS (International Organisation of Pension Supervisors). It has undertaken work to analyse the main governance-related problems identified by pension supervisory authorities globally, and how these are being dealt with.[20]

The IOPS notes that, due to the crucial role of the private pension systems within the financial markets and their increasing importance as a source of retirement income for individuals, the effective supervision of pension funds is becoming ever-more important. Ensuring that pension funds are properly run has become a great concern to supervisory authorities, and hence they increasingly focus on the oversight of pension fund governance mechanisms. This is particularly important where supervisory authorities have adopted a 'risk-based' supervisory approach, as this allows much of the responsibility for risk management to rest with the individual pension fund companies themselves, while the supervisory authority verifies the quality of the fund's risk management processes and adapts its supervisory stance accordingly.

Supervisory authorities have to ensure not only that proper structures and mechanisms for pension fund governance are in place, but also that they are working effectively. To this end, the full range of supervisory tools – licensing, monitoring, communication, analysis, intervention and correction – have to be deployed.

---

20 Mandatory Provident Schemes Authority of Hong Kong, 'Supervisory Oversight of Pension Fund Governance', IOPS Working Papers on Effective Pension Supervision, No. 8 (Paris: IOPS Publishing, 2008), www.iopsweb.org/dataoecd/6/63/41269776.pdf.

IOPS members have stated that the major governance issues they face are the competence/expertise, accountability and internal control of the governing body. These issues have grown in importance as the complexity of the operations and investment of funds has increased and the legislative environment in many countries has developed, hence raising the level of competence and expertise required of governing bodies. Supervisory authorities have noted also that the shift from DB to DC plans has implications for pension fund governance and supervision, as the nexus of supervision shifts from controlling agency risks to managing systemic financial and operational risk. Again, supervisory authorities are particularly concerned with conflicts of interest relating to external, commercial, governing bodies (especially in some countries, related-party transactions).

Competence/expertise governing body

Some supervisory authorities are strengthening (or at least clarifying) their fit and proper requirements to help deal with the challenges posed by the competence and expertise of the governing body. For example, since 2004 pension fund trustees in Australia have had to be licensed, which has reduced the number and increased the ability and knowledge of the trustee community. The skill and competence of the governing body is usually assessed by the supervisory authority during the licensing process (the Dutch Central Bank, for example, undertaking an 'integrity and competence' assessment of persons nominated for an appointment to a position involving policy-making at a financial institution).

Most supervisory authorities also assess the governing body's competence on an ongoing basis, through regular communication, quarterly reports, etc. – often within the framework of the overall risk assessment of the fund. They can then intervene and use their powers and sanctions if they feel that the governing body is below par, or not acting in the interests of the fund's members – in some cases, removing or appointing members to the governing board.

When it comes to the competence of the governing body, supervisory authorities are also increasingly concerned to check that the board is not 'captured' by experts and is able to understand the advice it receives – an increasingly challenging task as the investment advice they receive and decisions they are expected to make become increasingly difficult for 'lay' board members to understand. Some supervisory authorities require a written record of the advice received, and may scrutinise this themselves. In other jurisdictions the pension supervisory authority may check the contracts with outside, outsourced service providers. If poor advice or conflicts of interest are uncovered, penalties can be imposed on the governing body or third party.

Accountability

Regarding the second governance problem identified by the IOPS – i.e. the accountability of the governing board – its members advise that this can be reinforced by an independent voice or a representative of pension plan stakeholders on the governing body. For example, the mandatory provident funds in Hong Kong, China have to have an independent director on their board, whilst the boards of industry and company pension funds in Australia require equal representation of employers and employees. The authorities in Germany take a different approach, with a 'two-tier' governance structure ensuring that a supervisory board oversees the day-to-day managing board of *pensionskassen* and *pensionsfonden*. An Annual General Meeting of fund members also provides oversight in countries such as Germany and Luxembourg.

Supervisory authorities check that such representation requirements are being met, either during the licensing process or on an ongoing basis, such as in reviewing pension fund annual reports. Penalties can be imposed if the requirements are not met, and in extreme cases, some supervisory authorities can remove or appoint members of the governing body if they consider that the board is not fully accountable.

Further important tools for improving accountability are transparency and disclosure.[21] Some authorities check all documents to be released by a pension fund before publication, whilst others undertake random checks or follow up complaints. In-depth examinations of information sent to pension plan members sometimes form part of an on-site examination of the fund, whilst auditors can also be important sources of checking whether disclosure requirements have been met. Where the supervisory authority is unhappy with the information disclosed, they can require clarification or rectification, and impose penalties for persistent or major offences.

IOPS members note that communication with the governing body and service providers can be an effective way of enhancing these parties' understanding of relevant disclosure requirements (for example, the supervisory authority in Jamaica organises numerous workshops and seminars to educate trustees and other pension stakeholders).

Finally, supervisory authorities rely on independent third parties to apply oversight to pension fund governing bodies, and thereby enhance their accountability. As the OECD 2009 governance guidelines state, auditors (external and internal), actuaries and custodians should have whistle-blowing responsibilities. Some authorities (for example, the Dutch Central Bank) hold

---

21 A. I. Rinaldi and E. Giacomel, 'Information for Members of DC Pension Plans: Conceptual Framework and International Trends', IOPS Working Papers on Effective Pension Supervision, No. 5 (Paris: IOPS Publishing, 2008), www.iopsweb.org/dataoecd/7/16/41269701.pdf.

regular meetings with these professionals to help to ensure that their role is understood. Penalties can be imposed on third parties who fail to fulfil their responsibilities.

Internal controls

The quality of internal controls is also of major concern to IOPS members. The regulation and supervision of these varies.[22] In some countries, internal controls are embedded in the organisation and functioning of the pension fund, whilst elsewhere a separate internal control unit is required. Supervisory authorities also place requirements on pension fund internal control systems. For example, the Mexican supervisory authority imposes a specific structure of internal controls (including specified oversight committees, a compliance officer, etc.), whilst the Australian supervisor provides guidance on principles, leaving detailed mechanisms to the trustee's discretion and judgment.

An assessment of the fund's internal control mechanisms usually forms part of the licensing process – and indeed is recommended in the OECD/IOPS Guidelines on the Licensing of Pension Entities (hereafter, OECD/IOPS Guidelines 2008).[23] The OECD/IOPS paper 2009 highlights other supervisory mechanisms for overseeing these internal controls, from using internal audit records, to self-assessment declarations by governing bodies, external audits, on-site inspections and dummy trades.

The internal control systems of pension fund service providers may also pose a threat to the funds. Supervisory authorities often seek to monitor the internal control systems of these service providers (either by themselves, by way of the fund's management or by liaising closely with other supervisory authorities).

The governance of Pension Supervisory Authorities

In addition to looking at the governance of the pension funds they oversee, IOPS has looked at the authorities' own governance arrangements.[24] The governance, oversight and performance measurement of financial supervisory authorities are increasingly being recognised as important topics – not least due to the current financial crisis and perceived problems in (and lack of) the regulatory oversight of financial institutions. As supervisory authorities

---

22 See OECD 2009 governance guidelines (fn. 19 above); and F. Stewart, 'Pension Funds' Risk-management Framework: Regulation and Supervisory Oversight', IOPS Working Papers on Effective Pension Supervision, No. 11 (Paris: IOPS Publishing, 2009), www.iopsweb.org/dataoecd/31/33/43946778.pdf (hereafter, OECD/IOPS paper 2009).

23 See www.oecd.org/dataoecd/7/34/40434531.pdf.

24 See Stewart, 'Pension Funds' Risk-management Framework', cited above fn. 22.

increase their oversight of pension fund governance, the spotlight has rightly been turned onto their own arrangements.

Building on work by the International Monetary Fund (IMF),[25] the good governance of pension supervisory authorities can be summarised in four categories:

- *independence*: requiring clarification of the authority's responsibilities and powers, processes for appointing its governing board and the ability to secure resources and operate without undue influence;
- *accountability*: involving external audits, suitable internal organisation and measuring performance;
- *transparency*: ensuring that the authority's objectives and achievements are understood, and that a consultative relationship with industry is established; and
- *integrity*: requiring codes of conduct, discretion to apply powers, internal controls and competent staff.

An IOPS survey of its members found that they broadly comply with these main categories.

It is difficult to measure the effectiveness of pension supervisory authorities as it is hard to determine the 'counter-factual' (i.e. what did not happen) or screen out the effects of external factors. IOPS advises supervisory authorities to establish a range of performance measures which cover: *effectiveness* (outcomes against the authority's high level objectives); *efficiency* (for instance, using the authority's credibility or reputation with key stakeholders as a proxy); and *economy* (for instance, cost per inspection or overhead cost relative to operational activities). The IOPS recognises that further work is needed in this area.

Regulation and supervision of pension scheme governance in the United Kingdom

Regulatory context

The UK private pensions system comprises some 62,000 occupational pension schemes[26] sponsored by one or more employers, and personal pensions provided by insurers, often facilitated through a group arrangement with an employer. The two types of provision have distinct regulatory and supervisory arrangements.

25 See M. Quintyn, 'Governance of Financial Supervisors and Its Effects – A Stocktaking Exercise' (IMF Institute, International Monetary Fund, 2007), www.suerf.org/download/studies/study20074.pdf.
26 According to TPR's Annual Report and Accounts for 2009–10, in March 2010, there were around 47,500 registered occupational DC schemes, 6,300 DB schemes and 1,800 hybrid schemes.

Personal pensions are subject to financial services legislation. Occupational pension schemes are run by pension trusts subject to trust law. Pensions legislation has overlaid both types of law, so as, in particular, to:

- enable pension schemes to contract their members out of the state second pension and consequentially claim rebates from the government, subject to complex regulation;
- help ensure that DB plan designs deliver worthwhile benefits, for instance by indexing benefits to inflation;[27]
- prevent theft from or abuse of schemes, in response to the Maxwell affair in the early 1990s, which exposed the vulnerability of occupational pension schemes to abuse by an unscrupulous employer (and the Goode report[28] which in its wake considered how regulation could be strengthened); and
- respond to the failure in the early 2000s by some DB schemes to provide members with the benefits promised.

Hence much UK pensions legislation is intended to prevent fraud or other abuses of pension assets and to minimise the risk that promises will not be honoured. It provides in particular for:[29]

- registration of occupational pension schemes;
- vesting and preservation of pension benefits;
- restrictions and consultation on modification to scheme rules;
- the conditions governing contracting out from the state second pension;
- pension sharing on divorce;
- the DB promise – its indexation to inflation and cash-equivalent transfer values;
- how DB liabilities should be valued and funded, and how deficits and surpluses should be handled (occupational schemes only);
- the duty on employers and associated companies and persons to underwrite the DB liabilities of the occupational pension schemes they sponsor;
- timely paying over of contributions by the sponsoring employer;
- reporting breaches of legislation to the supervisory authority (whistleblowing) and other reporting by occupational pension schemes;
- cross-border activities within the European Union;
- winding up of occupational pension schemes; and
- aspects of occupational pension scheme governance (see below).

27 The requirement for indexation is now limited to an increase of 2.5 per cent per year.
28 Report of the Pension Law Review Committee, chaired by Professor Roy Goode, 1993.
29 In the absence of any consolidation of pension legislation, reference needs to be made to four main Acts of Parliament and hundreds of subsidiary regulations with later legislation often amending earlier legislation. The Acts are the: Pension Schemes Act 1993, Pensions Act 1995, Welfare Reform and Pensions Act 1999 and Pensions Act 2004. It should be noted that substantial parts of the legislation do not apply to public sector schemes.

Since 2006 there has been a unified regime of tax incentives covering occupational and personal pensions. An important aspect of the regime is that at least 75 per cent of the accrued pension savings at retirement (no earlier than age 55) should be drawn down as income over the remainder of the retiree's life, necessitating either scheme provision of a pension (for DB schemes) or, for DC schemes, the purchase of life annuities or regulated income, draw-down products.[30]

The Financial Services and Markets Act 2000, and regulations and rules made under that Act, regulate the providers of personal pensions and the personal pensions product, and hence their governance. This is outside the scope of this chapter, but some regulation, for instance that applying to the timely paying over of contributions, applies to all types of pension product.

In addition, legislation to encourage participation in private pensions has:

- required employers with five or more employees to make a pension scheme available; and
- established a simplified contractual pension product, the 'stakeholder pension', aimed at employers or employees new to pension provision[31] with specific regulation of design, charges and disclosure.

The Pensions Act 2008 substantially increases participation requirements. All employers will in due course have to auto-enrol qualifying employees into a qualifying pension scheme (phased in from 2012 to 2016[32]), although employees can then opt out. The opt-in/opt-out process will be repeated every three years. Employers can auto-enrol into an existing (or a new) occupational pension scheme or personal pension arrangements, so long as the schemes meet legislatively specified criteria. Otherwise employees will auto-enrol into a new DC scheme, 'personal accounts' run by a government-appointed board of trustees, NEST (National Employment Savings Trust). In legal form this will be an occupational pension scheme, but without restrictions on who can join it. The eventual aggregate contribution rate will be 8 per cent of qualifying earnings[33]

---

30 The requirement does not generally apply where the accrued savings are below a specified amount (£18,000 in 2010–11) or for pension pots of under £2,000 arising from an occupational pension fund. Regulated draw-down is allowed only to the age of 75, at which point the balance must be annuitised or transferred to an 'alternatively secured pension' which is more tightly regulated. Draw-down is seen as a realistic option only for larger pension pots, say above £90,000 (HM Treasury, 'The UK Pension Annuities Market: Structure, Trends & Innovation' (HM Treasury, January 2009)). The requirement to annuitise by age 75 will be removed from April 2011.

31 Stakeholder pensions can also be sold directly to members of the public.

32 According to the Employers' Duties (Implementation) Regulations 2010, employers with 50,000 or more employees must comply at specified dates during 2012. The threshold number of employees becomes progressively smaller, reaching 50 in 2014 and extending to the smallest employers thereafter. These dates may be subject to change.

33 Qualifying earnings are any gross earnings between £5,035 a year and £33,540, including earnings that are not currently pensionable. The thresholds are based on earnings levels in 2006–7 and will be increased before the reforms are implemented and annually thereafter.

taking account of contributions from taxation, but the 3 per cent employer contribution will be phased in until 2017. The employee contribution will be 4 per cent.

Institutional context

The Department of Work and Pensions (DWP) is responsible for regulatory policy for occupational pensions, emphasising the importance played by the second pillar in social welfare policy. HM Revenue & Customs (HMRC) supervises the compliance of pension schemes with the legislation governing tax incentives. Since 2005 there has also been a Pension Protection Fund (PPF), established to provide compensation in the event that an employer sponsoring a DB scheme becomes insolvent and the scheme has insufficient funds to pay the benefits due. The PPF is funded by a largely risk-based levy on pension schemes that are not purely DC.

The United Kingdom has had a stand-alone supervisory authority for occupational pensions since 1996, initially the Occupational Pensions Regulatory Authority (OPRA) and since April 2005 the Pensions Regulator (TPR).[34] TPR's statutory objectives are to:

- protect the benefits of members of work-based pension schemes;[35]
- promote good administration of work-based pension schemes;
- reduce the risk of situations arising that may lead to claims for compensation from the PPF; and
- maximise employer compliance with the employer duties introduced through the Pensions Act 2008 and with the safeguards against prohibited recruitment conduct and inducements to opt out of pension saving.[36]

In practice, TPR has some regulatory powers, as it can issue codes of practice, subject to legislative safeguards over consultation and parliamentary approval.[37] Codes provide practical guidance on the requirements of pensions legislation and set out the standards of conduct and practice expected of those subject to these requirements. The standards set out in a code are intended to be consistent with how a well-run pension scheme would choose to meet its legal requirements. Codes often expand on intentionally vague terms in legislation, such as 'appropriate' or 'timely'. They are not statements of the law and there is no penalty for failing to comply with them. Nor need all

---

34 The powers and functions of OPRA were set out in the Pensions Act 1995, as subsequently amended. The additional powers and functions of TPR, together with most of its objectives, are set out in the Pensions Act 2004. Its last objective, and associated powers, was provided by the Pensions Act 2008.

35 This combines two objectives in the Act which cover members of occupational pension schemes and members of contractual schemes where the employer pays over contributions.

36 This objective was added by the Pensions Act 2008.

37 A code of practice is brought into force by a statutory instrument laid by the government.

provisions of a code be followed in every circumstance, although alternative approaches nevertheless need to meet the underlying legal requirements. When determining whether the legal requirements have been met, a court or tribunal must take any relevant codes of practice into account. TPR has issued 12 codes to date.

The Financial Services Authority (FSA) is responsible for the regulation and supervision of financial services companies providing personal pensions, including their market conduct. This means that the FSA and TPR have complementary supervisory responsibilities for those personal pensions provided through the workplace (and indeed all stakeholder pensions). The FSA also supervises the provision of life annuities bought by retirees or schemes that are winding up or divesting themselves of some of their liabilities. It is not yet clear how these arrangements will change with the proposed abolition of the FSA.

A separate Pensions Ombudsman handles complaints about the administration of any occupational or personal pension scheme, so long as the complainant has gone through any legally mandated internal dispute resolution procedures The Pensions Advisory Service (TPAS), an independent non-profit organisation that provides free information, advice and guidance on the whole spectrum of pensions, helps scheme members navigate through the complaints process.

UK regulation of occupational pension scheme governance

Trust law remains pre-eminent, with most UK pensions legislation focusing on the pension plan, what can and must be promised and how it should be funded. There have, however, been two waves of legislation relating to pension trust governance. The first responded to perceived gaps in trust law following the Maxwell case and the second, which came into force from 2005, made explicit some requirements considered implicit in trust law so as to ensure compliance with the Institutions for Occupational Retirement Provision (IORP) Directive, and tightened the law relating to the funding of DB pension schemes and employer support of them. The provisions include:

- **Composition** – requiring schemes generally to have at least one-third of trustees to be member-nominated.[38] While the government is empowered to increase the ratio to 50 per cent, such a move appears to be in abeyance.[39]

---

38 Pensions Act 1995, Occupational Pension Schemes (Member-Nominated Trustees and Directors) Regulations 2006 and Code of Practice 8. Where there is a corporate trustee body, at least one-third of the body's directors should be member-nominated.
39 The rules of a few schemes already require them to have 50 per cent of trustees to be member-nominated.

- **Propriety** – barring classes of people (for example, criminals, bankrupts and professional advisers) from being trustees and providing for trustees to be removed, suspended or disqualified where appropriate.[40]
- **Trustee knowledge and understanding** – requiring that individual trustees have appropriate knowledge and understanding of the law relating to pensions and trusts, the principles relating to the funding of occupational pension schemes and the investment of the assets of such schemes.[41]
- **Process** – permitting decisions to be taken by majority voting and requiring meeting minutes and proper books and records to be kept and money to be kept in separate bank accounts from those of the employer.[42]
- **Professional advisers** – requiring schemes to appoint an auditor and actuary (unless exempted), specifying the qualifications, appointment and resignation processes for all professional advisers, and requiring schemes to take professional advice on investment matters.[43]
- **Investment decisions** – requiring schemes to have a statement of investment principles (SIP), reviewed at least every three years (or after a significant change in investment policy) and apply the prudent person principle, such that investments are properly diversified, predominantly in regulated markets and appropriate to the liabilities.[44] Legislation does not interpret the principle in a specific way except that schemes must have no more than 5 per cent of investments in the sponsoring employer and may hold derivatives only for risk reduction or effective portfolio management. Borrowing is prohibited, which excludes some types of complex transactions. Trustees are allowed to delegate responsibility for investment decisions to a sub-committee or a fund manager (the only trustee function that can be fully delegated).
- **Internal controls** – must be established and operated to ensure that schemes are administered and managed in accordance with scheme rules and the law.[45]
- **Disclosure** – schemes must prepare an annual report, including audited accounts, in accordance with legislative requirements. They must also provide members with specified annual disclosures relating to their benefit entitlements, and provide on request specified scheme documents, including scheme rules and annual reports.[46]

40 Pensions Act 1995.
41 Pensions Act 2004 and Code of Practice 7.
42 Pensions Act 1995 and Occupational Pension Scheme (Scheme Administration) Regulations 1996.
43 Pensions Act 1995.
44 Pensions Act 1995 and Occupational Pension Schemes (Investment) Regulations 2005.
45 Occupational Pension Schemes (Internal Controls) Regulations 2005 and TPR Code of Practice 9.
46 Pensions Act 1995 and regulations made under this Act, as amended.

● **Internal disputes resolution** – legislation requires a process to be in place, but leaves flexibility as to what is appropriate for each scheme.[47]

Supervision of occupational pensions governance in the United Kingdom

The mission of TPR is to 'work to improve confidence in work-based pensions by protecting members' benefits and encouraging high standards and good practice in running pension schemes'. From its inception it was intended to be risk-based, and this ethos underpins its approach to supervision. It seeks to target resources on areas which pose the greatest risk, ensuring its actions are proportionate, consistent, accountable and transparent (in line with the government's Principles of Good Regulation). Its operational strategy is to 'Educate, Enable' and 'Enforce' where it is appropriate and proportionate to do so.[48]

A major focus has been on the risk that DB pension schemes are wound up with insufficient funds to pay promised benefits, hence creating a call on the PPF. This has been tackled by seeking to ensure that trustees agree with the employer(s) a prudent funding objective that is appropriate to enable the scheme to meet its liabilities as they fall due, taking account of the risks to the scheme, with a recovery plan that ensures that any deficit against the objective is eliminated as quickly as is reasonably affordable for the employer.

The interpretation of subjective terms used in legislation, such as 'prudent', is left to the discretion of trustees – there is no formal funding standard – but TPR have issued a code of practice and a statement on the factors that would trigger supervisory attention, such as funding objectives below a specified level or recovery plans longer than ten years. TPR has also encouraged a focus on mortality assumptions reflecting the latest understanding of increasing longevity.

TPR has paid particular attention to the assessment and monitoring by trustees of the strength of the employer (employer covenant) both in relation to the triennial valuation of scheme assets and liabilities, from which the funding objective and recovery plan derive, and where there is a material change in the employer's circumstances or the status of the pension scheme as a creditor. TPR has worked with trustees where corporate transactions potentially weaken the relative status of the pension scheme debt on the employer, and monitors the market to assess the risk of new products and strategies as they emerge. It has therefore on occasion used its powers to prevent employers from avoiding the pensions debt and issued guidance on scheme abandonment and transfers out of pension schemes.

---

47 Pensions Act 1995, as inserted by s. 273 of the Pensions Act 2004 (as amended). Code of Practice 11 provides guidance on timeliness.

48 Further details of TPR's strategy can be found in its Corporate Strategy 2008–12, published in October 2008: www.thepensionsregulator.gov.uk/docs/corporate-strategy-2008-2012.pdf.

In relation to DC, TPR is committed to raising standards in the key areas where it feels that members may not be served in the way that they should be: member communication, administration (especially record-keeping), investment, and charges and choice of retirement options. For instance, TPR has focused on enabling informed member choices at retirement and improving the quality of employer engagement in DC pension provision. This included a thematic review of retirement literature used by schemes as members approach retirement. Furthermore, TPR's attention to the quality of record-keeping (see below) is particularly relevant to DC schemes.

TPR does not so much supervise schemes as ensure that trustees are effectively supervising their schemes in line with their fiduciary duties. Hence, effective governance is central to the achievement of TPR's objectives. TPR has focused in particular on:[49]

- **Trustee knowledge and understanding** – Trustees who are equipped to discharge their responsibilities effectively are central to TPR's strategy. TPR's code of practice sets out what individual trustees are expected to know and understand, while its 'trustee toolkit' provides an online learning resource covering the full scope of the requirement.

- **Conflicts of interest** – The consequences of not managing conflicts appropriately can be severe, with trustees inadvertently or deliberately making decisions which are not truly in the best interests of members. TPR has issued guidance on this subject, and expects that conflicts should be identified in good time and managed effectively, and has accordingly issued guidance covering trustee and adviser conflicts.

- **Monitoring the employer covenant** – TPR commenced consultation in June 2010 (final guidance published November 2010) on draft guidance for trustees on monitoring employer support: covenant, contingent assets and other security.

- **Relations with scheme advisers** – TPR has recognised that expert advice is essential for schemes to be well run and has issued guidance on the selection, appointment and monitoring of advisers.

- **Administration** – Recognising in particular, the evident variability of administration standards and quality of record-keeping, TPR has issued specific guidance on record-keeping with targets for the accuracy of common data which schemes must hold. Where schemes fail to put adequate plans in place to resolve data issues, TPR will require them to improve.

- **Internal controls** – TPR Code of Practice 9 expands on the legislative requirement (Occupational Pension Schemes (Internal Controls) Regulations 2005), in particular by recommending that trustees put in place risk identification and

---

49 These priorities are largely taken from TPR's report on 'How the regulator will promote better governance of work-based pension schemes', October 2007, www.thepensionsregulator.gov. uk/docs/governance-discussion-paper-report-Oct07.pdf; and their Corporate Plan 2010–13, www.thepensionsregulator.gov.uk/docs/corporate-plan-2010-2013.pdf.

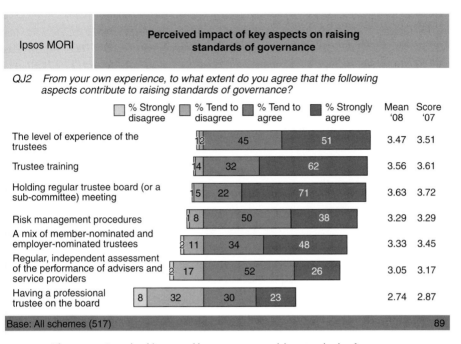

Figure 2.1 Perceived impact of key aspects on raising standards of governance
Source: TPR Governance Survey 2008, conducted by Ipsos MORI.

management arrangements and identifying the types of risks which schemes should seek to control. Recognising that many of the issues dealt with by its case teams have their root cause in an inadequate system of controls, TPR published revised guidance in 2010 identifying areas it regards as particularly important and control procedures it expects trustees to operate.

● **Governance during wind-up** – bearing in mind the length of time (over ten years) taken by some scheme wind-ups in the past, the aim is for the key activities in wind-up to be completed within two years.

TPR has addressed the scope for employers to secure good governance of contract-based provision, for instance by issuing guidance on (voluntary) management (oversight) committees.

TPR's approach to governance has been to educate and enable trustees in relation to these issues and intervene where serious problems become evident. To help inform the development and implementation of its governance strategy, TPR conducts annual surveys of pension fund governance in the United Kingdom. These have identified factors that contribute to higher governance standards, notably regular trustee board meetings, trustee training and the level of trustee experience.

Table 2.1 TPR 2009 Scheme Governance Survey						
Does the board of trustees …	*All schemes %*	*All DB schemes %*	*All DC schemes %*	*Small (12–99) %*	*Medium (100–999) %*	*Large (1,000+) %*
Have a means of identifying and recording potential conflicts of interest for each trustee?	68	79	49	57	75	87
Have a specific policy to manage trustees' own conflicts of interest as they have arisen?	63	73	43	50	71	83
Keep and maintain a register of trustees' interests?	52	60	36	41	57	72
None of the above	22	13	39	32	15	7

Base: All schemes except frozen and fully insured (n=772)
Source: TPR, 'Occupational pension scheme governance: A report on the 2009 scheme governance survey' (conducted for TPR by IFF Research), Table 6.

TPR's surveys show that governance standards have risen in recent years. There is, however, an emerging gap between governance standards of smaller and larger funds, with the former struggling in particular with issues such as keeping documented internal controls, addressing trustee learning gaps and ensuring a high standard of member communication. Smaller schemes also struggle to hold regular meetings and are less likely to have formal mechanisms for dealing with conflict of interest. When coupled with the higher relative costs of running smaller schemes, this is a key issue both in the United Kingdom and globally.

Conclusions

Improving governance remains a challenging task for pension funds and their regulators and supervisors worldwide. While recent regulatory and industry initiatives have improved the situation, there are still many cases of under-performance driven by bad governance practices. Some types of serious governance failure could be prevented through wider stakeholder representation on the governing body, higher levels of expertise – which may be achieved via training as well as greater use of independent, professional trustees – and effective codes of conduct that address conflicts of interest. Specific governance mechanisms for DC pension plans (such as oversight committees, safe-harbour rules and increased supervisory oversight) are also required. Finally, encouraging consolidation of pension plans would help to improve governance standards.

UK regulation and supervision has risen to many of these challenges, especially in relation to the composition, competence and impartiality of the governing board. The large number of relatively small schemes remains an issue and the United Kingdom has yet to emulate, for the generality of DC provision, the safe-harbour rules introduced in the United States.[50] The substantial differences between the regulation and supervision of trust-based and contract-based schemes differentiate the United Kingdom from most other countries.

50 The regulation of stakeholder pensions has similarities with the safe-harbour rules.

3

Pension funds and the capital markets

BARRY RILEY

Pension funds and long-term investment

It is estimated[1] that pension funds globally manage investments aggregating some $20,000 billion. In the United Kingdom, the figure is less than $2,000 billion, but pension funds are still major players in the sterling markets. How pension schemes are governed in terms of investment strategy can therefore be extremely important for the efficiency and structure of the global capital markets.

Pension funds have enjoyed the status of being the ultimate in long-term institutional investors (although in recent years certain sovereign wealth funds have acquired a potentially similar position). It can be argued that pension funds have the long-term strength to accept short-term risks, especially in the equity markets. However, the application of this approach has varied greatly over recent decades. Recently, mainly due to rising costs and tougher regulation, many corporate sponsors have begun to consider winding up their pension schemes or buying out part of their pension liabilities through transactions with insurance companies. Such measures emphasise the short rather than the long term.

At one time in the early 1990s, the average exposure of UK defined benefit pension funds to equities reached 80 per cent. This was clearly a risky strategy, but one that was generally thought at the time to be justified by the relative historical returns which had been achieved by various asset classes in the period from 1950 onwards.

Actuarial valuation formulae were designed to support this degree of risk-taking. Valuation of equities was primarily based on dividend income (in an extension of the principle of valuing long-term fixed income bonds on their interest payments). Dividend income was much more stable than share prices. Actuaries, for whom pensions consultancy became a very big activity in the second half of the twentieth century, surpassing the profession's traditional business and employment base in life assurance, were keen to support

1 Watson Wyatt, '2009 Global Pension Assets Study', available at www.towerswatson.com.

sponsors in providing pensions, on a voluntary basis, over the very long term; in the circumstances, short-term solvency crises arising from occasional stock market crashes were largely ignored.

The assumption of high investment returns on risky assets was one of several factors which enabled the apparent cost of pensions to be kept down: the budgeted cost of the typical 1960s pensions promise was about 12 per cent of pay (of which employers bore about 8 percentage points and employees the rest, although this varied from scheme to scheme).

Emerging from the post-war environment

Back in the immediate post-war environment, corporate pension schemes (of which there were relatively few at the time) rarely invested more than 20 per cent of their portfolios in equities. The mindset of institutional investors at the time was very much influenced by the memory of difficult economic conditions in the 1920s and early 1930s (together with the residual influence of the panoply of controls introduced during the Second World War). Equities were regarded as being very risky, while bonds – especially government bonds – had proved to be solid investments during a deflationary period.

But post-war conditions were to prove very different. There was to be consistent economic growth and almost uninterrupted inflation (at modest rates to begin with, but rising to double-digit levels in the 1970s). The relaxation of price controls and property development restrictions progressively released value in equities which had been suppressed. However, conventional wisdom was very slow to catch up with the new economic reality.

A key figure in the progressive change in sentiment that developed was George Ross Goobey, who in the late 1940s was appointed as manager of the Imperial Tobacco pension scheme. His own independence of thought was important to his emergence as a pioneer. It was also fundamental, though, that he was backed by a very supportive board of trustees. The location of the fund in Bristol, quite far away geographically from the consensus-ruled City of London, was also significant.

Ross Goobey noted that in the late 1940s equities offered much higher yields than bonds. He once observed that he was 'like a child in a sweetshop who discovers everything is for sale at knockdown prices'. His risk-tolerant strategy soon began to pay off and was noted by the managers of other pension funds.

During the 1950s, the average annual real return on UK equities was 13.7 per cent, and dividend growth also became strong as corporate profits grew and wartime controls were gradually relaxed: in 1951 a Conservative Government was elected and promised a 'bonfire of controls'. Meanwhile, inflation was progressively eroding the real value of bonds: the real return on gilt-edged bonds in the decade was *minus* 2.3 per cent, annualised. In 1950, more than one-half of the equity market was owned by private individuals, but institutional

Table 3.1 Beneficial ownership of UK equities 1963–2008 (%)						
	1963	*1975*	*1989*	*2000*	*2006*	*2008*
Individuals	54.0	37.5	20.6	16.0	12.8	10.2
Insurance companies	10.0	15.9	18.6	21.0	14.7	13.4
Pension funds	6.4	16.8	30.6	17.7	12.7	12.8
Other UK holders	22.6	24.2	17.4	9.6	19.8	22.1
Foreigners	7.0	5.6	12.8	35.7	40.0	41.5

Source: National Statistics.

investors became progressively gripped by what was dubbed a 'cult of the equity'. By the end of the century, personal investors directly owned less than 20 per cent of the market and institutions dominated.

After the war, government bonds were highly rated for their security, but equities were regarded as risky and dividend income as vulnerable. But as time passed the risk of inflation, on the one hand, and the potential rewards of growth, on the other, became factored into the prices of securities. By 1959, UK equities were near the top of a great bull market and in August of that year the yield on equities fell below that on gilts, at a crossover point of 4.76 per cent. Markets had entered the era of the 'reverse yield gap', which was to last for many decades (although with occasional brief re-reversals after 2000).

However, the UK stock market was volatile. This was a period of 'stop-go' economic policies as governments responded to repeated crises for sterling as the balance of payments dipped into deficit: there were sharp bear markets for UK equities in 1961 to 1962, 1966 and 1969 to 1970. There followed in due course a particularly severe bear market in 1973 and 1974, and a spectacular – if short-lived – market crash in 1987. Equity-based pension fund investment strategies could only be sustained with the support of actuarial valuation models which largely ignored short-term price fluctuations. British pension funds managed to survive a solvency crisis in the late 1970s, although sponsors had to raise their contribution levels substantially for a while: between 1975 and 1980 the average employer contribution rate rose from 7 to 11 per cent according to the annual survey by the National Association of Pension Funds.

How pension schemes provided finance for growth

The switch into equities had largely been driven by the relative returns on bonds and equities. But as the average equity allocation headed towards 60 per cent in the early 1980s, another rationalisation began to appear. This was that it was natural for British companies to support each other through the capital markets, and specifically by investing in equities. Pension fund savings should be used to finance the corporate sector's growth.

There were some similarities to the arguments which had been used in Germany after the war for the development of self-invested corporate pension schemes in which contributions were retained on balance sheets. Indeed, the rate of industrial growth in Germany had been the envy of the world in the 1950s and 1960s and the heavy flow of capital from pension contributions was thought to have been an important factor. But the German system was flawed. The problem of bankruptcy risk was tackled by a national guarantee scheme in the 1970s. But there remained the drawback that the capital was largely retained by big, well-established companies and was not available to small and new enterprises. As the corporate sector landscape began to change rapidly by the 1980s, through radical developments in technology and in the management structure of industrial organisations, which tended to become much more dispersed, the disadvantages of the German approach became more obvious.

A market-based approach, as practised in the United Kingdom and various other countries, such as the United States and the Netherlands, had the advantage of providing diversification. Indeed, investment by pension funds in the sponsor's own equity became increasingly frowned upon, because of bankruptcy risks and conflicts of interest between sponsors and trustees, although self-investment was quite common at one stage (and in a number of cases the pension funds were initially endowed by new sponsors with gifts of some of their own shares). Capital tended to flow from the funds of big, established employers into the shares of smaller and newer companies, thus aiding industrial dynamism and innovation.

An equity-based strategy could therefore be viewed by consultants and trustees as representing sound governance, so long as the reporting and regulatory frameworks were supportive (that is, temporary downside volatility could be tolerated). The pursuit of high returns was also clearly in the interest of the scheme sponsors in that the long-term cost of pensions was likely to be kept low. This was increasingly important because from the 1970s onwards there were regular changes to pensions legislation which generally had the effect of raising costs: for example, there were measures to protect the pensions of 'early leavers' and to provide a degree of inflation-proofing for pensions in payment. All the time, too, life expectancy was rising, imposing unexpected further burdens on pension schemes. By the 1990s, the underlying cost of pensions had climbed to something like 25 per cent of pay, but for a while sponsors were floating happily and unsuspectingly on an equity market bubble.

Pension schemes in the great equity bull market

A long equity bull market began in 1982; despite interruptions it was to persist until 2000. Soon the scheme deficits and extra employer contributions of the late 1970s were left behind and surpluses began to appear. During the 1980s

31

and 1990s, UK pension funds achieved real returns of some 10 per cent annually on their overall portfolios (including bonds and property). This was an exceptional period: a reasonable expectation, on the basis of a century of data, would have been for perhaps 6 per cent on equities and 2 per cent on government bonds. Many sponsors began to award themselves 'contribution holidays' and the average employer contribution rate declined to 6 per cent of wages by 1991.

During the 1990s, a debate began to develop amongst academics and actuaries about the sustainable level of the 'equity risk premium': this is the extra return to be received by investors in equities relative to the return on risk-free assets, commonly defined as treasury bills. This extra return compensates investors for bearing the risks involved in substantial price fluctuations. But the premium may vary substantially over time.

A paper[2] produced in 2002 by three academics from the London Business School (Elroy Dimson, Paul Marsh and Mike Staunton) calculated a global equity risk premium on the basis of data extending all the way back to 1900. Using 102 years of data lends authority, but the time span leaves room for criticism that structural changes may distort the calculations; for instance, the statistics for Germany had to be omitted for the period of hyperinflation in the early 1920s, and it is arguable that there may be survivor bias in the statistics because substantial countries such as Russia and China disappeared from the database as a result of Communist revolutions.

At any rate, the statistics showed that the global annualised equity risk premium (covering data from sixteen countries) was 5.9 per cent as an arithmetic mean and 4.6 per cent as a geometric mean. The United Kingdom was closely in line with this worldwide figure, but US equities performed slightly better (at an arithmetic average premium of 7.5 per cent). The authors concluded that exceptional factors may have boosted equity market performance in the second half of the twentieth century. Looking ahead, they expected arithmetic risk premia to lie in a range of 3.5 to 5.25 per cent, such levels being much lower than general expectations in academic literature during the latter part of the twentieth century.

Indeed, the Dimson, Marsh and Staunton research was published fairly near to the start of a poor period for equity markets. Some years later, early in 2009, a chapter entitled 'The Lost Decade', written by Tim Bond, head strategist at Barclays Capital, was published in the annual *Barclays Equity Gilt Study*.[3] This chapter described how the period between 1999 and 2008 turned out to be one of the worst in a century for equity returns. In that decade, the annualised return on UK equities was just 1 per cent, implying a negative

---

2 E. Dimson, P. Marsh and M. Staunton, 'Global Evidence on the Equity Risk Premium', (2003) 15 *Journal of Applied Corporate Finance* 27.

3 T. Bond, 'The Lost Decade' in Barclays, *Equity Gilt Study 2009* (Barclays Capital, February 2009).

equity risk premium. Only in the decade from 1965 to 1974 had UK equity returns previously been as poor. However, Tim Bond said it was wrong to conclude that equities were unattractive; rather, there had been a correction from overvaluation in the late 1990s and future returns were likely to be much higher.

A lesson for pension fund managers is that equity markets are subject to substantial distortions of price over periods of a decade or more compared with what might be regarded as underlying fair value. Moreover, strategists are acutely aware that when an asset class performs strongly, its proportion of the portfolio by value will tend to rise unless consistent principles of rebalancing are applied. This rebalancing requires the partial sale of high-performing asset classes and increases in the weightings of underperforming ones. But in practice it is difficult to apply this kind of independent thinking; there is very strong pressure on fiduciaries (and on the pension consultants who advise them) to stay closely in line with the peer group. This herd instinct helps to explain the enormous shifts in pension fund investment asset allocation that have taken place over the decades.

Until the 1950s equities were generally regarded as too speculative to account for a substantial part of large institutional investment portfolios. But strong market performance forced a change of attitude. According to figures published by UBS Asset Management, the average UK pension fund allocation to equities was 50 per cent at the beginning of 1980 and the proportion increased to 72 per cent by the end of the decade, before finally peaking at 81 per cent in 1993.

An important influence on this final flowering of the 'cult of the equity' was the shift in the structure of the asset management industry. Historically, many pension funds had been internally managed, like that of Imperial Tobacco, or contracted out to life insurance companies. But in the 1970s and 1980s trustees increasingly hired external managers, usually merchant banks or City of London stockbrokers, because as corporate advisers and brokers they had strong connections with the senior management of listed companies. By the 1990s, independent specialist managers began to come into the picture as well.

The big managers, such as Mercury Asset Management, originally part of S. G. Warburg, Schroders and the stockbrokers Phillips & Drew (which later became UBSAM) offered so-called 'balanced' strategies across different asset classes. But in practice they won competitive mandates on the basis of performance figures and so they were drawn inevitably towards the asset class which was the best performer in the short to medium term: as the 1980s progressed, it became clear that this class was equities.

Moreover, equity portfolios had become increasingly international, a change that had been inevitable ever since the removal in 1979 of 'investment dollar' controls on investment, which required the purchase of currency at a premium, part of which had to be surrendered on the proceeds of eventual sales. By the mid-1990s, 40 per cent of equities in UK pension fund portfolios were from overseas. In actual fact, that may not have been the full story in terms of economic fundamentals, as an increasing number of companies listed on the London Stock Exchange were themselves foreign, or at least they traded mainly overseas. So any suggestions that UK pension schemes were somehow collectively supporting British industry were becoming outdated. There was also a challenge to the dividend-based actuarial valuation model, which could not be plausibly applied to mixed global portfolios.

Attention switches to liabilities and bonds

Eventually, by the mid-1990s, the consensus was starting to shift. Trustees and consultants began to become concerned that they had lost control of asset allocation. One reason for their anxiety was that important changes were taking place in the structure of liabilities. As schemes matured, they were paying out more in pensions and reserving proportionately less for the very long-term liabilities associated with young employees.

The merits of matching assets and liabilities were increasingly considered. Bonds were seen to offer a good match for pensions in payment: indeed, inflation-linked government bonds offered the only available hedge against inflation risks which were accumulating in UK pension schemes because of the limited price indexation (LPI) protection (inflation-proofing up to a 5 per cent ceiling) required by legislation in the 1980s to be provided on pensions in payment. Actuaries were instrumental in persuading the British Government to begin to issue inflation-linked gilt-edged, the first issue being of Treasury 2 per cent Index-linked Stock 1996 in 1981, this being initially available only to pension funds. Historically, equities had been seen as offering a hedge against inflation, but this could not be seen as at all reliable in the short to medium term: equities were severely damaged by inflation in the 1970s. From the 1980s onwards, index-linked gilts began to offer an alternative, and better, inflation hedge. Figures published by the WM Company,[4] which measures pension funds, show that British pension funds' allocation to index-linked gilts rose from 2 to 12 per cent on average between 1990 and 2008. During the same period, the total allocation to bonds increased from 13 to 35 per cent.

In theory, government bonds are the safest assets available to pension funds, although there is a price in the form of low coupons. Corporate bonds offer rather higher yields, but the premium reflects credit risk which may become important at times of crisis, causing yield 'spreads' to widen and imposing greater price volatility. The yield 'spread' also includes a liquidity premium because most corporate bond issues are difficult to trade, certainly compared with gilts. However, so long as the accounting standards include a discount rate

---

4 WM Performance Services, *UK Pension Funds Annual Review 2008* and earlier years, circulated to clients of the WM Company.

Table 3.2 Average UK pension fund investment strategy across major asset classes

Year-end	UK equities	Overseas equities	Equities Total	Bonds	Cash	Property
1962	47	–	47	51	2	–
1963	47	–	47	51	2	–
1964	46	–	46	50	2	2
1965	47	–	47	48	3	2
1966	43	1	44	49	2	5
1967	47	1	48	45	2	5
1968	54	1	55	36	3	6
1969	52	1	53	36	3	8
1970	50	2	52	34	4	10
1971	56	2	58	31	3	8
1972	57	4	61	25	5	9
1973	48	4	52	26	8	14
1974	34	4	38	27	16	19
1975	45	5	50	26	9	15
1976	44	5	49	28	7	16
1977	45	4	49	28	6	17
1978	45	5	50	28	6	16
1979	45	5	50	26	7	17
1980	46	8	54	25	4	17
1981	45	10	55	23	4	18
1982	44	12	56	25	4	15
1983	45	15	60	23	4	13
1984	49	14	63	21	4	12
1985	51	14	65	21	3	11
1986	53	16	69	18	4	9
1987	54	13	67	18	5	10
1988	52	16	68	16	6	10
1989	52	20	72	13	6	9
1990	52	18	70	13	7	10
1991	55	20	75	13	4	8
1992	56	21	77	12	4	7
1993	57	24	81	10	4	5
1994	54	23	77	13	4	6

Table 3.2 *(cont.)*						
Year-end	UK equities	Overseas equities	Equities Total	Bonds	Cash	Property
1995	55	22	77	14	4	5
1996	53	22	75	14	6	5
1997	53	20	73	15	7	5
1998	51	20	71	19	5	5
1999	51	24	75	17	3	4
2000	49	23	72	19	3	5
2001	46	25	71	20	2	6
2002	39	25	64	26	2	7
2003	39	28	67	24	2	6
2004	37	29	66	24	2	7
2005	33	32	65	24	2	7
2006	31	32	63	24	2	8
2007	25	31	56	30	3	7
2008	21	29	50	35	3	7

Sources: UBSAM Pension Fund Indicators/WM Performance Services.

for liabilities linked to the AA-rated corporate bond yield, a pension scheme holding large volumes of corporate bonds will reduce the volatility of its solvency measure. (There are, however, concerns amongst accountants regarding whether a corporate bond yield is theoretically valid for this purpose, and a future switch to a risk-free discount rate, such as a government bond yield, is possible.)

Another drawback of corporate paper is that the term of the borrowing tends to be fairly short, so it may be difficult to achieve a good match against the liability profile. The increasing demand by pension funds for very long duration has encouraged European governments in recent years (particularly including the British Government) to extend their borrowing terms from a previous maximum of 25 years to 30 and even 40 years.

Apart from inflation risk, government bonds are also subject to political risks which may be manifested as manipulation in the markets. In the United Kingdom's gilt-edged market, the most notorious historical case of this was when the Chancellor of the Exchequer, Hugh Dalton, pursued a 'cheap money' strategy in the immediate post-war period: in 1946, the government issued what became known as 2.5 per cent Daltons, which over the next few years were to lose a great deal of money for anyone misguided enough to buy them.

US Treasury bond yields were also held artificially low in the immediate post-war period.

In fact, government-fixed interest bonds proved to be very poor investments for pension schemes throughout the period up until the late 1970s, when inflation was allowed to rise. Eventually, however, a serious global attack on inflation was led by Paul Volcker as chairman of the US Federal Reserve and the new British Government under Margaret Thatcher gave support. In a period of declining inflation, government bonds delivered very high real returns for the next 20 years (although not quite as high as the returns on equities). By the turn of the twenty-first century, pension funds in the United Kingdom were recovering much of their confidence in bonds. However, political risks began to appear again. By 2008, government borrowing was rocketing in volume and, much as in the late 1940s, official intervention was being used as a means of holding down long-term bond yields – this time using the policy label of 'quantitative easing'.

Entering a period of turmoil

From the mid-1990s onwards, the whole process for determining asset allocation began to unravel. For the British actuarial profession, a landmark was the presentation at the Institute of Actuaries in April 1997 of a Sessional Paper[5] called 'The Financial Theory of Defined Benefit Pension Funds'. The three authors – Jon Exley, Shyam Mehta and Andrew Smith – directly attacked the conventional belief that equities were 'natural' assets for DB pension funds and instead recommended bond-based strategies. They said they wished to rescue DB pension schemes from the dire consequences of unanticipated and unrewarded risks, an aspiration which seemed provocative and fanciful at the time, but not in the light of what happened subsequently.

In May 1997, the Labour Party won a general election and within a few months the new Chancellor of the Exchequer, Gordon Brown, had entered the picture by launching his notorious £5 billion a year tax 'raid' on equity dividends received by pension funds. This was represented as partly an attempt to discourage British companies from paying high dividends rather than retaining the funds and investing in expansion. But more importantly, it amounted to the imposition of a 'stealth' tax on pension scheme surpluses which, had more rigorous valuation techniques been employed, would never have been claimed to exist.

Meanwhile, the equity market was moving into the final dangerous stage of its long bull market. The technology-based bubble which dominated the final two or three years of a bull market lasting 18 years was clearly irrational and British pension funds were highly exposed. Some degree of adjustment was

---

5 J. Exley, S. Mehta and A. Smith, 'The Financial Theory of Defined Benefit Pension Funds', (1997) 3(4) *British Actuarial Journal* 835–966.

being made as between 1993 and 1998 the allocation of pension fund portfolios to bonds nearly doubled from 10 to 19 per cent, but it was too little, too late, and there was no escape.

At around this time, the accountants were moving into action. Previously, they had been content to leave much of the financial reporting by pension schemes to the actuaries. But the accountants were becoming concerned by the scale of financial risks of many kinds, for instance, in banking and other financial sectors, as well as in corporate pensions. They were turning towards 'fair value' methods, which increasingly marked assets to market prices or, where they were not available, to some other suitable measure of current worth.

In 1999, IAS 19 was launched, followed by a separate but similar UK standard FRS 17, which was phased in after 2001. Under FRS 17, assets were marked to market annually and the AA-rated corporate bond yield was introduced as a discounting factor for liabilities. The effect was to increase the observed financial risks of corporate pension plans, due to both equity price volatility and the extent of mismatching against bonds. Annual surpluses or deficits were not credited to or charged against earnings, but were stated in the profit and loss account. A number of large British companies became exposed as having pension deficits approaching or even exceeding the market capitalisations of the sponsoring enterprise: examples included British Telecom and its public sector ex-stablemate the Post Office, while British Airways was scathingly described as a small airline struggling to feed a huge pension fund.

The timing of the crackdown by the auditors was unfortunate, given that equity markets crumbled between 2000 and 2003. Within the short space of two or three years, the comfortable, and even embarrassing, surpluses of DB pension schemes in the 1990s abruptly disappeared. British schemes were overwhelmed by a series of highly damaging developments:

- dividend income taxes, costing around £5 billion a year from 1998;
- the halving of share prices from a peak in early 2000;
- falling bond yields (which raised the present value of liabilities);
- highly adverse longevity trends, with life expectancy rising by something like two years per decade; and
- relatively new statutory controls on solvency because the Pensions Act 1995 had introduced the concept of a Minimum Funding Requirement, subsequently replaced by the measures in the Pensions Act 2004.

New definitions of scheme solvency

While pension actuaries continued to calculate scheme solvency on a smoothed basis, usually every three years, three other measures of solvency came into vogue. One was the FRS 17 formula and a second, even less flattering version, was the full buy-out valuation representing the difference between a scheme's assets and the cost to the company of buying out the liabilities through an insurance company. The other definition of solvency appeared in the Pensions Act 2004, legislation which introduced the Pensions Regulator (TPR) and the compulsory solvency insurance agency the Pension Protection Fund (PPF). Section 179 of the Act defined the valuation of liabilities for PPF purposes.

The section 179 valuation is slightly more favourable for pension schemes than the FRS 17 version, mainly because the PPF does not pay out in full the pensions promised by bankrupt sponsors. For example, the TPR's *Purple Book 2007*, an annual publication,[6] estimated that in March 2007 the DB sector's aggregate buy-out deficit was £400 billion and the FRS 17 deficit was £86 billion, but on the section 179 basis there was actually a surplus of £52 billion. However, these values can fluctuate widely, both absolutely and in relative terms, as is demonstrated by the fact that two years later the *Purple Book 2009* calculated that the section 179 funding position had sharply deteriorated to a deficit of £200 billion, while the FRS 17 deficit had actually fallen a little to £54 billion. Meanwhile, the buy-out deficit had climbed to £571 billion. Some of these variations may have reflected changes in the pension schemes universe from year to year. But the main factors were equity market levels (particularly low at the March 2009 valuation date, before a very sharp move upwards) and fluctuations in the relationship between gilt-edged bond yields and corporate bond yields.

As a result of all of these problems, the risk framework for pension funds was transformed at the beginning of the twenty-first century. Until the 1990s, pension funds were among the most risk-tolerant of investors and they became the dominant owners of equities. The increasing internationalisation of port-folios also meant that their influence was spreading: UK pension funds, and US funds too, became very important investors in major listed companies in Continental Europe, for example, filling something of a gap because domestic, risk-friendly investors had always been scarce in countries such as Germany and France.

Quite quickly, pension funds were becoming risk-averse. The changes in the United States were progressing a little more slowly, especially in terms of accountancy, but were going in the same general direction as in the United Kingdom. At the beginning of 2000, the average UK fund's exposure to equities was 75 per cent of the total portfolio, but by 2009 it was falling below 50 per cent, taking strategy back roughly to where it had been 50 years earlier.

A reassessment of equities

This disillusionment with equities arose partly because equity market returns became so poor. As already discussed, the ten-year period up to 2008 was one

---

6 TPR, *Purple Book 2007*, www.thepensionsregulator.gov.uk/docs/purple-book-2007.pdf; and TPR, *Purple Book 2008, 2009, 2010*.

Table 3.3 UK self-administered pension funds net investment in equities (£ billion)			
Year	UK equities	Overseas equities	Total equities
2000	–7.2	–11.8	–19.0
2001	0.2	16.5	16.7
2000	–10.9	15.6	4.7
2003	–8.5	4.9	–3.6
2004	–17.7	7.2	–10.5
2005	–17.7	–0.2	–17.9
2006	–17.7	1.0	–16.7
2007	–27.6	–6.5	–34.1
2008	–5.3	–10.1	–15.4
2009	–6.6	2.4	–4.2

Source: National Statistics.

of the worst in history for global equities: only periods including the great slump of the 1930s or the inflationary crisis of the 1970s were as bad. There were simple economic explanations for market weakness during those previous times, but in contrast the 1999 to 2008 decade was a very buoyant period for the global economy (although leading up to a nasty recession).

Why did equities perform so badly during these years of apparently favourable conditions? A simple explanation is that there was a necessary correction of the notorious stock market price bubble which peaked in the year 2000. But it is worth looking for reasons why the price level of the global market strayed so far away from fair value. This is important because pension funds themselves may have played a significant role.

Pension funds were influential in pumping up the equity markets during the 1980s and 1990s. They bought shares from other kinds of investors, including private individuals and governments (which took the opportunity offered by strong demand from investors for risk capital by embarking on a privatisation spree). They then began to undermine equities in a swing of the pendulum; corporate sponsors decided to retreat from defined benefit pensions (thus reducing the flow of contributions) and, moreover, the trustee boards turned increasingly towards liability-matching strategies, which involved ever-greater allocations to fixed-income securities. More detailed risk analysis procedures have also presented trustees with an opportunity to consider in more detail their approach to various specific risk exposures: equity market risk, bond mismatching risk, inflation risk, foreign exchange rate risk and (to enter a very sensitive area for trustees) sponsor risk. There are also various regulatory risks, including those related to the PPF. And there is a kind of elephant in the room, in the form of a huge exposure in most schemes to longevity risk, in respect of which various techniques are being developed. Such an analysis of various specific risks may open up the possibility that derivative markets could be used to control overall scheme risks. Trustees have to be confident, however, that they have enough internal and external expertise and advice to take decisions on technically obscure matters.

The increasing pressures on pension funds since the late 1990s have caused sponsors and trustees to think more carefully about governance issues relating to investment strategy. Risk analysis, asset-liability matching and the possible contribution of investment specialists through an investment sub-committee of the trustee board have become important subjects. These are discussed in detail in Chapters 11, 12 and 13.

Pension funds as suppliers of risk capital

The changes in pension fund investment strategy invite the question of what will happen to equity markets in the future. If pension funds not only shrink in size, as appears to be happening, but withdraw almost completely into bonds and other low-risk assets, the global markets may run short of risk capital. True, there are other categories of equity investors which are growing in influence, including sovereign wealth funds and private equity funds. But they remain very modest in size compared with pension funds and they may introduce new risks of a political or speculative nature to the markets.

Any shortage of equity capital could pose a particular problem over the next few years as the corporate sector globally is likely to require large volumes of new equity risk capital in order to replace the excessive debt built up during the credit bubble period, which peaked in 2007. Extra funds will also be required in order to finance recovery after the global recession.

The main characteristic of pension funds as investors is that they often have very long time horizons. Each scheme has a different maturity profile depending on the structure of the membership. But younger employee members are accruing benefits to be received 50 or even more years into the future. However, retired members with pensions already in payment have immediate income rights that can more suitably be matched against a bond portfolio of limited duration.

Equities can be regarded as investments with very long or even infinite duration. From this approach developed the now rather old-fashioned argument that equities provide a suitable match for pension scheme liabilities, at least for those with very long maturity. The difficulty with such arguments is that, in practice, equity portfolios are turned over rather quickly and the concept of duration is difficult to apply. After all, managers of equity portfolios normally define their performance targets in terms of short-term deviations from the market indices and the long term is left to take care of itself.

Nevertheless, the poor combination of return and volatility delivered by listed stock market investments over the past decade has triggered some new thinking. The question is whether commitments should be made to long-term projects, of which various infrastructure schemes provide perhaps the best examples. The whole area of renewable energy is a central part of the discussion; certain alternative assets such as timber forests also have potential.

And even in the more conventional listed equity market some managers are offering a long-range approach in which there is little or no attempt to trade individual stocks, but considerable research effort is put into the identification of companies which will prosper over periods relevant to the liability-matching objectives of immature pension plans. Such strategies can be regarded as reducing the long-term risks and taking advantage of the inherent risk toleration of pension funds. But there are big practical difficulties. There will always be a need for the managers to react to unexpected events, as they arise. Moreover, as long as valuations are carried out in the usual way at one-year intervals, there will be persistent high volatility to worry sponsors, regulators, fiduciaries and plan members.

The search for alternative asset classes

Perhaps extensive diversification of risky projects and investments will provide part of the answer. Some US funds – especially college endowment funds, which have somewhat similar objectives to pension funds – have adopted strategies of investing in illiquid asset classes (ranging from private equity to timber forests) with supposedly low correlation. At the same time they have avoided mainstream asset classes such as listed equities and government bonds. For ten years until about 2006, endowments such as those of Harvard and Yale earned spectacular returns from this.

The rationale for such strategies was based primarily on considerations of value and the duration of liabilities. A big college endowment fund (or a pension fund) does not require high liquidity in its investments, so to invest in the most liquid asset classes implies that it is paying a price for an unnecessary investment characteristic. Other kinds of investors – such as banks, mutual funds and private investors – can be left to pursue the liquidity that they need.

However, when endowment funds focus on alternative assets, they are entering what may turn out to be something of an investment jungle. Hedge funds are sometimes described as 'absolute return' funds, which may imply that they target fairly steady investment returns – say in the range of 10 to 12 per cent a year – almost regardless of whether the major asset classes are affected by bull or bear markets. Somewhat similarly, private equity funds profess to take corporate assets off the listed markets and develop and restructure them so as to create enhanced value. Several years later they can be sold to trade buyers or refloated as listed entities at values that are not linked to the general ups and downs of equities, but rather to the skill of the private equity specialists.

Table 3.4 Yale Endowment Fund annual return on assets (%)					
Years ended 30 June	*2005*	*2006*	*2007*	*2008*	*2009*
	22.3	22.9	28.0	4.5	−24.6

However, sceptics of these 'alternative' asset classes point out that a major factor in hedge fund and private equity strategies is high leverage. Is their major objective to leverage returns in bull markets? If so, bear markets are bound to cause them major problems. It is certainly not the general rule that hedge funds as a group can perform as well in bear markets as good markets – an original claim of the pioneer hedge fund manager Alfred Jones in the 1960s when he developed the idea that general market risk could be hedged out completely. Most hedge funds reported negative returns in 2008 when the markets were disrupted by the effects of the credit crunch.

At any rate, hedge funds and private equity funds come in all shapes and sizes, and degrees of client-orientation and even honesty. It requires a great deal of skill and hard work, not to mention intuition, to avoid the crooks like Bernard Madoff and pick the very best operators. The range of returns achieved by individual hedge funds and private equity funds is very varied, and the best performers are often closed to new business anyway. These are not open, regulated investment markets, but are more in the nature of business networks which are best left to those who have special knowledge and well-established contacts. Small pension schemes have the opportunity to invest on a lower risk basis in funds of hedge funds, but these are costly vehicles; the returns are usually fairly modest and it is not clear that they are uncorrelated with the returns on the major asset classes, notably equities.

The top endowment funds, in developing alternative strategies, had the field largely to themselves for some years and picked the best performers. Latecomers to these alternative asset classes tended to pick second-rate funds and experience corresponding poor returns. In any case, something of a bubble was developing in alternatives, including most commodities, from 2005 onwards and the claimed high returns of the leading endowments owed much to unsustainable price momentum as copycat investors tried to force their way into illiquid investments. Eventually, the bubble burst.

The damage became painfully apparent in the financial year 2008 to 2009 (endowments often draw up their accounts at the end of June, the close of the academic year). Harvard's fund reported a negative investment return of 27 per cent as almost all of its asset classes – especially private equity – suffered heavy declines. At Yale, the result was similar, with a negative return of 25 per cent. These losses were probably about twice as great as those typically borne in that period by more conventional funds invested mainly in listed equities and fixed interest bonds.

Table 3.5 Yale Endowment Fund asset allocation at the peak value of $22.8 billion in June 2008 (%)	
Absolute return	25.1
Domestic equity	10.1
Fixed income	4.0
Foreign equity	15.2
Private equity	20.2
Real assets	29.3
Cash	–3.9

However, this bad year came after a very successful decade. In the ten years ending 2007/08, Harvard achieved an annualised investment return of 13.8 per cent, and Yale one of 16.3 per cent. For comparison, the return obtained by the average UK pension fund over the same period was only about 4 per cent. Not only pension schemes but also rival academic institutions, including Oxford and Cambridge in the United Kingdom, became very jealous of this apparent ability by the stars of the Ivy League to create wealth and they have also set up endowment funds. But the risks of a shift into illiquid assets of uncertain value have become apparent.

For the likes of Harvard, this crisis in the alternatives was a financial embarrassment which might reduce the flow of scholarships and research grants, while also delaying new building projects. However, for pension plans subject to increasingly tight regulation, the consequences might well be much more serious: for example, sponsors might be required to subscribe more funds. As the regulation of life insurance and pension funds has developed, since the 1990s, the analysis of price, volatility, liquidity and risk has become more rigorous and comprehensive. Governments, regulators and statutory guarantee funds will not allow investment institutions to make up their own rules and pin their own value estimates on assets which are unsellable in most conditions.

New approaches to risk

The traditional philosophy underlying British pension fund trustee behaviour has been that it has been appropriate to accept substantial investment risks because the upside gains will be beneficial both to the sponsors and the scheme members, while the downside risks can be borne by the sponsors – who, after all, raised their contribution rates sharply in the late 1970s and again after the turn of the century. But in recent years, many sponsors of defined benefit schemes have been backing away from this implied promise by closing pension plans in stages. The first step is to close to new employees, the second to close to all new accrual and the last step may be to transfer the scheme to a life company.

It is interesting to see how the methodical Dutch have addressed these issues. The Dutch regulators treat corporate pension schemes very much like life insurance companies. Schemes in the Netherlands are allowed to invest in volatile assets such as equities, and many do. But they are required to put up extra regulatory capital to cover the equity risk. In effect, sponsors are not permitted to fill any gaps that appear in the funds as they arise, but they have to cover the downside risk of equities in advance.

A consequence of such safety-first measures is to raise the cost of covering the pension promise. In the United Kingdom and United States, the problem was aggravated in the wake of the 2008 credit crunch by the decision to adopt policies of quantitative easing – meaning the official purchases of bonds on a massive scale in order to monetise the financial system. This had the side-effect of lowering government bond yields, or at least holding them below their natural levels. Such a phenomenon clearly suited governments which had enormous borrowing programmes in the bond markets. But it was damaging for investors, especially pension funds.

Not only did bond income tend to fall, but when pension plans were subject to the newer financial reporting standards – such as FRS 17 in the United Kingdom – their surplus/deficit calculations were adversely affected. For a while, they were being hit twice: firstly, by the weakness of equity prices and secondly, by a decline in bond yields, which had the effect of increasing the present value of their liabilities. By 2009, the equity market was recovering fast, which reduced the deficits but did not really help solve – in fact, may have aggravated – the underlying problem of the long-term volatility of equities.

Given the risk and solvency issues of pension schemes, any strength in equities may have two consequences. Firstly, it will obviously enhance the rather faded appeal of equities as an asset class. But, secondly, trustees and sponsors may see a bull market as providing an opportunity to sell out. In any fundamental change in long-term strategy, such as a switch from equities to bonds, short-term market timing intrudes as a complicating but important factor. In the United Kingdom, the equity market sell-off by pension funds, which became pronounced from the late 1990s onwards, might continue for a number of years to come. Equities could become very cheap again, as they did in the early post-war period and again in the late 1970s.

Consequences of pension scheme closures

The pressures on DB corporate pension schemes in the United Kingdom, and also the United States, have become extreme. Most schemes are closed to new entrants and increasing numbers are shutting to new accrual by existing members. The whole sector may be quite rapidly restructured into closed funds on a run-off basis and invested in liability-matching bonds.

True, there are other types of pension providers in existence, or planned. Defined contribution corporate plans have existed on a small scale for many years and recently have been more widely set up as alternatives to the now-closed DB schemes; there are a few stakeholder plans, relics of an earlier unsuccessful government attempt to prop up the corporate pension framework; several types of personal pension plans are popular; and a highly ambitious and mandatory Personal Accounts scheme, called NEST (National Employment Savings Trust), has been planned by the government to reach people not already covered by pension schemes, to be introduced by a date which was originally 2012, but which has slipped further into the future. Might these various funded pension arrangements provide a replacement demand for equities? The trouble is, they are all focused on individuals and most private investors are highly risk-averse and will be reluctant to invest in volatile listed equities (let alone in shadowy long-term projects). Moreover, the history of mutual funds shows that most investors get their timing in the volatile equity market badly wrong, buying near the cyclical tops and selling close to the bottoms in a way which leads to severe underperformance compared to long-term equity market returns.

The danger of a gap in the capital markets

If DB schemes exit equities, and other pension funds fail to take up the slack, an important gap could appear in the capital markets. There would be favourable opportunities for other types of long-term investors, including private individuals, corporates, private equity funds and sovereign wealth funds. For governments in general, there might be nationalisation opportunities, reversing some of the privatisation that has been common over the past 30 years during the heyday of pension funds. In due course, depending on the buoyancy or otherwise of the global economy, a period of high equity market returns might well commence: this happened between 1952 and 1972, and again between 1982 and 2000.

Fluctuations in the capital markets are inevitable and can usually be absorbed by informed users. However, there is a possibility that the markets could become stressed and might cease, for a time at least, to provide a necessary flow of risk capital to the corporate sector. Pension funds over the decades have proved to be supportive investors. Alternative owners of corporate equity such as private equity funds or governments might try to pursue aggressive or politically motivated agendas. It is time for some considered thinking on the consequences of discouraging pension funds from investing in the global equity markets. The world needs stable, long-term investors in risk. But an important proportion of them are in effect being regulated out of the equity asset class.

Perhaps it is the high price volatility of conventional listed equity stocks that is at the heart of the problem. Should there be a greater emphasis on less risky securities such as convertibles? Might it be practicable to invent other classes of participating risk capital that would be less volatile? Would regulators or accounting standard setters be impressed enough to relax the rigour of their solvency tests? There is a growing need for a debate here.

Meanwhile, the traditional governance issues for pension schemes have become distorted. For many decades, equity investment appeared attractive as part of the pursuit of very long-term strategy. Today, however, fiduciaries, sponsors and regulators have become preoccupied with much shorter-term matters involving deficits, scheme closures, buy-outs and restructurings. Risk has been shunned and asset-liability matching has become the dominant theme.

4

Social responsibility and fiduciary duties of trustees

PAUL WATCHMAN

> Many assumptions underlying the way economists, policymakers and regulators have traditionally viewed pension schemes no longer apply.
>
> K. Johnson and F. Graaf[1]

Fiduciary duties of pension fund trustees have been described as a 'ramshackle concept',[2] a Gothic legal edifice of great antiquity which no longer has much to offer as a model to delineate the duties of pension fund trustees.[3] Therefore, to financial or investment experts living in the twenty-first-century, post-Sarbanes-Oxley world, discussion of fiduciary duties in the context of modern pension fund management may appear to jar. However, why should the fiduciary duties of pension fund trustees be thought of as a historical relic when they appear to sit happily as part of the duties owed by a company director to his or her members? Indeed, so much so are fiduciary duties of company directors regarded as relevant and necessary to good corporate governance that they were codified by recent UK company legislation.[4] Part of the explanation surely lies in the fact that pension funds have developed rapidly in the latter part of the twentieth century. From humble beginnings as simple trust-based legal entities, pension funds have become very sophisticated and complex investment vehicles. In fact, pension funds are now major players in the global investment market and in some cases a dominant force in local or regional investment markets.

To give some idea of the scale and recent rapid growth of the global investment industry, it may be helpful to compare International Finance Services London (IFSL) estimates of the values of the investment market and in particular pension funds for 2005 and 2008. The UNEP FI Freshfields Report,

1 K. Johnson and F. Graaf, 'Modernising Pension Fund Legal Standards for the Twenty-First Century', (2009) 2(1) *Rotman International Journal of Pension Management* 44.
2 R. Lee, 'In Search of the Nature and Function of Fiduciary Loyalty: Some Observations on Conaglen's Analysis', (2007) 27 *Oxford Journal of Legal Studies* 327. See also M. Conaglen, 'The Nature and Function of Fiduciary Loyalty', (2005) 121 *Law Quarterly Review* 452.
3 J. Langbein, 'Questioning the Trust Law Duty of Loyalty: Some Interest or Best Interest?', (2005) 114 *Yale Law Journal* 929.
4 Section 172(1) of the Companies Act 2006.

based on IFSL data, stated that in 2005 the value of invested funds worldwide was $42 trillion.[5] By 2008, IFSL reported that, after a 19 per cent fall in value in 2008, the global investment industry conventional investment value was $61.6 trillion. Of this sum, pension fund investment accounted for $24 trillion, whereas insurance funds and mutual funds accounted for US $18.7 and $18.9 trillion respectively. Another important fact provided by IFSL on pension fund investment value was that in 2008 the United States dominated the pension fund market. In that year, the United States had $15.26 trillion under management. To give some idea of the scale of US domination, the United Kingdom – by far the next largest country for pension fund investment – had $2.66 trillion under management.[6]

Historical origins of fiduciary duties

> Those who cannot remember the past are condemned to repeat it.
>
> George Santayana[7]

Claims have been made that the concept of fiduciary duties can be traced back to the Bible,[8] Roman law[9] and the crusades.[10] Whatever their provenance, there can be no doubt that, originally at least, fiduciary duties were the creation of judges, not legislatures.[11] However, they became over time a set of obligations laid down by the judiciary or the legislature to regulate what was perceived as a special relationship of trust and honour between fiduciary and beneficiary. It is common, for example, in such relationships to find the fiduciary vested with very broad discretion to act to protect or enhance the interests of the beneficiary, albeit the extent of discretion open to a fiduciary may be limited by an investment plan, contract or statute.[12] Equally, it is generally the case that a beneficiary or beneficiaries had scant contractual rights to supervise management of assets by the fiduciary or obtain redress against the mismanagement of assets by the fiduciary. This apparent imbalance in power and vulnerability of the beneficiary to fraud or theft gave rise to a recognition by the judiciary in some legal jurisdictions, in some instances later supplanted or supplemented by trust law or by legislative definition, providing a raft of fiduciary duties circumscribing

---

5 UNEP FI/Freshfields, A Legal Framework for the Integration of Environmental, Social and Governance Issues into Institutional Investment' (October 2005), p. 20 (hereafter, Freshfields Report (2005)). All sums are expressed in US dollars unless otherwise stated.

6 www.ifsl.org.uk, Fund Management 2009 (October 2009).

7 G. Santayana, *The Life of Reason* (New York: Dover Publications Inc., 1980), vol. 1, ch. 12.

8 Matthew 25, Verses 14–30.

9 *Institutes of Roman Law by Gaius*, with a translation and commentary by Edward Poste, 4th edn (Oxford: Clarendon Press, 1904).

10 A. Hudson, *Equity & Trusts*, 4th edn (London: Cavendish Publishing, 2005).

11 R. Lee, 'Rethinking the Content of the Fiduciary Obligation', (2009) 73 *The Conveyancer and Property Lawyer* 236.

12 E.g. the Japanese Welfare Pension Insurance and *Le Fonds de Réserve pour les Retraites*.

that special legal relationship of trust and honour between the parties.[13] These fiduciary duty rules set down by judges to regulate such special relationships required a very high degree of responsibility on the part of the fiduciary or trustee, much stricter than the morals of the market place in the words of Mr Justice Cardozo,[14] as a necessary protection against a strong temptation on the part of the fiduciary or trustee towards theft or fraud.[15]

In the twentieth century, there developed a fundamental challenge to the traditional concept of fiduciary duties insofar as the pension fund industry and the financial investment market were concerned. Changes in pension fund demand and the need for greater sustainability of finance and investment of pension funds particularly and the entry of new investment vehicles, instruments and practices led to an investment industry revolution.[16] Before examining this revolution, it is necessary to describe the nature of the fiduciary duties of pension fund trustees.

The fiduciary duties of pension fund trustees[17]

Something stricter than the morals of the market place.

Mr Justice Cardozo[18]

To understand the development of modern fiduciary duties of pension fund trustees, it is necessary to examine the leading cases and provide an outline of their nature and content. In the United States, the modern prudent investor rule[19] provides some clarity on the nature and content of fiduciary duties of pension fund trustees. However, the position in the United Kingdom has been muddied for some time by a misunderstanding or limited reading of *Cowan* v. *Scargill*.[20] The arguments against the common misperceptions of this case are laid out in detail in the Freshfields Report[21] and will not be rehearsed fully

---

13 Companies Act 2006, s. 172(1) sets out in legislation the fiduciary duties of company directors. A proposal to define the fiduciary duties of pension fund directors during the passage of the Pensions Bill was resisted by the government on the ground that pension fund trustees had wide discretion to take account of matters, such as ethics, without breaching their fiduciary duties.

14 Mr Justice Cardozo: 'Many forms of conduct permissible in a workaday world for those acting at arm's length are forbidden to those bound by fiduciary ties. A trustee is held to something stricter than the morals of the market place. Not honesty alone, but the punctilio of an honor the most sensitive, is then the standard of behaviour.' *Meinhard* v. *Salmon* (1928) 164 N.E. 545 at p. cited by Johnson and Graaf, 'Modernising Pension Fund Legal Standards', cited above fn. 1, p. 46.

15 *Ibid.*

16 R. Sullivan and C. Mackenzie, *Responsible Investment* (Sheffield: Greenleaf Publishing, 2006).

17 R. Lee, 'Rethinking the Content of the Fiduciary Obligation', cited above fn. 11.

18 Cited above fn. 14.

19 UNEP FI/Freshfields Report (2005), cited above fn. 5, p. 8.

20 [1984] 3 WLR 501; [1985] 1 Ch. 270. See also *Martin* v. *Edinburgh DC* (1988) SLT 328; and *Harries* v. *Church Commissioners for England* [1992] 1 WLR 1241.

21 Cited above fn. 5, pp. 88–90.

here. Suffice it to state that even the judge in this case, Megarry V-C, expressed doubt some years later that *Cowan* v. *Scargill* did no more than echo settled law on fiduciary duties rather than expanding them to what became an accepted investment industry myth of the need for profit maximisation in respect of each and every transaction.[22]

As the law in relation to the fiduciary duties of pension fund trustees is far from clear, reference should also be made to guidance issued by regulatory bodies. For example, the US Department of Labor (DOL) issues guidance on fiduciary duties[23] and the OECD issues guidance on fund management generally,[24] both of which provide guidance on fiduciary duties and the modern prudent investor test.

From a reading of the US,[25] English and Scots case law and a review of legislation and regulatory guidance on fiduciary duties and pension fund trustees, a core of common law fiduciary duties applicable to a pension fund trustee (the fiduciary duties of company directors differ, as do the duties of other types of fiduciary) may be suggested to include the duties of loyalty, good faith, protection of the pension fund's beneficiaries' (both present and future) best interests, fairness, prudence and acting for a proper purpose. To these may be added other ancillary fiduciary duties, such as the duty to diversify to spread risk, which, however, may also be seen by some as part of the core duty to act prudently. A further example of where an ancillary fiduciary duty may be regarded not as an ancillary duty, but as a core fiduciary duty in its own right is the duty to monitor, communicate and influence. This relatively new requirement of pension fund trustees to monitor the activities of the asset manager and the companies' stocks and shares in which they invest and communicate their findings with the beneficiaries has been stated by the DOL to be consistent with the discharge of the fiduciary duty of pension funds[26] and clearly forms an important part of the active duties imposed on pension fund trustees by Principles for Responsible Invesment (PRI).[27]

---

22 R. E. Megarry, 'Investing Pension Funds: The Mineworkers' Case' in T. G. Youdan, *Equity, Fiduciaries and Trusts* (Scarborough: Carswell, 1989), p. 115.

23 PWBA Office of Regulations and Interpretations, Advisory Opinion (DOL, May 28, 1998) (Calvert Letter).

24 OECD, Guidelines for Pension Fund Governance, 5 June 2009; and OECD, Recommendation on Core Principles of Occupational Pension Regulation, 5 June 2009.

25 See, e.g. the Freshfields Report (2005), cited above fn. 5, pp. 102–16 and the following cases: *Associated Students of Oregon* v. *Oregon Investment Council* (1989) 82 Or. App. 145, 728 P.2d.30; *Board of Trustees of Employee Retirement System of the City of Baltimore* v. *City of Baltimore* (1989) 317 Md. 72; 562 A.2d. 720; *Withers* v. *Teachers Retirement System* (1978) 447 E. Supp. 148 (SDNT); and *Blakenship* v. *Boyle* (1979) 329 E. Supp. 1089, 1112.

26 US Department of Labour, *Meeting Your Fiduciary Duties* (October 2008), www.dol.gov/ebsa/pdf/fiduciaryresponsibility.pdf.

27 UNEP FI, PRI, Principles (2006): Principle 2 (active ownership), Principle 3 (disclosure), Principle 4 (promotion of principles) and Principle 6 (reporting).

Given the generality and vagueness of fiduciary duties, they may be seen to overlap, and in some cases conflict, to some extent. Therefore, it is not surprising that not all commentators agree as to the exact nature and content of the fiduciary duties of pension fund trustees.[28] Likewise, there is disagreement as to whether each duty is to be given equal priority or weight. Yet, as a pension fund is an investment instrument in general, the fundamental duty of pension fund trustees must be the proper fiscal management of the fund to provide reasonable returns to the beneficiaries according to the terms of contractual agreements between the trust and asset managers, such as investment mandates and investment management contracts.[29] Additionally, it may be noted that the discharge of fiduciary duties, such as the duty to act fairly, may give rise to an unavoidable conflict of interest between present and future beneficiaries of the trust fund.[30] Finally, the organic nature of fiduciary duties may lead to changes in the definition of the legality of fiduciary duties to reflect changes in social values[31] and what may be regarded as, for example, prudent or fair investment practice.[32] It also suggests that given the organic nature of fiduciary duties and changes in social mores and civil society beliefs and practices, the legal application, interpretation and development of the list of core and ancillary fiduciary duties may never be regarded as finally complete.[33]

It is worth mentioning those fiduciary duties which may be regarded as a challenge to the integration of Environmental, Social and Governance (ESG) considerations into mainstream and pension fund investment decision-making.

---

28 Cf. Freshfield Reports (2005) and (2009); B. J. Richardson, *Socially Responsible Investment Law* (Oxford: Oxford University Press, 2008); B. J. Richardson, 'Do the Fiduciary Duties of Pension Funds Hinder Socially Responsible Investment?', (2007) 22 *Banking and Finance Law Review* 145; B. J. Richardson, 'Putting Ethics into Environmental Law', (2008) 46 *Osgoode Hall Law Journal* 243; Megarry, 'Investing Pension Funds', cited above fn. 22; Langbein, 'Questioning the Trust Law Duty of Loyalty', cited above fn. 3; J. Langbein, 'The Uniform Prudent Investor Act and the Future of Trust Investing', (1996) 81 *Iowa Law Review* 641; R. Lee, 'Rethinking the Content of the Fiduciary Obligation', (2009) 73 *The Conveyancer and Property Lawyer* 236; C. Woods, 'Funding Climate Change: How Pension Fund Fiduciary Duty Masks Trustee Inertia and Short-Termism' in J. Hawley, S. Kamath and A. T. Williams (eds), *Institutional Investors, Risk/Return Tradeoffs and Corporate Governance Failures* (Philadelphia, PA: University of Pennsylvania Press, 2011, forthcoming); R. Thornton, 'Ethical Investments: A Case of Disjointed Thinking' (2008) *Cambridge Law Journal* 412; and J. H. Farrar and J. K. Maxton, 'Social Investment and Pension Fund Trusts', (1986) 102 *Law Quarterly Review* 32.

29 *Cowan* v. *Scargill*; *Martin* v. *City of Edinburgh*; and *Harries*, all cited above fn. 20. J. H. Langbein and R, A. Posner, 'Social Investing and the Law', (1980) 79 Michigan Law Review 72.

30 *Cowan* v. *Scargill*, cited above fn. 20.

31 *Roberts* v. *Hopwood* [1925] AC 575; *Prescott* v. *Birmingham Corp.* [1955] Ch. 210; and *Bromley LBC and Greater London Council* v. *Secretary of State for the Environment* [1982] 2 WLR 62.

32 Johnson and Graaf, cited above fn. 1, p. 45.

33 Freshfields II Report (2009).

The duty to act for a proper purpose of the trust

As can be seen from *Cowan* v. *Scargill*,[34] it is the duty of pension fund trustees to act for the proper purposes of the trust. Much then will turn on the wording of the objectives of the trust and the investment plan. Yet in *Cowan* v. *Scargill*,[35] it can be seen that the courts will be reluctant to allow trustees to distort trust investment by indulging in financing political beliefs or placing ethics before financial sustainability. The Freshfields Report questioned whether taking account of ESG considerations breached fiduciary duties where there was a business case and added that failure to take account of ESG could itself be a breach of fiduciary duties.[36] Moreover, on a careful reading of case law, the Freshfield Report added that this restriction did not apply to church or issue trusts ('crusader trusts'), which in declining to invest in certain industries such as armaments, land mines, paper and pulp, timber, tobacco, oil and gas or alcohol were in fact acting not only for the proper purposes of the trust, but to invest in these industries would be against the *raison d'être* for the trust. Examples of such 'crusader' trusts include the Church of England, Salvation Army or British Heart Foundation. It may be that the Freshfields Report was too conservative in its view of the critical distinction between 'crusader' trusts and non-crusader trusts on this issue. The UK and other governments, by way of support for this argument, have pointed to ethics being a proper consideration for pension trusts notwithstanding their status as 'crusader' or non-crusading trusts.[37] Equally, other academic and industry commentators have suggested that there are ample legal grounds without reliance on the business case for pension funds to have regard to ethical considerations as part of their investment decision-making process.[38]

Duty to act in the best interests of the beneficiaries

A leading, if not the paramount, fiduciary duty of pension fund trustees is to act in the best interests of all classes of beneficiaries.[39] Beneficiaries include present and future beneficiaries.[40] Furthermore, it should be noted

---

34 Cited above fn. 20.
35 *Ibid.*
36 Freshfields Report (2005), cited above fn. 5, p. 86, fn. 339 and p. 88, fn. 355.
37 DOL, Calvert Letter, cited above fn. 23; and speeches by Government Ministers and representatives during the Pensions Bill debate, discussed below.
38 C. Joly, 'Ethical Demand and Requirements in Investment Management', (1999) 2(4) *Business Ethics: A European Review* 199; C. Joly, *The Greening of Financial Markets, Finance for Sustainable Development Testing New Policy Approaches* (New York: United Nations, 2002), pp. 283 ff; Richardson, *Socially Responsible Investment Law*, cited above fn. 28; and Richardson, 'Putting Ethics into Environmental Law', cited above fn. 28.
39 HM Treasury, *Institutional Investment in the United Kingdom: A Review* (London: HM Treasury, 2001), para. 5.89 (hereafter, Myners Report).
40 *Cowan* v. *Scargill*, cited above fn. 20.

that the best interests of the beneficiaries is not defined as or necessarily is the best 'financial' interests of the beneficiaries.[41] In fact, there is often an inherent conflict between the best interests of present beneficiaries, who are drawing pension fund benefits but no longer contributing to a pension fund, and future beneficiaries, who are contributing to the pension fund but not withdrawing benefits from it at present. This tension in holding an appropriate balance between classes of beneficiaries is apparent also as part of the obligation of pension fund trustees to act fairly between the beneficiaries.

Some support for the inclusion of ESG considerations as part of the fiduciary duties of pension fund trustees in the United Kingdom, it is submitted, may be derived by reference to pension law, company law and the speeches of the UK pension ministers during the passage of the Pensions Bill.[42]

UK pensions legislation requires pension fund trustees to ensure that there is a written and updated statement of investment principles (SIP) that governs decisions about investment relating to the pension scheme.[43] Added to that requirement are the duties on pension fund trustees to state in the pension scheme's SIP the extent (if at all) to which their selection, retention and realisation of investments has taken account of social, environmental or ethical considerations and their policy (if any) in relation to the exercise of the rights (including voting rights) attaching to those investments.[44]

Section 172(1) of the Companies Act 2006 states that the basic duty of a company director is to 'act in a way that he or she considers in good faith would most likely promote the success of the company for the benefits of its members as a whole'. Section 172(1) requires company directors in discharge of this basic duty to have regard, amongst other matters, to the following considerations:

- the likely consequences of any decision in the long term;
- the interests of the company's employees;
- the need to foster the company's business relationships with suppliers, customers and others;
- the impact of the company's operations on the community and the environment;
- the desirability of the company maintaining a reputation for high standards of business conduct; and
- the need to act fairly as between members of the company.

---

41 Lord Hoffman, *Nestle* v. *National Westminster Bank* [1993] 1 WLR 1260; and Lord Murray in *Martin* v. *City of Edinburgh*, cited above fn. 20, at 334.

42 Lord McKenzie and Rt Hon. Michael O'Brien, *Hansard*, (HL) 7 October 2009 and *Hansard*, (HC) 21 May 2008.

43 See s. 35 of the Pensions Act 1995 and s. 244 of the Pensions Act 2004.

44 Occupational Pension Schemes (Investment) Regulations SI 3127/1996; and Occupational Pension Schemes (Investment) Regulations SI 3378/2005.

As discussed below, the UK Government declined to encapsulate the fiduciary duties of pension fund trustees in the same way during the passage of the Pensions Bill. However, the fiduciary duties of company directors to company shareholders are widely recognised as being at best as extensive as and certainly no less onerous than the fiduciary duties that are owed by pension fund trustees to the fund beneficiaries. Added to this statutory precedent are the speeches of the UK pensions ministers, approving ESG, including ethical considerations, as relevant, pension-fund-trustee, decision-making considerations for all pension funds. Each of these factors, it is submitted, lends support to ESG being lawful considerations for UK pension fund trustees in discharging their fiduciary duties towards the trust fund beneficiaries.

Duty to act prudently

The final fiduciary duty of pension fund trustees to be examined in the context of the legality of ESG considerations is the duty of prudence. The duty to act prudently relates both to the level of risk a pension fund trustee may find acceptable and the concentration to be applied by pension fund trustees in discharging other fiduciary duties, such as the duties of skill, care and diligence. Regulations issued by the DOL under the Employment Retirement Income Security Act 1974 (ERISA) define the fiduciary duties of a pension fund trustee as being discharged 'with respect to a plan with the skill, care *and prudence*, and diligence under the circumstances then prevailing that *a prudent man acting in a like capacity and familiar with such matters* would use in the conduct of an enterprise of a like character and with like aims'.[45] The qualification to these duties, 'like capacity and familiar with such matters', is cited by Myners as the 'prudent expert' rule.[46] However, prudence also requires the pension fund trustee in discharge of this fiduciary duty to apply necessary professional skills or seek professional advice,[47] diversify investment in accordance with modern portfolio theory,[48] consider the suitability of each investment,[49] take account of relevant considerations and disregard irrelevant considerations,[50] and act reasonably.[51] It has been argued elsewhere that it is highly imprudent for

---

45 Department of Labor, 44 FR 37225, 1979 (emphasis added).

46 HM Treasury, *Institutional Investment in the United Kingdom: A Review (Myners Report)* (London, 2001), para. 2.34. See also HM Treasury, *Myners Principles for Institutional Investment Decision-Making: Review of Progress* (London, 2004) and (London, 2008).

47 Trustee Act, s. 1; and *Barlett* v. *Barclays Bank Trust Co. (No. 1)* [1980] Ch. 515.

48 Lord Hoffman, *Nestle* v. *NatWest Bank*, cited above fn. 41.

49 Pension Act 1995, s. 36; Trustee Act 2000, s. 4(3)(b); and *Harries*, cited above fn. 20.

50 *Re Hastings Bass* [1975] Ch. 25; and *Abacus Trust Co. (Isle of Man)* v. *Barr* [2003] EWHC 114 (Ch.).

51 *Associated Provincial Picture Houses* v. *Wednesbury Corp.* [1947] 2 All ER 680.

pension fund trustees in discharging this principal fiduciary duty to ignore ESG considerations[52] or climate change.[53]

The organic nature of fiduciary duties

On the question of the nature of fiduciary duties in general, it is important to note a key assumption based on case law. This assumption is that it is reasonable to infer that neither their legal definition nor the interpretation of the legality of the acts and omissions in discharge of the requirements of fiduciary duties is static or incapable of augmentation or reduction. Fiduciary duties are hence organic in nature. Fiduciary duties may be seen to alter periodically, to reflect: first, changes in social values; second, changes in investment practice; and third, what may be described broadly as technological changes. However, it should be noted that changes in fiduciary duties and changes in social values, market practices or technological changes are unlikely to be automatic or contemporaneous. This is due to the inherent and deeply conservative nature of the investment industry and the attachment of the judiciary to historical and legal precedent. Given these predilections of judges, asset owners and managers, there is a material time lag between change and recognition of its impact on the legality of pension fund trustee fiduciary duties.

On changes in investment market practices as opposed to changes in social values, it is well known that in investment decision-making excessive prudence as well as a lack of prudence can lead to unnecessary financial loss. For example, a failure to diversify risk by investing in different asset classes (such as equities, bonds, cash or currencies) in accordance with modern portfolio theory may be imprudent.[54] Nevertheless, excluding categories of assets to minimise loss may be equally imprudent.

The most obvious and important change in pension fund investment practice in recent years has been adoption of PRI by the pension fund industry. These principles are discussed below. However, for the present it may be worth mentioning that by 2008 PRI had been adopted by over 360 leading institutional asset owners, investment managers and practice service partners, representing US $14 trillion of assets: a sea change in what is one of the most conservative global investment industries.

Recent developments: the pension fund industry in the twenty-first century

At the heart of this chapter is an assessment of current responsible investment practices adopted widely by an influential group of members of the modern

---

52 Freshfields Report (2005), cited above fn. 5.
53 A. A. Calvello, *Environmental Alpha: Institutional Investors and Climate Change* (New Jersey: John Wiley, 2010), p. 101.
54 Lord Hoffman, *Nestle* v. *NatWest Bank*, cited above fn. 41.

pension funds industry. This assessment also entails examination of contemporary investment practice in the context of fiduciary duties of pension fund trustees. It considers whether, after the creation of and wide acceptance by the pensions industry of PRI and acceptance of the necessity for pension funds to exercise social responsibility in their investment processes and decision-making generally, there is a need for further change. Moreover, it demonstrates that account should be taken of the constant growth and development of pension funds, the progressive concentration of shares in their ownership, the evolution of new products by the pension fund industry and the challenge of the increasing longevity of the population and thereby the dependence of increasing numbers of pension fund beneficiaries. Finally, in assessing the modern pension fund industry, the recent deep and almost unprecedented global meltdown of financial institutions of 2008 to 2009 and subsequent credit crunch cannot be ignored.

These are important but admittedly not the only relevant considerations. The global meltdown of leading banks and other finance houses, for example, did result in a stark light being projected on financial sustainability. However, it also illuminated other dark, cribbed and confined spaces of investment practice – for example, dubious practices such as rewarding asset managers with cash bonuses for short-term returns. The financial meltdown and credit crunch also resulted in a sharper and more expanded public focus and debate about investment and rewards that some private investment vehicles had hitherto enjoyed.[55] Questions fundamental to the pension fund industry were also repeated with greater vigour and imbued with a sense of urgency. For instance, the place of ethics and morality of investment decision-making, the balance between short-term investment returns and long-term financial sustainability, and the impact of extra financial considerations in respect of company value.

Therefore, it would be wrong to infer that concerns about pension fund investment are a twenty-first-century phenomenon. Issues relating to the unchecked and growing power of pension funds are not new, nor is the testing of the ethics of investment and reward systems. Due to increasing concentration of ownership of stocks and shares in the hands of relatively few global pension funds,[56] the market influence of pension funds, almost like the imperium of the Roman Empire, was noted and debated by the economic, legal, investment and political communities for some time.[57] In the past five years

---

55 See, e.g. the interrogation of senior bank officials by the Select Committee on Trade and Industry.

56 K. Johnson and F. Graaf, 'Modernizing Pension Fund Legal Standards for the Twenty-First Century', (2009) 2(1) *Rotman International Journal of Pension Management* 44, fnn. 6 and 7 cite that pension funds in the United States in 2006 accounted for 38.3 per cent of institutional investor public equity holdings, totalling US $10.4 trillion, and that in 2007 the average pensions assets to GDP for all OECD countries was 76 per cent.

57 M. Friedman, 'The Social Responsibility of Business to Increase Its Profits', *New York Magazine*, 13 September 1970; and Langbein and Posner, 'Social Investing and the Law', cited above fn. 29.

especially there have been important challenges, one of the most important being the challenge to pension fund industry orthodoxy that fiduciary duties applicable to pension fund trustees require them to maximise profits. In effect, they are like Ulysses' crew, stuffing their ears with cloth to protect themselves from hearing the siren songs of ESG considerations,[58] corporate responsibility[59] or ethical concerns.[60]

The Freshfields Report

> The single most effective document for promoting the integration of environmental, social and governance (ESG) issues into institutional investment has arguably been the 'Freshfields Report'.
>
> UNEP FI, Fiduciary Responsibility[61]

In 2005, Freshfields were commissioned by the UNEP FI Asset Management Working Group (AMWG) to consider the following question:

> Is the integration of environmental, social and governance issues into investment policy (including asset allocation, portfolio construction and stock-picking or hand-picking) voluntarily permitted, legally required or hampered by law and regulation primarily as regards public and private pension funds, secondarily as regards insurance company reserves and mutual funds?[62]

In raising these questions, the AMWG also indicated its wish to understand whether the commonly held view that fiduciary duties require a portfolio manager solely to pursue profit maximisation is a correct interpretation of the law or whether acting in the interests of beneficiaries can also incorporate other objectives.

In effect, the principal findings of the Freshfields Report turned the world of pension fund investment trustees and asset managers on its head. Rather than denying the need to take account of ESG considerations, the report argued that it was necessary for the investment industry to have regard to ESG considerations as additional valuation tools. Fiduciary duties provided a checklist for the fiduciary rather than obstacles to taking account of ESG in mainstream investment. The report also cautioned pension fund trustees and their asset management advisers that a failure to take account of ESG considerations

---

58 Freshfields Report (2005), cited above fn. 5; and Calvello, *Environmental Alpha* cited above fn. 53, p. 101.
59 Calvello, *Environmental Alpha*, cited above fn. 53, p. 317.
60 See, e.g. Richardson, *Socially Responsible Investment Law*, cited above fn. 28; and C. Joly, 'Ethical Demands and Requirements in Investment Management', (1999) 2(4) *Business Ethics: A European Review* 199–221.
61 UNEP FI, 'Fiduciary Responsibility – Legal and Practical Aspects of Integrating Environmental, Social and Governance Issues into Institutional Investment' (Geneva: UNEP FI, 2009), www.unepfi.org/fileadmin/documents/fiduciaryII.pdf, p. 13.
62 Freshfields Report (2005), cited above fn. 5, p. 6.

where there appeared to be a nexus with value could be a breach of fiduciary duties:

> Institutional investors who hide behind profit maximisation and the limits supposedly placed by their legal duties as fiduciaries do so at their own peril. There is no legal bar to the integration of ESG considerations into investment decision-making (provided the focus is always on the beneficiaries' best interests) and indeed failure to have regard to such considerations where there is a proven link between an ESG consideration and investment value may itself amount to a breach of fiduciary duties by the pension fund trustee or on his behalf by an asset manager.[63]

Although at the time the Freshfields Report appeared to be radical, what it stated about the fiduciary duties of pension funds rapidly and unexpectedly, without great opposition from the pension funds industry, at least that part of the industry which was not based in the United States,[64] became the new orthodoxy. No longer was it possible for pension fund trustees and asset managers to dismiss ESG considerations as irrelevant to mainstream investment practice.

Principles of responsible investment

> If we are to build a more successful, vibrant, modern economy we can no longer afford to view economic success as being in conflict with social and environmental goals. On the contrary these goals must be seen as integral to economic success and the very essence of sustainable development.
>
> Mike O'Brien, UK Minister of State for Pensions[65]

This trend towards incorporating ESG into mainstream investment decision-making was reinforced by the success of PRI, which provided a new blueprint for pension fund investment and management. PRI have six principles, including commitments on the part of signatories to incorporate ESG into investment analysis, decision-making, and active ownership policies and practices; disclosure of ESG issues by investment entities; acceptance and implementation of the principles by the investment industry; and reporting activities and progress towards implementing the principles.

The importance of PRI cannot be exaggerated because they gave the imprimatur of leading global pension funds and asset management to ESG incorporation. No longer was it possible to argue with any degree of industry consensus that ESG was not a relevant consideration for investment practice when the industry leaders had themselves decided that it was relevant to mainstream investment decision-making. It must be stated that other factors also assisted PRI in achieving acceptance of ESG into mainstream investment decision-making. Of those other factors, including voluntary initiatives by financial

63 Freshfields Report (2005), cited above fn. 5, p. 145.
64 See, e.g. Richardson, *Socially Responsible Investment Law*, cited above fn. 28, p. 206.
65 *Hansard*, (HC) 21 May 2008.

institutions and federal and state legislation, by far the most important were climate change and the meltdown of the financial industry.[66] Faced with the destructive proof of global warming in the form of extraordinary natural disasters and unparalleled losses and debts in the financial industry, it became increasingly difficult for investors to ignore ESG.

Fiduciary Responsibility Report: 'Freshfields II'

> ESG issues are not peripheral but should be part of mainstream investment decision-making processes across the industry.[67]
>
> Achim Steiner, UN Under-Secretary and Executive Director,
> UN Environment Programme

The 2009 UNEP FI Fiduciary Responsibility Report is in part a follow up to the Freshfields Report of 2005, which concluded that 'integrating ESG considerations into an investment analysis so as to more reliably predict financial performance is clearly permissible and is arguably required in all jurisdictions' covered by the report.[68] The 2009 report focuses on the two most important of the nine jurisdictions covered by the 2005 Freshfields Report: the United States and the United Kingdom.

The 2009 report details a number of important developments since 2005: first, the widespread adoption by the financial investment industry of PRI;[69] and second, important policy statements made during the passage of the Pensions Bill in 2008 by the UK Government Pensions Minister, Lord McKenzie, that fiduciaries must take account of ESG and even ethical considerations in making investment decisions:

> There is no reason in law why trustees cannot consider social and moral criteria of financial returns, security and diversification. This applies to trustees of all pension funds.

> It is an obligation on pension fund trustees not simply a right or option to state in their Statement of Investment Principles what the fund's guidelines are on responsible investment and what extent social, environmental or ethical considerations are taken into account.[70]

Ministerial statements whatever their context and ministers however august do not amount to a change in the law. Some weight may be given to these statements in interpreting the fiduciary duties of pension fund trustees. It is

---

66 P. Q. Watchman, 'The Case for Climate Change as the Paramount Fiduciary Issue Facing Institutional Investors' in Calvello, *Environmental Alpha*, cited above fn. 53, p. 101.
67 'Greening the World's Multi-trillion Dollar Investments Gets Asset Managers' and Legal Backing', www.unepfi.org/fileadmin/documents/fiduciaryIIpress.pdf (14 July 2009).
68 Freshfields Report (2005), cited above fn. 5, p. 13.
69 See, e.g. PRI Annual Report 2009, which reports 538 signatories in May 2009 responsible for ownership or management of in excess of US $18 trillion.
70 *Hansard*, (HL) 7 October 2008.

necessary to understand the context in which they were made. The fiduciary duties of company directors had been codified in legislation by the Companies Act 2006[71] as stated and amendments to the Pension Bill to achieve the same statutory effect of pension fund trustees' fiduciary duties had been put forward. In essence, the government were trying to persuade those lobbying for this change that it was unnecessary because pension fund trustees already had power to have regard to ESG considerations without breaching their fiduciary duties. By attributing this right and duty to all pension funds, Lord McKenzie, Secretary of State for Pensions put forward a far wider case than that advanced by the 2005 Freshfields Report. The 2005 report accepted only that crusading charities, such as church and health charities, had unfettered discretion to have regard to ESG in the absence of a business case. It was not absolutely certain that a non-crusader pension fund, such as an occupational pension fund, could take account of morals or ethics in investment or divestment decision-making without transgressing its fiduciary duties.[72]

The 2009 Fiduciary Responsibility Report is not limited to a follow-up report on the 2005 Freshfields Report. The 2009 report provides sample ESG provisions for investment mandates and investment management contracts. Sustainability of long-term investment has replaced the need to maximise short-term profits. Investment mandates include ESG and questionnaires are provided to establish good ESG management practice by asset managers. Based on the radical changes in terms of adoption of ESG integration under PRI and the investment industry, the 2009 Fiduciary Responsibility Report puts forward further legal developments on fiduciary duty and ESG issues since 2005. There is a potential further proactive responsibility on financial advisers and asset management companies to raise ESG issues when rendering investment advice to clients:

> [There is a] very real risk that [the financial advisor] will be sued for negligence on the grounds that they failed to discharge their professional duty of care to the client by failing to raise and take account of ESG considerations.[73]

Finally, the 2009 Fiduciary Responsibility Report goes further than the 2005 Freshfields Report. It argues on the basis of the legislative changes of company director fiduciary duties that as the codified statutory duties of company directors include a duty for directors in carrying out their business to have regard to community and environmental impact, it was not beyond argument that pension fund trustees should be subject to similar duties. The special, long-term nature of the relationship between trustees and beneficiaries of the pension fund and the need for long-term sustainability of pension fund investments

---

71 Companies Act 2006, s. 172(1).
72 Freshfields Report (2005), cited above fn. 5, p. 86.
73 UNEP FI, Fiduciary Responsibility (2009), cited above fn. 61, p. 16.

point towards the fiduciary duties of pension fund trustees being more onerous than those of company directors.

Active ownership of pension fund assets

The concept of active share ownership is central to the regulatory framework for the governance of listed companies in the UK. Directors are required under law to act in the interest of the members of the company (shareholders) and under Section 172 of the Companies Act 2006 are expected to pursue 'enlightened shareholder value' in order to promote the long term success of the company.

Shareholders in turn are expected to take action where they believe that the directors are not best serving their own or the interests of the beneficial owners (including pensioners, insurance company policyholders and unit trust investors) and the law provides them with voting and other rights to enable them to do so.[74]

The 2009 Fiduciary Responsibility Report was, as was the 2005 Freshfields Report, well received by the investment and pension fund industries. It would be wrong to suggest that the 2005 report and the 2009 report were the only sources which highlighted serious industry deficiencies or promoted radical changes in investment practice. The work of Fair Pensions,[75] Mercer,[76] Ceres[77] and the Railpen/HSBC/Linklaters consortium[78] may be cited, amongst others, as important milestones on the road to integration of ESG into mainstream investment decision-making. Nor had the AMWG been ploughing a lonely furrow. The Norwegian Government Global Pension Fund, one of the largest pension/sovereign funds in the world, has been leading the way through its Ethical Committee in applying ESG to their investment and divestment decisions. In recent years, the Norwegian Pension Fund has divested its share holdings in major international mining, tobacco, munitions, armaments and food retail companies on ESG or ethical grounds.[79] The P8 and the Prince of Wales' Trust have also been active in promoting responsible investment.[80]

---

74 Financial Reporting Code, Consultation on a Stewardship Code for Institutional Investors (January 2010), paras. 1.1–1.2.

75 Fair Pensions, *Responsible Pensions?* (London: Fair Pensions, April 2009).

76 UNEP FI and Mercer Investment Consulting, *Demystifying Responsible Investment Performance: A Review of Key Academic and Broker Research on ESG Factors* (Geneva: UNEP FI, 2007).

77 Ceres, *Corporate Governance and Climate Change: The Banking Sector* (Boston: Ceres, 2008)

78 Railpen, HSBC and Linklaters, *Climate Change Investment Risk Audit: An Asset Owner's Toolkit* (London: Linklaters, November 2009).

79 See, e.g. Norges Bank Investment Management, *Government Pension Fund Global Annual Report 2009* (Oslo: Norges Bank Investment Management, 2009).

80 *Prince's Pension Plan for the Planet* (London: HRH Prince of Wales, 5 December 2008).

Pension fund governance

There are other important catalysts to the reform of institutional investment. These cluster around the Myners review of institutional investment in the United Kingdom,[81] the Walker review on corporate governance in UK banks and other financial entities,[82] the work of the Investment Governance Group (IGG)[83] and the Financial Review Council (FRC).[84] Each of these bodies found deficiencies in modern pension fund management and other investment practices. The picture painted by these reports was not unlike the painting kept covered by Dorian Gray. These reports portrayed asset managers as behaving like lemmings over an extended period of time.[85] Their cravings for short-term reward appeared to have displaced their contractual duties to their clients to link investment performance and strategy to long-term pension fund objectives.[86] The reputation of pension fund trustees was also far from untarnished:[87] amateur rather than expert, untutored and steadfastly ignorant rather than knowledgeable, passive rather than active, under-resourced rather than supported adequately. From these reports a consensus developed that the pension fund and investment industry was a patient in need of treatment. The question is and remains: who will carry out the treatment and will it be effective in providing firm foundations for recovery?

Conclusions

> The [pension fund] industry's 'incentive structure' is flawed – the rewards and sanctions facing industry participants are not appropriate and so participants are incentivised to act in ways that will ensure that the system remains prone to periodic crisis.
>
> Watson Wyatt[88]

81 Myners, *Institutional Investment in the United Kingdom* (London: HM Treasury, 2001, 2001, 2004 and 2008); and Lord Hoffman in *Nestle*, cited above fn. 41.
82 D. Walker, *A Review of Corporate Governance in UK Banks and Other Financial Entities* (London: HM Treasury, 16 July 2009).
83 Investment Governance Group, *Response to Myners 2008* (London: HM Treasury, 2008).
84 Financial Review Council, *Consultation on a Stewardship Code for Institutional Investors* (2010); and *FRC Review of the Combined Code: Final Report* (December 2009), p. 1.
85 Johnson and Graaf, cited above fn. 1, fn. 1.
86 See, e.g. 'Goldman's Responses on Relations with Clients', *New York Times*, 19 May 2010; 'Goldman Lobbies Against Fiduciary Reform', *Financial Times*, 12 May 2010; 'Wall Street Derivatives Sales Flaws After SEC Golman Suit', *Bloomberg Business Week*, 2 January 2010; D. Hoffman, 'Did Goldman Sachs Breach Their Fiduciary Duty to CDO Investors', *Wall Street Cheat Sheet*, 23 February 2010; 'Fiduciary Duty and Sophisticated Investors', *Securities Law Prof Blog*, 4 May 2010; and 'Goldman Sachs Bankers Disagree on Duty to Clients', *MarketWatch*, 2 June 2010.
87 See, e.g. NAPF, 'Pension Scheme Governance – fit for the 21st century?' (London: NAPF Discussion Paper, July 2005).
88 Watson/Wyatt/*Financial Times*, 'Defining Moments: The Pension and Investment Industry of the Future' (London: Watson Wyatt Ltd, July 2008).

For a large part of the pension fund industry and the financial investment industry, the last five years have witnessed fundamental change. Some of the issues are still being worked through by national governments and the investment community, for example, accountability, transparency, appropriate risk and rewards, sanctions and the place of responsible investment.

Market understanding of fiduciary duties has changed. They are no longer regarded by the investment industry as insurmountable obstacles to responsible investment or ESG-driven investment. Rather, it is appreciated that fiduciary duties can be enabling and used lawfully as part of a larger decision-making framework or process to ensure the best interests of the beneficiaries. The *raison d'être* of pension funds is to provide financial support to beneficiaries, but the best interests and best financial interests of the beneficiaries are not necessarily the same.

Where does pension fund reform go from here? How does it match modern pension fund management with a need for sufficient protection of beneficiaries? How does it balance the discretion of pension fund trustees maximising financial return with socially responsible investment? A number of basic reforms may be suggested for consideration.

First, a simplification of the fiduciary duties of pension fund trustees may be undertaken. This may be achieved, borrowing heavily from the United States, by adopting a comprehensive, modern prudent mantest or by a restatement of the principal fiduciary duties of pension fund trustees (to act for a proper purpose and on behalf of all beneficiaries and to act loyally, with prudence and fairness) with greater clarity of the meaning. Second, a hierarchy of duties and the relationship between these fiduciary duties may be created. It could also be achieved without difficulty by the investment industry reaching consensus as to what these duties entail at present.

Third, notwithstanding the positive findings on ESG and investment, legislative reform is required to define the scope and nature of pension fund trustee fiduciary duties. This can be achieved by codifying and setting out in statute the fiduciary duties of pension fund trustees. This need, if anything, is greater than the need to set out in legislation the fiduciary duties of company directors, a matter which was conceded by government and addressed in the United Kingdom by the Companies Act 2006.

Fourth, it is not enough for governments to provide legally non-binding advice in Parliamentary or other fora. This dilemma of pension fund trustees should be removed by a clear legislative provision making it lawful for pension fund trustees to have regard to ESG, ethics or other stated relevant and material investment considerations.

Fifth, the requirement to have regard to ESG, including ethical considerations, should also be reinforced by other legislative and regulatory requirements. Norwegian legislation sets out the investment powers and structure of the Norwegian Global Pension Fund. This may provide some parts to construct an adaptable pension fund model and decision-making structure. These allow pension fund trustees expressly at present to have regard to non-financial criteria to prepare an investment policy without breach of fiduciary duties or for investment and divestment on ethic grounds. The UK legislative duties of pension funds under pension legislation in terms of statement of environmental and social impacts in investment plans which provide greater ESG transparency in respect of investment and pension fund accountability for investment should be adopted, reinforced and extended generally to ensure that pension funds satisfy these obligations in practice and cannot, as they do at present, merely pay lip service to these objectives.

Sixth, investment mandates and other relevant contracts between pension funds and asset management companies should contain provisions requiring ESG considerations to be taken into account. The precedents set by AVIVA, PRI, 'Freshfields II' or the French retirement reserve fund include these requirements.

Seventh, pension fund trustees and asset managers acting with the requisite level of skill, care and diligence should be indemnified against legal action as provided for under Manitoban legislation.[89] It should be made plain to asset managers and other investment advisers by legislation or, pending legislative reform by professional guidance notes issued by regulators, for example, the Securities Exchange Commission (SEC) or Financial Services Authority (FSA) or professional financial investment bodies, that they may be held liable for professional negligence if they are not proactive in discussing and monitoring the potential impact of ESG on investment values with existing and potential investors.

Eighth, advocates of PRI should work closely with national pension fund and financial services regulators, such as the DOL or the FSA, to produce authoritative research reports and guidance for pension fund management and investment.

An example of such guidance may be a reformulation of the businessman rule as guidance for pension fund trustees, which might emphasise the fact that judges do not second-guess business or investment decision-making. Investment decisions are not therefore assessed with the benefit of hindsight, but against reasonable standards of decision-making and the knowledge and experience of the pension fund trustees at the time the decision was made. Judges, however, if not interested in the merits of the decision or the weighting given to each relevant and material investment consideration, are very focused on the process by which the decision was made. Investment, it should be stressed, is an art not a science, despite the extensive use of mathematical and economic modelling in the investment industry, and therefore pension fund trustees and asset managers have considerable latitude to get investment decisions wrong without any suggestion whatsoever of breach of fiduciary duties.

89 See, e.g. Manitoba Trustee Act 1995, s. 79(1).

There is a need for greater investment market acceptance of the necessity and benefits of consultation. This includes consultation by pension fund trustees of their beneficiaries and greater owner activism on the part of pension fund trustees and their asset managers. It may be difficult to remind pension fund trustees in whose name they act. Equally, companies need to acknowledge pension fund ownership and that pension funds can make or break companies by investing in or divesting their shares. Finally, consideration should be given to whether ESG considerations should be required for other investment models. Care should be taken because not all investment models are appropriate ESG vehicles. However, governments which bailed out the financial sector in 2009 may wish to consider, in light of the financial meltdown of leading banks, what may have been the outcome if ESG considerations had been properly taken into account. It may be that for other investment models ESG considerations could have provided a more appropriate investment focus than that which was used recklessly in relation to derivatives and other financial instruments which resulted in an almost unparalleled financial crisis.

5

Good trusteeship

EDDIE THOMAS

Governance of pension schemes has developed mainly as a result of experience with defined benefit schemes and it is these schemes which comprise the background to most of this chapter. However, the principles of good governance generally apply to defined benefit and defined contribution schemes alike.

Moving towards better governance

The requirement for good governance has increased considerably in recent years. The governance expectations of companies are set out in the Combined Code. Corporate governance received close attention in the 1990s and, following the failures of BCCI and Polly Peck, recommendations for improving and applying the Code were made first by Cadbury, later by others including Greenbury, Hampel, Smith, Turnbull and Higgs.

Pension schemes did not receive the same attention until the Maxwell scandal catapulted them into the limelight in 1990. The complete failure of governance exposed in this particular case shocked business, the public and politicians alike and gave rise to the Goode Committee report[1] and the wide-ranging reforms of the Pensions Act 1995 that followed.

By analogy with the definition of corporate governance given by Cadbury, pension scheme governance may be defined as 'the system by which pension schemes are directed and controlled'. The Maxwell case was astonishing in the extent of the failure, or absence, of the system of control for Mirror Group pension schemes. In their evidence to a Commons Select Committee, former trustees of these schemes described how their meetings had been run in stark terms:

> The style of the meetings was that you would be kept waiting around for hours, including senior Directors and Editors of newspapers, and suddenly he would appear in his shirt sleeves and conduct two hours of business in five or six minutes. You just could not raise matters, they were steamrollered through. The helicopter would arrive, and out he would go

---

1 Cm. 2342 (HMSO, September 1993).

in a puff of smoke, and you were left asking, 'what was that about?' At one stage we asked for verbatim minutes to be taken, because we were so unhappy that minutes as recorded did not agree with all our understandings of what happened at the meeting. Often minority viewpoints frequently expressed by myself and other trustees were just simply not recorded and there was no comeback. We could protest, but still we were not able to get meetings scheduled, we could not raise agenda items and we could not get the minutes published. There was also quite a lot of manipulation in the way the meetings were held. They could be held at two days' notice, with no access to the previous minutes, no agenda, and the reports and valuations were placed before you at the meetings. It is very difficult to wade through all that detailed information at one minute's notice.[2]

This was, of course, a rare example, but it did illustrate graphically what in the extreme might go wrong, and the extent to which some pension scheme trustees were disempowered by employers who regarded the pension scheme as part of the company entity. If articulate journalists could not exercise their trustee role properly, what chance had lesser mortals of doing so?

Structure, composition and operation of trustee boards

Structure

The Goode Committee concluded in its report that the trustee structure was appropriate for pension scheme governance (some argue that, for defined contribution schemes, a contract-based structure would be better) and today nearly all private sector pension schemes are still established under trust with individual trustees or a trustee company. In this chapter, the model where the trustee is a company is assumed, usually a direct or indirect subsidiary of the principal employer. The directors are referred to as 'trustees' or 'trustee directors', the company as 'the trustee' and the board of the company as 'the trustee board'. Where the word 'trustee' is used, it is taken to mean a pension scheme trustee unless the context indicates a wider interpretation.

Although there are many similarities between a corporate trustee structure as adopted by the majority of larger pension schemes and the structure usual for smaller schemes where individuals act in a personal capacity, it is worth noting the differences. For example, under a corporate structure:

- transferring assets is easier;
- changing trustee directors is easier;
- deeds usually only require two signatures; and
- generally, trustee directors are better protected from personal liability.

2 Evidence to House of Commons Select Committee.

Under an individual structure:

- there are no filing requirements with the Companies Registry (but this is not onerous); and
- it may be more difficult for the sponsor to remove individuals, or to change the trustee structure (see also 'Independence and liability' below, this chapter).

There is no doubt that the trustee model of governance takes time and effort, but it can be very cost effective for larger schemes. For smaller schemes, finding the resources for effective trustee governance can be difficult, and the expense is often disproportionate to the size of the scheme. The requirements of good governance apply to large and small schemes alike, and there is a clear need for better standards among smaller schemes where many of the problems considered by the Pensions Regulator seem to arise.

There are also many public sector schemes established under statute and some unfunded schemes which do not have trustees. These latter schemes are not the subject of this chapter.

Composition and operation

Given the responsibilities falling on a trustee board, it is essential that its size and composition are carefully considered. Consideration should be given to the number of trustee directors, the company-appointed/member-nominated split, the method of choosing member-nominated directors (MNDs), term of office, the participation of executive staff of the sponsoring employer, who the chairman (a person of either gender!) should be, and whether to have 'independent' trustee directors.

Typically, trustee boards vary in size between six and twelve members. In the author's view, this range is the best for effective governance. Larger boards can be unwieldy with the danger that members do not feel involved, while smaller boards can struggle to cope with the work and have difficulty in obtaining a quorum. It is usual for company-nominated directors (CNDs) to be in the majority (subject to having at least one-third of the board as MNDs to comply with legislation),[3] but there are schemes where there is parity between CNDs and MNDs, with the balance being held by independent trustees or a chairman with a casting vote (usually a CND). However, it is worth noting that trustee boards rarely need to vote.

Ideally, members should be chosen for the contributions they can make rather than as representatives of any particular interest group, but this is easier said than done. The legal requirement for choosing MNDs is that candidates should be nominated by a process involving at least all the active and pensioner members of the scheme (or an organisation that adequately

---

3 Pensions Act 2004, ss. 241 and 242; and SI 2006/714.

represents them), and selection should be by a process in which some or all of the members of the scheme are eligible to participate. Holding an election among the membership does not necessarily produce suitable trustees, and there is an argument for a selection process (in which members participate), either as a first stage prior to an election or in place thereof. The use of selection committees has become common, but often members of the scheme have been in the minority on these committees. In the author's view, it is important that the composition of such committees is balanced, but it is recognised that this may be difficult to achieve, especially if all MNDs are standing for re-election at the same time.

Trustees other than MNDs are customarily appointed by the employer. As CNDs form the majority on many trustee boards, their selection is extremely important in determining the character of the board. It is helpful if CND vacancies can be filled after discussion of requirements between the chairman of the trustee board and the company. The appointment of senior employees, such as the finance director, who may at times be conflicted, and employees who are unlikely to be able to dedicate the necessary time required for being a trustee, should be avoided.

It is important that trustees should be willing and able to engage fully in the affairs of the trustee board. This includes preparing for and attending meetings regularly, undertaking regular training to understand and keep up to date with the complex issues involved, and contributing impartially to discussions. Trustees may be called upon to discuss matters such as the award of an ill-health pension in a complicated case, the extent to which derivatives should be used in their investment strategy, the selection process for member-nominated trustees, whether to insure a part of the liabilities, and whether employer proposals for financing a deficit are acceptable. Few trustee directors can master all such matters, so it is necessary that collectively the board should possess a balanced range of skills and experience and that its members work well together.

A good chairman makes all the difference to how a trustee board operates. Some of the qualities required are universal, but others are more particular to pension schemes. Specifically, to be effective in this role, a chairman needs a broad understanding of pension schemes derived from experience, preferably of several schemes, and an ability to engage on particular issues in discussion with the employer. To this end, successful completion of the Pension Regulator's e-learning Trustee Toolkit[5] (or its equivalent) would seem to be an essential requirement. An important role for the chairman of a pension scheme is to ensure good liaison with the company and it is unlikely that this will happen unless the person chosen is acceptable to the company. On the other hand, the chairman should also be credible in the eyes of members. The more senior the person in the company, the less likely this is to be the case. Choices which have worked well are a recently retired senior executive of the company, or an independent trustee approved by the company.

There should be a process for reviewing the individual performance of trustee directors. Areas to consider include attendance at meetings and participation in discussions. Helpful suggestions for improvement often emerge from reviews and the chairman can play a key role in leading the process and in any follow-up actions that are taken. A trustee board should also consider periodically making a formal assessment of its own effectiveness as a decision-making body. The best way to do this would be against a set of formal objectives, although few trustees have this currently.

Duties and responsibilities of trustees

Prudent man

The legal concept of 'trusteeship' and of a 'trust' is well understood in English law. The current understanding of the general duties and responsibilities of trustees was largely developed in the nineteenth century in court judgments in relation to family trusts and further codified in the Trustee Act 1925. The principles that were established later came to be applied to pension schemes when these became more common in the earlier part of the twentieth century. For a long time, the key concept of a 'prudent man' sufficed as a definition of a trustee's duty of care. This is that a trustee has a duty to exercise reasonable care and show the prudence and diligence that an ordinary man of business would exercise in the management of his or her own affairs, and to exercise any special skills that he or she may possess. Pension scheme trustees operated in a non-contentious environment and their actions were not closely scrutinised or regulated. Such pension legislation as there was related to fiscal matters rather than matters of governance.

Trustee knowledge and understanding (TKU)

Over the last 30 years the environment has changed significantly. There have been numerous legal cases involving pension scheme trustees acting either as plaintiffs or as defendants, and the issues contested have concerned a wide range of matters. In addition, Parliament has on several occasions legislated on matters relating to the duties and responsibilities of pension scheme trustees (as opposed to trustees in general), notably in the Pensions Acts of 1995 and 2004.

Good governance requires a familiarity with the trust deed and rules of the particular scheme. The trust deed and rules (and any supplementary deeds) are the governing documents of a pension scheme, defining inter alia the purposes of the scheme, eligibility for membership, the benefits to be provided, contributions to be paid and the powers conferred on the trustees. Trustees should be familiar with these documents and always refer to them when asked to make unusual or difficult decisions, especially where the exercise of a discretionary power is concerned. There is a statutory requirement that trustees must be conversant (have a working knowledge) with the trust deeds and rules (and, for a corporate trustee, the memorandum and articles of association), the Statement of Investment Principles and the Statement of Funding Principles.

The Pensions Act 2004 established the Pensions Regulator (TPR – the successor to the less powerful Occupational Pensions Regulatory Authority) and this has marked a new chapter in pension scheme governance. TPR has extensive powers to intervene in the running of a pension scheme if things go wrong, but an important part of its remit is to promote high standards of scheme administration and ensure that those involved in running pension schemes have the necessary skills and knowledge. To this end, TPR has issued codes of practice providing practical guidance on the requirements of pension legislation and setting out the standards of conduct and practice expected of trustees and others. These may be found on TPR's website.[4] The current codes are listed at the end of this chapter.

A central requirement of current legislation introduced by the Pensions Act 2004 is that individual trustees of an occupational pension scheme must have appropriate knowledge and understanding of the law relating to pensions and trusts, the principles relating to the funding of occupational pension schemes and the investment of the assets of such schemes. TPR's Code of Practice No. 7 (paragraph 30) explains this requirement. It states:

> The breadth of the knowledge and understanding achieved should be sufficient to allow trustees to understand fully any advice they are given, to challenge that advice if it seems sensible to do so and to enter fully into all decision-making processes.

TPR has developed a comprehensive e-learning toolkit for trustees,[5] with its own 'Certificate of Successful Completion', and has become increasingly active in pointing out for trustees areas where standards need to improve. TPR's view is that the toolkit is required study for new trustees unless they can find a suitable equivalent learning programme. Many larger schemes now expect existing trustees to have completed the toolkit, and there is strong pressure from TPR for existing trustees to do so.

In addition, trustees must be aware of the Pensions Ombudsman, whose remit is to investigate and decide complaints brought by any party with an interest in a pension scheme. The majority of cases have been brought by members against trustees and concern individual benefit entitlements. The Pension Ombudsman's decisions have a judicial character.

Accountability

Those charged with governance must be aware of who their stakeholders are. In other words, to whom are they accountable? For pension schemes, the

4 See www.thepensionsregulator.gov.uk.
5 See www.trusteetoolkit.com.

pre-eminent answer is the 'members' of the scheme. A good trustee board will first and foremost consider the implications of its actions (or non-actions) on the members. It will ensure that members are regularly informed of how the scheme is financed and run, the security for benefits, benefit entitlements and any choices members may make, who the trustee directors are and to whom members should apply for more information. Since 2004, members have had the right to participate in the nomination and selection of not less than one-third of the individual trustees or trustee directors (prior to that date there were arrangements for MNDs, but there was an opt-out provision that was widely used) so that trustees might be considered to be more accountable than before to members. However, MNDs do not have any statutory powers over and above those conferred on other trustee directors. Exceptionally, the trust deed and rules of a scheme may confer special powers on certain trustee directors, but for the most part trustee directors must consider themselves as representing the same interests irrespective of the manner of their appointment.

Members' interests are also protected in other ways, by TPR, the Pensions Ombudsman and the Pensions Advisory Service (TPAS). These bodies cannot and should not be a substitute for knowledgeable trustees acting with integrity.

Another important stakeholder is the sponsoring employer (or employers where there are several), not least because it 'underwrites' the pension scheme and would normally be liable for any shortfall if the scheme were to be 'wound up' (when pension schemes were thought to have surpluses, an interest of the employers was in any refund of assets not required to secure benefits on a winding-up). The management of the relationship between the trustee and the sponsoring employer should be one of the main concerns of trustee directors and can often be a source of difficulty, not least because some of the trustee directors may hold senior positions within the sponsoring company and have been appointed by the sponsor. It is essential that trustee directors have a clear policy in the event that conflicts of interest arise for any of them and there may be times when a trustee director should not participate in discussions or decisions. In the extreme, it may be appropriate to resign.

Since the Pensions Act 2004 came into force, the Pension Protection Fund (PPF) and TPR are clearly stakeholders in a loose sense of the word. The TPR's statutory responsibilities include protecting the interests of members of work-based pension schemes and reducing the risk of situations arising that may lead to claims for compensation from the PPF. Therefore, TPR has an interest in ensuring that pension schemes are as well funded as they can be.

Many trustee directors are not remunerated directly for acting as such. Others are remunerated indirectly by the employer because the role is seen as part of their employment, or directly by the employer as part of the costs of running the scheme. As there is no requirement to publish the source or amount of the remuneration of trustees, arguably they are less accountable than directors of public companies.

Looking after stakeholders' interests

In this section, some of the issues which arise in looking after the interests of the main stakeholders – the members and the employers – are considered.

Members' interests

Looking after members' interests may not be straightforward. For instance, the interests of members who are employees of the company may be quite different from those of pensioners who are no longer working for the employer. It may serve the interests of active members that the scheme continues, but of pensioners that it be discontinued – good trustees must be able to balance competing interests fairly. Trustees may also have a practice of awarding discretionary benefits, for example, pension increases. Should they continue to do so without additional contributions from the employers if the scheme is in deficit? What are the right terms for benefit options, for example, commutation of pension at retirement, or transfer payments made when members leave and opt to move their rights elsewhere?

Another difficult area concerns the merger of schemes. A sponsoring employer may wish to rationalise pension arrangements under one trust, but if the trusts they plan to merge have different levels of solvency, this may not be in the interests of the members of the better-funded scheme. Transactions between schemes within the same commercial group need very careful consideration. Where the schemes have the same trustee, arrangements may have to be made to ensure that the interests of the different memberships are represented separately.

Although it is rarely an issue now, in the 1990s when pension schemes enjoyed surpluses, trustees often had to consider the effect of the admission of new participating employers. Cases arose where, following the acquisition of a company, the new owners sought to use the surplus in the acquired pension scheme for their own employees' benefits, often diluting the security for existing members' benefits and reducing the expectation of discretionary benefits, for example, pension increases. In such situations, trustees *must* obtain legal advice so that they are fully aware of their duties and powers. A full understanding of the relevant provisions of the trust deed and rules is paramount.

Trustees should ensure that they communicate regularly with their members in a way in which members can understand. That is easier said than done, and a high standard of communication is only achieved with much thought and work. The main form of communication has been written material. Larger pension schemes are using websites to good effect, but very few schemes facilitate direct access to the trustee board in the way that stakeholders of public companies have access to their boards at annual general meetings.

It is also important that trustees are aware of and agree communications to members for which they are responsible and seek to ensure clarity of ownership between these and statements which are the employer's. A case which reached the High Court (*Steria* v. *Hutchison*)[6] involved confusion over pension rights arising from statements in a pension scheme booklet which had not been properly considered by the trustee, and letters to members from the pensions manager issued on company paper.

Employers' interests

The conduct of the relationship with the employer is a key consideration for defined benefit scheme trustees. It is common for employers to provide services to the trustee board. In doing so, there is a danger that the trustees approach their role with the mind-set that the pension scheme 'belongs to the employer' and is 'a part of the business' rather than with the attitude that it is a separate entity for which they are legally responsible. This is not to say that the employer is not a key player, especially in a defined benefit scheme (less so in a defined contribution scheme). Good governance depends on trustees being able to maintain the right balance between dependence on the employer and independence from the employer; this balance can be harder to achieve the more the trustee looks to the employer to provide services.

Trustees are required to obtain the employer's agreement to the method and assumptions used for calculating the technical provisions (the present value of the liabilities of the scheme), the statement of funding principles, the recovery plan and the schedule of contributions.[7] They must also consult the employer before a statement of investment principles is prepared or revised.[8] They are required to monitor the strength of the employer 'covenant', which is best done with the employer's co-operation. It is important that there are recognised channels for consultation, and the role here for the chairman of the trustee board and for trustee directors who hold senior management positions within the company is significant. While currently employed senior company executives may find it difficult to devote the time needed to trusteeship, and conflict issues may pose difficulties for them, a recently retired senior executive who has easy access to senior management can be invaluable on the trustee board as a bridge between the board and the company.

The interests of the employer or, in a multi-employer scheme, the employers, are less clear than the interests of the members and have at times posed severe difficulties for trustees of defined benefit schemes. The outcomes of cases that have been decided in the courts have usually preferred members' interests over employers' interests and have often highlighted the difficulties for trustees in balancing these interests. The issues are usually financial, concerning contributions, 'ownership' of surpluses, responsibility for deficits and the degree of investment risk acceptable. The key concern for trustees

6 *Steria Ltd and others* v. *Hutchison and others* [2006] EWCA Civ 1551.
7 Pensions Act 2004, s. 229(1).
8 Pensions Act 1995, s. 35(5)(b).

underlying all such questions is the extent to which the financial needs of the pension scheme should take priority over the financial needs of the employer's business. Trustees have to decide how far to 'push' the employer for contributions and in so doing often have to consider what the effects might be on the employer's attitude to the continued provision of benefits. Individual trustee directors may have quite different perspectives on this question and may need guidance on what they should and should not consider. In such situations there is an important role for the chairman and the view of an independent trustee.

Key issues on the trustee agenda

Unlike a company, a pension trustee board does not have numerous staff at its disposal. This means that trustee directors are likely to be more involved in the details of running their pension scheme than company directors, who normally have an executive on whom they can rely and to whom they delegate day-to-day operational matters. Some trustees are quite involved in running the scheme, especially trustees of medium and smaller schemes, where the costs of using external resources can be disproportionate to the size of the scheme. A danger for trustee boards is that they become too involved in minutiae and do not pay enough attention to strategic questions.

Key issues for trustees vary from scheme to scheme and over time. A good trustee board will be aware of the important issues affecting schemes at any time and will ensure that it considers their relevance for its own scheme. It will avoid its agenda being dominated by detail to the exclusion of more important matters. A main objective for trustees should be to ensure that, in the long term, the scheme will have sufficient resources to pay all the benefits promised to members under the rules of the scheme; this requires having a long-term, strategic view on funding, investment and the covenant of the employer.

One of the greatest challenges for trustee boards, most of whom are faced with significant deficits in their schemes (however these are measured), is to reconcile the tension between their need for a long-term strategy for funding and investment, and the tendency for companies (especially quoted companies) to manage to short-time horizons that are governed by stock market expectations and the perceived needs of shareholders. This tension is clearly expressed when companies argue that cash is better invested to grow the business and thereby enhance the covenant than being invested in the pension scheme where it is 'locked away'. The concern of many finance directors is that trustees are too cautious, that substantial deficit contributions eventually may turn out not to have been required, and that it will not be possible then to return surpluses to the company. While these concerns are understandable from a company perspective, the argument provides little reassurance for trustees unless accompanied by a clear commitment to the payment of contributions, both concerning timing and amount.

A strong covenant per se is good, but there is a limit to the extent to which trustees should rely on 'good faith'. The fortunes of companies can change quickly and unexpectedly, and managements change too. In the event of a hostile takeover, there is no guarantee that the new management will abide by the good intentions of past management. Commitments therefore need to be enforceable and provided by an entity of substance if trustee boards are to agree to any significant deferment of deficit contributions (or, indeed, significant levels of investment risk). These commitments can take various forms, including charges over company assets, a formal agreement covering long-term funding objectives,[9] escrow arrangements, guarantees and so on. Trustees will need negotiating skill, tenacity and patience to achieve results, but in the author's mind there is no doubt that the end results can be significant.

Investment strategy stands alongside funding strategy in importance. Again, there is often tension between trustees' expectations and the expectations of companies. Trustees are required to be prudent, and will not want to run unnecessary investment risk. Companies, on the other hand, have a natural aversion to assets that are not 'working' and so are more inclined than trustees to favour 'return-seeking' asset classes which carry higher expected returns that it is hoped will contribute to reducing deficits. The dilemma for trustees is to what extent they should agree to a higher risk investment strategy. They have the comfort of knowing that the final decision rests with them,[10] but the question is so closely linked with covenant strength and funding strategy that the views of the employer inevitably must be taken into account.

The third area of strategic importance for trustees is assessing the strength of the employer covenant. It is unfortunate that this has come to be considered as a major concern for trustees. The concept of funded pension trusts started life on the premise that this was the best way of providing security for pension promises because it enabled employees to be given security for retirement income independently of their job security. So employees might lose their jobs, but not their pensions as well. The situation today is that this fundamental concept has been compromised, and a strong employer covenant is regarded by many as an acceptable substitute for full funding using a strong valuation basis. Trustees must consider the viability of the employer on whom they will depend for many years to meet pension deficits. Getting the assurances needed is a sensitive area for trustees and may require significant resource. Some companies cooperate willingly in providing information, but others regard this as unnecessary, raising concerns about confidentiality, disclosure of price-sensitive information, giving preference to creditors and so

---

9 For instance, an agreement that the long-term funding strategy is to achieve a position where the scheme is 'self-sufficient'. Agreement on the level of reserves to satisfy 'self-sufficiency' should be included, and one objective would be to reach a position where the scheme is no longer relying on the covenant of the company for benefits that have accrued.

10 Pensions Act 1995, s. 35(4).

on. It is also an area which can pose difficulty for individual trustee directors who hold senior positions in the company. Conscious of these difficulties, TPR has been consulting on draft guidance for trustees on monitoring the employer covenant, contingent assets and other security, and further information may be found on the Regulator's website.[4]

Getting support and help

The extent to which trustees delegate varies and depends on the composition and character of the trustee board. The resources available to trustees are mainly from professional advisers and service providers, and the sponsoring employer.

Professional advisers and service providers

Trustees rely to a great extent on professional advisers and service providers. This is especially so in matters of law, administration, and funding and investment policy. Trustees also have come increasingly to use professional advisers to monitor the strength of the employer covenant. Managing these relationships well is an important part of good governance and one in which trustees should actively participate (rather than relying on the employer to do it). Trustees who rarely see their legal adviser are less likely to be aware of what their trust deed and rules require of them when difficult questions arise than trustees who invite their lawyer to meetings to participate in relevant discussions. At the other extreme, trustees must avoid being overwhelmed by advisers. It is important to strike the right balance between relying on professional advice unquestioningly and not taking advice at all, and this is best achieved by having trustees who are familiar with the issues and have the confidence to challenge advice intelligently.

The quality of the relationship with, and the standard of the advice received from, an adviser is enhanced if clear terms of reference have been agreed both for the relationship and for specific project work. Advisers should be certain of what is asked of them, generally and in relation to particular issues. There should be an understanding whether they are expected, on the one hand, to initiate discussions (being 'proactive') or, on the other hand, to give advice only when asked to do so. Proactive advisers are likely to attend board meetings frequently and participate in general discussions. Trustees need to be alert to the danger of paying for generic advice that they do not need. Generic advice can be helpful in educating trustees when they are in unfamiliar territory, but it can sometimes be used by advisers as a substitute for addressing the difficult questions. At the end of the day, trustees are there to make decisions and need advice that helps them to reach conclusions, not to pass exams.

Relationships will be enhanced if they are reviewed from time to time. Good advisers initiate this themselves and seek assurances about the quality, relevance, clarity and timeliness of advice, as well as the trustees' perception of value for money. It is common for trustees to conduct a wider review at longer intervals, say between three and five years, including considering other firms, but these reviews usually only result in a change in appointment if there is serious dissatisfaction with the service that has been provided.

Some sponsors use their own advisers in order to be independent of the trustee. There are times when this is clearly necessary, but there are dangers too that different advisers can get stuck in unproductive disagreements that have no practical benefits for members.

The majority of advisers have sought to limit liability in various ways for the advice they give.

There is a danger that standards will tend to be lower where less is at stake for the adviser. Advisers who require liability caps which are substantially below a realistic level of potential loss are not to be preferred.

Investment manager relationships are the most difficult of all to manage. Each manager has its own investment style and internal systems and these need to be understood before making an appointment. It is counter-productive to try to fit a manager into a mould in which they are not comfortable and it is best to avoid too many restrictions in the terms of the manager agreement. Once a manager has been appointed, trustees have to decide how to monitor performance. Lord Myners, an adviser to the government on investment and financial matters, argued that managers are inhibited by not having security of tenure and that longer-term contracts are needed so that a manager's strategy has a chance to prove its worth. While this may suit managers, it sits uncomfortably within a responsible governance structure. It is hard to see how trustees who have entrusted millions of pounds of assets to a manager can sit back and wait passively for results. Active monitoring is essential, and while it is not ideal to make judgments based on short-term results, trustees inevitably must take account of these. If trustees lose confidence in a manager's ability to meet agreed investment targets, the proper course of action is to move the assets elsewhere and they should be able to do so without restrictions.

Regular meetings with investment managers are an essential part of the governance process, but these can be time consuming and are not easily accommodated within normal trustee meetings. Many trustees have formed investment committees and delegated significant powers to them. It is possible for such committees to co-opt members with specialist investment expertise, and so long as a committee includes trustee directors and reports regularly to the trustee board so that 'ownership' of major investment decisions is not lost, this approach can work well.

A trustee is required to have an investment strategy and investments that are suitable for the scheme.[11] The trustee must decide what asset classes are the most appropriate and the proportions of the total fund invested in each.

11 Pensions Act 1995, s. 36(2)(b).

Investment consultants have developed sophisticated models to illustrate the expected returns and volatility of different asset strategies, but there is a danger that trustees are overwhelmed by complexity, terminology and choices offered. It is in this area, more than any other, that the benefit of 'knowledge and understanding' is most apparent, and trustees should ensure that they understand the choices available and are able to say why they have chosen a particular option.

The sponsoring employer

Apart from allowing employees to act as trustees, the main areas of support provided for trustees by employers are administrative and secretarial. The practice of having in-house departments to manage the investments of the company pension scheme has all but disappeared, but some companies do employ a chief investment officer to oversee investment matters and report to the trustee board.

A main concern for trustees in relying on employer support is that the extent of delegation to the employer is understood, and that all concerned on the employer's side are clear (and make clear to others) when they are acting for the trustees. This is important when appointing and instructing advisers and trustees should ensure that it is always made clear that they are the client. For administration of benefits, best practice is to have a formal written agreement between the trustees and the employer as is normal with a third-party provider. The agreement would cover matters such as the services that will be provided, the service standards required and reporting. Another concern is the relationship with the pensions manager, who will usually have a dual role, supporting and advising both the company and the trustee board. Most of the time this is not a problem, but in the event of a negotiation or a contentious matter arising between the trustee board and the company, the position of the pensions manager needs to be considered and a decision may have to be made that he or she can participate for one party only on the matter.

Independence and liability

Independence

A growing number of trustee boards, especially those of larger funds, have independent trustees, meaning trustees who have no connection whatsoever with the corporate group which sponsors the pension scheme. There is no question that independent trustees, and especially those who act as such in a professional capacity, bring particular qualities and character to a trustee board. They are increasingly being used. The level of expertise now required of trustees and the time involved makes the appointment of a professional independent trustee particularly appropriate.

However, the question of independence is wider. All directors should feel that they are able to put the interests of members of their scheme first, and not be swayed by considerations relevant to any other interest group or stakeholder. To a large extent, this can be achieved by training, by requiring trustees at the beginning of each meeting to disclose any new potential conflicts of interest or any actual conflicts, by having a written policy for dealing with such conflicts, and by avoiding particular appointments, for example, the chief executive Officer (CEO) and the finance director of the sponsor. Although it is generally true that trustee directors are able to put aside the manner of their appointment when sitting at the trustee table, it is sometimes difficult for CNDs to 'forget' that they are employees of the company, and for MNDs to forget that they are also employees or pensioners. Having an independent trustee who can act impartially can help considerably.

A trustee company is usually a subsidiary of the employer so that, technically, the employer could replace the trustee company (and all of its directors with it) with a trustee company formed more to its liking. This has very rarely happened, but it is a risk of which trustees should be aware in stressed situations. A way around this potential problem is to make the trustee company independent of the employing group by issuing shares to a small number of shareholders. Again, independent trustee directors can play a useful role here. In one particular case, an approach to TPR is known to have helped to protect the position of the trustees.

Liability for decisions

There is a danger that trustees will conduct their business with an eye to making 'safe' decisions, i.e. decisions that will expose the trustee board to the least possible risk of being criticised for maladministration or for negligence. This is a danger which professional trustees, from whom a higher standard of care is to be expected, particularly should guard against. Such a cautious approach to trusteeship can lead to decisions being deferred or not being made at all.

The risks for the trustees of an ongoing scheme can be overstated, however, and there are usually significant protections on which they can and should rely. Although there has been an increase in the number of cases coming before the UK courts involving pension scheme trustees, the courts have been reluctant to find trustees liable who have followed a 'proper process' in making their decisions. In this context, 'proper process' includes taking appropriate professional advice, establishing the relevant facts, acting in accordance with the trust deed and rules and with legislation, and not acting perversely. Provided the process is correct, an error of judgment does not render trustees liable; their performance is judged not with the benefit of hindsight, but by whether they made a reasonable decision given the circumstances that existed at the time. On the other hand, trustees run risks if they are motivated by considerations other than their beneficiaries' best interests. In *Cowan* v. *Scargill*,[12] it was held that 'best interests' meant 'best financial interests' and that the defendant union trustees of the Mineworkers' Pension Scheme were in breach of their fiduciary duty as trustees in attempting to impose restrictions on the way in which pension fund monies were invested by prohibiting overseas investments and investment in energies directly competitive with coal.

Pension scheme trust deeds commonly contain protections for trustees in the form of indemnities from the employer and exoneration clauses. Exoneration clauses provide that trustees will not be liable except in very limited circumstances such as 'wilful neglect or default'. Although it has been questioned whether such clauses should be allowed, the courts have generally upheld their effectiveness. They are particularly useful in situations where the employer has gone into liquidation and is therefore unable to give an indemnity. A disadvantage of exoneration clauses from the beneficiaries' point of view is that it is they who may suffer since there is no remedy for a loss. An indemnity from a solvent employer does not suffer from this disadvantage and may therefore be preferred. However, following changes introduced by the Companies Act 2006, care needs to be taken in drafting such indemnities where the trustee company is a subsidiary of the company providing the indemnity.

Many trustees have some form of insurance cover. In terms of governance, insurance may be seen as a better form of protection than exoneration or indemnity clauses in the trust deed because losses are compensated, thereby increasing the resources available to the scheme. Trustees are now able to effect policies specifically designed for the needs of a pension scheme. These may include cover for losses even where there is no legal liability and cover for the cost of indemnities provided by the employer. Another important element of cover is for legal expenses which may be incurred in defending a claim. Other considerations are the extent to which cover survives the termination of the trust and the resignation or retirement of a trustee director. Premiums are often met by the employer, but if they are to be paid from trust assets trustees should confirm that they have the power to do so.

Section 33 of the Pensions Act 1995 effectively provides that an exoneration clause or an indemnity from scheme assets cannot cover losses due to a failure by trustees to exercise skill in the performance of their investment functions. However, trustees may derive protection through an indemnity from the employer or from an insurance policy. The Pensions Act 1995 also provides statutory protection for trustees who have delegated making investment decisions to an authorised investment manager, provided they have taken steps to satisfy themselves that the manager has appropriate knowledge and experience for the job and they monitor the manager's competence. In view of the size of the assets for which trustees are often responsible, it is clearly vital that procedures are established to ensure that these requirements can be satisfied. Few,

---

12 [1984] 2 All ER 750; [1984] IRLR 260.

if any trustees, will themselves have the knowledge or experience required, or the systems or research available, to make investment decisions. Even if these requirements could be satisfied, most trustees would not want to run the liability risks. This is one reason why in-house investment departments of some larger pension schemes have all but disappeared.

Trustee boards should ensure that their decisions are taken at properly convened meetings and are recorded in the minutes. While it is not necessary to record all of the reasons for a decision, the minutes should refer to the advice and other papers received, note the names of the participants and record that a full discussion of the relevant facts took place. Often, it is necessary for trustee decisions to be taken outside formal meetings: there should be properly documented, delegated powers enabling individuals, be they trustee directors or others, to do so and the extent of the delegated powers should be made clear. Such decisions should be reported at the next formal trustee meeting.

Conclusion

It will be clear from the preceding sections of this chapter, and from other chapters in this book, that the responsibilities faced by pension scheme trustees today are massively different from ten, or even five, years ago. Being a trustee of a pension scheme now is time consuming, requires a high level of knowledge and understanding and, above all, calls for the exercise of judgment on many complex matters. No matter how much professional advice is available, answers are often not clear cut and choices still have to be made. Many schemes have considerable deficits so that relationships with sponsoring employers who pay contributions have become a key concern for trustees. As long-established defined benefit schemes become more and more mature, and less and less relevant to businesses, these relationships will be tested to the utmost. Schemes that have good governance are more likely to be able to secure the additional funding needed to enable delivery of the full benefits promised to members than those that do not.

Appendix

The Pension Regulator's Codes of Practice (as at April 2011)

1 Reporting breaches of the law
2 Notifiable events
3 Funding defined benefits
4 Early leavers
5 Reporting late payment of contributions to occupational money purchase schemes
6 Reporting late payment of contributions to personal pensions
7 Trustee knowledge and understanding (TKU)

8 MNT/MND – putting arrangements in place
9 Internal controls
10 Modification of subsisting rights
11 Dispute resolution – reasonable periods
12 Circumstances in relation to the material detriment test

6

Conflicts of interest

IAN GAULT, SAMANTHA BROWN AND SUSANNE WILKINS

Introduction

In essence, a conflict of interest will arise where one party owes obligations to two or more other parties and the interests of those parties conflict. Whilst the potential for conflicts of interest has always existed in the occupational pension scheme regime, the risk of such conflicts arising has increased in recent years. Changes in the scheme funding and section 75 debt regimes, the existence of scheme funding deficits and the introduction of the Pensions Regulator (TPR) and the statutory codification of conflicts in the Companies Act 2006 have all played a part. The heightened risk of conflicts arising calls for a heightened awareness amongst trustees, employers and their professional advisers as to how to manage these risks. In this chapter we consider the framework surrounding conflicts of interest and the practical implications for pension scheme governance.

The legal framework

Conflicts of interest at common law

Conflicts of interest can arise in situations in which relationships between parties are governed by fiduciary obligations. The principles of fiduciary obligations have developed from the relationship of principal and agent and consequently are frequently framed as obligations owed to a principal by his or her fiduciary. In essence, these obligations will exist where one party has 'undertaken to act for or on behalf of another in a particular matter in circumstances which give rise to a relationship of trust and confidence'.[1] Whilst there are a number of settled classes of relationship in which fiduciary obligations are, without question, owed by one party to the other – such as trustees to beneficiaries,[2] solicitors to clients[3] and company directors to

---

1 *Bristol & West Building Society* v. *Mothew* [1998] Ch. 1 at 18.
2 *Keech* v. *Sandford* [1726] EWHC Ch. J76.
3 *Nocton* v. *Lord Ashburton* [1914] AC 932.

their company[4] – these categories are not finite and fiduciary obligations may arise in a number of other scenarios.

In *Bristol & West Building Society* v. *Mothew*, Lord Justice Millet described the obligations of a fiduciary in the following terms: 'a fiduciary must act in good faith; he must not make a profit out of his trust; he must not place himself in a position where his duty and his interest may conflict; he may not act for his own benefit or the benefit of a third person without the informed consent of his principal'. These obligations can be encompassed under the general obligation to act with undivided, single-minded loyalty to the principal. In the context of a pension scheme trustee, this can be a complex area and the nature of the duties owed by a trustee are likely to depend upon the powers which he or she is exercising. However, in broad terms, the obligation of loyalty is often considered under two heads: the duty to ensure that there is no conflict between the fiduciary's duty to his or her principal and his or her own self-interest (the 'self-interest conflict'); and the duty to ensure that there is no conflict between duties owed to different principals (the 'duty/duty conflict').

Self-interest conflict

An individual who owes fiduciary obligations cannot act in circumstances where his or her own self-interest could conflict with the interests of his or her principal. This principle is founded on the concept that an individual will be unable to withstand the temptation to pursue his or her own interest. There are, however, certain exclusions to this rule. The three most widely used exceptions are set out below:

- **Informed consent of the principal**
  A fiduciary can continue to act if the principal has given his or her express authorisation to this. In order for the principal's consent to be effective, the fiduciary must disclose not just the fact that he or she has an interest in the transaction, but also the nature of that interest.
- **Consent of the person creating the fiduciary position**
  A fiduciary will also be excused from compliance with the strict rule where the person creating the fiduciary position was aware that the fiduciary would, or could, have a conflict between his or her duties to his or her principal and his or her own self-interest, and either expressly or implicitly consented to and authorised the existence of the conflict.
- **Court sanction**
  The third exception to the strict prohibition is for the sanction of the court to be given to the fiduciary continuing to act notwithstanding the existence of the conflict.

---

4 *Guinness plc* v. *Saunders* [1990] 2 AC 663.

Duty/duty conflict

A fiduciary is also prevented from acting in cases where he or she owes duties to two principals and those duties conflict or could conflict. This strict principle is sometimes referred to as the 'double employment rule' and will apply whenever a fiduciary 'puts himself in a position where his duty to one principal may conflict with his duty to the other'. It is not necessary for there to be an actual conflict between the interests of the principals – a potential conflict is sufficient for a breach of duty to arise.

There are certain exceptions to this rule. The most widely used of these is that of informed consent. A fiduciary will not be in breach of this rule where he or she has obtained the informed consent of each of his or her principals to his or her continuing to act. However, even where the fiduciary has obtained the informed consent of his or her principals, he or she will nevertheless be constrained from acting for both in two circumstances:

- **The 'no inhibition rule'**
  The fiduciary must be able to act in the best interests of both of his or her principals at the same time and cannot promote the interests of one at the expense of the other. If he or she is unable to act in this way he or she will be in breach of the no inhibition rule and the informed consent of his or her principals will be insufficient to excuse the existence of his or her conflict.
- **Actual conflict**
  A fiduciary cannot act where the interests of his or her principals are actually in conflict.

Whilst informed consent is sufficient to enable a fiduciary to continue acting in circumstances where the interests of his or her principals *might* conflict, in the event that the potential conflict becomes an actual conflict, or he or she is unable to act in the best interests of both principals at the same time, the fiduciary must stop acting for at least one, and sometimes both, of his or her principals. Fulfilment of his or her duty of loyalty to one principal will not be a defence to a breach of his or her duty of loyalty to the other principal.

Confidentiality

The fiduciary's duty of loyalty also often gives rise to questions regarding the extent to which a fiduciary is under a duty to transmit information learned from one principal to another principal. The question will most often arise where the fiduciary is acting in a dual capacity and in performing his or her role for one principal comes into possession of information which it would be in the interests of the other principal to know. The obligation to share confidential information with a principal is a feature of the fiduciary's obligation of undivided loyalty and a fiduciary must therefore disclose information which it is in the interests of his or her principal to know.

Legal challenges and remedies

The remedies available in the event that a fiduciary has acted where he or she has a conflict of interest will depend upon whether the conflict has resulted in a breach of fiduciary duty. A breach of fiduciary duty will arise where his or her conflict has resulted in a breach of his or her obligation of loyalty, for example, where there has been a breach of the double employment rule and the fiduciary has not obtained the informed consent of his or her principal to his or her acting. Where, however, there has been no breach of the double employment rule, but the fiduciary has not complied with the principles of no inhibition or the actual conflict rule, then this will not automatically constitute a breach of fiduciary duty.

If there has been a breach of fiduciary duty, the transaction in question will be voidable at the direction of the principal. Whether it is in fact possible for the transaction to be rescinded will depend upon it being possible for both sides of the transaction to be undone so that the parties are in the position they were in before the event in question took place.

If it is not possible to undo the transaction in question, equitable compensation may be available if the principal has suffered loss.[5] Equitable compensation is intended to make good a loss suffered by the beneficiaries which was caused by the breach.

An alternative remedy is for the fiduciary to be required to account for profits (i.e. to give to the principal any monetary advantage from which the fiduciary has benefited as a result of his or her breach). However, this remedy will usually only be available where the fiduciary has preferred his or her own self-interest in such a way that he or she has profited from the funds of his or her principal (for example, from trust assets).

The statutory obligation to avoid conflicts of interest

Whilst the duty to avoid conflicts of interest has existed in common law for many years, there has historically been no statutory prohibition on conflicts of interest. However, the Companies Act 2006 has now codified the common law requirements in relation to company directors and places a statutory obligation on a director to 'avoid a situation in which he has, or can have, a direct or indirect interest that conflicts, or possibly may conflict, with the interests of the company'.[6] This obligation is stated expressly to include both a conflict of the director's interests and his or her duties, and a conflict of his or her duties (i.e. the self-dealing conflict and the duty/duty conflict).[7]

5 Breach of the double employment rule will not always result in loss. See *Bristol & West Building Society* v. *Daniels* [1997] PNLR 323; and *Bristol & West Building Society* v. *Fancy and Jackson* [1997] 4 All ER 582 at 614.
6 Companies Act 2006, s. 175.
7 The provisions of s. 175 of the Act do not apply to conflicts of interest arising in relation to transactions or arrangements which the director may enter into with the company, which give rise to separate obligations under the Act.

The obligations imposed by the Companies Act 2006 and the actions which can be taken to comply with these requirements are discussed further below.

The trustee perspective

Of all governance issues, conflicts of interest can be particularly difficult for trustees to manage because they affect individual trustees rather than the whole trustee body. In the context of pension scheme governance, trustees should be aware of the potential for conflicts to arise between: (i) their individual interests and their duties as trustees; and (ii) different duties which they owe. Conflicts may arise in particular in the circumstances described below.

The self-interest conflict

Where the trustee is a member of the scheme

Given the scope of the self-interest conflict (see above), where a trustee is also a beneficiary of the pension scheme, on the face of it there will be a risk of his or her own self-interest conflicting with that of the membership more generally. This can arise in particular where an active member trustee is asked to take a decision which could benefit different categories of members in different ways. In the past, such difficulties often arose in the case of a distribution of surplus; however, a topical example in current times would be a decision to close a scheme to future accrual.

Given the statutory requirement for member-nominated trustees, the difficulties raised for member trustees by the self-interest conflict are now addressed, at least to some extent, in section 39 of the Pensions Act 1995, which disapplies the 'no conflict' rule to member trustees. The effect of section 39 is to prevent a trustee from being prohibited from acting in circumstances in which the exercise of his or her powers would give rise to a potential conflict between his or her personal interest and his or her duties to beneficiaries.

Whilst section 39 prevents the trustee from being prohibited from acting, it does not go so far as to enable automatically a trustee to benefit from the scheme. This means that where trustee decisions are taken which result in a member trustee benefiting from the scheme, it will still be necessary for the trustees to demonstrate that the power in question has been exercised for a proper, rather than improper, purpose.[8]

The duty/duty conflict

Where the trustee is a director of the employer

It will usually be in the interests of the trustee board to benefit from the expertise and business insight afforded by having a director of the principal

8 *Hillsdown Holdings plc* v. *Pensions Ombudsman* [1997] 1 All ER 862.

employer amongst its number. However, trustees who are also directors of the principal employer owe fiduciary obligations to the company[9] as well as to the scheme beneficiaries. This means that conflict issues can be acute for these individuals and will usually require careful management.

Although the fundamental objective of both trustees and company is to provide benefits to the members of the scheme, there are many circumstances in which the interests of the company and trustees can diverge, particularly in difficult economic climates. Examples of such circumstances include corporate restructurings, payment of section 75 debts, scheme funding and benefit design. In matters of scheme funding, in particular, the interests of the employer and trustees can polarise and it will often be the case that the trustees' and company's views on the amount and pace of funding required will differ. If there are divergent views and negotiations between the parties, a trustee will not be able to act on both sides of the debate and steps should be taken to manage the conflict.

The conflict issues which arise for directors acting as trustees are explored further below. However, it is insufficient for the employer alone to manage the conflict and the individual trustee will need to take steps to ensure that he or she is not in breach of the double employment rule in his or her position as a trustee. This may necessitate taking the steps described below.

Where the trustee is a senior employee of the employer

The generally accepted position is that an employee will not automatically be regarded as owing fiduciary obligations to his or her employer, under either common law or the Companies Act 2006.[10] However, a fiduciary relationship can arise if the particular terms of the employee's contract of employment require the employee to act in the interests of the employer. The extent to which fiduciary obligations are found to exist is likely to depend, inter alia, upon the particular duties in question, the extent of autonomy exercised by the employee and the control or direction extended by the employer. Given these characteristics, the existence of a fiduciary relationship with the employer is more likely to arise for a senior employee than a junior employee.

From the perspective of an employer-nominated trustee who is not a company director, whether conflict issues could arise for him or her is likely to depend upon the extent to which as a matter of his or her employment contract he or she has duties to pursue the employer's best interests in relation to the pension scheme. For example, the position of a senior treasurer with delegated authority to negotiate and agree pension scheme funding on behalf of the company is likely to differ significantly from that of a senior IT employee who performs no functions in relation to the pension scheme or other financing issues.

---

9 *Aberdeen Railway Co.* v. *Blaikie Bros* (1854) 1 Macq 461; and more recently in *Guinness plc* v. *Saunders*, cited above fn. 4.

10 *University of Nottingham* v. *Fishel* [2000] ICR 1462.

The discussions below regarding conflicts which can arise for a company director who is also a trustee also indicate that such conflicts can arise equally for senior employees. Whether this is the case in practice will depend upon the nature of the employee's duties to the employer. However, it is nevertheless a risk of which employer trustees should be aware.

Where the trustee is a trustee of another scheme

Where companies operate more than one pension scheme, it is not unusual for there to be common trustees of the schemes, particularly employer-appointed representatives. This in itself is not a difficulty on an ongoing basis. However, trustees should recognise the potential for conflicts to arise in the event of negotiations between the two trustee boards. This can be a particular issue on scheme mergers where trustees will often seek indemnity and warranty protection from each other in the merger agreement. In such cases, individual trustees should ensure that they are not negotiating with themselves and steps should be taken to manage conflicts appropriately. It is unlikely that a trustee would be able to engage in such discussions in his or her capacity as trustee of both schemes.

Where the trustee represents a particular constituency

Where a trustee is elected to represent a particular constituency (for example, a trade union representative) that will not in itself usually be sufficient to give rise to a conflict situation for that trustee, as he or she will not necessarily owe fiduciary duties to members of his or her constituency. However, the trustee will nevertheless be required to comply with the equitable principles of decision-making and exercise his or her powers for a proper purpose, rather than to promote the interests of his or her constituents.

Managing conflicts of interest

A failure by trustees to take adequate steps to manage the risk of conflicts of interest arising may result in the trustees' decision being set aside or personal liability for the trustees for having acted in breach of fiduciary duty and/or trust. It is therefore an important part of scheme governance to ensure that appropriate measures are in place for managing trustee conflicts of interest. This is an area which has attracted heightened focus in recent years and is a topic on which TPR places particular emphasis.

Pensions Regulator guidance

Trustees should be aware of and familiar with TPR's Guidance on conflicts.[11] The guidance does not provide a blueprint for managing conflicts, and recognises

---

11 Conflicts of interest Guidance from the Pensions Regulator (October 2008), www.thepensions
   regulator.gov.uk/guidance/guidance-conflicts-of-interest.aspx.

that the reasons for conflicts arising and the manner in which they should be managed will be scheme specific. The Regulator identifies five principles which trustees should adopt:

- trustees should understand the importance of conflicts of interest, including understanding the nature of the duties which can give rise to conflicts, and must seek appropriate legal advice;
- trustees should take steps to identify potential future conflicts as well as conflicts which have already arisen and maintain registers of interests and conflicts;
- trustees should have in place procedures for evaluating, managing and avoiding conflicts of interest;
- trustees should ensure that they manage the risk of conflicts arising for their advisers in order to ensure that the trustees are able to obtain appropriate advice; and
- trustees should document and apply a conflicts policy to assist in their management of conflicts.

There is no automatic sanction for breach of TPR's guidance. However, where the Regulator considers that conflicts have not been appropriately managed, it may take 'appropriate action'. This can include issuing an improvement notice (requiring the trustees to take steps to manage their conflicts). TPR also has power to appoint independent trustees where it is satisfied that it is reasonable to do so in order to protect the interests of the scheme members generally.[12] This power was exercised by the Regulator in the case of the GEC 1972 Plan (the Telent pension scheme) as a direct consequence of a failure to manage conflicts of interest appropriately.[13]

Conflicts policies

As part of their scheme governance arrangements, trustees should ensure that they have procedures in place for identifying, monitoring and managing conflicts of interest. Best practice at the time of publication suggests that this will include devising and adopting a conflicts policy and maintaining a conflicts register. These should be maintained and reviewed periodically.

Steps which can be taken to manage conflicts of interest

The existence of a conflict or potential conflict for a trustee does not mean that the trustee must automatically cease to act. Rather, it requires that steps are taken to manage it appropriately. What steps are appropriate are likely to depend

---

12 Pensions Act 1995, s. 7.
13 See the Reasons of the Determinations Panel dated 7 November 2007, following the compulsory review of the decision made at the Special Procedure hearing on 19 October 2007 in respect of the GEC 1972 Plan.

upon the nature of the conflict and the identities of the individuals involved. It will often be appropriate for one or more of the following steps to be taken:

- the conflicted trustee may excuse him- or herself from the relevant discussion and decision-making;
- use of a sub-committee excluding the conflicted individual;
- resignation of the conflicted trustee; and/or
- appointment of an independent trustee.

These options are considered further below.

Excusing the conflicted trustee from the relevant discussion and decision-making

A conflicted trustee can abstain from discussions and decision-making relating to the matter in which he or she is conflicted. In order for this approach to be effective at all, the scheme trust deed and rules must allow meetings to be quorate without the participation of the conflicted trustee and for decisions to be taken by a majority of trustees. In the event that unanimous trustee agreement is required, abstention will not be possible.

Even if he or she abstains from the relevant decision-making, the conflicted trustee nevertheless remains a trustee and should therefore continue to act in the best interests of beneficiaries. This means that if the conflicted trustee possesses information which would be relevant to the trustees' decision-making, this should nevertheless be shared with the trustee board, in order to ensure that the trustee board is able to consider all factors which are relevant to their decision. For this reason, this option will not always be effective where the conflict has arisen for a company-appointed trustee who holds sensitive information about the company which would be relevant to the trustees' decision-making, such as the finance director. This is discussed further below.

Use of sub-committees

An alternative option is for the trustee body to delegate decisions relating to the particular matter to a sub-committee of trustees which does not include the conflicted trustee. For this approach to be effective, the trust deed and rules must permit delegation.

Resignation of the conflicted trustee

Where a trustee conflict is so acute that it would be impracticable for the conflict to be managed effectively in any of the ways discussed above, it may be necessary for the trustee to resign. The risk of such acute conflicts arising and resignation being required is a relevant consideration which should be borne in mind when trustees are being appointed.

Appointment of an independent trustee

The appointment of an independent trustee as an additional member of a board of trustees will not of itself absolve any individual trustees of conflicts of interest. However, the presence of an independent trustee on a trustee board may assist in monitoring conflict issues and ensuring that they are addressed appropriately. It can also assist in ensuring that the trustee board remains quorate without the participation of the conflicted trustee.

Employer issues

Background: the employer's perspective

Although the primary regulatory focus is on ensuring that pension scheme trustees can identify and manage conflicts of interest, the employer also has to negotiate the employer/trustee conflicts minefield.

From a purely practical point of view, the employer will often have a key role in appointing and removing trustees (subject to the statutory member-nominated trustee requirements).[14] Typically, scheme rules vest the power of appointment in the employer with the result that the employer is able to determine the make-up of the majority of the trustee body.[15]

Trustees are also responsible for the operation of a major element of employees' remuneration packages, with all the attendant implications for employer/employee relations. Therefore, the make-up and conduct of the trustee body will be of significant interest to the scheme's sponsoring employers.

Perhaps most significantly from an employer viewpoint: employers can incur huge liability in respect of defined benefit pension schemes, and the extent of this liability is influenced to a considerable degree by trustee powers, decisions and policies. Typically, trustees have powers to direct the scheme's investment policy; their agreement will also be required to any scheme amendments (including amendments to close the scheme to future accrual), scheme mergers and buy-outs. Trustees also have significant powers in relation to scheme funding, including a key role in agreeing the rate of employer contributions to the scheme and in agreeing funding targets and actuarial assumptions with the employer.[16]

---

14 See s. 242 of the Pensions Act 2004 and the Occupational Pension Schemes (Member-nominated Trustees and Directors) Regulations 2006 (No. 714). TPR has also issued a code of practice on putting member-nominated trustee arrangements in place (No. 8, in force from November 2006).

15 Under SI 2006/714, at least one-third of the trustee body must be nominated and selected by the scheme membership. It is likely that this will be increased to one-half in due course.

16 Scheme rules may even give the trustees sole power to set employer contributions; this unilateral power survives the introduction of the scheme-specific funding regime.

It addition, trustees have a crucial role in various types of corporate transactions; for example, through their powers to determine investment strategy and to call in so-called 'section 75 debts' from the scheme's participating employers.

In short, the scheme's status as an (usually major) unsecured creditor of the employer, coupled with the legislative/regulatory trend towards increased trustee activism (itself backed up with significant powers entrenched in scheme rules and, to some extent, legislation), mean that there is an understandable desire by the employer for its interests to be represented on the trustee body. Conversely, it is this emphasis which makes it increasingly difficult for directors/senior employees of the employer to act as trustees of defined benefit pension schemes.

Naturally, the employer has a vested interest in the trustee body containing an appropriate degree of skill and expertise; a well-run scheme, operated within the parameters of a sound governance policy and featuring high quality decision-making will maximise efficiency and minimise costs. This convergence of interests means that it does not necessarily follow from the debtor/creditor status of the employer/trustees that the two parties must adopt constantly adversarial positions. There continues to be scope (in theory at least) for directors and senior employees of the employer to act as trustees.

Some of the difficulties involved with dual roles, and the potential to resolve them, are explored from an employer's perspective below.

Where the trustee is a director of the employer

There is a perceived benefit to both the employer and trustees from having a director or senior employee of the employer on the trustee body of a defined benefit pension scheme (in terms of contributing both expertise and through factual knowledge of the employer's outlook, plans and financial position). However, the individual concerned would owe duties to both the employer and the trustees.

Fiduciary duties: their existence is not fatal to dual roles

Where the potential trustee is a director of the employer, he or she would be a fiduciary (in respect of both the employer and as a trustee) and would owe fiduciary duties to both parties. Fiduciary duties may also be owed by a senior employee, depending on the nature of his or her role and functions (see above). However, the existence of fiduciary duties to the employer does not mean that the director or senior employee cannot act as a trustee if he or she is able to manage those duties. Note, however, that particular issues arise in relation to confidential information (see below).

The Companies Act 2006: conflicts must be authorised by the company

The Companies Act 2006 imposes a duty on directors to avoid actual and potential conflicts of interest.[17] The Act also makes it clear that this duty applies to the exploitation of information.[18] However, the conflict can be authorised by the company's directors[19] provided that nothing in the company's constitution would invalidate the authorisation[20] and that the quorum requirement is met without counting the vote of the interested director.[21]

In respect of a private company which was incorporated before 1 October 2008, advance authorisation can be by the board of directors (in which case shareholders must pass an ordinary resolution permitting the authorisation, which then endures as long as the facts and circumstances of the conflict remain the same) or via changing the company's articles of association to allow the conflict.[22] It is also possible for shareholders to authorise the conflict by ordinary resolution or to ratify it after the event (subject to restrictions).

Where the director of an employer company seeks to become a trustee of the company's pension scheme (whether it is constituted as a body of individuals or as a corporate trustee), it will be necessary for the potential conflict of interest situation to be authorised by the employer company by one of the above methods.

Where the trustee body is set up as a company, it will also be necessary for the trustee/directors to consider the implications of the Companies Act 2006. However, the extent to which the conflicts of interest provisions are relevant to trustee companies is the subject of debate, especially as the ability to enforce the provisions lies with the company itself (subject to certain derivative action rights also introduced by the 2006 Act, under which shareholders can enforce the duties).[23]

The trust deed and rules: authorisation clauses

Companies (and their directors or senior employees considering accepting a position as a trustee) should also cast a critical eye over any clauses in the scheme's trust deed and rules which purport to authorise conflicts of interest.

17 Section 175(1) provides that 'A director of a company must avoid a situation in which he has, or can have, a direct or indirect interest that conflicts, or possibly may conflict, with the interests of the company'. Note that these provisions only apply in relation to where the situation arose on or after 1 October 2008. These provisions also do not apply to senior employees.
18 See s. 175(2).
19 See s. 175(4)(b).
20 See s. 175(5). This statement applies to private companies – it is necessary for a plc to have an express provision in its constitution authorising the use of this process.
21 See s. 175(6).
22 It will still generally be necessary for the directors to consider the conflict matter (and in some cases resolve to authorise the conflict).
23 In the case of pension scheme trustee companies, the shareholders are usually members of the employer's corporate group.

Such clauses are potentially very useful, but in most cases it is not clear to what extent the standard express authorisation clauses in trust deeds would be held to cover director trustees in respect of their duties owed to their employer. Standard clauses typically only cover conflicts of interest and not conflicts of duty.

Conducting negotiations: the general position

In *Hillsdown Holdings plc* v. *Pensions Ombudsman*,[24] the High Court had to consider the position of a company director (who was also a trustee) who took part in negotiations on the distribution of surplus on behalf of the trustees.

The court accepted that the conduct was not self-dealing (and, therefore, that the negotiations should not be set aside automatically). However, the case suggests that, in the absence of an express provision which permits a trustee to act in negotiations with the employer notwithstanding his or her status as a senior employee or director of the employer, there may be a presumption of bias unless it can be proved that the decision reached by the trustees was reasonable and proper.

The position of the finance director

Prior to the Pensions Act 2004 and the accompanying trend towards greater trustee independence and activism, it was not uncommon for an employer's finance director to sit on a trustee board. Those who are in favour of this approach can find support in a Technical Release issued by the Institute of Chartered Accountants in 2007, which took the view that there is no inherent problem with finance directors acting as trustees, notwithstanding their proximity to key company decisions which affect the pension scheme.

However, many would argue that an inherent conflict arises where the employer and trustees are negotiating on matters with direct financial implications (for example, setting employer contribution rates or engaging in negotiations on other aspects of the scheme-specific funding regime[25]). It is difficult, therefore, for a finance director to act as a trustee during negotiations when he or she may not only have an interest deriving from his or her role as finance director in minimising employer expenses, but will also be privy to confidential information as to the company's financial circumstances and plans.

24 [1997] 1 All ER 862.
25 This was introduced by the Pensions Act 2004. A central tenet of the regime is that key matters relating to scheme funding are generally (subject to certain exceptions) set through agreement by the employer and trustees. Such matters generally include setting employer contribution rates, the actuarial assumptions to be used and calculating the scheme's 'technical provisions' (broadly, its liabilities).

Assuming, therefore, that it would be very difficult for the finance director to participate in scheme-funding negotiations, the question arises as to whether he or she can act as a trustee in relation to other matters and recuse him- or herself from acting in respect of financial matters.

This continues to be a matter for debate. However, many consider it to be unwise for a finance director to act (or to continue to act) as a trustee. One key reason for this view stems from the fact that the finance director will be privy to high-level financial information about the company, its plans generally and in relation to the pension scheme. In a regulatory environment which encourages ongoing scrutiny of the employer covenant and which expects this scrutiny to permeate into many aspects of the operation of the pension scheme (for example, TPR's guidance to trustees to seek appropriate mitigation on the occurrence of a materially detrimental event),[26] it is extremely difficult for the finance director to refrain from breaching his or her duties to at least one of the parties (see below).

On the issue of funding negotiations generally, it is important for the employer to plan for a proper commercial arm's-length negotiation with trustees who are likely to be independently advised and determined to fight their corner on any difficult issues. To this end, it is generally good practice for employers to obtain their own separate legal and actuarial advice at an early stage, especially if the scheme's actuarial valuation is likely to disclose a substantial deficit.

Whether the issues described above will apply to senior employees involved in the finance function for the employer will depend upon the scope of the senior employee's role in relation to the employer (see above).

Confidential information

The strict legal position (based on non-pensions cases) is probably that a trustee's fiduciary duties generally require him or her to disclose to his or her co-trustee and/or use for the benefit of the scheme relevant information acquired in his or her capacity as director or employee whether or not it is confidential to the employer. This is likely to be most relevant to directors and senior employees who come into possession of sensitive or confidential information on a day-to-day basis, but could apply equally to junior employees. This means that if a director/senior employee fails to disclose the information to his or her co-trustee, he or she may be in breach of his or her fiduciary obligations as a trustee. Equally, if he or she discloses the information, he or she may be in breach of his or her duty of confidentiality to the employer. This disclosure dilemma can be managed by entering into a confidentiality agreement (see below). However, this type of conflict will be particularly difficult

26 See TPR's clearance guidance, revised in June 2009.

to overcome for a finance director, in light of the relevance and sensitivity of the information he or she holds.[27]

Confidential information issues are most likely to be a problem where a director or senior officer is potentially involved on both sides of a negotiation. Note that a conflicted trustee who does not participate in the relevant trustee decision-making arguably remains under a duty to disclose relevant information to his or her co-trustees.

It is vital that this issue be considered before it arises in practice; it is very difficult to unravel this particular type of conflict. One possible way of managing the conflict is to incorporate into the trust deed a clause which expressly releases the conflicted trustee from any duty of disclosure to co-trustees if he or she elects not to participate in the decision-making process. Again, this may severely restrict the role of a trustee who is also a finance director of the employer (or who holds any other position with the company by virtue of which he or she is privy to confidential financial information), given the pervasive nature of finance/covenant issues in the operation of pension schemes.

Confidentiality agreements

Entering into a confidentiality agreement, in which trustees agree not to disclose confidential information, is viewed as generally helpful as part of a conflict-management strategy, although it falls well short of being a panacea. However, from the employer's viewpoint, a confidentiality agreement may be essential if information to be disclosed to the trustees includes commercially (or price-) sensitive information (as would usually be the case when conducting a covenant review).

Increasingly, employers are favouring putting a standing confidentiality agreement in place, covering all information that may from time to time be disclosed to trustees. This avoids the risk of delay if trustees need to be approached urgently on any particular issue, such as a corporate transaction. However, the employer should ensure that any standing agreement is sufficiently flexible to allow additional conditions to be imposed if, for example, particular information to be disclosed in the context of a proposed transaction is especially sensitive.

There are also other pitfalls for the unwary. For example, employers need to bear in mind that confidentiality agreements can be difficult to enforce against lay trustees. In addition, the existence of a confidentiality agreement cannot absolve the trustees from their duty to disclose information where a failure to disclose would be a breach of trust or a breach of pensions legislation.

---

27 In practice, a conflict only arises where the information at issue is material to the trustees (i.e. it would reasonably be expected to affect the decisions made by the trustees). A conflict also only arises where the information has not been generally disclosed to the trustees.

Furthermore, as TPR points out in its guidance on conflicts of interest, confidentiality agreements do not deal with the conflict itself: they allow disclosure of information. It may still be necessary to manage the conflict.

If information is particularly sensitive, the employer may prefer not to give full disclosure to trustees, but may instead opt to restrict disclosure to the trustees' advisers (for example, this will be possible where it is provided as part of a covenant review).

Duty under regulations for the employer to disclose information to trustees

Employers should bear in mind that regulations impose a general duty on current and former employers to disclose (on request) to the scheme's trustees such information as is required for the performance of trustee duties (or for the performance of the professional advisers' duties).[28]

There is also a more specific requirement for employers to disclose the 'occurrence of any event relating to the employer which there is reasonable cause to believe will be of material significance in the exercise by the trustees … or professional advisers of any of their functions'.[29]

These duties were sometimes overlooked until TPR cited them in its code of practice on scheme-specific funding, specifically in relation to trustees obtaining the information necessary to assess the employer covenant.[30]

Critical events

As a general point, governance arrangements (including those dealing with conflicts) should be sufficiently robust to be able to be effective on the occurrence of critical events, such as if the employer is the target of a takeover bid or where the company experiences serious financial difficulties.

Where a company is on the brink of insolvency, it may be difficult for any director to continue to act as a trustee of the pension scheme. Directors will have duties to the employer's creditors on a possible insolvency and must be careful not to favour one creditor over others. They are also likely to be in the difficult position of having to manage the company, seek independent advice on the financial position of the business and avoid wrongful trading.

Adviser issues

In addition to concerns about their own conflicts of interest, employers and trustees also need to be vigilant as to whether their professional advisers (such

---

28 Regulation 6(1)(a) of the Occupational Pension Schemes (Scheme Administration) Regulations 1996 (No. 1715).
29 Regulation 6(1)(b) of the Occupational Pension Schemes (Scheme Administration) Regulations 1996 (No. 1715).
30 Regulatory Code of Practice 03; 'funding defined benefits'.

as legal advisers, actuaries or accountants) have a conflict of interest (either generally, or in relation to particular issues or events). Clearly, the advisers themselves also have an important role to play in disclosing and managing any conflicts which may arise.

Identifying conflicts

A conflict may arise wherever the role of the adviser may affect the independence of the advice given. The conflict can exist for the duration of a particular transaction or negotiations on a particular issue, or it can be an enduring conflict.

This section considers primarily conflicts which arise when professional advisers act for both the employer and trustee (although conflict issues relevant to employers and trustees do not arise uniquely in this form; witness the position of a lawyer who advises trustees and also a different professional adviser to the scheme (for example, a custodian)).

Certain conflicts will be more transparent to employers and trustees than others: for example, a legal adviser who had previously advised both the employer and trustees on general issues, but whose clients now take adversarial positions on a significant issue. In this situation, the adviser will be unable to continue to act for both parties in relation to the contentious issue. However, they may be able to continue to act for one of the parties; whether this is appropriate will depend on (amongst other things) the nature of the issue, the views of the parties and the measures put in place by the adviser to prevent the misuse of any confidential information. It may also be possible for the adviser to revert to acting for both the employer and trustees when the contentious issue has been resolved. Again, whether this is appropriate will depend on a number of factors.

It should also be noted that, in order to help trustees to identify and manage conflicts of interest, regulations effectively provide that certain professional advisers[31] must notify pension scheme trustees of any conflict of interest to which they are subject in relation to the scheme as soon as they become aware of its existence.[32]

Professional advisers who are members of (and regulated by) a professional body will, in any event, usually also be subject to guidance issued by that body

---

31 Legal advisers, fund managers and, broadly, actuaries, auditors and custodians. See s. 47(3) of the Pensions Act 1995 and reg. 2 of the Occupational Pension Schemes (Scheme Administration) Regulations 1996 (No. 1715).

32 The Occupational Pension Schemes (Scheme Administration) Regulations 1996 (No. 1715). These set out certain formalities in relation to the appointment and removal of certain professional advisers. On receiving the notice of their appointment, the adviser must acknowledge in writing receipt of that notice (within one month). In that acknowledgement, the professional adviser must confirm in writing that he or she will notify the trustees of any conflict of interest to which he or she is subject in relation to the scheme immediately he or she becomes aware of its existence.

on conflicts of interest,[33] and must also act in accordance with their common law duties as fiduciaries. Disclosure of the conflict to the affected parties will be a fundamental requirement.

However, notwithstanding these safeguards, it is still ultimately the responsibility of the trustees to identify conflicts and to manage them appropriately.

Guidance from the Pensions Regulator

In its October 2008 guidance on conflicts, TPR acknowledges that adviser conflicts are likely to arise and sets out some best practice points for trustees. Trustees should:

- actively manage their relations with advisers to ensure that advisers are able to provide independent advice;
- require their advisers to declare any conflicts that may arise in respect of their engagement on a timely basis;
- consider in advance whether conflicts make it undesirable for a particular adviser to be appointed or continue to act for them, in circumstances where a conflict with a sponsoring employer may arise;
- evaluate the nature of the conflict, where a conflict has been declared, and determine an appropriate course of action; and
- where applicable, understand the reporting lines and conflicts that the in-house pensions manager and secretariat may have.

The trustees can demand and expect full cooperation from their professional advisers, who should also be able to demonstrate to the trustees that they have effective conflict-management procedures in place.

Confidential information

Where a conflict arises (whether isolated or enduring), professional guidance generally dictates that the professional adviser can either cease to act for both parties or cease to act for one (the 'cessation party'), but continue to act for the other (the 'continuing party'). It may even be possible for a firm of professional advisers to continue to act for both parties where effective information barriers are put in place (see below). However, this latter approach is increasingly rare.

One key factor relevant to whether the adviser can carry on acting for the continuing party is the extent to which they are in possession of confidential information through their work for the cessation party (and the extent to which that information would be useful to the interests of the continuing party).

In these circumstances, the best solution may be for the adviser to cease to act altogether. However, it is also possible for the adviser to use internal

---

33 E.g. the Law Society and the Financial Services Authority have professional guidelines on this issue.

safeguards to ensure that there is no misuse of confidential information. This may enable them to carry on acting for the continuing party.

For example, the adviser may be able to put information barriers in place whereby different personnel are allocated to deal with the continuing party (compared to those who dealt with the cessation party). Non-public information relating to the cessation party could be physically secured (that is, locked away with highly restricted access); electronic data could be secured with passwords. Traditionally, information barriers have been a popular way of dealing with the confidential information issue, especially in relation to larger firms of professional advisers, where it is feasible physically to separate files and run separate teams of advisers and support staff where appropriate.

However, there are also certain difficulties with this approach and care must be taken to ensure that any solution is compatible with the adviser's fiduciary duties (especially, in relation to disclosure of information), as well as with legal and regulatory requirements.

Where an 'isolated issue' conflict subsides (for example, because the issue is resolved), it may be possible for the adviser to resume acting for one or both of the parties. Again, whether this is appropriate will depend on a number of factors, including whether difficulties arise because an adviser who acted for a continuing party has become privy to confidential information during the transaction/issue which will be relevant to relationships going forward.

Acting for the employer and trustees: market practice

In light of the increased regulatory emphasis on trustee professionalism, independence and activism, it is becoming less commonplace for trustees and employers to share the same advisers. This trend has been helped by the increasing number of situations (in particular the introduction of the scheme-specific funding regime and TPR's moral hazard sanctions) which necessarily take on a more adversarial character, given that they involve negotiations on material financial issues.

Conclusions

As will be clear from the discussion above, the risk of a conflict arising permeates many areas of the running and operation of occupational pension schemes. Indeed, it can be seen as an unavoidable feature of the relationship between an ongoing scheme and its sponsoring employer. Clearly, it will be in the interests of all concerned to ensure that the relationship works smoothly and that legal requirements and principles of good governance are observed. If this is to be achieved, trustees, employers and professional advisers need to be aware of the issues and take steps to ensure that potential conflicts are recognised and managed effectively.

7

The pension scheme in the employment package

WYN DERBYSHIRE, STEPHEN HARDY AND DAVID WILMAN

Any contemporary comprehensive analysis of pension scheme governance requires knowledge not only of pensions and trust law, but also an understanding of the treatment of pension schemes in the wider employment law context. At the end of the day, pension schemes are effectively vehicles whereby employers and employees can make provision for the financial needs of employees and their dependants in later life. This is true even in the case of the self-employed, whose pension provision will generally take the form of personal pension schemes. However, this chapter focuses on the employer–employee relationship and its interaction with the trustees of employer-sponsored occupational pension schemes.

Key to understanding the tri-angular relationship between employees (and former employees), their employer and trustees is recognition that accrued pension rights under an occupational pension scheme typically take the form of:

- rights arising under the pension scheme trust that can be enforced by the relevant employee(s) as a beneficiary of the pension trust against its trustees; and
- contractual rights arising under the contract of employment entered into between the employee and employer.

As far as an employee's beneficial rights are concerned, these will be enforceable, in principle, against trustees through the courts in the same way as the rights of any beneficiary under any trust, subject to the usual vagaries of trust law. However, in some respects a disgruntled beneficiary of a pension scheme (who need not, of course, be an employee, or even a former employee – he or she may be a spouse, for example) is more fortunate than the beneficiary of a (non-pension) trust in that that statute affords the individual additional methods of making his or her case, for example, by allowing him or her access to an independent disputes resolution procedure that trustees must follow and the ability to bring a claim (at no cost) before the Pensions Ombudsman should his or her complaint fall within the Pensions Ombudsman's jurisdiction.

An alternative or additional avenue that an employee (or former employee) may explore if he or she perceives that his or her pension rights are being infringed is the possibility of pursuing a claim against his or her employer (or former employer) under the provision of his or her contract of employment. This immediately raises the issue of whether pension rights are contractual in nature. Despite occasional attempts by employers to argue that they are not, it seems likely that in at least the majority of pension disputes the rights will be deemed to be contractual in nature.

Fundamentally, it may be that those rights are express in nature, either in the written provisions of the contract of employment, or in some ancillary document such as a staff handbook, explanatory booklet or supporting letter that an employment tribunal or court would have little difficulty in determining should be regarded as being incorporated into the contract of employment. However, even in the absence of such express provisions (and details of pension benefits are rarely expressly spelt out in their entirety in employment contracts), basic employment law principles would dictate that simple membership of an occupational pension scheme over a period of time is capable of creating implied contractual pension rights built up by custom and practice. The nature of those rights will to some extent depend upon the exact circumstances of the relevant pension scheme, but a court is unlikely to have difficulty in determining that an employee who has been a member of a pension scheme for a period of time (which need only be a few months) has at least an implied contractual right to be a member of that scheme, albeit subject to its governing provisions from time to time. Consequently, an employer would be ill advised to assume automatically that the absence of any express provisions dealing with pensions in an employee's contract of employment necessarily means that the employee has no contractual pension rights at all.

In addition to these two strands of pension right enforceability, it is also important to recognise the relationship between the sponsoring employers of the pension scheme and its trustees. This relationship is largely dictated by pensions and trust law and is enshrined in the pension scheme's trust documentation, which will largely dictate the nature of that relationship. Thus, the trust documentation will typically set out a variety of powers and legal obligations imposed on the employer and/or the trustees, and practitioners refer to the 'balance of power' between the two parties when discussing the ability (or inability) of a particular party to exercise (or prevent the exercise of) a power or function arising under the scheme's trust documentation.

By way of example, a pension scheme's amendment power will usually be exercisable by the employer, but require the prior consent of the trustees (or vice versa). Even where on the face of the trust documentation one party might appear to have the unrestricted ability to exercise (or not exercise) a particular power (for example, the employer's ability to appoint and remove trustees (apart from member-nominated trustees, who generally cannot simply be removed at will by an employer)), in practice the ability of the party with the power will frequently be restricted by operation of law. For instance, in the example just cited (the power to appoint and remove trustees), the employer's power will be fiduciary in nature and thus cannot simply be exercised for trivial or unjustifiable reasons (and any attempt to do so could lead to the employer's actions being challenged in the courts).

Likewise, most pension schemes are drafted on the basis that the employer is itself a contingent beneficiary of the pension scheme, a factor which should be borne in mind by trustees when considering the exercise (or non-exercise) of any unilateral power they may have. Therefore, trustees do owe some measure of responsibility to the employer under general trust law principles.

Variation of rights

The importance of recognising that pension schemes operate within both a pension law context and an employment law context is perhaps most apparent when one considers making possible changes to pension scheme rights, and especially when those changes are detrimental to the interests of a scheme's beneficiaries. When considering such changes, it is important to identify whether the proposed changes will impact pension rights which have already accrued prior to the date of the change, future pensions rights (that is, pension arising in respect of future service), or a mixture of the two.

As is well known, and regardless of the employment law aspects, worsening pension benefit rights which have already accrued can be very difficult to achieve without express member consent due to the provisions of section 67 of the Pensions Act 1995. Furthermore, some amendment powers include built-in prohibitions upon them being utilised to worsen accrued benefits. As a consequence, such variations are in fact quite rare. More common are changes that affect only future pension benefit rights. Generally speaking, section 67 of the Pensions Act 1995 will not prove an obstacle to varying future pension rights; however, there are other potential difficulties within both the pensions law and the employment law arenas.

Within the pensions law arena, the principal difficulty usually faced by employers who seek to vary adversely future pension benefits (for example, by closing a scheme to future accrual or worsening future benefit accrual rates, etc.) is ensuring that the relevant pension scheme's amendment power can be operated so as to introduce the desired change into the scheme's trust documentation. Occasionally, amendment powers are encountered that specifically prohibit the worsening of future benefits (or only permit such a step with the consents of affected members). However, even where this is not a factor, not only will a scheme's amendment power generally be considered a fiduciary power (and thus can only be exercised for its proper purpose), but its exercise will usually be conditional upon obtaining the agreement of both the employer and the trustees of the scheme. From the perspective of the trustees, they should only be willing to agree to the exercise of the power if they are satisfied that its exercise is in the best interests of their beneficiaries (which can translate as being 'the least worst option' in the case of detrimental changes such as those mentioned above). Employers who plan to worsen members' benefits should thus be prepared to be challenged by the trustees to justify why the changes are needed before consent to exercise of the amendment power is granted.

Historically, it was fairly common for benefit changes to be introduced by exercise of the relevant scheme's amendment power alone, with members simply being informed of the prospective (detrimental) alterations to their pension benefits. Often, members were not even asked to provide express consent; from an employment law perspective, the effect of this was that the employer effectively made unilateral adverse changes to an employee's contract of employment. Unless active members objected in such a way as to demonstrate that they refused to accept the change (which seldom occurred), members would eventually be deemed to have accepted the change to their service conditions by reason of custom and practice.

Today, however, members (and unions) are far more aware of their employment rights, and generally speaking, any employer wishing to make detrimental changes to a pension scheme (such as scheme closure) must consider not only the pensions law aspects (i.e. persuading trustees that they should agree to the proposed changes to the scheme's trust documentation), but also the employment law aspects.

From the employment perspective (and the viewpoint of the employer), there are, in principle, four separate possible 'methods' which may be adopted to vary an employee's contractual pension rights (for example, when seeking to close a scheme to future accrual or to otherwise worsen future benefits):

  (i) Route 1 – there may be an express clause in the employee's contract of employment or handbook or other documentation that permits the employer to change the contractual terms;

 (ii) Route 2 – each employee may explicitly consent to the change to the contractual term;

(iii) Route 3 – the employer may seek to impose unilaterally the change to the contractual term (and the employees do not object); or

(iv) Route 4 – the employer may elect to terminate (dismiss) the employee on notice and re-hire on new contractual terms.

Route 1 – express variation clause

Employment contracts may contain a term which expressly permits the employee to remove or amend benefits at the employer's discretion. Clearly this may be helpful in relation to implementing the changes, but employers should be aware that the existence of such a clause does not give an employer the 'green light' to go ahead with the proposed changes without further consideration for a number of reasons. Firstly, even where there is the contractual flexibility to amend or remove benefits, this right will be interpreted restrictively by employment tribunals and the courts (particularly where it is widely drafted, rather than limited and specific). Secondly, an employer also remains under a duty not to breach its implied duty of mutual trust and confidence towards each employee, so that in exercising any contractual variation clause, the employer should do so in a reasonable manner. A unilateral decision to change the benefits as proposed, without prior warning, discussion or consent, is unlikely to be a reasonable exercise of the contractual variation clause. As such, despite the fact that there is a flexibility clause in the employment contracts, the basic rule remains that an employer cannot unilaterally change terms and conditions of employment without the risk of employment claims.

Route 2 – seek employee's consent

The second method, and arguably the better methodology from a legal perspective (if not always the most practical), is to seek each employee's consent to the contractual variation. This may be achieved by way of initial discussion with the employee (which would itself constitute a 'consultation'), during which a letter documenting the change would be handed to them. The letter should propose the change, and set out timing and the effect (if any) on their terms and conditions. The employee would be asked to sign and return a duplicate copy to their employer indicating their acceptance of the change to their contractual terms. Having signed to that effect, the employee's contract will be deemed to be amended from the date of the change. So long as the information provided has not been misleading and the employer has not applied undue pressure, the change will be valid and the risk of any claim minimised.

Route 3 – gain implied consent

The third approach is to impose the change without express consent and if the employee continues to work under the new arrangements, over time, the employee will be deemed to have impliedly consented to the change.

However, this approach is not without a number of difficulties. Firstly, the employee may claim that the employer has acted in a manner that has breached the term of mutual trust and confidence which is implied into every contract of employment. The employee would be required to resign (generally very quickly after the change, but this is not always the case) and claim breach of contract and, if the employee has one year or over of continuous service (in the absence of any other potential issue such as discrimination), constructive dismissal for a repudiatory breach of the employment contract (see the section on damages below). The employer may mitigate this (to a degree) by providing the employee with a new contract of employment on the new terms; whilst the employee is under a duty to mitigate his or her loss, there is no requirement for the employee to accept work provided by an employer who has acted in such a way.

The second difficulty with this approach is that it can take a significant period of time before the employer gains a degree of certainty over whether or not the change has been impliedly accepted, because it is not until it is tested by an employee in an employment tribunal or the courts that this issue becomes clear.

On the other hand, the implied consent route may have advantages in certain circumstances. It is likely to be quicker than seeking express consent and, if the change to the pension scheme is only minor in nature, and the pension consultation requirements (see below) are not triggered, then the risk of an employee resigning and bringing a claim is minimal, especially in a difficult employment market.

Route 4 – dismiss and re-hire

The final option is to dismiss the employee on notice (to avoid contractual notice claims) for 'some other substantial reason' (being one of the potentially fair reasons for dismissal) and then immediately re-hire that employee on the new contractual terms. Although there is still a possibility that the employee may bring a claim for unfair dismissal, this route has the advantage that it gains a degree of certainty immediately because individuals will either accept or reject the new terms and, assuming there is a good reason to make the change to the pension scheme and a properly organised and effected consultation process followed by a fair process on dismissal, the employer will minimise the potential litigation risks.

Consultation

There are potentially a number of consultation obligations that may be required prior to implementing any pension change or effecting a change in an employee's terms and conditions of their contract of employment. These can arise either as a consequence of pensions legislative requirements ('pension consultation obligations') or as a result of obligations arising in the employment law arena ('employment consultation requirements'). Primarily, of course, the employment consultation process (and indeed the pensions consultation process) is a matter of concern for the employer rather than the trustees – nevertheless, trustees will usually be anxious to ensure that the employer has fully complied with its duties in this regard, particularly in circumstances where, depending on the results of the consultation exercise, they may actively consider the exercise of one or more of their powers (for example, giving their consent to the exercise of the pension scheme's amendment power). Consequently, it is important that trustees as well as employers understand the operation of the pension and employment consultation processes.

Pension consultation obligations

Pension consultation obligations may arise under the provisions of the Occupational and Personal Pension Schemes (Consultation by Employers and Miscellaneous Amendment) Regulations 2006. Specifically, employers are

109

required to consult affected employees in relation to a 'listed change' where employers have 50 or more employees involved. Such 'listed changes' include, but are not limited to: increasing normal pension age; closing a scheme to new members; stopping an employer's liability to make further contributions; stopping further benefit accrual by existing members; and reducing employer contributions or increasing employee contributions. Broadly speaking, if an employer is making an adverse change to a pension scheme's benefit structure, it is likely that the regulations apply.

In terms of process, there is a minimum period of 60 days for genuine consultation. No 'starting point' is specifically identified, although employees and employee representatives are required to be given certain information about the changes before the commencement of the pensions consultation process. This information includes a description of the proposed listed change and an explanation of its effects on the scheme and the members, details of any relevant background information and a timescale for introducing the proposed changes. Longer periods of consultation are permissible and, if possible, no decision should be made (or at least confirmed) until the end of the collective employment consultation period (which we discuss below) to ensure any collective employment consultation amounts to a genuine consultation. The pensions consultation requirement captures both active members and prospective members, which is a potentially wide group – for example, employees in a waiting period, or who are admitted automatically after a certain period of service, or who may join subject to employer consent.

If there are existing employee representation arrangements in place under which there are employee representatives, and the proposals fall within their scope, the employer should comply with such arrangements. Otherwise, an employer has the choice of consulting with trade union representatives in respect of members covered by the recognition agreement, or the affected members themselves (if this is provided for in a negotiated or pre-existing agreement). If that still leaves some employees unrepresented, it is recommended that an election is held to appoint representatives in respect of such employees. However, there is no obligation to do so and the remaining employees can be consulted directly.

A process of pension consultation should then follow. The parties are under a duty 'to work in a spirit of co-operation, taking into account the interest of both sides'. However, there is no requirement to reach agreement, provided that the employer considers the responses it receives in relation to the proposed changes before deciding to go ahead and make the changes. In any event, the consultation process must last at least 60 days.

Failure to comply with these requirements could lead to enforcement action by the Pensions Regulator, following a complaint by an employee representative and/or an affected member of the pension scheme. In particular, although the Regulator cannot reverse a change that has been made, it can issue an improvement notice, setting out required steps. Failure to comply with an improvement notice could lead to a fine and/or the imposition of a financial penalty (where there is no reasonable excuse for a failure to comply with the consultation obligations). The fine is a maximum of £5,000 where the employer is an individual, or £50,000 where the employer is a company.

Employment consultation obligations

In addition to the potential pension consultation obligations, there may be obligations to consult under employment law. Firstly, there may be obligations under an information and consultation agreement under the Information and Consultation of Employees Regulations 2004. These regulations would only apply to negotiations if an information and consultation agreement had been formally initiated by the employing company or the employing company had received a request by at least 10 per cent of the employees (subject to a minimum of 15 and a maximum of 2,500). Secondly, there may be a contractual obligation to consult in the employment contracts, staff handbook(s) or elsewhere. Finally, there may be an obligation to do so under any trade union or collective agreement(s) that apply. The actual requirement to consult will depend on any agreement concerned.

From the individual consultation perspective, when effecting any change to an employee's contractual terms of employment, it is recommended that consultation occurs on an individual basis as a matter of good practice (and necessity in some cases). Additional employment consultation obligations arise in relation to route 4 – the dismiss and re-hire route – and these are set out below.

Overlap of consultation obligations

It is debatable whether the pension consultation can effectively be run concurrently with the employment consultation process. The safest approach is likely to be to wait until pension consultation is complete in so far as the minimum 60 days have elapsed (but not an announcement on the decision) prior to starting any employment consultation. If it is necessary to commence the employment consultation process earlier, it may be commenced simultaneously with any pensions consultation. However, any communications made to employees as part of the consultation processes have to be dealt with carefully in order to avoid any implication that either consultation exercise was a 'sham'. The key (in relation to both pensions and employment consultations) is to ensure that it is clear to the employees that a final decision has not been taken pending the completion of the consultation exercise and that any comments they make will be given legitimate consideration and a fair response.

Other potential consultation obligations

In addition to the consultation requirements set out above, there are specific (additional) requirements if an employer intends to dismiss and re-hire one or more employees. If the proposal to dismiss affects more than 20 employees, collective consultation obligations under the Trade Union and Labour Relations Act 1992 (hereafter, TULRCA 1992) will be triggered. This is because employers are obliged to consult collectively where they 'propose to dismiss as redundant 20 or more employees at one establishment within a period of 90 days or less'.[1] The statutory definition of 'redundancy' is a dismissal 'not connected with the individual worker concerned'.[2] This definition will also include dismissals which may be regarded under the Employment Rights Act 1996 as being for 'some other substantial reason', which would include the dismissals envisaged under the proposal.

Such collective redundancy consultation must commence 'in good time' and before any final decisions on the dismissals have been made, otherwise the consultation will be ineffective for not having been undertaken 'with a view to reaching agreement' over ways of avoiding the dismissals.

Collective redundancy consultation involves several steps. The first is the election of employee representatives (unless there is a recognised trade union covering all of the employees). There are specific rules regarding the election of employee representatives and for the process to be effective: these should be complied with. Secondly, there is a requirement to inform the Department of Business, Innovation and Skills within a particular timescale and a failure to do so is a criminal offence. Thirdly, there is a requirement to give written notice of the potential redundancies, and certain statutory information to, and to consult with, the union/elected representatives (and also individually with affected individuals in one-to-one meetings), about a number of issues, including the reasons for the 'redundancies' or in this case dismissals, the classes of employees to whom the dismissals shall apply and why those employees have been selected. It may be, of course, that the changes only affect a small portion of that employer's workforce. Fourthly, the consultation must commence in good time and where the employer is proposing to dismiss 100 or more employees within a 90-day period, consultation must begin at least 90 days before the first dismissal takes effect and where the employer is proposing to dismiss between 20 and 99 employees in a 90-day period, consultation must begin at least 30 days before the first dismissal takes effect. Finally, the employer should confirm the new terms and notice arrangements in writing with the affected employees.

Depending on how the collective consultation meetings progress, the employer may commence an individual consultation process during the latter part of the collective consultation period, with the announcement that they intend to terminate each individual's employment on notice. Currently, the ACAS Code of Practice on Disciplinary and Grievance Procedures applies to such a process and employers should take a careful note of its contents and any

1 TULRCA 1992, s. 188(1).
2 TULRCA 1992, s. 195.

other procedure set out in their staff handbooks. The process must be 'fair' for any subsequent dismissal for 'some other substantial reason' to be deemed fair.

Notice should be given after the collective and individual consultation processes are complete and not before, unless employee representatives agree (in writing) that all matters of the collective consultation have been dealt with and there is no further need to consult collectively.

Clearly, this is a significant exercise to undertake and most employers would at least attempt to gain express consent (route 2 above) in the first instance, if time permits, prior to undertaking an exercise of this nature to minimise any unfair dismissal risks.

Other commercial matters

It is worth noting at this point that in addition to the legal considerations outlined below, when choosing a particular route, there are also commercial issues to consider and this may affect the choice of approach.

Changing pensions terms could detrimentally affect employee motivation levels and morale, and could also impact on employee loyalty going forward. Employers who explain clearly why they are taking such steps, and manage the process of obtaining consent appropriately (see below) are more likely actually to obtain consent from employees and limit any negative commercial impact.

It would be sensible in most cases for employers to approach such changes as a 'selling' exercise, and incentives and inducements may significantly increase voluntary acceptance rates in the case of route 2 and minimise risks in the case of the other routes.

Employers (and trustees) should be aware that a failure to get the overall consultation and process right and to gain acceptance may result in either a class action brought by a large number of employees or trade union action, both of which could be very damaging from both a financial and publicity aspect. Whilst class actions are likely to be rare, trade union action is much more common and at the time of writing, several unions are applying significant pressure to a number of employers who are intending to or have implemented changes to employees' pensions arrangements. Having said that, it is worth noting that actions that might have been difficult for employers and trustees to contemplate 20 years ago (for example, the closure of defined benefit schemes to new entrants and the halting of future pension accrual) under such schemes have become much more common in recent years and news that their employer is contemplating such a step will come as less of a shock to employees and trustees than might have been the case in the past.

Pensions issues on terminations of employment

One of the most difficult aspects of pensions issues in the employment law context is that of calculating the value of the loss of pension rights in relation to a loss of employment claim. Again, although primarily an area of concern for employers and employees, trustees also need some familiarity with these issues. Various approaches can be adopted as regards the treatment of pension rights upon terminations of employment, depending upon the nature of the employment claim and the type of pension scheme under consideration. It should be noted that this can be a very complex area and, whilst the overall approach remains the same, there are differences introduced on a fairly frequent basis as the result of developing case law. Further, the approach outlined below does not take into account employment aspects such as how likely it was that the employee in question was going to be dismissed. Specialist (for example, actuarial) advice should always be sought when assessing the quantum for any claim.

Redundancy is the dismissal of an employee as a result of the closure of the business or function which results in a diminution for the employee to carry out work of a particular kind or at a particular workplace. Where an employee is entitled to compensation for redundancy, his redundancy payment will be calculated by reference to a statutory calculation mechanism which takes into account factors such as the age of the claimant, his or her length of continuous employment and his or her gross average weekly pay (subject to a maximum of £400 per week with effect from 1 February 2011).

The definition of 'pay' for these purposes (set out in the Employment Rights Act 1996) does not make any allowance for the value of pension contributions in the case of a defined contribution occupational pension scheme, a personal pension scheme or a stakeholder scheme (or pensions accrual in the case of a defined benefit occupational pension scheme). Consequently, a claimant's pension entitlement in the event of redundancy will depend upon the governing provisions of his or her pension scheme (and possibly any contractual rights he or she may have in relation to redundancy).

Generally, unless the claimant has already attained his or her normal pension date (NPD) and is able to claim a retirement pension 'as of right', the relevant provisions in the scheme documentation will be the 'early leaver' provisions. Thus, he or she will be entitled to the various protections offered by the law to early leavers (for example, a deferred pension with a statutory cash equivalent transfer right if he or she is treated as having more than two years' qualifying service under an occupational pension scheme), and if necessary the claimant can enforce those rights by means of claims brought before the Pensions Ombudsman or the courts.

A dismissal is unfair if it is for an unfair reason, and/or the dismissal procedure is unfair, either automatically or otherwise. Although the remedies available for unfair dismissal include reinstatement and re-engagement orders, in reality the most likely remedy to be awarded by a tribunal when it finds that a claimant has suffered unfair dismissal is an award of compensation. Such compensation for unfair dismissal claims will generally take the form of a basic award and a compensatory payment.

Basic awards are calculated in a similar, but not identical, way as redundancy payments and do not take account of pension contributions or the accrual of pension benefits.

So far as the compensatory award is concerned, this may include an element intended to provide compensation for the loss of pension rights, if the tribunal considers this to be just and equitable. Such an award is subject to a cap (of £68,400 at the time of writing). Historically, tribunals have often found the quantification of pension losses a difficult area and to assist in their deliberations a set of guidelines ('Employment Tribunals – Compensation for Loss of Pension Rights' – hereafter, 'the guidelines') has been prepared by the Government's Actuaries Department. Now in their third edition, the guidelines suggest two alternative approaches to assessing pension loss: the 'simplified loss' and the 'substantial loss' approaches.

The guidelines suggest that the simplified loss approach will be appropriate in most cases, with the substantial loss approach being reserved for use in cases when the person dismissed has been in the respondent's employment for a considerable time, where the employment was of a stable nature and unlikely to be affected by the economic cycle or where the person dismissed has reached an age when he or she would be unlikely to seek new employment save for the fact of the dismissal.

However, the guidelines also stress that the decision as to whether in any particular case it is more appropriate to adopt the simplified loss approach or the substantial loss approach is, ultimately, a matter for the tribunal.

Simplified loss approach

The simplified loss approach requires three sets of calculations:

- loss of enhancement of accrued pension rights;
- loss of pension rights that would have accrued between the date of dismissal and the date of the tribunal hearing; and
- loss of future pension rights that would have accrued between the date of the hearing and the date of the claimant's retirement.

Calculating the loss of enhancement of accrued pension rights poses (relatively) little difficulty if the relevant pension scheme is a defined contribution scheme (i.e. a defined contribution occupational scheme, a personal pension scheme or a stakeholder scheme), since the claimant's 'pensions pot' remains (or at least may remain) invested as it would have done but for the unfair dismissal.

Matters are more complicated in the case of a defined benefit scheme, because if there had not been an unfair dismissal the value of any future pay increases that the claimant might have received may (and generally would) have increased the value of his or her accrued pension rights (i.e. the pension accrued in respect of service prior to the dismissal). On the other hand, as a deferred pensioner, he or she would be entitled (at least) to the statutory revaluation of his or her deferred pension from the date on which he or she became a deferred pensioner (i.e. the date of the unfair dismissal) until the date on which his or her benefits come into payment. Other (potentially unquantifiable) factors may also be relevant.

In order to address these difficulties, the guidelines effectively suggest that either no compensation for the loss of enhancement of accrued pension rights should be awarded at all, or use should be made of an actuarial method (involving the application of multipliers as described in the guidelines) in order to determine the value of the compensation that should be ordered. The guidelines suggest that no compensation should be awarded where the claimant is within five years of his or her NPD, or where the employment would, in any event, have terminated within one year.

As regards the issue of loss between the date of the dismissal and that of the hearing, again there is usually little difficulty in assessing the value of the loss in relation to a defined contribution scheme. Defined benefit schemes again pose problems, and the guidelines suggest (whilst recognising that this is a technically incorrect approach) that the simplest way of addressing this issue is to base compensation for pensions loss in respect of the period between the dismissal and the hearing upon the notional contributions the employer would have made to the scheme had the claimant continued in employment.

The issue of calculating future pensions loss can be particularly problematic. Factors to be taken into account may include: possible future pay increases; the likelihood of the claimant actually joining the pension scheme (if, for example, he or she is currently in a membership waiting period); the probability of him or her remaining an active member of the scheme until his or her NPD; and (in cases where the claimant finds or is likely to find replacement employment) the nature and quality of the pension provision (if any) offered by his or her new employer as compared with that offered by his or her former employer. Other factors may also be relevant.

In practice, tribunals are frequently left with little option other than to consider all available evidence regarding what was likely to occur in the future in relation to the claimant's pension and then reaching a decision as best they can as to the future loss he or she has sustained. In this regard, the guidelines suggest that where the period of loss of future employment is unlikely to exceed two years (for example, because the tribunal considers that the claimant is likely to find comparable new employment within a two-year period), the employer's contributions (or notional contributions in the case of a defined benefit scheme) should be used as the basis for calculating the loss of future pension rights, with the application of a discount to allow for accelerated receipt. However, in circumstances where the pension loss arises in respect of a period that is greater than two years, the results of the simplified loss approach calculations may be perceived as being increasingly arbitrary, and in such circumstances, the tribunal may conclude that the substantial loss approach is more appropriate.

Substantial loss approach

The substantial loss approach depends upon the use of actuarial tables set out in the guidelines to determine the value of the pension loss attributable to the dismissal. Consequently, the substantial loss approach does not require the loss of enhancement of accrued rights, the loss of rights in respect of the period between dismissal and the hearing date or the loss of future pension rights to be calculated separately.

In the comparatively rare event that a tribunal issues a re-engagement and reinstatement order, the claimant should (in principle) simply be treated as if he or she had not left the pension scheme.

Pension claims in wrongful dismissal cases

In contrast to unfair dismissal claims, in claims relating to wrongful dismissal (i.e. the dismissal of an employee without cause in breach of a notice period or the improper premature termination of a fixed-term contract) the principal remedy is damages. Such damages will normally be calculated as being equal to the salary and other benefits to which the claimant would have been contractually entitled in respect of the period from the employment's termination to the date on which the employer could legally have brought the employment to an end had there not been an improper (premature) termination of the contract (the 'claim period'). The purpose of such damages is to place the claimant in the position he or she would have been in had the contract been performed as it should have been, always subject (of course) to the duty on the claimant to mitigate his or her loss.

The starting point for any calculation of the pension loss sustained in respect of a defined contribution scheme will be employer contributions that should have paid to the scheme in respect of the claimant during the claim period. In principle, allowance should also be made for the investment returns that the (unpaid) contributions would have earned in the scheme over the claim period, although this can on occasions be difficult to assess without the benefit of specialist financial advice.

If the wrongful dismissal claim involves a defined benefit scheme, the claimant's loss will be: (i) the loss of pension accrual over the claim period (since the claimant would have ceased to accrue benefits under the scheme as an active member upon ceasing to be an employee); and (ii) (where the claimant was legally entitled to future pay increases during the claim period) the effect of pay increases upon the value of the pensions accrued prior to the date of termination.

In certain circumstances, pension loss may also include the loss of life cover (i.e. death-in-service benefits) during the claim period. This will be particularly relevant if the claimant dies during the claim period without a settlement having been reached (although in such circumstances, the principle of loss mitigation would suggest that the claimant may be penalised if he or she does not establish his or her own replacement life cover, unless he or she has good reason for not doing so, for example, because a medical condition effectively makes him or her uninsurable).

Allowance should also be made (in the case of a contributory scheme) for the fact that the claimant would have had to pay member contributions to the pension scheme had he or she in fact remained an active member of it during the claim period. In practice, the calculation of pension loss may require actuarial assistance, and in some negotiated settlements, the parties agree simply to calculate the pension loss by reference to the (notional) employer contributions that would have been paid in respect of pension accrual over the claim period, regardless of the nature of the pension scheme and the presence (or absence) of other complicating factors.

As a general point, it should be noted that if it is agreed that compensation for pension losses sustained during the claim period should be paid directly to the claimant, consideration should be given as to whether allowance should be made for accelerated receipt. In many cases, however, it is agreed by the parties that any compensation for pension loss should be paid directly to the pension scheme (either as a special contribution or (in the case of a defined benefit scheme) in order to fund an augmentation of the claimant's accrued pension rights) since this will usually be more tax efficient for both the claimant and the employer. It is important to note that trustee consent is likely to be required in respect of any augmentation of benefits under an occupational pension scheme. Moreover, where the claimant was highly paid and/ or has already accrued a considerable pension entitlement under a registered pension scheme (or schemes), care needs to be taken to ensure that such an augmentation or special contribution can be paid without incurring tax charges under the registered pension scheme regime. It should also be noted that some settlements of dismissal claims involve the employer consenting to the provision by the employer's occupational pension scheme of an early retirement pension. If such an approach is contemplated, it is important that the employer reviews the governing provisions of the pension scheme to ensure that such an offer is within its power to give and does not (for example) require the consent of the trustees of the scheme. If trustee consent is required, such consent must be obtained before a final settlement is entered into with the claimant.

Lastly, it should be remembered that where the claimant is entitled to a pension as of right (i.e. without the consent of the trustees, the employer or indeed any other party), the pension payments so received cannot be offset against any wrongful dismissal award.

8

Employer support and the development of the sponsor covenant concept

PAUL THORNTON AND DONALD FLEMING

The need to incorporate the 'sponsor covenant' and to take account of the impact of corporate events on the pension scheme's position has long been implicit in trustee decision-making. However, it is really only in the last five years that this has been explicitly a key agenda item for trustee boards, not least through the encouragement and formal pronouncements of the Pensions Regulator (TPR). Having a framework for assessing and reviewing the covenant is now an integral part of good scheme governance because it puts trustees in a good position to make appropriate decisions about scheme funding and corporate events which may affect the employer's ability to fund their scheme.

With trustees increasingly expected by TPR not just to establish a framework to monitor the sponsor covenant, but also to have a 'seat at the table' alongside the company's other major stakeholders, the relationship between the trustee board, the employer and third parties has changed. We consider in this chapter how the concept of the 'sponsor' or 'employer' covenant and the changes in relationships and expectations placed on trustees are affecting scheme governance.

We begin by examining the nature of a pension scheme's relationships with its corporate sponsor and other relevant parties, how these relationships have changed and what this means for trustee behaviour. We look at different perspectives on the concept of the sponsor covenant, a development which is fundamentally changing the way in which trustees relate to the sponsor company, and how trustees deal with changes to the covenant. We then examine the key areas of an emerging governance model.

Pension scheme relationship with corporate sponsor and other parties

The key pension scheme relationships are highlighted in Figure 8.1.

The sponsor and its owners and lenders

The sponsor company is established under company law with a board of directors which owes fiduciary responsibilities to its shareholders (whether these

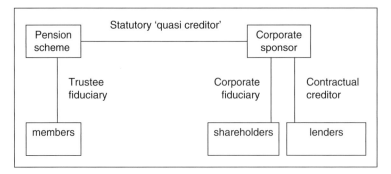

Figure 8.1 Key pension scheme relationships

are other group companies or external owners), although the 2006 Companies Act has introduced some modest duties towards other stakeholders, including the pension scheme. The sponsor's relationship with its bank lenders, bond-holders and trade creditors is established by the terms of the contract and is a debtor–creditor relationship.

The pension scheme and its members

The relationship between a pension scheme and its members is grounded in trust law. The scheme assets (whether originating from the sponsor or from portfolio growth) are held under trust by the trustees, separately from the sponsor company's business assets. The trustees owe fiduciary responsibilities to the scheme members. It is not uncommon for a corporate entity to act as trustee, with the persons who act as trustees being directors of this entity.

The pension scheme and its sponsor

One or more companies will be party to the scheme's trust deed and rules as 'participating employer', with the contractual responsibility for making contribution payments. While the relationship is therefore in the nature of a debtor–creditor one, the perceived soft pension promise of this 'debt' long obscured this technical reality. The current status of the pension scheme as a quasi creditor reflects the progressive hardening of the pensions 'promise' over recent years: under the Pensions Act 1995 a statutory employer debt (known as a 'section 75' debt) is triggered when the company ceases to participate in a scheme. The debt was originally calculated on the Minimum Funding Requirement (MFR) basis and its impact in practice was limited. However, 2003 regulations mean that, for a solvent employer which winds up its DB scheme, an employer debt is now triggered which is calculated on a basis which equates to the cost of buying an annuity contract with an insurance company and is much more expensive.

The pension scheme as a creditor

The pensions 'promise' is no longer in any sense an informal, paternalistic undertaking. The Pensions Act 2004 established the Pensions Regulator, which stressed the concept that the relationship between a pension scheme and its corporate sponsor is a creditor relationship. It stated that a pension scheme in deficit should be viewed as a material unsecured creditor of the sponsor and that trustees should therefore learn from the way in which a bank with a large unsecured loan would look to negotiate with a company. In its June 2009 Clearance Guidance, TPR stated that: 'Trustees and employers should recognise and understand that a scheme in deficit on any basis should be treated in the same way as any other material creditor.'

For a large number of companies, the pension scheme in deficit is the largest creditor of the company relative to other unsecured creditors and in many other cases it is a material amount. However, the pension 'creditor' has special characteristics which distinguish it from other types of creditor and which have implications for the trustee stance, as follows:

- *Legal underpinning*: while obligations to the pension scheme, like those to lenders, are governed by the contractual terms, pension scheme obligations have evolved within the context of pensions and trusts and have been heavily affected by statute; moreover, unlike banks and bondholders, pension schemes have their own regulator to support them.
- *Quantification*: a bank makes a loan on pre-agreed terms and the maximum amount and maturity of the debt is known at any given time; a bond is for an amount which can be ascertained at the outset. The amount of the pension debt is often the subject of considerable debate between pension trustees and sponsor. This is exemplified by the difference between the actuarial valuation bases used for the technical provisions required for funding purposes and those used for financial reporting in a company's accounts.
- *Maturity*: the pension scheme is likely to be the company's longest-term liability, but its maturity is not fixed.

So there are limits to the analogy with other corporate creditors. Most companies now acknowledge the analogy between bank/bond debt and pension debt, but would still regard pension debt as different from 'real' cash finance provided to the company for it to invest in the business, given that the amounts involved are subject to actuarial estimates and are not firm figures. Nonetheless, the analogy holds true in terms of how creditor participants behave: bank and bond creditors themselves increasingly view the pension creditor as a competing claimant, particularly in corporate restructurings and distress situations, and TPR views it this way. It is fair to say that this now reflects how many large pension schemes and their sponsors behave in practice.

Need for trustees to be engaged with the sponsor

The post-2004 regulatory regime provides for situations in which clearance may be appropriate in order to provide companies with certainty that TPR will not exercise its enforcement powers, notably to issue a contribution notice or financial support direction. The fact of this regulatory framework for clearance of itself requires trustees to be continuously and actively engaged participants, addressing issues and asking questions that, in many cases, have not been raised with the sponsor company before, such as:

- How strong is the sponsor covenant and what can it afford?
- What is the trustee board's position on a proposed major corporate disposal?
- How should the trustees react to a credit downgrading of the company?
- What should the trustees' position be towards a bank refinancing?
- How does the company's financial, business and operational strategy affect the scheme?
- How should the trustees react to a change of ownership of the company?

This has behavioural implications for the trustee role and its relationship with the sponsor. With considerable impetus from statements and guidance from TPR, a market practice is developing whereby trustees are expected to engage proactively with the sponsor on an ongoing basis to monitor their exposure to the sponsor covenant and to take appropriate steps where there is a possible threat to the scheme's funding position. Further, trustees have the right to be provided with relevant financial information in order to do so. This represents a real change from the previously somewhat paternalistic approach to information sharing.

This in turn places new demands and responsibilities on trustees, most critically when the sponsor is in financial distress:

- *Acting responsibly*: in the first place is the need to engage responsibly with the sponsor with due reference to corporate timetables and its own governance – it will usually be necessary to establish a sub-committee with authority to engage and pursue matters with the sponsor subject to full trustee board approval rather than waiting for the next scheduled trustee board meeting.
- *Acting proportionately*: trustees need to keep a sense of proportion in assessing the likelihood of risks and their potential impact on the scheme, and on their course of action.
- *Confidentiality*: the sharing and dissemination of confidential information about the company's finances or its business plans (for example, plant closure plans) is a very difficult issue for many trustee boards given the conflicted roles and positions held by some trustees. Nonetheless, trustees are expected to adhere to high standards and those who breach this duty are at risk of not being considered 'fit and proper' persons.

Changing advisory dynamics

It is to be expected that the pension scheme's professional advisers will be intimately involved with trustee decision-making. Given the technical complexity of many areas around pensions and the expertise required, the distinction between receipt of advice which enables a board to take informed decisions and reliance on an adviser's views can sometimes be a fine one. The 2004 Pensions Act reinforced the former: formal responsibility for core decisions, even on some technical matters such as actuarial assumptions, rests with the trustees. (The precise balance of responsibilities between trustees and scheme actuary can vary, however, particularly in some longer-established schemes, depending on the specific terms of their trust deed and rules.)

Regulatory guidance and the stress on 'Trustee Knowledge and Understanding' develops this approach. The trustee board is expected now to be 'conversant' not only as previously with its scheme, the law and investment and funding principles, but also with the financial and commercial prospects of the company. This presents some trustee boards with challenges where those on the board who are most likely to have considerable experience of such matters (typically the finance director, treasurer, company secretary, HR director and pensions officers) may feel that they must stand aside from potentially contentious discussions with the employer over scheme funding because of conflicts of interest, or where the member-nominated trustees may feel the need to acquire some deeper understanding of the employer's business and financial model.

Of course, prudent trusteeship, even in the new regulatory environment, does not require every trustee to be an expert in pensions and trust law, fund management, accounting, actuarial analysis and corporate finance; but it does look for the trustee body to appreciate the extent of its collective expertise and to seek appropriate independent advice where necessary. Even where there is particular expertise within the board, trustees often feel more comfortable in using that expertise to challenge an external adviser than to rely on a fellow trustee to provide the appropriate comfort on a specific area and it is therefore crucial that all of the trustees have the confidence to ask the right questions of their advisers – and of the company and its advisers. TPR is seeking to improve the quality of pension scheme governance and administration and has stressed the importance of trustee boards taking independent advice where appropriate, particularly in relation to the assessment of the sponsor covenant.

In addition to the relationships described, it is important for the trustees to take an overall view of how the pension scheme sits with the employment and industrial relations considerations for the employer, and how the risk which the pension scheme represents to the employer's business is managed by the company. These aspects are dealt with in other chapters of this book.

The history of many pension schemes and their relationships with employers often reflects the attitudes of a past, more paternalistic, age. As this chapter should show, trustees are no longer entitled to take such attitudes for granted.

The analytical standpoint and the sponsor covenant

From an analytical viewpoint, the pension trustee is required to assess the strength of the 'sponsor covenant', a term of art which has conventionally been described as the willingness and ability of the sponsor company to support the pension scheme, but is being redefined as the sponsor's legal obligations to the scheme and its (current and prospective) financial position. This means considering the legal support structure provided by a corporate group and its ability to generate profits and cash in order to pay ongoing pension contributions and to address deficit funding; it also requires an assessment of the position on insolvency in terms of recoverability of the full (buyout) deficit. The trustees need to approach this in a balanced way; for instance, making a sensible assessment as to the likelihood of insolvency in the short to medium term.

From the perspective of the chief executive or finance director, the focus is to operate the business so as to generate the best return on the capital invested in it. That capital will be provided typically from a mix of equity shares and debt and, in some cases, from instruments (such as preference shares) which have characteristics of both.

Equity share capital is essentially 'risk' capital: the shareholder can benefit from growth in the price of the shares and in dividend income; but there is no set date by which share capital has to be repaid, and there is a risk of receiving nothing in insolvency. The shareholder is vulnerable to a collapse in the ongoing value of the investment, i.e. the share price, or a cut in dividend income.

Debt capital has a different risk profile: the lender does not seek to share in the upside if the business performs well, but the price of this is predictability in interest payments which cannot be varied by the corporate borrower and the return of its capital on a known date. Debt ranks above equity on insolvency.

Debt finance is typically cheaper than equity, but the theoretical risk of insolvency increases with higher levels of debt finance (i.e. increased gearing) because in extremis the lender can call in its loan. Hence, conventional corporate finance theory will seek to strike an appropriate financing mix for the particular business. This has important consequences for trustees' stance towards their sponsor: as quasi creditors, their role is not to take equity-type investment risk. This informs the trustees' critique of management which is more from the viewpoint of a creditor than an equity investor. They need to be dispassionate – although this is sometimes misread as unsupportive. Assessing the value of the sponsor company is a relevant, but secondary, factor in the trustees' assessment of the covenant – unless the value of the company is clearly smaller than the size of any pension deficit, in which case it becomes of primary importance.

Fragmentation of stakeholder constituencies

The distinction between debt and equity finance is not always clear-cut. The capital markets are themselves increasingly fragmented, comprising stakeholder constituencies with distinct claims and viewpoints. For instance, there are different types of bank lenders – some lend on an 'asset-backed' basis, and will look to the security in the tangible assets, while others will lend on an unsecured basis. In the most complex financing structures, a restructuring may involve some or all of: senior bank lenders, mezzanine lenders, hedge funds and junior ranking bond holders. Each of these parties will have different priorities and interests and, as such, will have varying negotiation tactics. The debt market is also seeing the entrance of new players into the market such as private equity sponsors using funds to buy into distressed situations, which adds another dynamic and negotiation position to the situation.

TPR and the PPF are active participants in many major restructurings and, indeed, if, how and when to involve them are important tactical considerations for all parties. The further the company is along the 'distress' spectrum, the more the PPF becomes a potential player. Factors, amongst others, that will be considered by all parties during negotiation include: the value of the underlying business/assets; the ranking of each party and its debt; legal and security rights – any ability to trigger insolvency; the basis of calculation of the pension deficit and how this compares to earnings, cash flow or level of bank or bond debt or the market/asset value; overall financing costs (including pension deficit payments) – the current level compared with forecast cash flow generation and proposed level of new financing costs; and other aspects of the restructuring plan, such as disposals and application of proceeds. In some cases, the trustees may have the unilateral right – not to be exercised lightly – to wind up the scheme (a so-called nuclear option), thus triggering a section 75 debt, which could be such as to render the sponsoring company insolvent.

So, commensurate with trustee powers are responsibilities; with the pension scheme embedded as a stakeholder, the trustees have to understand the consequences of taking actions, or indeed of not taking actions, and how they sit in relation to each of the other stakeholder constituencies.

Key factors in covenant assessment

Corporate structure

The pension scheme may originally have been established with one or more companies within the group (participating employers) supporting the pension scheme, one of which may have a central administrative or commercial role (the principal employer). Over time, parts of the group may have been sold or grown through acquisition, or there may have been a reorganisation of the group structure to suit tax planning or strategic re-structuring. The shape of the corporate group providing legal support for the pension scheme may today be quite different from that originally intended.

The scheme's trust deed and rules may specify limits to the extent of each participating employer's liability towards the scheme. TPR will expect the trustees and their advisers to assess the extent of support provided by the respective employers within a group and the legal relationships between them. The Regulator's enforcement powers (including financial support directions and contribution notices) start with the underlying entity, although they can 'pierce the corporate veil' to extend beyond this to other group companies and entities. (The potential extent of these powers has prompted some private equity bidders to seek clearance, concerned to avoid the risk of enforcement across their underlying investor funds.)

The extent to which the covenant strength of the wider group can be taken into account is often a critical judgment, particularly in covenant assessments involving large global corporations.

Capital structure

The trustees need to understand how the sponsor group finances itself. In terms of the debt structure, this includes the nature and composition of its borrowings, the maturity profile, scope for further borrowings, nature of the lender(s), terms (for example, covenants, security) and sensitivity of credit ratings. In terms of equity finance, it is important to understand who owns or controls the company, and what the competing claims of capital expenditure and investment, dividends and payments to shareholders are.

Financial performance

At the core of the sponsor covenant is the ability of the sponsor to generate cash and support the scheme. At one level, this is simply the ability to pay ongoing company contributions. In the context of the triennial actuarial valuation, where there is a funding deficit the trustees will address the question of how the funding deficit can be addressed over a specific recovery period. Unless the deficit can clearly be paid off at once, the process is a form of debt re-scheduling. These issues are therefore about the affordability of pension scheme funding.

The task for trustees and sponsor in reaching an agreed scheme recovery plan is to determine a level of deficit recovery contributions which is 'reasonably affordable'. This is looked at in the light of the other claims on cash flow: capital expenditure, investment plans, working capital, financing costs and dividends. Realistically, no company will be able to project accurately its profitability and cash-flow requirements for as long a period as even a decade, never mind more extended periods.

The trustees' assessment is necessarily a matter of judgment, but also needs to be balanced – a stronger performing company may be able to afford to pay more into the scheme under a shorter recovery period than a weaker one and the credit risk is higher the longer the contribution horizon, but the trustees must take care not to 'kill the golden goose'.

Financial position in insolvency

Trustees need to establish a reference point in terms of where the pension scheme 'debt' sits as a balance sheet item and their ability to recover the section 75 debt on insolvency of the sponsor.

Typically, the scheme is classed as an unsecured creditor: on insolvency the insolvency practitioner will assess all of the assets and liabilities of the company and seek to pay off the liabilities from realisable assets. The order in which this is done will be determined by the legal claims of the respective creditor groups and insolvency law. The insolvency context shows most acutely the position of the pension scheme as a formal creditor.

Business environment and strategic challenges

Covenant assessment is inherently a matter of judgment: a view of reasonable affordability looks at past trends and the sponsor's track record, but also at its prospects.

The competitive environment in which the company operates is highly relevant to assess the financial 'risk' exposure. The covenant framework needs to establish the extent to which the business is cyclical and its longer-term growth prospects (including such factors as brand strength and market share).

The way in which senior management responds to the business environment through its stated strategy will have a considerable effect on the financial position of the company. It will also determine the shape and viability of long-term sponsor support. Covenant assessment therefore requires some consideration of the track record of current management in achieving its strategic objectives. This also highlights how closely trustees and the covenant adviser need to engage with senior management to gain a proper view of the strategic challenges which they face.

Towards a new model for trustee engagement

As we have seen, the recognition of the pension scheme as a quasi creditor has largely been prompted by changes in law and regulation. This is reflected in terms of a more business-like, less paternalistic approach from company boards, particularly where the scheme is closed to accrual or where the scheme was acquired as part of a larger corporate acquisition and the new parent group has few emotional links to the scheme.

Trustee boards are developing governance structures to reflect the new realities. The position of 'insiders' such as the finance director or treasurer on the trustee board is increasingly accepted as a conflicted one, most acutely when there is a corporate event or a scheme event such as a recovery plan negotiation. In some cases, those conflicted can stand down from participation during such events, although this can be an awkward compromise and the perception as much as the actuality of conflict of interest often leads to them to stand down from trusteeship altogether.

Where detailed, complex analysis and discussion is required on a more intensive basis than through the full trustee board schedule, the use of a standing sub-committee works well. So, for example, the use of investment sub-committees is increasingly complemented by risk monitoring and covenant monitoring sub-committees.

An interesting development, seen to date only in the largest schemes, is the creation of a quasi-autonomous management structure for the pension scheme, with a scheme chief executive responsible to the scheme for its overall management; this parallels the development of the in-house chief investment officer. This is perhaps an indicator of a possible way to reconcile the conflicts inherent in the 'part-time' trusteeship model with the full-time expertise needed to run the largest schemes.

As the concept of covenant assessment becomes embedded in trustee governance, so the appropriate management of confidential financial information becomes important. Although trustees have the right to seek appropriate information to carry out a covenant assessment, the specific information requirements will be the subject of discussions with the sponsor on a case-by-case basis, perhaps leading to an informal agreement to share agreed information, a written protocol or even in some situations a legal agreement which documents the respective parties' obligations similar to the information undertakings in a bank facility agreement.

When the trustees and their financial advisers come to assess or monitor the covenant, the question as to what information is available will arise. Where the parent company is listed on a major stock exchange, there will be a considerable amount of information in the public domain available to investors and also bondholders (such as credit ratings). In some cases, stakeholders such as bank and bond creditors might have (under confidentiality) access to more detailed financial information relevant to their positions. The trustees or their covenant adviser will seek to establish a dialogue with senior management on at least the basis of openness which they have with stock market and credit market analysts on a regular basis and perhaps on the basis of information shared with the banks. This ideally involves detailed one-to-one meetings with relevant members of the senior management team.

Laws and stock market rules seek to put all investors on a level playing field and prohibit selective briefings which place one party in a better, 'insider', position than others. They also regulate the frequency and time periods within which certain types of information should be disclosed to the markets. The extent to which (typically financial) information is 'price sensitive' and whether it can or should be disclosed publicly or privately with investors, lenders and analysts is an extremely delicate matter which, for listed companies, can require considerable coordination and dialogue amongst the senior management team (including the chief executive, finance director, company secretary, investor relations and corporate treasurer), their corporate broking, financial PR and (in some cases) legal advisers. Market practice changes over time – for instance, the detailed terms of a company's bank facility have not tended to be provided publicly to the stock market; however, during the recent financial crisis stock market participants became concerned about covenant breaches and sought this type of information, which itself became price sensitive for some companies. Disclosure of pension valuation bases (i.e. the trustee's actuarial valuation, not just the company's accounting valuation) is increasingly sought by equity investors and analysts. This is the level of disclosure to which trustees and advisers are increasingly working.

Information-sharing arrangements therefore need to take account of legitimate company senior management concerns regarding potentially price sensitive information and how that information is used by other stakeholders. Sharing sensitive information which has an employee impact (for example, plant closures) with the trustee board, some of whom may be affected personally or through other roles, such as trade union representation, also presents challenges of confidentiality and conflicts of interest.

It is increasingly common for management to require trustees to sign confidentiality agreements in relation to all information shared with them. However, there is still sometimes reluctance to share sensitive information relating to employees across the trustee board. Selective disclosure to a sub-group or the chairman can itself place these parties in a difficult position as to whether to share that information with their trustee colleagues. These challenges are not insurmountable, but require sensitive handling in coordination with legal and financial advisers.

Governance around communication protocols is still evolving – but there is some 'bootstrapping' – as levels of communication and transparency with trustees increase, what constitutes reasonable market practice itself evolves.

Corporate events

Impending corporate events such as bids, disposals and demergers pose a key issue of principle for trustee governance: how far should trustees seek to be actively involved by having a 'seat at the table' and, once at the table, what should they seek to achieve?

If a corporate event is potentially materially detrimental to the funding position of the pension scheme, the trustees have a legitimate interest in being involved, in line with the pension regulatory framework. That involvement extends to seeking 'mitigation' for the detriment. TPR has repeatedly stated its approach as being an umpire, not a referee; although there will be situations where its view as to the adequacy of mitigation offered or the appropriateness of assumptions is determinative, and there is an inherent tension with its responsibilities towards the PPF. This indicates a regulatory approach that seeks to promote trustee behaviour and good governance, rather than specific outcomes.

Mitigation

If trustees are really to learn from bankers, the expectation is that they will look at the techniques used by bankers in loan documentation, such as those used to minimise risks arising from changes to the basis on which the facility was initially made available. For instance, the corporate borrower will covenant to inform the lender(s) of changes in its financial position through regular testing of specified financial metrics (such as interest cover and net debt to profitability). Such commitments are known as 'information covenants'.

Lenders will also look to protect their credit exposure in insolvency through security over assets. The value of this security will be protected through restrictions on the borrower's ability to raise new debt or provide security (known as a 'negative pledge'). Guarantees may also be required from entities within the borrower group.

A number of major companies have entered into agreements with their pension schemes which provide legally binding restrictions such as these, indeed sometimes the pension scheme is itself a party to inter-creditor agreements involving the lending group.

Structures such as escrow accounts have been developed to improve the funding position of the pension scheme consistent with the sponsor's concerns over trapped surpluses. TPR has promoted consideration of 'contingent assets' such as these and we expect this to be a continuing area of innovation. Applying the principle of proportionality, though, means that a highly structured contingent funding agreement may be appropriate in some contexts for some large schemes with identified sponsor risk exposures, but it is unlikely to be appropriate for all schemes.

Companies in restructuring or distress

Trustees face the same difficult judgmental issues as bankers when the company is in a restructuring or distressed situation: whether to continue the ongoing exposure or to take more immediate action, including potentially triggering insolvency (perhaps through the pursuit and crystallisation of a section 75 debt). The trustees' task is made more challenging by the nature of their fiduciary obligations to members and the need to ensure that entry into the PPF is not compromised.

The pension scheme's own constitution can require the trustees to make judgments of critical importance to the employer, a prime example being the so-called 'nuclear option' mentioned above: in some cases the trustees have powers or discretions to wind up the scheme in certain circumstances, triggering a buy-out debt on the employer. The consequences of this can be extreme, perhaps triggering a cascade of cross-defaults under banking and debt agreements or a collapse in investor confidence, leading to group-wide insolvency.

It is in the context of restructurings and major events that the limits to the 'trustee as banker' analogy become clear. Trustees must assess the impact on scheme funding of such events. If they view them as detrimental to the scheme's position, they have the right to use the tools available under their trust deed and rules and the pensions regulatory regime. However, with rights go responsibilities – while a banker might act single-mindedly to protect its credit exposure, a trustee board must weigh up the impact of its decisions if they will inevitably cause a corporate insolvency or collapse in shareholder support for the sponsor. Trustees must balance short-term considerations against the desirability of ensuring a strong, ongoing covenant from a continuing business in future years.

Support for the trustees' position in corporate events

The trustees' ability to engage with restructurings and major corporate events such as bids, disposals and demergers derives from the clearance regime, and TPR's expectation that the trustees will have come to a considered view as to the effect of an event which is potentially materially detrimental to scheme funding (a 'type A event') or its effect on a scheme recovery plan. Where the sponsor is a larger listed company and the trustees' position is material to the share price, the trustees' decisions will likely be the subject of market scrutiny and comment by equity analysts. This indicates how the views of the pension trustees can now themselves be price-sensitive or can affect the outcome of a takeover bid. It is in the takeover context that the company board's obligations towards its shareholders (a relationship subject to company law and market responsibilities such as those imposed by the UK Listing Authority and the Takeover Panel) can trump communications with, and responsibilities towards, its pension scheme. In such a situation, trustee involvement is often determined by the bidder (for example, if it is a precondition of the bid), but where this is not the case, trustees may have to act tactically (for example, using press campaigns) to get the 'seat at the table' with the bidder.

Other issues

Dynamic covenant monitoring

There is as yet no established market practice as to how closely a trustee board should monitor the financial performance of the sponsor group. The scheme's constitution provides a staring point: for instance, some trust deeds and rules empower the trustees to wind up the scheme if they believe that there is no reasonable prospect of the deficit being made up. It makes sense for the trustees to monitor financial performance and the risk of such a position being imminent. However, the concept of dynamic covenant monitoring owes more to regulatory impetus; in an environment where valuation is market based and where the asset/liability position is monitored on a regular basis, it is anomalous not to monitor the sponsor covenant also on a regular basis.

In a reflection of corporate governance for listed companies, best practice for trustee boards is to establish a risk-management framework through which the covenant is monitored on a regular basis. This framework includes sponsor covenant risk, funding risk and investment risk – areas which are intrinsically linked: the ability of the company's finances to cope with the downside risks of investment performance failing to match funding assumptions is in turn affected by the degree of prudence in the funding assumptions. During an actuarial valuation, these factors are explicitly considered when agreeing the appropriate degree of prudence in the actuarial assumptions.

The Regulator has reinforced (in recently published guidance) the importance of having a framework for assessing and reviewing covenants, including monitoring and support mechanisms contingent on events happening. Trustees should regard this as important to the security of the scheme as monitoring fund performance.

Risk assessment

The concept of 'enterprise risk management' – the identification, monitoring and management of the risks to which an organisation is exposed – is increasing in prominence within corporations. Underlying the concept of covenant assessment is the assessment of the exposure to the corporate risk borne by a pension scheme. This risk is often financial, but can arise from a variety of other factors, such as political, environmental or business accidents. It is likely that sponsor covenant assessment will broaden to address non-financial risk assessment and there are grounds for seeing a more holistic view of pension and covenant risk taking shape. Already this is seen in scheme de-risking exercises.

De-risking

Risk analysis is at the core of the developing governance model. During the life of a pension scheme, the trustees bear covenant risk: the risk that the sponsor will not be able to stand behind the funding of accrued benefits. A full buy-out of the scheme transfers sponsor covenant risk to risk on the buy-out provider. A partial buy-in reduces sponsor covenant risk, but does not transfer that covenant risk: the scheme remains exposed to sponsor covenant risk for the uninsured portion and indeed for the insured portion until individual annuitisation; this is because the bulk annuity contract is technically just another investment of the scheme.

Buy-in and buy-out processes are sometimes complicated by a debate as to whether the sponsoring company or the trustees should manage and 'own' the evaluation process. From the above analysis and the authors' practical experience of such processes, both boards have a legitimate interest in the choice of provider and core annuity contract terms. As a scheme investment, this falls within the trustees' authority; but the residual covenant risk remains with the sponsor. A joint working sub-committee of the two boards can usefully take such a process forward.

Advisory roles

Even were there to be a single right answer or solution to scheme funding, it would soon be superseded. Few businesses remain unchanged over years, never mind decades; so it is a mistake to assume that the profile of their obligations and the relationship between the company, banks, shareholders, bond and pension creditors and other parties will not change over time. The legal, pensions regulatory and accounting framework highlights the simple point that trustees need to address the company's and scheme's position on a dynamic basis, reacting to and being prepared for changes in circumstances. This affects the trustees' relationships with all of their professional advisers, requiring a more integrated, ongoing use of such resources. There is also another dynamic at play: where an event has a potential effect on the sponsor covenant or there is a scheme-related event such as a recovery plan, it is increasingly the norm that sponsor and scheme will deal with this through separate teams of professional advisers, excepting some areas of actuarial analysis that have been carried out on a common platform.

Conclusion

Pension scheme trustees have fiduciary responsibility for substantial asset portfolios and the delivery of the pension promises they have been set aside for. They have a duty to deal with the company in as business-like a fashion as the bondholders, bank lenders and other stakeholders, and they have the right to be treated accordingly.

9
Establishing the funding requirements of pension schemes

MARTIN SLACK

This chapter considers the technical elements that go into an actuarial valuation of a defined benefit pension scheme – that is a scheme that promises to pay future benefits, regardless of the actual experience. There are a number of legislative processes surrounding valuations under the Pensions Act 2004 in particular, but these are not considered in depth here.

What is an actuarial valuation?

An actuarial valuation is an exercise for putting a current value on the liabilities of a defined benefit pension scheme and, in some cases, calculating a future contribution requirement. The value may be compared with the value of the available assets in order to determine a surplus or deficit. The future contribution requirement may be the amount needed to meet additional liabilities as they accrue, with an adjustment to allow for the removal of any surplus or deficit.

An actuarial valuation involves consideration of future issues that are, to a varying extent, unknown – for example, what aggregate pension amounts will be paid each year and what financial conditions will pertain – it therefore requires the use of a range of assumptions. There is no single correct, or even appropriate, set of assumptions and it is this range of possible assumptions that results in a potentially wide range of results for an actuarial valuation.

There is thus no single surplus or deficit within a pension scheme; it will depend upon what liabilities are being valued and what assumptions and methodologies are being used for the valuation. Referring to a scheme deficit without specifying the assumptions behind the calculations is therefore meaningless.

Objective of a valuation

Valuations may be undertaken with a number of objectives.

Funding

Historically, an actuarial valuation would be completed solely for the purpose of setting a future contribution rate – this may be referred to as a funding, or

134

ongoing, valuation. The outcome of a funding valuation is typically a contribution rate in two parts: a regular contribution to meet the accrual of future pension rights and an adjustment designed to amortise any surplus or deficit over an appropriate period. A surplus or deficit on a funding basis simply means that the funding to meet future pension scheme liabilities is either ahead or behind a planned timescale.

Solvency

A solvency valuation is a comparison of the assets with the amount required to secure the liabilities on a minimum risk basis – this may be taken as the cost of securing the liabilities with an insurance company.

Accounting

From around 1988, UK quoted companies have had to complete an accounting valuation under an accounting standard. The requirement for companies in other jurisdictions will vary. Accounting valuations provide information on the pension scheme to shareholders of the sponsoring company. The results are of no relevance to contributions or security.

Under the first UK standard – SSAP 24 – there was some actuarial judgment over the method and assumptions to be used; the later, and current, standards prescribe the method and give much less discretion over the most material assumptions.

Statutory

From time to time, government, or regulators, have required special valuations. These are valuations where the method and assumptions are laid down by regulation and therefore require very little actuarial judgment.

Historically, HM Revenue & Customs required a valuation to assess whether there was an excessive surplus, but this is no longer required. The Minimum Funding Requirement (MFR) applied from 1997 to 2005 and, from 2005, valuations for the Pension Protection Fund (PPF) were introduced. These PPF valuations are used in the normal course of proceedings to calculate the PPF levy (referred to as section 179 valuations), although a special valuation also applies when a scheme winds up to see whether it is eligible for entry to the PPF (section 143).

Legislative background

Funding valuations

Pre Pensions Act 2004

Prior to the Pensions Act 2004, the principal legislation affecting funding valuations was the requirement to complete one at least every three years and latterly for the actuary to produce a certificate covering the adequacy of the contributions being paid. There was no direct interference with the setting of assumptions. Some schemes chose to use the MFR basis for funding valuations on the basis that this was a prescribed minimum.

Post Pensions Act 2004

The Pensions Act 2004 established TPR and gave it powers and responsibilities in relation to funding valuations.

The Act put specific responsibility on trustees to set the assumptions, rather than the actuary or the employer, although, depending on the terms of the trust deed, they must seek the agreement of the employer.

TPR has issued guidance on setting assumptions, with clear pointers towards the use of prudent assumptions. It has established triggers which are used to identify valuations which it might consider not to be sufficiently prudent.

The value of the liabilities used for a valuation under the Pensions Act 2004 is referred to as the 'technical provisions'.

Trust deed

All trust deeds should include a requirement for regular valuations with the objective of updating the employer contribution requirement.

Some trust deeds may set out great detail on the valuation process, including who sets the assumptions. All deeds will state how the employer contribution rate is determined; examples would range from the employer or trustees having a unilateral decision, some process for reaching agreement or for the actuary to decide. The Pensions Act 2004 overrides a deed that gives the employer the unilateral decision and will now impose trustee agreement.

Actuarial guidance

The actuarial profession has issued a number of guidance notes covering actuarial valuations – now replaced by guidance from the Board of Actuarial Standards. However, these generally cover the reporting of actuarial advice, rather than the setting of assumptions. The one exception was Guidance Note 27, which, with government direction, set the assumptions for MFR valuations. This has now been withdrawn.

Accounting valuations

Accounting valuations are controlled by accounting standards. The first UK standard was SSAP 24: introduced in 1988, replaced from 2001 by FRS 17 and now generally replaced by IAS 19. These standards prescribe the methodology to be used and give clear direction on the setting of assumptions, with the ultimate decision being with the directors of the company, having taken actuarial advice.

Solvency valuations

The Pensions Act 2004 requires the actuary to produce an estimate of the solvency valuation as part of the normal valuation process. There is no prescription of the assumptions to be used, but it would be normal to have regard to estimates of insurance company buy-out terms.

Responsibilities

Clearly, the actuary is a key individual within the valuation process. The actuary's skills and experience are vital to identify the decisions required to complete the valuation process and to advise on, or choose, appropriate methods and assumptions. The actuary will then complete the necessary calculations by applying the methods and assumptions to the data provided and advise on the possible courses of action.

For a funding valuation, the trustees of the scheme play an essential part. Under the Pensions Act 2004, they control the choice of methods and assumptions and will either need to agree these with the employer, or, if the trust deed gives them the power to set contributions unilaterally, to consult the employer before reaching a decision. In either case, the trustees will need to rely on actuarial advice as to the range of appropriate methods and assumptions and the potential consequences of the final decisions.

For a funding valuation, the employer will either need to agree, or be consulted over, the methods and assumptions to be used. However, for an accounting valuation, the choice of assumptions (the method is set out in the accounting standard) is for the directors, after having taken actuarial advice.

Under the Pensions Act 2004, TPR could set the funding assumptions if the trustees and employer are unable to agree and can also require the trustees to reconsider the assumptions if it considers that they are not sufficiently prudent.

Achieving agreement on the methods and assumptions can be a long and difficult process, particularly where the contribution levels are very material for the employer, or the employer wishes to make benefit changes to reduce the long-term costs. The Pensions Act requires that valuations are completed within 15 months of the valuation date; practical experience is that many valuations use up most of this period.

Data

There are three key elements of data required for a valuation: data on the membership; data on the benefit calculation rules to allow the future benefits to be calculated; and data on the current assets.

Membership data may come in raw form, for example, in the form of individual member information, including dates and, for current employees, salary information; or in a partly processed form, for example, as accrued pensions for sub-groups of members. With the former, the actuary will need more detail

137

of the benefit structure to convert the raw data into prospective pensions. For all but the largest schemes, it would be most common to work from raw membership data as this will generally allow greater flexibility with the valuation calculations.

The actuary will need to apply certain checks to the data provided to confirm that there are no obvious errors or omissions. A reconciliation with data provided for previous valuations is an important part of this process, not least because it may identify members whose details appear to have been lost (or suddenly found – the late discovery of a group of members, typically deferred pensioners, not included in previous valuations is not unknown).

For a formal funding valuation, the actuary will need audited scheme accounts, if these are available. For other valuations, a statement of the total asset value may be sufficient.

Valuation process

The actuary will normally process the valuation in one of two ways. The first, and more traditional approach, is to calculate valuation factors that combine the various membership and financial assumptions and to apply these to pension amounts calculated from the membership data.

The second is to take the membership data and membership assumptions and then calculate the expected future benefit cash flows. These cash flows can then be discounted explicitly using the financial assumptions. Such an approach allows more flexibility in the valuation calculations.

With current IT resources, it is usually possible to produce valuations on a number of different sets of assumptions relatively easily. The more time-consuming part is the checking and processing of the membership data.

Valuation method

A valuation will need to use a particular valuation method. The valuation method essentially relates to the method for determining the future benefits that will be valued for those members who are still accruing benefits.

The first distinction relates to the allowance for future salary increases – relevant where the benefit calculation is based on salary at the point of retirement or leaving service. A 'current' method of valuation will not allow for future salary increases (at least to the extent that salary increases might exceed the rate at which the accrued benefit is automatically re-valued). A 'projected' method of valuation will include an allowance for future salary increases up to the point of retirement, or earlier death or leaving.

A current valuation will show a smaller deficit/larger surplus than a projected valuation.

The second distinction relates to the allowance for future benefit accrual. Most methods ignore future accrual when calculating the surplus or deficit, but it is sometimes appropriate to determine the surplus or deficit including future accrual, but also taking credit for a predetermined level of future contributions from the members and the employer. This is referred to as an 'aggregate method'.

Where future accrual is ignored in the deficit or surplus calculation, there is still a choice over the calculation of the future service contribution rate. The most common practice is to calculate an annual rate which, on average, should be sufficient over the period to the next valuation date. For schemes that are open to new members, the contribution rate may be expected to remain reasonably stable over this period, so the rate may be calculated as the rate required for just one year (a 'unit' rate). For schemes no longer open to new members, the contribution rate will typically be expected to increase as the average age of the members increases (as the future benefits are discounted for a shorter period); a level contribution rate can be calculated that allows for this, either over a short period, or until the last member is expected to retire or leave. This period is referred to as the 'control period'; where the control period runs up to the last member retiring, the method is referred to as 'attained age'.

The method chosen will not usually affect the valuation of the liabilities for deferred and current pensioners, as their benefits are fully determined. The exception could be where there are material discretionary benefits, such as post-retirement pension increases; a current method may exclude such increases whereas a projected method may not.

Historically, for funding valuations, there was freedom over the choice of valuation method; under the Pensions Act 2004, technical provisions are required to be calculated on a projected method, with the exception that any discretionary pension increases can be ignored.

Accounting valuations must be on a projected method, whereas solvency valuations will be on a current method.

Assumptions

As an actuarial valuation involves calculations relating to unknown future events, a vital part of the process is the setting of assumptions regarding those events.

In many areas, although the precise future is unknown, it is possible to be reasonably confident about the range in which the actual experience might fall. This results in the concepts of prudence and best estimates. A prudent assumption would be one where it is perceived to be more likely that the actual outcome will be more favourable than that assumed, rather than less favourable. A best estimate assumption is one where it is perceived to be equally likely that the actual outcome will be more or less favourable.

The required assumptions fall naturally into two parts: the assumptions affecting the timing and amount of future benefit payments (the membership assumptions) and the assumptions that affect the conversion of those future payments to a current value (the financial assumptions).

Membership assumptions

The principal membership assumptions will cover issues such as: mortality pre and post retirement; rates of retirement by age; rates of leaving service by age; rates of salary increase; and rates of pension increase. In addition, assumptions may be made over the exercise of member options, in particular exchange of pension at retirement for a lump sum. A 'rate' of retirement or leaving means the proportion of members reaching the given age who retire or leave in the following year.

For the larger schemes, guidance on appropriate assumptions can be obtained from analysing recent experience. However, it will always need to be borne in mind that past experience may not be a reliable indicator of future experience.

Mortality – general

For most schemes, the starting point for setting a mortality assumption will normally be to look at the available standard mortality tables. Various bodies publish tables of mortality experience drawn from differing sub-groups of the population. The Office of National Statistics publishes tables based on the total UK population and sub-groups based on location and socio-economic class. This analysis demonstrates that mortality experience is not homogenous and that there are a number of factors that can influence the mortality experience of sub-groups. For example, the life expectancy for 65-year-old men living in West London can be ten years more than those living in parts of Glasgow. Analysis of tables for different periods also demonstrates how mortality has changed over time.

A second useful source of mortality data is the Continuous Mortality Investigation (CMI), a body sponsored by the Faculty and Institute of Actuaries. The CMI historically analysed mortality data collected from participating life insurance companies, but more recently has also collected, and analysed, pensioner mortality data from occupational pension schemes – the latter referred to as 'SAPS'. The CMI has published a number of standard tables over the years based on sub-groups of the measured population – the naming convention is logical, but complex. For example, the PNA00 tables relate to the experience of insured pensioners ('P'), retiring normally ('N') with the experience weighted by the amount of pension ('A') over the period 1999 to 2002 ('00'); 'M' or 'F' would be added for males or females. The more recent SAPS tables have the rather simpler nomenclature of 'S1', with sub-groups depending on whether the experience relates to pensioners who retired normally or early due to ill health.

The first part of setting a mortality assumption is thus to select an appropriate standard table that best reflects the likely current mortality experience of the relevant members of the scheme. A better fit can be achieved by applying an adjustment to the standard table; the two common adjustments being either to use the table data for a different age from the actual age of the member: an adjustment of –1 means that for a 65-year-old member of the scheme, the mortality is assumed to follow that of a 64-year-old under the table. The second method of adjustment is to apply a percentage loading: a 90 per cent adjustment means that the chance of dying in a year is taken as 90 per cent of the chance under the standard table.

For pensioner, or post-retirement, mortality, the assumption should also recognise that the standard tables represent mortality experience at a particular time; there is now overwhelming evidence that mortality rates are improving (i.e. the chance of dying at a particular age is reducing) and are likely to continue to improve. Some allowance for this would therefore invariably be included. The allowance is inevitably a matter of judgment, but a number of techniques have been developed. These are discussed below under post-retirement assumptions.

The mortality assumption may thus be expressed as a base table (reflecting expected current mortality) and an allowance for future improvements.

Mortality – pre retirement

Pre-retirement mortality is not usually a very sensitive assumption – although specific benefit liabilities may arise on death before retirement (for example, a lump sum), other benefit liabilities are extinguished (for example, the retirement pension). Only the very largest schemes are likely to have sufficient data to establish scheme-specific experience and therefore for most schemes it would be typical simply to use one of the standard tables.

Mortality – post retirement

For the largest schemes, say over 10,000 pensioners (although it is the number of pensioner deaths that is really relevant), current mortality experience can be assessed from the scheme's own data. This experience would normally then be used to determine a suitable standard base table, with or without an adjustment.

However, typically there is not sufficient data available to give a reliable guide to actual experience. In this case, a good starting point will be to analyse the distribution of the membership by socio-economic class, as the population tables demonstrate that there is significant correlation between socio-economic class and life expectancy – occupation is the principle determinant of socio-economic class. A proxy for socio-economic class, if that is not available, can be the member's postcode, leading to the concept of postcode profiling.

Any analysis of current pensioner data only gives a guide for the mortality of current pensioners; in setting an appropriate assumption for other members, consideration will need to be given as to whether there has been any change in the make-up of the employee base – for example, a move from blue to white collar employees. This may require different assumptions for current pensioners and current non-pensioners.

For post-retirement mortality, the need for an assumption for future improvement is difficult to deny. Some of the standard published tables include a modest implicit allowance for future improvements – essentially by providing a chance of death by both age and year of achieving that age. This gave rise to the use of a suffix to the table: 'B' meaning that the assumption reflected the chances of death at each age using each member's year of birth to assess the year in which that age was achieved (so the suffix 'B35' meant born in 1935); 'C' meaning that the chance of death was taken from a fixed year (so 'C00' meant the chances of death at each age in 2000); and 'U' meaning that the future chances were taken using the table starting in a particular year (for someone born in 1935, 'B35' and 'U00' would be the same for someone aged 65 in 1999).

However, for the PA92 tables, published by the CMI in 1999, an additional allowance for future improvement was introduced: the so-called cohort allowance. This assumed temporary additional rates of improvement in mortality over three alternative periods, giving rise to the short, medium, and long cohort. Although the actual cohort assumptions put forward were recognised as being interim and based on limited actual experience, the cohort concept could be explained by post-war improvements in health care and general life style. The medium cohort quickly became a common allowance, possibly simply because it was the middle one rather than there being any particular evidence to support it.

Within the last few years, more sophisticated assumptions for future improvements have been introduced: the simplest is to continue a minimum rate of improvement once the cohorts run out – the so-called 'floor'. The most recent assumes a short-term trend from an estimate of the current rate of improvement to a long-term rate, with a superimposed 'wobble' to allow for a cohort effect.

The range of different allowances for future improvements has resulted in a confused naming convention. It is perhaps better to accept this convention as a means to enable actuaries, and other mortality experts, to understand each other, rather than attempting to explain it.

Retirement and leaving service rates

Few employee members will remain employed until their Normal Retirement Date and therefore assumptions can be made for rates of retirement and leaving service by age. In practice, the need for these rates will depend on the benefits provided; for example, where early retirement benefits reflect the value of the benefit payable from Normal Retirement Date, the assumption for early retirement may have little effect on the valuation result.

Salary increases

An accounting or funding valuation will, if on a prospective basis and where benefits are linked to final salary, include an allowance for future salary increases when valuing the benefits for current employee members.

This will usually be defined relative to the assumption for future price inflation and may include an allowance for both general increases applicable for all employees and promotional increases.

Pension increases

Where future pension increases are fixed, for example, at 3 per cent per annum, then no assumption is necessary as the future is known.

More typically, future pension increases will be linked to future price inflation, with minimum and/or maximum increases applying in each year. The statutory minimum for pension accruing from 1997 to 2007 can be referred to as '5 per cent LPI': the increase in each year is in line with increases in the retail price index (RPI), with a minimum of 0 per cent and a maximum of 5 per cent. From 2007, statutory increases are '2.5 per cent LPI'. Schemes may have overriding provisions, for example, minimum increases of 3 per cent.

It would be usual for the assumptions to allow for any minima and maxima. The assumed rate for future price inflation is an average and, whereas that average may be between the minimum and maximum, it is expected that there will be individual years when inflation may be below the minimum or above the maximum. For example, for pension increases at 5 per cent LPI, if the expected average RPI is 3.5 per cent per annum, the expected average pension increase may only be 3.2 per cent per annum.

Proportion 'married'

This assumption relates to the proportion of cases when a dependant's benefits will be payable on a member's death. The assumption should reflect the scheme's definition of dependant, as clearly for a scheme that only pays to the legal spouse, a lower proportion will be appropriate than for a scheme that pays to a wide class of dependants. The most accurate approach would be to assume a variable proportion married by age at death; in practice it is common for simpler assumptions to be used, such as an average proportion applicable as at the valuation date, and then to make some allowance for dependants predeceasing the member.

Commutation

Commutation is the practice of surrendering pension on retirement for a lump sum. The current terms for commutation may be such that allowing for commutation reduces the value placed on the liabilities; however, consideration needs to be given as to how the current terms might change in the future, so taking full credit for commutation on current terms might result in an under valuation. Where current terms are financially neutral, allowing for commutation may not change the value placed on the liabilities, but will produce a better estimate of the pattern of future cash flows, where that is used for other purposes.

Expenses

Although not strictly a benefit of the scheme, a valuation (other than an accounting valuation) should have regard to the likely expenses that may have to be met from the scheme. These would include the expenses of administration, as well as adviser fees and general trustee expenses. They may also include the expenses of winding up the scheme at some point in time.

PPF levy

Although the levy is strictly payable by the scheme trustees, it may not be practical to allow for it in a funding valuation, as it is difficult to make a sensible assumption for its future amount. The amount will depend firstly on how much the PPF wishes to collect (which is a function of the PPF's own experience and its estimates of future demands on the PPF). Secondly, the allocation of this levy between schemes currently depends on each scheme's own PPF funding level (ascertained by a section 179 valuation) and the perceived financial strength of the employer (for which the Dun & Bradstreet 'failure score' is currently a major input). To estimate any one of these for more than a year ahead, never mind all three, is simply not possible. Many schemes thus require the sponsoring employer to pay the PPF levy as an addition to any other contributions, rather than making what could be very spurious assumptions.

Financial assumptions

It is now almost universal for the financial assumptions to be set by reference to market conditions – the so-called 'mark to market'. For such valuations, the value placed on the liabilities can then be compared directly with the market value of the assets. Up until the end of the 1990s, it was common to base funding valuations on assumed long-term conditions and to 'adjust' the actual value of the assets to a value that was considered to be consistent with those long-term conditions. Although this practice resulted in more stable contribution requirements, the asset adjustments required became quite extreme and very reliant on particular assumptions on elements, such as future dividend growth from equities. As a result, the methodology became discredited.

Whilst easier to understand, mark-to-market valuations do result in much more volatile valuation results, which, for funding valuations in particular, can cause difficulties.

Price inflation

The assumption for future price inflation directly affects the future benefits that are to be valued, as most of those are now linked directly, or indirectly, to the RPI. However, the assumption may not, in practice, have that much impact on the overall valuation result, as the discount rate used to discount those future benefits may itself be linked to the expectations for future price inflation. Nevertheless, most valuations will make an assumption for price inflation.

The starting point for this assumption will be the gilt markets and, in particular, the difference between the fixed-interest gilt yields and the index-linked gilt yields – with the latter giving RPI-linked returns, this difference is an indication of the market assessment of future RPI. As gilt yields can vary by duration, it will be important to look at yields at a duration that is appropriate to the liabilities being valued. In the extreme, a different assumption can be used for the benefit payments due in each future year to reflect this. These duration-dependent rates can be obtained from yield curves available from the Bank of England and other sources.

There is a practice of making a small adjustment to the implied RPI rate, or rates, to allow for an 'inflation risk premium'. The rationale for this is that investors will want a margin from their expected rate of RPI to reflect future uncertainties. In theory, this premium could be positive or negative, but a positive adjustment would be unusual. Where an inflation risk premium is applied, it should be consistent with the minimum risk discount rates – see below. The risk-free value of an RPI-linked benefit is obtained by discounting the current benefit amount at the index-linked yield. Increasing the benefit by an RPI assumption that is less than the difference between the fixed and index-linked yield and then discounting that increased benefit by the fixed yield will produce a lower value. This would be an underestimate of the risk-free value.

The inflation risk premium should therefore properly be considered in the context of the discount rate and the allowance for investment risk. If there is a mismatch between the split of the liabilities between real and fixed liabilities and the split of the assets between real and fixed assets, then considering whether there is an inflation risk premium may be appropriate.

Discount rates – general

A key part of any valuation is the discount rate; that is the rate at which the amount of benefit payable at a future date is discounted to give a current value.

For a solvency valuation, the discount rate will be close to the gilt yield (fixed or index-linked as appropriate) – again with an eye on a consistent duration – as the purpose is to produce a minimum risk valuation.

For an accounting valuation under FRS 17 or IAS 19, the discount rate is currently prescribed as the yield on 'AA' corporate bonds of appropriate duration. Until the 2008/09 credit crisis, there was very little variation in this yield across the available bonds and thus little variation in the discount rates used at any particular time. With the volatility and uncertainty resulting from the crisis, a wide range of yields opened up. Choosing the appropriate yield therefore became a little more difficult and no doubt some directors would have been in discussion with their actuaries and auditors over the discount rate to use.

Discount rates – funding valuations

For a funding valuation, the discount rate is perhaps the assumption that results in the most discussion.

The principle of applying a discount rate to a future cash flow is to unwind the investment return that could be earned on monies invested now to meet that cash flow; if the discounted value is then invested in a way which earns the discount rate, it will accumulate to an amount equal to the benefit payment when the payment is due.

For funding valuations, where the purpose is to calculate the contributions to be paid to meet future benefit payments, it is relevant to consider how the current assets and future contributions will be invested and what investment returns might be earned. A higher level of future investment return can be allowed for by using a higher discount rate; this will reduce the contribution rate emerging from the valuation on the simple premise that more of the monies needed to pay benefits will come from future investment returns.

The consideration of potential future investment returns should thus fall into two parts: the first is to consider the likely future investment strategy, in particular the split between return-seeking assets, such as equities, and lower risk assets, such as bonds; the second is to consider the expected return from the various asset classes and, importantly, how much of that return to anticipate when setting the discount rate. It is common to refer to the discount rate as an 'assumed' investment return; in practice, the assumed return should be higher than the discount rate, as not all of the assumed return from return-seeking assets should be anticipated in the discount rate.

With many pension schemes now closed to new members, and indeed a number now being closed to future accrual, it is likely to be unrealistic to assume that schemes will not change their investment strategy over time. It would be a very high risk strategy to retain a high allocation to return-seeking assets as the scheme membership becomes dominated by current pensioners and investments need to be realised to raise the money to pay benefits. Various techniques have therefore been developed to allow for changing investment strategies over time as the membership matures.

The most common technique – and one that has been in use from the early to mid-1990s – can be referred to as the 'pre-post' method. The implicit overall strategy behind this method is that there will be one sub-strategy for the assets needed to back the current pensions in payment from time to time – typically a low-risk strategy; and another for the assets needed to back the prospective benefits for those members not yet retired – typically a higher risk, return-seeking strategy. For a pension scheme closed to new members, such a strategy would, over time, move increasingly into a low-risk strategy, and eventually, once all members have retired, it would be totally low risk.

Other techniques are available that have a similar effect of reducing the reliance on high-risk, return-seeking assets over time.

For closed schemes, it may also be relevant to make an explicit assumption for the scheme winding up at some future date and seeking to secure remaining benefit payments by the purchase of insurance contracts. It may be unrealistic to assume that both the trustees and the sponsoring employer would be willing to accept the risk and expense of running a pension scheme the sole purpose of which is to provide pensions for former employees.

Finally, if the trustees are only willing to invest in risky assets while they have a financially strong sponsoring employer, the long-term assumption for the allocation to such assets should reflect their long-term views of that financial strength.

It is not necessary for the assumed strategy to mirror directly the expected actual strategy, although in many cases it will. The assumed strategy represents one which the scheme would be able to afford to adopt if the contributions resulting from the valuation were paid in practice and the assumed rates of return were earned. It would clearly be wrong to assume a strategy with a higher allocation to return-seeking assets than is likely to happen in practice, as it will then be difficult to achieve the required investment returns. However, it would not be uncommon for the assumed strategy to have a lower allocation than in practice – this provides a potential source of additional investment returns that, if delivered, would allow future contributions to be reduced.

Having selected an assumed future investment strategy, the next stage is to consider the expected returns from that strategy. Trustees should take advice from both the actuary and investment consultant as to the likely expected returns from the various asset classes, usually expressed as additional returns over the minimum risk return from gilts. The expected return from equity-type investments could typically be in the range of 3 to 4 per cent per annum over the minimum risk return. The expected additional returns from other asset classes may be lower. Care needs to be taken not to assume, without thought, that expected returns from current assets will continue to be available in the future. A recent case in point has been corporate bonds, where the prospective yield increased dramatically relative to gilts in response to the credit crisis; it could be unrealistic to assume that such yields would continue once markets stabilise. Although the high yield may be achieved on stocks held at the time, most corporate bonds are short term and would need to be replaced as they mature with bonds at lower yields.

Once an expected return has been identified, the remaining issue is to determine how much of that return to anticipate in the discount rate and hence in the contribution rate. It is possible to construct models of the expected distribution of the return over time and the discount rate may be set at a level that the distribution suggests has a high confidence of being achieved. For example, for equity investment, the confidence of achieving 2 per cent per annum over gilts over a ten-year period may be of the order of 70 to 75 per cent, which may be considered adequate. That is not to say that the actual return will not be less than this. For a greater confidence a lower excess over the gilt return should be used. However, 100 per cent confidence is not achievable while there is investment in return-seeking assets.

The choice of confidence level should be influenced by the assessed financial covenant of the sponsoring employer, as too low a confidence level (i.e. anticipating too much of the expected return) increases the chance that the contributions set at the valuation will be insufficient and will therefore need to be increased at the next valuation. The greater the doubts about the employer's future, the greater the confidence needs to be that the contributions will be sufficient, and so the lower the proportion of expected additional returns that should be anticipated.

Recovery plan

The recovery plan is the term used under the Pensions Act 2004 to define the plan for removing any deficit revealed at a funding valuation. The valuation process described above will result in a funding deficit or surplus and a contribution rate to meet the future accrual of benefit. The final stage is to calculate the additional contribution, or reduction in contribution, to 'correct' the deficit or surplus.

Deficit correction

The initial level of any annual deficit contribution emerging from the calculation will depend on:

- the target period over which the deficit is to be eliminated (the 'recovery period') – the longer the period, the lower the initial annual deficit contribution;
- whether the contribution will be fixed in amount, or increase in line with the salary roll, or some index (for example, RPI) – in general if the contribution is to increase it will start from a lower amount; and
- whether any credit is to be given for expected investment returns in excess of those anticipated in the main valuation calculations.

Recovery period

TPR initially set a 'trigger point' of ten years, indicating an expectation that recovery periods should not exceed this, although it also stated that trustees should seek to set deficit contributions at as high a level as the sponsor can reasonably afford. This might suggest a lower recovery period if the sponsor has sufficient resources.

As larger deficits emerged following the credit crisis, TPR suggested that it was preferable to respond to the sponsor's requests for lower contributions by increasing the recovery period, rather than reducing the deficit by weakening the assumptions used for the valuation.

Allowing for additional investment return

Where the discount rate for a funding valuation has been set at a more prudent level than could be justified from the actual investment strategy being adopted, some trustees agree to allow for some of that prudence when setting the deficit contributions. In other words, they are willing to expect that some of the deficit will be funded from investment returns not needed to support the valuation rather than from deficit contributions. This is clearly sacrificing some of the prudence in the valuation and thus reducing the chance that the deficit will be funded by the end of the recovery period.

Allowing for uncertainty

As any actuarial valuation relies on assumptions about future events, there can be no certainty that those assumptions will be borne out in practice and thus that the results of the valuation are 'correct'.

For funding valuations in particular, it is therefore important to understand the potential consequences of that uncertainty. This can be demonstrated in a number of ways:

- By showing the effect of simple changes in the assumptions – for example, allowing for different pensioner mortality, or changing other membership or financial assumptions.
- By simple scenario testing – that is by considering what the position might look like at a future date (for example, the next valuation) if the experience up to that date follows particular scenarios. The range of scenarios considered should include favourable and unfavourable outcomes (for example, the return from return-seeking assets significantly exceeding, or falling below, the allowance in the valuation). It may also be possible to consider the impact of changes in gilt yields and inflation experience.
- By running multiple simulations that allow for random uncertainty. This is the most sophisticated approach, although it requires an 'economic model' that is able to simulate future financial conditions in a consistent way. By running projections in a number of simulated projections, such an exercise can show the potential range of the funding level in future years and, potentially, the range of contribution rates that might be required at future valuations. Such an exercise would demonstrate that taking a more prudent approach reduces the chance, and the effect, of having to increase contributions at future valuations. Such an exercise is essentially a traditional asset liability modelling exercise, and bringing it into the valuation process highlights the connection between funding valuations and investment strategy.

Documentation

The final stage of a funding valuation exercise is the documentation. Under the Pensions Act 2004, trustees are required to prepare three documents, in addition to the valuation report:

- a statement of funding principles, recording the methods and assumptions used for the calculation of the technical provisions, i.e. for the valuation;
- a recovery plan, setting out the proposal for funding any deficit – this is not required if there is no deficit; and
- a schedule of contributions, setting out the contributions to be paid for the greater of a period of five years or the recovery period.

It would be usual for the employer to agree these documents, although if the trustees have unilateral power to set contributions under the rules of the scheme, it is not strictly necessary.

The actuary will need to provide two certificates: the first that the technical provisions have been calculated in accordance with the statement of funding principles and the second that the contributions in the schedule of contributions are such that the scheme 'could be expected' to be funded fully by the end of the period covered by the schedule. The actuary will also produce a final valuation report setting out the background to, and results of, the valuation calculations, although in practice much of this advice should have been provided over the period of discussion leading up to the final decisions on the valuation being taken.

The value of the technical provisions, including the key assumptions used, and any recovery plan have to be submitted to TPR.

Conclusions

There is no single result from an actuarial valuation in the form of a deficit or surplus. The result will depend on the purpose of the valuation – solvency, accounting, statutory or funding – and, for funding valuations in particular, the assumptions used.

Whereas many of the assumptions may be similar for all valuations – it is difficult to justify material differences in, for example, the pensioner mortality assumption (other than on grounds of explicit differences in prudency) – the discount rate will be the most significant variation. For non-funding valuations, there may be little room to vary the discount rate, but for funding valuations, deciding the discount rate(s) may be the most significant and difficult decision and should be considered in conjunction with the current, and expected future, investment strategy.

10
Effective oversight of pension administration

AVGI GREGORY

Introduction

Trustees have a responsibility under pensions legislation to ensure that pensions administration is run effectively, whether it is carried out by the sponsoring employer or by a third-party administrator (TPA). However, frequently, pensions administration gets relatively little attention from trustee boards, compared to other trustee responsibilities such as investment and funding.

Errors and maladministration can damage scheme, employer and trustee reputation. Furthermore, errors can be very costly to resolve, involving significant effort from trustees, lawyers and other advisers.

Trustees not only have a legal responsibility, but they also have a moral obligation to members, many of whom find pensions complex and difficult to understand. Trustees should ensure that members' benefits are calculated and paid in a timely and accurate way. Administration is the most significant, and often the only, point of contact between the beneficiaries of a pension scheme and its trustees; members will frequently judge a scheme and its trustee board by the quality of its administration.

Perhaps more pertinently, the Pensions Regulator (TPR) has been given a statutory objective to promote, and improve understanding of, good administration, and therefore will use a number of means to increase trustees' ability to oversee pensions administration effectively.

In this chapter, the term 'trustee' should be taken to mean 'trustee director' where the trustee of a scheme is a corporate trustee.

What is good administration?

As a minimum, good administration requires compliance with legislation and the scheme's trust deed and rules. It involves:

- accurate record-keeping and maintenance of members' data;
- prompt and robust collection and investment of contributions;
- accurate calculation and payment of benefits; and
- effective communication with members and statutory bodies.

151

Within these constraints, the quality of pensions administration frequently reflects the employer culture. So, for some pension schemes, good administration includes high levels of contact with members, high-quality communication material and a good degree of pensioner liaison. For other schemes, little more than 'minimum compliance' administration is provided.

Whether the service required is at the 'minimum compliance' end of the spectrum or the 'Rolls-Royce' end, it should always be robust enough to ensure that payments are calculated and paid correctly, and that operational risk to trustees, employers, members and indeed the scheme is kept as low as possible.

The trustees need proactively to consider and decide on the quality and service levels of the administration they require, and preferably agree those with the sponsoring employer.

In summary, a scheme that is considered to have good administration should be able to demonstrate that:

- it is compliant with statutory requirements, and with the trust deed and rules;
- a comprehensive agreement between the trustees and the administrator (external provider or sponsoring employer) is in place, covering service scope and levels;
- administration and other activities actually meet the requirements of the service agreement;
- the service offers good value for money to both trustees and sponsoring employer;
- communication between trustees, the sponsoring employer and the administrator is frequent and clear;
- trustee reporting is consistent, regular and sufficient;
- administration tasks are completed promptly, in a controlled manner and fully recorded;
- payments are made/received promptly, accurately and are properly recorded;
- member correspondence is clear and concise;
- operational risks are regularly reviewed, understood and well controlled;
- business continuity arrangements are in place and well tested;
- data is held securely and is maintained in good order;
- the administrator regularly assesses and implements improvements to its processes and technology, with such changes being implemented cost effectively, smoothly and without affecting 'business as usual';
- skills of administration staff are kept up to date and appropriate development programmes are implemented; and
- management processes are in place to ascertain the performance of administration against agreed service level agreements.

Clarity of responsibilities

Trustee board

The trustee board has the ultimate responsibility for the effective running of their scheme's pensions administration; trustees are accountable under law and to the members. Trustees must ensure that the scheme is effectively administered in all reasonable circumstances and, in particular, that they are satisfied with the quality of scheme records and service delivery.

While much of the pensions administration activity might be delegated to others (both day-to-day oversight and the administration itself), the trustees must ensure that this delegated activity is conducted in line with their requirements and should regularly receive reports to ensure that both the delivery and strategy are satisfactory and meet their stated objectives.

Administration objectives must be regularly reviewed and agreed (either by the trustee board, or by a delegated committee), and any new trustees should be clear of their responsibilities for pension administration. Any delegated activity should be clearly defined.

Many schemes have delegated the oversight of pensions administration to a committee (frequently called the operations or administration committee), the remit of which may also include accounts, discretionary decisions, communications and other operational matters. Given the increasing attention paid to administration by TPR, the Pensions Ombudsman, the Pension Advisory Service and even the press, proper oversight should provide reassurance to both trustees and members.

In considering the performance of the administration, whether in-house or outsourced, trustees need to examine regularly and carefully whether or not:

- the scheme is being administered (at the very least) in compliance with legislative and statutory requirements;
- the administration is being carried out in accordance with the trust deed and rules, and any service level agreement;
- errors are promptly identified and rectified, and do not indicate systemic problems;
- members receive correspondence and payments in a prompt and timely manner;
- payments and information are sent to regulatory and statutory bodies promptly and accurately; and
- the performance is accurately, honestly and concisely reported upon.

A manager from within the administration team should regularly report to the trustee (typically monthly or quarterly) on performance and progress. Many trustees find that it is often reassuring to include a statement of compliance with each report.

153

Sponsoring employer

The sponsoring employer has a number of responsibilities and activities to carry out, although they are fewer if the pensions administration is outsourced to a TPA.

If the appointment of the administration team (internal or external) is made directly by the employer, a robust service level agreement must be drawn up between trustees and employer. Such agreements are not always present, and even when they do exist, they tend to lag behind the scope and effectiveness of agreements between trustees and external providers or TPAs.

The process of establishing a good service level agreement provides a means to discuss and reach agreement on issues where there is a difference of opinion between employer and trustees concerning the quality and scope of the administration (perhaps on response times, quality/content of communication material or pensioner liaison). In terms of robustness and risk appetite, however, both employer and trustees usually hold similar views on operational matters.

Occasionally, there are instances where trustees have delegated administration to the sponsoring employer, and the employer has then sub-contracted the administration to a TPA, with no formal contractual relationship between the trustees and the TPA. Such a governance structure can make it difficult for the trustees to drive service requirements and the only option, where service is below trustee expectations but acceptable to the employer, is for the trustee to terminate the administration relationship with the sponsoring employer and make direct alternative arrangements. Inevitably, this is an unsatisfactory state of affairs, so trustees must ensure that they have a robust administration governance structure in place and service level agreements are regularly reviewed and discussed.

Employers and trustees must discuss and agree who will meet the costs of administration. Costs are either paid directly by the employer or the trustees; in the latter case administration costs are treated as scheme expenditure and paid from the scheme's assets, in which case scheme accounts and actuarial valuations need to reflect this. Whichever is the case, both employers and trustees have an interest in ensuring that the administration is delivered cost effectively and administration costs are well controlled.

A key operational responsibility for the employer is to provide a regular and accurate data feed for active scheme members, for example, salary, contributions, joiner and leaver information. For most schemes nowadays this feed is electronic and frequently automatic. The receiving pensions administration team/system will automatically process the feed, updating member data, adding new members and initiating leaver calculations. Any exceptions that fall outside pre-agreed tolerances will be highlighted, clarified and corrected by the administration team or the employer.

Pensions management team

Typically, in larger employers, it is the role of one or more employees to look after the pension scheme's day-to-day operations on behalf of the trustees. In smaller employers, this may fall to a single individual in the finance or HR department, or perhaps the company secretary. The administration-related role of this pensions management team may include:

- acting as the scheme secretary and dealing with the administration team;
- raising relevant and pertinent administration issues to the trustees;
- working alongside the trustee board and committee members to recommend administration strategy and relevant provider(s);
- overseeing or directing change projects, which may include outsourcing, insourcing or changing TPA;
- overseeing performance of either the TPA or the in-house team against the service level agreement (SLA);
- helping to ensure that flow of data from the employer to the adminis-trator runs smoothly and to resolve repeated errors that arise in active data;
- advising on particularly complex and difficult administration cases; and
- acting as a liaison between the trustees and the administrator.

Administration team

The administration team, whether in-house or within a TPA, has day-to-day responsibility for delivering the service to members and other stakeholders through activities such as:

- running the scheme so that it is compliant with legislative and trustee requirements;
- direct liaison with members, the sponsoring employer and other providers (such as the actuary);
- collection and reconciliation of all contributions and onward transmission to the investment managers;
- processing and recording of all member events, including issuing benefit statements and payment of benefits to members as they fall due;
- providing an online facility for members to obtain information about the scheme and to check their own pensions provision;
- maintaining up-to-date and accurate records for all members;
- pension scheme accounting and treasury services;
- provision of information for the employer's financial statements;
- statutory reporting and liaison with regulatory bodies;
- provision of regular reports to the trustees and employer; and
- production of the annual report and accounts.

Administration strategy

Insourcing versus outsourcing

It is important that the trustees ensure that the most appropriate service delivery strategy and administration governance arrangements are adopted for their scheme, taking into account factors such as: the employer's views; required service levels and desired member liaison; available skills and capability; technology; and risks. One of the key decisions is whether to carry out the administration in house (insourcing) or to contract a TPA to provide administration services (outsourcing).

The trustees need to be clear on what they expect from the 'pensions administration' partnership (internal or external). A summary of some of the advantages and disadvantages of in-house and outsourced administration is shown in Table 10.1.

Issues to consider when reviewing strategy

From time to time, trustees may wish to review whether or not they wish to retain the current method of administration service delivery, namely whether to:

● retain administration in house;
● move administration to an internal 'shared services' department;
● outsource for the first time;
● change outsourced provider; or
● 'insource', bringing an outsourced administration service back in house.

It is good practice for trustees to review their service delivery strategy from time to time. A review can also be prompted by special circumstances, such as:

● a drive by the sponsoring employer to outsource non-core business activity;
● staff issues, for example, the failure to attract and retain suitable administration staff or key staff are due to retire;
● system issues, perhaps with persistent problems, leading to the need to replace the system or sign a new contract;
● changes in the membership of the scheme, perhaps through merger or acquisition activity, or demographics;
● a change in circumstances at a TPA, such as a change in ownership, loss of key staff or persistent service non-compliance; and
● changes in a corporate contract to outsource HR and benefit administration services.

The outputs from a review of strategy can vary from maintaining the status quo, perhaps with a few improvements, to a complete change of administrator, or a system-replacement project. The bigger the change, the greater the potential disruption is likely to be and the greater the risks. Great care should be taken to ensure that decisions are based on proper research and careful

Table 10.1 Advantages and disadvantages of in-house and outsourced administration		
	In house	*Outsourced*
Advantages	Operational issues can often be addressed more quickly by an in-house team. Changes to processes as a result of scheme or organisation changes may be implemented more quickly and flexibly, and the cost of change is often subsumed in the running costs. If done well, in-house administration has the potential to offer good 'value for money' for medium/large schemes. The culture of the sponsoring employer, and the scheme, is more likely to be reflected by the pensions administration team.	The administration will be run by professional experts more capable of dealing with legislative changes. Technology and process changes resulting from legislation are applied across all clients, reducing risk and the learning curve. The employer may have a policy for outsourcing non-core activities. Service is less likely to be affected by difficulties in recruiting and training new staff. For small/medium-sized schemes, costs can be lower.
Disadvantages	Ongoing costs can be higher if there is high internal staff turnover or the need to invest in technology. Administration will often require more input and support from the pensions management team. The sponsoring employer may have a preference for outsourcing, particularly if there are few or no active members. Cost 'spikes' might occur due to occasional system changes. Good calibre staff may be difficult to recruit.	There is a strong requirement for good contract management skills, which are often lacking in pensions departments. Scheme- and organisation-driven changes are often less rapid and more costly, because they have to go through a change control process. Costs of non-standard services can be high and unpredictable. The culture of the employer and the trustee is less easily reflected within the pensions administration team.

consideration of all of the facts. Input and challenge should be sought from all key stakeholders.

When considering outsourcing, unless a full market review is conducted, accurate costs for comparing the various options are difficult to obtain. However, indicative costs can normally be sourced, in confidence, from the TPA market or via specialist advisers.

Any change of administrator will require careful planning, quality project management and adequate resource. Transition risk when outsourcing can be lower than first anticipated, given that the change would be carried out by professional TPA staff who will have well-established processes for such projects.

Outsourcing a pension administration function (and indeed, replacing an administration system) normally prompts an opportunity to cleanse thoroughly the data and review the processes and calculation routines. This needs to be factored in as part of the decision process.

Strong direction from a project owner within the employer should bolster success, whatever the transition. If outsourcing, then invariably control (and ultimately governance) mechanisms of the administration have to change, and staff skills will need to change to enable this to happen.

Depending on the method of outsourcing administration, it may be that existing staff choose not to, or cannot, transfer to the new administrator. In such a case, the loss of scheme knowledge and associated risks should be carefully considered and mitigation processes agreed.

Selecting an outsourced provider

The market

The outsourced pensions administration market is well developed, with broadly four kinds of market participant:

- actuarial firms and benefit consultancies who offer pension administration as a complementary service to their wide range of pension services;
- business process outsourcing organisations who offer pension administration as part of a wider HR outsourcing service;
- specialist pension administration firms or large pension departments owned by pension funds who offer pension administration to other schemes; and
- investment firms or insurance companies offering pension administration as part of a bundled service offering, typically for DC arrangements.

The outsourcing process

An outsourcing project will typically include the following steps:

Step 1: appoint a working group or sub-committee to oversee the process
The working group should represent the interests of the trustee, the members, the employer and the day-to-day pension management team. It must be able to inform the other trustees so that they can confidently support any recommendations made by the task group.

Such a working group is rarely larger than six people, and often consists of a pension manager, two or three trustees, an employer representative and a specialist consultant (although he or she should only offer advice).

Step 2: project planning The project should begin by defining the key objectives, the selection process and the key success factors. In outsourcing projects, typical *objectives* may include the following:

- defining the scope of what is, and what is not, to be outsourced;
- defining the key service levels and quality criteria;
- defining any time constraints and requirements relating to other projects, for example, issue of benefit statements;
- identifying strategic criteria for supplier selection;
- defining any cost constraints or expectations; and
- defining any requirements for data analysis and cleaning.

The selection process typically follows Steps 3 to 6 set out below.

Step 3: examine the market and decide on a list of providers to be invited to tender With so many providers in the market, it is sensible to try and identify a shortlist of suppliers that are most likely to meet the identified requirements and success criteria. With some specialist help, the aim is to draw up a list of providers who may be appropriate partners. The selection of this list can be by reference to several factors, depending on organisational priorities, such as:

- the provider's scale and capacity to meet the requirements;
- experience of dealing with schemes of similar size, design and complexity;
- the size of the provider's client base;
- the provider's financial health and ability to invest in developing their services and technology;
- location, especially if transfer of current staff under TUPE is a requirement;
- the number of administration and other professional staff; and
- other services that are offered.

Step 4: issue a request for information (RFI) or invitation to tender (ITT) If the list of potentially suitable providers is large, it is usual to issue an RFI. This is a short questionnaire designed to assess providers' capacity and broad capability to take on the business, following which a short-list can be selected. Once a short-list has been agreed, an ITT is issued. This is an altogether more extensive document, in response to which trustees should expect comprehensive proposals with service descriptions and costs. The ITT should be drawn up to provide enough detail to allow the potential providers to understand the complexities of the scheme and key requirements and to be able to provide reliable cost proposals.

Part of the tender process should include hosting a 'data room', which holds many of the relevant scheme documents. This saves sending out large amounts of scheme documentation, and can help with controlling confidentiality. Traditionally, this has been a physical data room within the employer's or scheme adviser's premises, but increasingly this is done electronically.

The questions and information requested in the ITT should clearly contribute to the decision-making criteria. Hence, these criteria (as well as the weighting or level of importance that will be given to each area of the tender) need to be developed alongside the ITT to ensure that the process is honest and auditable.

Step 5: manage the tendering process and evaluate the tenders The tendering process needs to be managed fairly and scrupulously, ensuring that all providers are given equal access to information, yet have confidence that their commercial information will remain confidential from their competitors. The process may include clarification meetings with the potential providers, presentations by them, site visits and taking up references with other clients, formally or informally.

Tender evaluation is often done by the working group, sometimes facilitated by an independent adviser. Detailed cost analysis is also carried out, including comparison with the costs of running the existing service, whether in house or outsourced.

The evaluation of tenders should lead to a preferred provider being identified (subject to contractual matters being satisfactorily resolved).

Step 6: review the contract and conduct due diligence Standard contractual terms vary significantly between providers. Trustees, often with the help of a sponsoring company procurement department, may have very specific ideas and requirements as to what should be included in a contract. For example, trustees might insist that penalty or incentive clauses are included to help to ensure performance meets the targets set. The tendering documents issued by the trustees or company may include a proposed contract, perhaps based on the Pensions Management Institute (PMI) Model Agreement (see the PMI website).[1]

It is essential that legal advice is obtained to ensure that the legal terms (whether proposed by the trustees or the provider) are fair and properly describe and support the intended business relationship. While this review can be done at a high level for all shortlisted providers at the same time as the tenders are being evaluated, it is more usually conducted with the preferred provider after the evaluation is complete.

Prior to signing contracts, the preferred provider may require a 'due diligence exercise' to ensure that there are no hidden surprises. The provider will review the scheme documents and spend time with the current administration team, in order to understand the processes and interfaces in order to appreciate exactly what is involved in the contract. This may result in a revision to the proposed terms of the contract.

The formal signing of the contract completes the tendering process.

---

1 See www.pensions-pmi.org.uk/index.php?option=com_content&view=article&id=177&Item id=54.

Step 7: implementation The new TPA should supply a suitable transition team and the trustees need to ensure that appropriate resources are available on behalf of the scheme. The TPA should be experienced in planning the transition and usually lead on the project planning and implementation. However, there will be many activities that fall to the trustees or current administrator, so leadership from the trustee side is also key. The implementation programme can include the following:

- presentations to staff affected by the change and addressing TUPE issues;
- data cleansing;
- setting up/transitioning technology;
- setting up and testing calculations;
- ensuring scheme rules are up to date and understood by the new provider's staff;
- agreeing and developing communication material (including web and paper media);
- training both new and transferring staff to carry out the new processes;
- transferring work in progress smoothly and successfully;
- transferring paper and electronic member and scheme files completely and accurately;
- establishing electronic data interfaces between payrolls, HR and the new administrator;
- instructing internal/expert auditors to review the transition and to sign off that the transfer was completed successfully;
- establishing a new contract management capability within the trustee or sponsoring employer; and
- establishing internal controls and reporting protocols.

Effective processes

Efficient end-to-end processes and technology form the backbone of effective administration. Increasingly, processes are driven by technology and the administrator's job is to check that the technology is working correctly. The impact of automation on governance arrangements cannot be underestimated. The processes and underpinning systems must be able to deliver reporting information to reassure trustees that the administration is compliant and being delivered to agreed service standards.

Workflow and electronic document management (EDM)

Crucial to effective and efficient administration is the ability to monitor and control workflow. Many in-house and external administrators have implemented both workflow and EDM systems. These now form the foundation of best practice administration, whereby each case (a piece of work relating to a member) is captured on the system at inception and then tracked all the way through to completion, including any accounting and payment tasks.

Workflow systems enable complex processes to be defined as a series of tasks, some automated by the system and some requiring action by the administrator, member or perhaps an external party such as an insurance company. Logic can be included so that only tasks relevant to the member's circumstances are carried out. Tasks where the administrator has no direct control of progress (for example, awaiting a response from the remitting scheme during a transfer in) can also be included, with automated chasers after specific periods.

Workflow design is a key project. Some departments prefer relatively few tasks per case, allowing the administrators to use their professional expertise as much as possible. Others like to automate as much as possible, relegating much of the administration activity to clerical duties. The type of scheme can be a major influence on the best approach.

Cases can be initiated by members (for example, a request for a transfer quote), administrators (for example, members reaching normal retirement age) or other systems (for example, a leaving service notification from a HR system). Cases and tasks are created/progressed not only through the receipt of post, but also through receipt of emails and web forms or information transferred electronically from other systems such as payroll and HR. A competent system should be able to handle all of these with a high degree of automation.

All incoming and outgoing communications are captured in the EDM system. For instance, incoming post is scanned and allocated (indexed) to appropriate members. An item of post may represent the completion of a task in a case (for example, await return of completed form) or a brand new case (for example, receipt of a transfer-out request form). The act of indexing automatically prompts the administrators to complete that task, or creates a new case as appropriate.

All of these cases and tasks are held in what can be thought of as a giant in-tray for the department. This is often split between the administrators/teams using various criteria, for example, employing companies or alphabetic by member name.

Each case, and task within a case, will be allocated a priority and target date, enabling the system to sort the 'in-tray' so that the most urgent work is selected first. Senior administrators may have the ability to override priorities if appropriate.

As tasks within the cases become due, they need to be picked up by the administrators. There are many ways of organising this, reflecting the management style of the department. Team leaders may allocate tasks to their administrators. Administrators might be allowed to select tasks from their team 'in-tray'. Some systems are able to assign tasks automatically ('workload balancing'). Good systems also know the capabilities of each administrator and only allow those with sufficient expertise to process any task.

Outgoing correspondence produced by workflows is stored automatically in the member's electronic file as it is produced. Administrators are therefore able to see all correspondence without leaving their desks.

Reporting

A good workflow system contains a complete picture of where every open case has got to, how long each component task took, who did it and what is due to happen next. All of these facts are reportable from the system. Hence, workflow systems are essential tools for reporting performance and managing the case work in compliance with:

- disclosure regulations;
- service levels agreed with trustees; and
- internally defined performance targets (for example, as part of a TPA quality management system).

A key reason for reporting is to demonstrate performance and it will typically comprise regular administration reports for scheme managers and trustees, such as:

- membership statistics;
- case-work turnover for all significant types of case;
- service quality in comparison with agreed targets;
- complaints;
- cash flow and contributions monitoring;
- significant activities (bulk communications with members, benefit statements); and
- confirmation that no regulatory breaches have occurred.

Another key reason for reporting is to manage the case-work so that the required service levels are met, typically including:

- work turnaround per team and individual administrator;
- number of tasks outstanding by type and due date;
- number of tasks outstanding by team; and
- schedule of forthcoming retirements.

With a good workflow system, reporting should be completely automated and most workflow systems will provide a comprehensive suite of standard reports. Nevertheless, as with all computerised processing, reports need to be tested and checked for reasonableness. Reports are often issued on the trustees' behalf and therefore the administrator should be able to reassure the trustees about all aspects of their delegated authority, for example, through clear signed statements of compliance. Reports should not need manipulation once run off from the administration or workflow systems.

Data management, security and data audits

The quality of a scheme's data is more important now than ever before. For DC schemes it was ever thus; DC administration is more akin to banking than traditional DB scheme administration and timeliness, and accuracy of data processing is paramount.

For DB schemes, data quality is also becoming paramount, for a number of reasons:

- As scheme deficits feature ever higher on corporate balance sheets, the quality of data that underpins valuations is increasingly critical. For schemes related to sponsoring employers which are ultimately registered with the US Securities and Exchange Commission, there is likely to be a legal requirement to assess the data management processes.
- As more scheme trustees and employers consider a buy-out of liabilities, potential purchasers will need to have a very accurate view of scheme data – far more so than for a typical valuation.
- The Pension Protection Fund (PPF) insists on a very high integrity of data for any schemes entering its protection; trustees of such schemes often have to spend considerable time and effort overseeing the cleansing of data and this has delayed the entry of some schemes into the PPF.

TPR is focusing on pension administration and record keeping. TPR updated its regulatory guidance on record keeping in June 2010.[2] This guidance details an approach to the testing and measurement of member record data. In particular, the approach is to measure: common data (of relevance to all schemes), conditional data (dependent on scheme type, structure and system design) and numerical data (to check the overall reasonableness of the test results). This is an area in which TPR will continue to review progress and publish further updates.

TPR intends to supplement the education by strengthening the regulatory approach. They will take enforcement action where the evidence they gather indicates a breach of pensions legislation. Where record-keeping problems are so severe as to indicate a failure to maintain adequate internal controls, resulting in a failure to administer the scheme in accordance with the scheme rules and the boarder requirements of the law, these schemes will be prime candidates for investigation.

Data security is a critical risk, receiving increasing prominence. Trustees must carefully consider the controls in place within the administrator, whether outsourced or in house. In the United Kingdom, many administrators have their services reviewed in line with the Audit and Assurance Faculty (AAF) 01/06 accounting standard. Data security will need to be viewed from a number of perspectives:

- Business continuity: does the administrator have a business recovery plan? Is it regularly tested?

2 See www.thepensionsregulator.gov.uk/guidance/guidance-record-keeping.aspx#s1657.

- Physical security: is electronic data held on machines that are suitably protected from being stolen, flooded or otherwise? Is physical (paper, fiche) data similarly protected? Are plans in place to deal with recovery of data should systems fail?
- Electronic security: is the data securely held and able to resist unauthorised remote and local access? Is the database structure clear and not susceptible to corruption? Many TPAs are regularly audited by data security specialists and their reports can be inspected on request.
- New data: is data that comes from authorised sources (for instance, corporate HR, or members themselves via a website) adequately verified before being added to the core scheme database?
- Historic data: is this relied upon for benefit calculations, or simply held for completeness? Is its significance properly documented?

A number of firms now provide data audit services. These firms have a variety of backgrounds: some are TPAs; some are professional service firms, such as actuaries or accountants; and some are specialist data audit and management firms. Such firms are often able to provide independent data quality checks using specialist analysis software. Trustees may find this useful, particularly during transitions of data through a change in administration system, outsourcing for the first time or a switch from one administration firm to another.

Interfaces with HR, payroll and regulatory bodies

Corporate payroll and HR interface data

For most schemes, regular data feeds from HR and payroll systems are carried out electronically according to an agreed specification. Where many payrolls are involved in submitting data (for example, industry-wide schemes), increasing use is being made of secure websites for loading and validating data files before submission. It is important that there is good communication between those responsible for the donor and receiving systems to ensure any changes in either system do not impact on the interface. Data transfers should always be validated, checking that new data is consistent with existing data and is within agreed tolerances (data changes normally cover salary changes, changes in working hours, joiners, leavers, change in status and so on). An annual check is useful to ensure that active member data held on the pension administration system agrees with that held by the sponsoring employer.

Web interfaces for members

Many schemes offer members online services where they can obtain quotes, see benefit statements and change some basic data. Trustees need to satisfy themselves that the administration processes ensure that any data changes made by members are correct.

165

Data sent to and received from external agencies such as HM Revenue & Customs (HMRC)

Schemes increasingly exchange electronic data with government agencies and other organisations such as tracing firms when pensioner members cannot be contacted. Such data is often bulk loaded and must be subject to the same rigour as bulk data loads from any other source.

DC unit prices

The loading of DC unit prices has been the cause of significant errors within administration. Rectification of problems with DC units is difficult, expensive and highly visible to members, requiring the administration system to 'roll back' all transactions back to the date of the original error.

Straight through processing (STP)

STP has been developed by the IMSDG (Investment Management STP Development Group), collaboration between the TPA and investment communities, to improve administration of DC schemes. It involves administration and investment systems interacting directly so that member instructions (for example, to switch from one fund to another) are carried out without manual intervention, avoiding delays and difficulties arising from transcription errors. This is particularly useful in that unit prices are no longer manually loaded into the administration system, avoiding the problems described above.

This technology is highly desirable from efficiency and member service viewpoints. It uses a standard called ViaNova and operates over the secure SWIFT network used by the banking community. However, it is still in its infancy and relies upon interfaces developed for each system. Trustees should satisfy themselves that any STP processes they intend to use are solid and that appropriate assurances are obtained.

Administration performance

Determining service levels

Typically, the relationship between trustees and the pension administrator will be subject to a service level agreement (SLA). Part of this agreement should set out the scope of service and the service level requirement. The SLA is often only reviewed at contract renewal time, and although it might not be required, trustees should consider including a clause allowing service levels to be reviewed more frequently within the contract period.

If a trustee board has delegated administration matters to a committee, then it will be this committee that will set objectives and agree terms of the SLA; otherwise, the board should consider setting up a working group to set administration objectives and agree service levels.

Many service levels are still based on turnaround times, but other methods of service level assessment should be considered, for example, quality measures, amount of reworking required or member satisfaction questionnaires issued after certain processes.

Regular, independent assessment, or 'member satisfaction audits', might also be used to assess performance quality.

Service level agreement

Typically, a SLA will include: parties to the contract; definitions; contract length; fees; insurance arrangements; banking; penalties if performance falls below par in an outsourced arrangement; contract cessation requirements; intellectual property rights; contractual compliance; confidentiality; and so on. The appendices will contain other crucial scheme governance documentation, including a schedule of service requirements covering topics such as:

- maintenance and updating of records;
- calculation of member benefits;
- general processing, including bulk processing, queries, complaints and appeals and dealing with regulatory authorities;
- communications (including web service to members);
- accounts services;
- pensioner payroll services;
- performance standards and quality;
- management services to the sponsoring employer and trustee; and
- security.

Other appendices might include:

- compliance requirement and sample certificate;
- key individuals from both parties, including escalation and payment authorities;
- sample documents and other related communication material; and
- change of control procedures.

Performance measures

Regardless of the turnaround times specified, and whether service is in house or outsourced, there is no reason why any targeted benchmark should not be 100 per cent in all cases. In principle, service should always be timely, accurate and easily understood by any recipient. Most TPAs and a large number of in-house functions aim to complete a task within five to ten working days. The exception is member deaths, which must be concluded in short order. Generally, timescales tend only to be extended during cases where there is reliance on another party for essential information that was not supplied in

167

Table 10.2 Example of a complaints log		
Level	*Complaint description*	*Activity*
1	Complaint has arisen from the member having misinterpreted or misunderstood information provided about the scheme, or the member may have provided incorrect information.	Complaint dealt with successfully by administration team – likely to be unjustified.
2	Complaint has arisen from the administration team having made an error or omission, and on investigation found to be justified.	Complaint required intervention of the pensions manager as is justified owing to error or omission. Error is corrected and member is compensated for any loss occurred.
3	Complaint started off at level 1 or 2, has failed to be resolved satisfactorily or may be a new and material complaint that requires the immediate action of the pensions manager or trustees.	Complaint escalated to trustees, and would normally trigger the internal dispute procedure – monitored via that procedure.

time. In any case, administrators should be monitoring overall case time, even if another party is due to carry out the next task.

As alluded to above, using turnaround times for tasks (cases may comprise several tasks) as the only key performance indicator is unlikely to be effective. Trustees should be working with their administrators to agree objectives and then measure performance of the service that is designed to meet those objectives. It is unusual for performance assessment to comprise only quantitative or qualitative measures and a combination of both, tailored for the trustees' requirements, will be needed.

As part of performance monitoring, the administrator must maintain a comprehensive issues and complaints log with three clearly defined levels of complaint or issue – this can be used as a management tool to identify patterns of issues that might require further action.

An example of a complaints log is set out in Table 10.2.

Operational risk management

- *Identifying risk*: Operational risk is as important as other areas of risk, such as investment or covenant risk. While the financial impact might not be as great as in other areas (although unmitigated operational risk can have significant financial implications), the time, effort and cost of sorting out problems can be considerable.
- *Statutory requirement*: The Occupational Pension Schemes (Internal Controls) Regulations 2005, which modified the Pensions Act 2004, require

Table 10.3 Risks related to administration matters

Risk	Possible types of control
Risk that existing controls are not operating effectively	Periodic control reviews with changes made on a timely basis
Risk of fraud (misappropriation of assets and fraudulent financial reporting)	Segregation of duties; frequent reconciliation procedures for cash and investment balances
Compliance/regulatory risk (failure to comply with scheme rules and legislation)	Compliance audits; stewardship and compliance reports from third parties
Non-compliance or maladministration by administration team or third-party advisers, e.g. outsourced administrators (poor record-keeping)	Peer review of key controls by administration team; authorisation procedures; periodic meetings between trustees and provider (when required); service level agreement reviews; performance appraisal of providers; internal quality review procedures by third-party administrators (i.e. independent control reviews – 'assurance reports')
Computer system and database failures	System recovery plans; data back-up procedures; password controls

that trustees should be obliged to consider risk across the schemes for which they are responsible. It states: 'The trustees or managers of an occupational pension scheme must establish and operate internal controls which are adequate for the purpose of securing that the scheme is administered and managed:

- *in accordance with the scheme rules, and*
- *in accordance with the requirements of the law.'*

The code of practice issued in line with the regulations expects that trustees will carry out full risk assessment of their schemes: 'Before implementing an internal controls framework, we recommend that the trustees should determine the various functions and activities carried out in the running of the scheme and then identify the key risks associated with those functions and activities.'[3]

Amongst eight risks listed by the code, five are directly related to administration matters.[4] See Table 10.3.

Trustees must therefore be able to demonstrate that a risk review has been carried out, and the accompanying guidance to the code of practice is helpful.

3 Regulatory Code of Practice No. 9, Internal controls, para. 21.
4 Regulatory Code of Practice No. 9, Internal controls, para. 26.

Administration risks need to be assessed methodically, and an estimation of the combination of potential impact and likelihood of a risk occurring will lead to a risk score that will indicate the urgency and importance of any action required. Another consideration may be timescale, or how soon is the likelihood of a risk becoming reality?

Managing and mitigating operational risk

There are several actions that could be taken to manage a specific operational risk down to an acceptable level. These include:

- **prevention** through the use of counter measures;
- **reduction** of the likelihood of the risk;
- **transference** through passing the risk to a third party, perhaps by outsourcing or the use of insurance;
- **contingency** measures planned and organised to come into force as and when the risk occurs; and
- **acceptance** where trustees decide to go ahead and accept the risk (perhaps other measures are too expensive).

From a trustee governance perspective, administration or operational risk ought to be actively overseen from within the trustee committee that monitors administration. This in turn ought to be part of the scheme's overall risk-management framework, ensuring an integrated approach.

Effective administration teams and accountability

An effective administration team will:

- have the right resources – numbers and skills;
- be well organised;
- be provided with regular and appropriate training;
- have clarity of reporting lines;
- be effectively led and managed; and
- have the right skills, right numbers and continuously improve.

Staff calibre

Significant staff turnover is not uncommon in pension administration teams and this highlights the need for resilient processes as well as a clear induction process; high turnover may be an indication of ineffective management or retention difficulties and is frequently a factor in poor administration performance.

Numbers

There is no clear benchmark for the required number of administrators for any given scheme. The ratio of members to administrators will depend on many factors, not least the degree of automation, scheme complexity, number of employer locations and payrolls and service levels to be provided. Trustees need to satisfy themselves that there are enough staff to cope with day-to-day business, and to help deal with periods of high workload, such as during a large redundancy exercise.

Training

All pension administration staff should undergo regular professional development. This could comprise a combination of internal training programmes and external professional exams. Administrators should consider taking Pensions Management Institute (PMI) exams and junior administrators should be encouraged to study for the Qualification in Pension Administration (QPA) or an equivalent qualification.

Team organisation and management

Trustees should reassure themselves that team structures are stable and robust, capable of managing day-to-day business, yet flexible enough to deal with periods of higher workload.

Knowledge management and succession planning are both important. Well-run administration functions should be rewarding places to work. Many schemes have long-serving administrators who have built up a high degree of knowledge, particularly of scheme complexities. Often this knowledge is only realised when the administrators leave, or when in-house arrangements are outsourced.

Trustees should therefore ensure that knowledge is properly documented and shared. Also, the trustee risk-management audits should challenge succession plans and ability to transfer knowledge.

Culture and values

However good the resources (technology and people), processes and documentation of service levels, ultimately it is the attitude, culture and values demonstrated by the administration team that has the most impact on quality and effective administration.

Trustees need to ensure that their values are communicated and thoroughly embedded within their administration team. This is more difficult when pensions administration is outsourced, but there are mechanisms by which this can be approached.

Values and behaviours can be demonstrated, and assessed, through:

- member care processes;
- innovation;
- attitude to change and development;
- attitude to problem solving; and
- communication style.

Interaction between trustees and administration team

Too often the trustees take insufficient interest in the staff administering the scheme on their behalf. Examples of improving the interaction between trustees and administration teams include:

- trustees setting up a committee to focus on administration and performance and having a regular dialogue with the administration manager; and
- holding trustee board meetings at the administrator's premises from time to time.

Management of conflicts and transparency

In-house administration departments are unlikely to have many conflicts of interest, although individuals may have personal, business and career relationships that may have an impact on particular projects. Such conflicts should be reported and actively managed.

Trustees should ensure that their administration team keeps all information confidential. A third-party administrator may be part of a firm providing advice in other areas, or to other clients, and steps should be taken to manage any potential conflicts of interest.

Many trustees take advice when considering outsourcing for the first time, or looking to move administration from one provider to another. They should take care to ensure that such advisers have no commercial relationships with TPAs and are unbiased in their dealings with them.

Engaging stakeholders and clear accountability

The administration team has to meet the needs of the members, the sponsoring employer and the trustees. Unclear reporting lines often result in poor administration performance, greater cost and higher levels of member complaints.

Outsourced pensions administration requires robust contract/client relationship management. Trustees must ensure that reporting and escalation relationships are clear, and that there is no risk of actions not being carried out because the reporting line is blurred or even non-existent.

The service level agreement will need to be monitored carefully and arrangements should be put in place for the administrator to report against its requirements. The trustees must review administration performance reports regularly, and act quickly to deal with any areas of concern that arise from such reports.

To end the chapter where it began, trustees have a responsibility to ensure that pensions administration is managed and carried out effectively. They are ultimately accountable to the members to ensure that their benefits are administered within agreed service levels and in accordance with scheme rules and legislation.

11

Investment governance of defined benefit pension funds

ROGER URWIN

Introduction

In institutional funds generally and defined benefit pension funds specifically, investment 'governance' describes the system of decision-making and oversight that is used to invest the assets of a fund. The responsibility for this investment role lies with trustees or other types of fiduciaries who are faced with high-level investment decisions (where they will typically take full responsibility) and more detailed implementation actions (where delegating to others is more likely to be used and the fiduciaries' role becomes one of framing the delegations and monitoring the actions of the delegated agents).

Investment governance, therefore, employs skills, resources and processes with the purpose of creating value for institutional funds.

There is a distinction between the inherited structure of investment institutions – normally framed by statute, property rights and covenants – and the governance of those institutions – framed by the rules and processes that sustain their performance.

Previous published research has demonstrated that good governance is required for funds to be effective and perform well in the competitive and complex environment of institutional fund management. Some prior research references include:

- *Fortune and Folly*[1] written in 1992 by two anthropologists (O'Barr and Conley), who suggested that funds were not managed for financial efficiency, but more for convenience of relationships with outside managers and the avoidance of risks from these relationships.
- In *Pension Revolution: A Solution to the Pensions Crisis,*[2] Keith Ambachtsheer demonstrated a 'governance shortfall' (the return foregone due to internal governance and management problems) between good and bad governance of 100 to 200 basis points per annum in his database of funds.

---

1 W. O'Barr and J. Conley, *Fortune and Folly* (Homewood, Illinois: Business-One Irwin, 1992).
2 K. Ambachtsheer, *Pension Revolution: A Solution to the Pensions Crisis* (New Jersey: Wiley Finance, 2007).

- In 'Best-Practice Investment Management',[3] the governance attributes of the world's leading institutional funds are categorised in research drawing on ten case studies from different countries and different types of funds which demonstrates how funds with strong governance have achieved a competitive edge.

For many pension funds, the governance problem is one of orchestrating collective action in a timely and effective fashion given the rigidities imposed by inherited systems of control. Such control is exercised through democratic committees not designed specifically for efficient decision-making with regard to complex investment instruments. This is especially important in that pension funds must be adaptive and responsive to market environments that seem to move at increasing speed. The challenge of institutional governance could be summarised in two parts: to facilitate adaptation to functional imperatives without changes to organisational design in the short term; and to build greater fitness to meet functional imperatives in the longer term through adaptation of organisational (re)design.

Many pension funds struggle with their responsibilities whatever their jurisdiction and inherited institutional form. However, it is not self-evident which precise governance configurations work best. If the United Kingdom and other countries are to redesign inherited pension and retirement income institutions to cope with twenty-first-century issues like demographic ageing, the sustainability of plan sponsors and the increasing premium on (and visibility of) financial performance, issues of governance design must be addressed.

The remaining sections of this chapter cover:

- governance and the trustees' responsibilities;
- the concept of the risk budget;
- the governance budget; and
- governance best practice and innovations in governance.

Governance and the trustees' responsibilities

Trustees must carry out a number of investment functions to fulfil their role. Such functions are best considered as a cycle (see Figure 11.1). Governance is at the centre of this cycle as it impacts upon the way in which decisions are reached, implemented and reviewed.

The trustees' responsibilities in this cycle can be divided into four main areas:

- high-level policy;
- high-level strategy decisions;

---

3 G. L. Clark and R. Urwin, 'Best-Practice Investment Management: Lessons for Asset Owners', White Paper, October 2007.

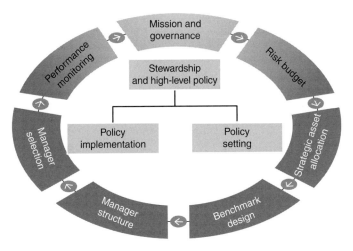

Figure 11.1 Trustees' investment functions

- implementing strategy; and
- monitoring responsibilities.

In designing governance and the allocation of responsibilities for the various activities, the trustees have four potential resources at their disposal:

- the trustee board itself;
- the investment committee where this is separate from the trustee board;
- executive and operational staffing – the 'executive function'; and
- outsourcing – external investment managers and other service providers.

For each stage in the cycle, good practice would involve making it clear who has responsibility for analysis and recommendations, who takes decisions and who implements those decisions.

In the United Kingdom, pension funds are required to maintain a formal statement of investment principles (SIP). It is normal practice for the following to be included in the SIP:

- *Investment decision-making process*: it should address issues such as who will set the investment strategy and what tools are used in setting it, who are the advisers involved and what the frequency of review will be.
- *Investment objective and strategy*: the current objectives and strategy should be included.
- *Implementation of the strategy*: included in this section should be the fund managers used and any agreement setting out their terms of reference and the manner in which the strategy is implemented.
- Policy on diversification, self-investment (where appropriate), the use of derivatives.

- Policy on social and environmental and ethical issues; and on ownership and corporate governance.

The Myners Principles are the accepted code of governance 'best practice' for UK defined benefit plans, but the use of the principles is voluntary in nature. Funds generally will report on their compliance with the principles and explain any areas of non-compliance. The six areas covered in the Myners Principles are:

- effective decision-making;
- clear objectives;
- risk and liabilities;
- performance assessment;
- responsible ownership; and
- transparency and reporting.

Risk budgeting

Decisions on how much risk to take in a fund and the deployment of that risk are critical to long-term value creation in a pension fund. Risk budgeting[4] provides a framework for guiding investment strategies consistent with the goals of the fund.

The risk budgeting approach can be summarised as:

- using fundamental asset class assumptions consistent with current market prices based on a market view of liabilities;
- building an efficient investment strategy out of all possible asset classes and strategies; and
- considering the achievement of both the trustees' and fund sponsor's goals.

The risk budget approach has gradually taken over as the dominant methodology for developing policy from its forerunner – asset liability modelling (ALM). Strictly, the ALM is part of the risk-budgeting approach being critical to the decisions that surround the amount of risk that a fund should take.

The models used in ALM work vary widely. Many are configured quite simply around an equilibrium structure in which returns and other stochastic variables are 'iid' (independent and identically distributed). But over time much more sophisticated versions may be used and arguably should be used that represent the more complex time series structures that govern the relationships between assets and liabilities in systems that are not in equilibrium, although may have tendencies to mean revert.

The global financial crisis has underlined the limitations of investment models generally. That said, the use of models is valuable provided the limits

4 See 'Risk Budgeting' in Watson Wyatt, *Remapping Our Investment World* (London: Towers Watson, October 2003).

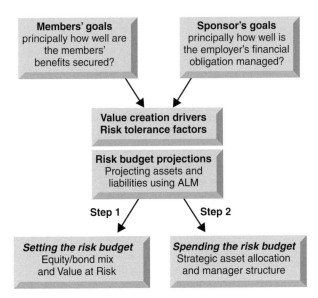

Figure 11.2 Summary of the risk-budgeting method

of its domain of applicability are understood. Further asset liability models in presenting longer-term outcomes appear to represent better the actual outcomes than the shorter-term models that are particularly vulnerable to regime changes and dual states.

The risk-budgeting method is summarised in Figure 11.2.

The risk budget analysis starts with specifying a fund-specific *liability proxy* to identify risk. The liability proxy is a portfolio that closely resembles the characteristics of the liabilities – which are cash payments to beneficiaries out into the future. As the goal of a pension fund is to meet these liabilities, the identified liability proxy portfolio can be thought of as the minimum risk portfolio. This would usually be a portfolio of high-quality bonds of appropriate term and inflation exposure to match closely the liabilities. Risk is then about departures from this portfolio, and is measured by the standard deviation of differences expected, or alternatively from a value-at-risk calculation.

The next step is to apply an asset model to the different strategies under consideration. We then compare the predicted risks and returns and determine our optimal strategy. Decisions then focus on where to deviate from this portfolio with a view to generating additional return and by how much.

This process starts with the overarching goal to maximise the investment return at an appropriate level of risk. The difficulty with this goal lies in the different definitions of risk that each stakeholder might use. All will be concerned with the benefit security, but whereas this will be the primary risk for members and consequently a key aspect for trustees, the company will also want to factor in the risks of not achieving attractive levels of contributions/ costs for the benefits paid.

The objective is to get both the trustees (representing the members' interests) and the company signed up to the *same* strategy. The key concept in this is signing them up to the same 'appropriate level of risk'.

A full perspective on how much risk might be appropriate requires a look at risk-tolerance factors related uniquely to each pension fund. Risk-tolerance factors are the specific characteristics of the fund that allow risk to be taken. As the health of a pension scheme's finances will always impact upon the operational efficiency of the sponsoring employer, this question must be assessed in the context of the company. There are three factors to be considered:

- *Covenant strength*: 'covenant' is defined as the willingness and ability of the sponsor to support the fund. A weak covenant would tend to argue in favour of a focus on the short term and a lower-risk approach, although issues of affordability of funding plans also arise.
- *Liability maturity*: some immature liability schemes will enjoy greater flexibility to sustain volatility of funding and/or contribution levels over time and can therefore exploit longer-term investment opportunities. In contrast, we would ordinarily expect very mature schemes to have a somewhat shorter-term focus and more limited appetite for risk.
- *Funding level*: the appropriate level of risk will be influenced by the funding level in a variety of ways on which it is difficult to generalise.

Setting the amount of risk to be taken requires a great deal of care by both parties – trustees and fund sponsor – and critically requires appropriate engagement between the two. The process should entail:

- joined-up decisions on current contributions and investment strategy; and
- decisions that encompass a plan of future funding and risk taking, often described as the 'journey plan'.

In advocating a partnership approach to strategy, we have to recognise that, when there is a weak funding position and potentially weak covenant, the trustee group have the key role.

When the fund is broadly in balance or in surplus, there can be a rough equilibrium of interests between the company and the members.

From time to time, however, this equilibrium of interests will be challenged. In times of deficit, what is good for the members may be against the company's interests and vice versa. Investment strategy under these conditions needs special care.

One critical aspect of this question is the extent to which the fund and its decision-takers can be viewed as competitively positioned to exploit risk. The investment challenge is difficult and fast changing and for appropriate returns to be captured certain competencies and disciplines will be necessary.

A relatively high hurdle is likely to be appropriate as the returns achieved must be sufficient for the risk taken. Given these points, the following are reasons why risk might be taken:

- investment risk can form part of a longer-term plan to repair a deficit or to build a margin to withstand future surprises;
- the higher returns possible from taking risk can reduce the sponsor's costs and will generally reduce accounting costs;
- investment risk and return can provide additional/increased benefits in a risk-sharing arrangement, like a cash balance plan or some hybrid plans; and
- companies are in the value creation business, so taking some risk may be seen as the natural position for the sponsoring employer.

This list provides a number of possible lines of support for taking some risk and most trustees and sponsors are likely to conclude that their mission is about risk-taking. The level of risk exposure and the type of risk exposure remain at issue. In particular, it must be remembered that to create real value after the cost of risk has been taken into account requires a margin of out-performance over low-risk strategies. This leads to the following three *value creation drivers* which, when present, suggest that risk can be productively employed for the benefit of both the members and sponsoring fund.

Risk-sharing over time

Risk-sharing is the first such factor. There are two important elements in this regard. The first is that there is some form of cross-generational risk sharing at work, i.e. different generations of both pension fund members and sponsor shareholders are prepared to accept some risk and are able to accept the consequences of 'taking the rough with the smooth'. Effective sharing of risk means that investment returns can be higher for the same level of risk. The second element is that to create value from risk over the long run, a degree of permanence will be required, allowing strategies to bear fruit and avoiding knee-jerk reactions. We might call this organisational staying power. It has to be acknowledged that this mind-set will be difficult to achieve in practice, particularly with the increasingly short-term pressures facing institutions and decision-takers.

Investment beliefs and long-term investment

This value creation driver concerns the 'investment beliefs' held, and the extent to which they can be used to make the case for pension funds as long-term investors competitively positioned to do better than short-term investors.

Pension fund boards and investment committees with well-developed and well-documented beliefs would tend to secure a competitive advantage over other investors.

Well-positioned governance

The quality of decision-taking is embedded in the governance of funds. Taking risk effectively requires governance resources to set strategy, and monitor and control progress. Governance resources can be mapped into a 'governance budget', which is comprised of the time devoted to investment matters, the investment skill of the individuals and the organisational effectiveness with which the time and skill are brought together. The investment world is dynamic and competitive and to secure a comparative advantage requires devoting more time (and/or resources) to investment, through raising the skill levels of the trustees or improving the organisational effectiveness. It is clear that any of these actions will probably require effort and additional cost, but the potential rewards in many instances will outweigh the cost.

Governance budget

The 'governance budget' framework helps the consideration of effective governance and the management of governance change. The 'governance budget' refers to the capacity to create value from effective actions in the chain of institution-defined tasks and functions. This concept is based on three principles:

- governance is a finite and conceptually measurable resource, and the size of this resource – the governance budget – is associated with expected performances and pay-offs;
- a certain size of governance budget is best matched with a certain investment style and strategy, consistent with other budgets that recognise limited resources and must be allocated skilfully; and
- there are ways to adapt the governance budget over time, with implications for likely investment performance and pay-offs.

Pension funds have three resources at their disposal to support them in making decisions: the time of the board and its agents, their expertise and their collective commitment – how productively the resources can be made to work collectively to a common cause. These three resources together constitute the governance budget, which directly influences the limits of what the fund can achieve.

The challenge to developing governance budget is significant in five areas.

Risk management

Decisions on how much risk to take in a fund and the management of that risk is critical to long-term value creation in a pension fund.

Taking risk effectively requires good governance to set strategy and monitor and control progress. Given that the investment world is dynamic and competitive, those governance resources need to be able to adapt to change to secure a competitive advantage.

Focus on an appropriate time horizon

The differences between short-term and long-term investing are significant.[5] Most institutional funds have a long-term investment mission. The governance challenge is generally to manage the long-term plan, but be resilient to the short-term pressures that build up from time to time.

Innovation capability

The concept of 'early mover advantage' in the corporate world is well known. In the context of investment markets, it relates to identifying and accessing successfully market and asset classes early in the cycle, ahead of the crowd.

Funds investing in newer, less popular asset classes, newer strategies or managers face many challenges. This places significant demands on governance, not least from the challenge of peer pressure.

Alignment with a clear mission

Institutional funds have difficulty with their mission. A particular complication for pension funds is their shared purpose. The role of a pension fund is to produce value propositions for both members and sponsor, but sometimes it will be difficult to satisfy both needs. A clear statement of goals is an important step to building alignment between the parties, so that the appropriate investment risk profile and strategy can be identified.

Best-practice funds tend to have not only a clear primary objective, but a number of defined secondary objectives which enable all parties to match operational goals with the mission.

Managing agents

In general, pension funds do not have the resources to manage all of their activities in house, and consequently employ agents in both advice and delegated roles. This exposes them to the risk that the agents' goals do not align with those of the pension fund.[6]

Governance is critical to monitor and control these misalignments, particularly with a large line-up of managers. Best-practice funds are experts in managing these agents and building good alignment.

Governance best practice and governance innovation

The governance best practice model referenced in this section is drawn from the paper 'Best-Practice Investment Management' referred to earlier, and

---

5 See Watson Wyatt, 'Long-Term vs Short-Term Investing' in *Changing Lanes* (London: Towers Watson, December 2004).
6 See Watson Wyatt, *Sales, Stewardship and Agency Issues* (London: Towers Watson, September 2007).

involved case studies on ten funds across the world that were cherry-picked for their exceptional reputation and strong, sustained performance. The ten comprise six pension funds, two endowments and two sovereign funds, located in North America (five funds), Europe (three funds) and Asia-Pacific (two funds). They are all large in terms of assets.

However, even these funds with exceptionally strong governance capabilities find it difficult to overcome certain constraints. The research shows that the most common constraints are inherited regulations and systems of control and the competing claims of multiple stakeholders. In addition, it shows that there is an unpreparedness in the industry to consider in-house resources as anything other than highly visible 'costs', whereas external spending on managers and transactions costs tend to be seen as 'performance benefits'. This has always seemed like an extreme case of tortured logic.

The central finding of the research was in isolating 12 best-practice factors as being indicative of future success in meeting institutional goals. Six of these are assessed as being within the reach of most institutional funds and are called *core attributes*: mission clarity; effective focusing of time; investment committee leadership; strong beliefs; risk budgeting framework; and fit-for-purpose manager line-up.

Six further global best-practice factors were isolated in the research and described as requiring significant resources, including an executive team, usually with a Chief Investment Officer (CIO). The research suggests that these *exceptional attributes* are not easy for most funds to achieve. They are as follows: highly competent investment executive; high-level board competencies; supportive compensation; real-time decision-making; exploit competitive advantage; and learning organisation.

In terms of structure, leading funds tend to split the key functions between a board, which governs, and an executive, which implements and manages. The board also appoints and supervises the CIO. In terms of people, the CIO will tend to have a very high degree of investment expertise, and be supported by strong researchers. Process-wise, leading funds are extremely skilled at maximising any sustainable comparative advantage that they have over competing funds, and tend to have impressively efficient decision-making structures.

The Clark/Urwin study identified 12 governance-related factors common amongst leading-edge funds. Six of these could be regarded as being core and within the reach of most funds.

A clear mission

As noted above, well-governed funds have a clearly defined set of goals, to which stakeholders are committed. The board and their staff understand what they are trying to achieve and how their strategy fits with these goals.

Effective focusing of time

In most circumstances, funds work within a constrained governance budget. Given these limitations, well-governed funds focus their resources so as to maximise the cost/benefit trade-off. Generally, less time could be spent on lower impact areas like monitoring managers, leaving more time to devote to asset allocation decisions where the impact is greater.

Leadership

Parallels can be drawn here with the corporate world. Strong leaders have the ability to create a positive culture, and organise the team into an effective and cohesive force. In the institutional funds setting, the key leader is generally the Investment Committee chairperson. In this role, the influence is considerable and best practice would be demonstrated by:

- dealing effectively with all stakeholders;
- addressing the institutional funds' challenges;
- creating a strong culture of responsibility and accountability for both board members and executive management; and
- mediating between the different styles of member on the committee.

Strong investment beliefs

Investment is essentially about making judgments and decisions in the present, typically with reference to the past, to cope with or exploit an uncertain future. Investors do this by using their underlying beliefs about how the investment world works. By beliefs, we mean certain axioms and conjectures about investment issues which can be drawn together into a coherent philosophy on investment. The quality of those underlying beliefs is a major determinant of success in investment.

Pension fund boards and investment committees with well-developed and well-documented beliefs would tend to secure a competitive advantage over other investors.

Risk budget framework

As noted above, decisions on how much risk to take in a fund and the management of that risk are critical to long-term value creation in a pension fund. Risk budgeting provides a framework for guiding investment strategies consistent with the goals of the fund. The funds in the Clark/Urwin study concentrated on management of both alpha and beta sources of return, and were clear on how to manage this mix consistent with their goals.

Manager line-up

To varying degrees, institutional funds will delegate portfolio management to external managers. Best governance practice suggests that this delegation should be covered by clear mandates which are aligned to the goals of the fund. The assessment of managers and products should be on a fit-for-purpose basis, focusing on investment efficiency after costs and considering alignment of the organisation to the fund's goals to achieve sustainability of performance.

Attention to the selection of managers is rarely matched in de-selection. In both cases, good processes are important. The industry has poor experience overall with hiring and firing managers.

There were six further governance factors identified in the Clark/Urwin study which are associated with the leading edge funds. These attributes differentiate the best-in-class funds from the rest.

Investment executive

There are strong arguments for separating governance into a governing function, which sets the framework, monitors and controls, and an executive function, which makes the decisions within the given framework and implements (or oversees implementation). Not only does this improve efficiency and accountability, but it also allows for the concentration of investment expertise within the executive function.

Research suggests that the majority of institutional investors fall short on this organisational design.

Best practice funds adopt a clear separation of governing and executive functions, with a strong culture of accountability. Furthermore, the executive function has a high level of investment competency, enabling the funds to implement and monitor complex investment arrangements.

Board selection and competence

These sound investment competencies are also observed at the board level of best practice funds. Board members ideally have strong numeric skills and the ability to think logically within a probability-based domain, such skills enabling the board to function effectively in its long horizon mission.

Supportive compensation

There are significant issues related to introducing effective compensation practices in institutional funds. Leading funds, however, have been addressing these issues at both the board and executive level, with some success in using compensation to attract appropriate skills and align actions to the goals of the fund.

Current practice among funds in general appears to result in significantly more being paid to external agents. There is scope to address this imbalance to some extent through greater use of internal resources, an approach which is becoming more widely adopted among the top funds.

Competitive advantage

As noted above, investment is a highly competitive activity. For funds to succeed, they need to be aware of their competitive advantages and disadvantages and adapt their decision-making accordingly.

Much of their competitive advantage will be built on a sound belief structure, but will also maximise their own particular areas of competence. It is equally important that funds should be aware of areas where they have no expertise and seek to limit their strategy accordingly.

Real-time decisions

Most funds are geared towards making decisions around a calendar-based series of meetings. Best practice funds, however, tend to have processes in place that enable decisions to be taken as and when necessary, based on investment market conditions. Making such a change from calendar to real-time focus involves more delegation and a clear definition of responsibilities.

Learning organisation

Best practice funds tend to be innovative. To be successful they need to operate in a culture that learns from experience. They also need to be willing to challenge conventional wisdom and deal enthusiastically with change.

Conclusion

The potential return advantage should be a strong motivator among pension funds to improve governance and then align it with investment strategy. However, it is clear that for many funds the 'governance gap' – insufficient governance for the complexity of investment strategy pursued – is widening due to lack of focus on these core attributes coinciding with the greater complexity of prime investment opportunities. Some investors will see merit in improving their governance arrangements by increasing the time they spend on investment issues, adding expertise and rethinking their organisational structures. However, it is unrealistic to suppose that all pension funds can better their arrangements to such an extent that they become high governance funds.

As such, governance is likely to become one of the bigger polarising factors among pension funds which would indeed be a welcome development.

There is strong evidence that investment success and value creation are driven by the quality of the decision-making involved. It follows that there should be a much stronger link between governance and investment strategy. The potential to destroy value through unsuitable investment strategies can be significantly reduced if pension funds are honest with themselves about their governance capabilities in the first instance. And if funds can start to treat governance as a variable and not a constraint, and make some moves in the direction of best practice, things could look altogether brighter for their considerable numbers of stakeholders. We are living through very challenging if not adverse investment conditions. Such times reinforce the idea that we should give more attention to the governance factor.

12

Hedging investment risk

DAWID KONOTEY-AHULU

Risk

The starting point for hedging investment risk in a pension scheme is the requirement to understand and manage the drivers of risk.

Firstly, it is crucial to understand those market factors that will exacerbate or reduce the deficit. Secondly, it is vital to manage the impact of those factors as far as possible.

A defined benefit pension scheme is behaviourally extremely complex. In the first place, the various *assets* held by the scheme have characteristics that can be very distinct: a building owned by the pension scheme behaves differently (in terms of fair value) from a portfolio of equities. A basket of index-linked gilts does not exhibit the same properties as a macro hedge fund or a holding of asset-backed securities. Even within asset classes, different individual assets have distinct characteristics.

In the same way, the liabilities are highly sensitive to some market changes (for example, long-term interest rates and inflation) and are insensitive to others (for example, equity prices). Then there are non-market factors (for example, longevity assumptions) which can have a profound impact on the present value of the liabilities and, therefore, the deficit or surplus of the scheme.

But that's not all. There is highly complex (and often poorly understood) correlated behaviour across the assets and liabilities. When interest rates rise, the value of a gilts portfolio will fall. When inflation rises, the value of an index-linked government bond will rise. When equities fall significantly in a short period, many other assets will do the same, but to a different degree. All of these effects can be mapped and analysed in what is known as a *covariance matrix*. But this rear view mirror cannot be relied upon accurately to predict the future, which often deviates from the past.

It is, therefore, particularly challenging to establish a risk-management framework. All pension schemes sign up to the principle that it is crucial to understand and manage 'risk', but beyond that there is plenty of differing opinion.

For example, how should a pension fund define 'risk'? In order to achieve badly needed returns on assets, one pension scheme's trustee board may regard as acceptable an investment that another set of trustees would consider imprudent. Because of the sheer number and complexity of influencing factors – funding level, strength of sponsor covenant, market conditions, level of governance and trustee expertise, extent of existing risk-management framework, etc. – it is simply impossible to prescribe a finite set of risk limits or acceptable asset classes. And yet, it has never been more vital to have a clear picture of risk and a carefully planned approach to risk management. The alternative – maintaining the status quo – is, for many pension schemes, simply not viable.

Now, risk – however defined – cannot be discerned in these markets in relying on any single set of risk parameters. There are several examples of pension schemes (and major financial institutions) that have suffered serious losses because they relied solely on a single risk measure that was, on its own, inadequate.

The risk analysis

As a first step in a basic risk analysis, it is helpful to use an asset/liability 'microscope' to determine the fund's sensitivity to micro-factors – which should be considered separately and then together. The results of this micro factor analysis usually contain a wealth of important information; magnification of the scheme's sensitivities highlights those exposures that are simply too large and have the potential to cause significant losses.

This first 'lens' or type of analysis is 'deterministic'. Deterministic analysis measures how the present value of the liabilities changes given a predetermined change in, say, the level of interest rates or inflation. Unlike 'stochastic analysis', which is run using forecasting simulations, deterministic analysis is run on a 'what if?' principle, i.e. it simply asks: 'What if this particular event, or change, occurs? How will it affect my scheme?'

Micro factor analysis highlights the impact on the liabilities of small changes in certain market factors on the aggregate liabilities, for example, small changes in interest rates, inflation or longevity assumptions. However, it is important to note that the behavioural characteristics of each *member class* within the plan are very different; it is necessary to apply the lens to separate component member classes – the *pensioners, actives* and *deferred members.* A tiny rise (or fall) in inflation, for instance, ripples through the future liability cash flows and changes their present value by a defined amount. A minute adjustment to the interest rate used to discount the cash flows due to tomorrow's pensioners measurably alters the present value of the liabilities.

Delta ladder

An important output of micro factor analysis, the delta ladder is based on deterministic analysis, and shows how the pension scheme's liabilities will

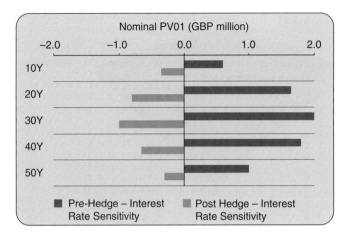

Figure 12.1 Delta ladder – example

change given a single basis point change in inflation and/or interest rates. The results can be broken out across different liability maturity 'buckets' to show how the change affects different sections of the scheme. For example, the delta ladder above shows the interest rate risk for liabilities in 10-, 20-, 30-, 40- and 50-year buckets.

The delta ladder highlights that the majority of the risk faced by a pension scheme is concentrated at the long end of the yield curve – the 30-, 40- and 50-year buckets. As a result, a change in the interest or inflation rate at the long end of the curve will have a significant impact on the present value of the scheme's liabilities. In current markets, this is very important as long-end interest rates continue to be highly volatile. This analysis is also instrumental in helping to outline the size and shape of a swap overlay that would be necessary to hedge fully the risk in each bucket.

Kite chart

The Kite chart (see Figure 12.2 below) is particularly helpful in micro factor analysis to illustrate how changes in the discount rate and inflation impact the present value of a scheme's liabilities; it demonstrates what happens to those liabilities when a portfolio is not hedged.

This highlights the *double negative convexity* of interest rates and inflation, and means that the liabilities will increase twice as fast for a given decrease in interest rates or increase in inflation as they will decrease in the event that interest rates increase, or as inflation decreases by that same given amount.

The second Kite chart (Figure 12.3) shows that a properly hedged portfolio is immunised from changes to both interest rates and inflation. This is an extremely important concept for trustees and sponsor, because it allows a pension scheme to reduce drastically exposure to two of the biggest risks it faces.

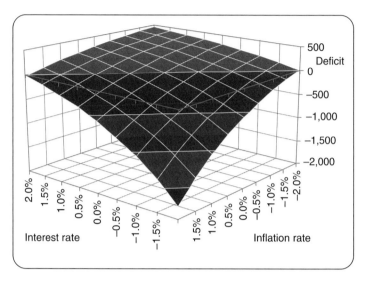

Figure 12.2 Deterministic liability rate analysis (un-hedged)

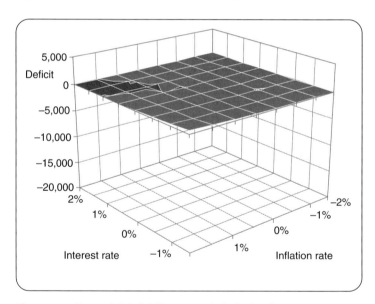

Figure 12.3 Deterministic liability rate analysis (hedged)

Liability profile

As the micro factor analysis explanation showed (see Kite charts, Figures 12.2 and 12.3), even small changes in inflation can have a significant impact on the funding level of an unhedged pension scheme. The liability profile

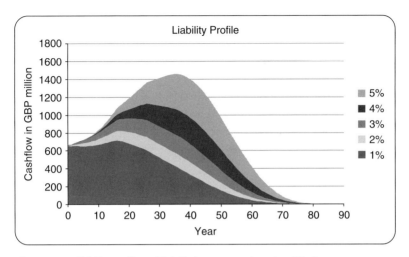

Figure 12.4 Liability profiles with inflation expectations (£ million)

(Figure 12.4) is an important output of any asset liability analysis, as it shows how a pension scheme's liabilities would be affected by incremental 1 per cent increases or decreases in inflation expectations.

It can be seen from the markedly different future cash-flow projections that relatively small, but prolonged, increases in inflation can result in significantly different liability obligations. This amply illustrates the need to manage inflation-linked liabilities.

All of this deterministic, micro factor analysis provides information on what the effect would be if an event *were to happen*. It does not, however, provide any information about the likelihood of those events happening, or the expectation of loss due to market movements. An important, complementary, second risk measure is Value-at-Risk or 'VaR'.

VaR provides a single minimum amount (the value) which the scheme might expect to lose (at risk), say, one year from now for a given confidence level. So, if the scheme's liabilities are £1 billion, its assets are £800 million and its one-year 95 per cent VaR is £300 million, then, simply, VaR ascribes a 5 per cent risk to the deficit increasing from £200 million today to £500 million or greater in a year's time.

Crucially, the VaR calculation relies on estimates of future volatility and correlation, together with an assumed probability distribution. Often, these are derived from historical information, and sometimes that historical data inaccurately forecasts the future. VaR also does not provide accurate information on how significant the 'or greater' loss may ultimately turn out to be, and a common error in relation to the use of VaR is to equate the VaR amount with a *maximum* (rather than a minimum) likely loss.

191

There are, consequently, many detractors of VaR, the most vocal of whom is perhaps Nassim Taleb. In his often quoted book, *Black Swan: The Impact of the Highly Improbable*, Taleb vehemently argues that users of VaR are typically lulled into a false and sometimes fatal sense of security about the future, since, he says, events perceived by a VaR model as impossible or extremely unlikely (black swans) are actually the main sources of risk.[1]

Taleb has a point in his criticism of VaR, but there is another perspective. In an article for the *New York Times*,[2] business columnist Joe Nocera interviewed several risk managers and quotes one:

> One risk-model critic, Richard Bookstaber, a hedge-fund risk manager and author of 'A Demon of Our Own Design,' ranted about VaR for a half-hour over dinner one night. Then he finally said, 'If you put a gun to my head and asked me what my firm's risk was, I would use VaR.' VaR may have been a flawed number, but it was the best number anyone had come up with.[3]

And that's the point. For all of its flaws, VaR provides useful additional information about the risk profile. In addition, VaR itself has several sub-lenses and risk 'filters' which help to build a clearer picture of where the scheme may find itself in the future. For example, whilst VaR only tells us the minimum loss we can expect, 'conditional VaR' goes one step beyond basic VaR and provides an *average expected loss* should the 'tail event' actually occur. This goes some way towards addressing Taleb's reasonable point that it is those 'tail events' – the black swans – that can really matter.

It is important for both trustee and sponsor to gain an understanding of the *probability* of certain events occurring in the future which may have an adverse (or beneficial) impact on the pension scheme. For example, if equity markets move significantly, how likely are interest rates, inflation or credit markets to follow suit? One can analyse the past and, in so doing, attempt to predict the future.

The first step in a VaR analysis is the calibration of the risk model. VaR is a powerful statistical measure of risk that can be shaped and adapted to produce different views of a scheme's risk. In its most basic form, VaR estimates the minimum loss that a portfolio may experience to a corresponding confidence level, but it can also be calculated using different methodologies, different time horizons and decay factors in order to generate a variance/co-variance matrix that will best suit the analysis needed for a particular scheme.

VaR models come in many shapes and sizes, and a brief description of different types of simulations is given below:

---

1 N. N. Taleb, *The Black Swan: The Impact of the Highly Improbable* (London: Random House, 2007).
2 2 January 2009.
3 "Risk Management" (2 January 2009), www.nytimes.com/2009/01/04/magazine/04risk-t.html?_r=1&pagewanted=1.

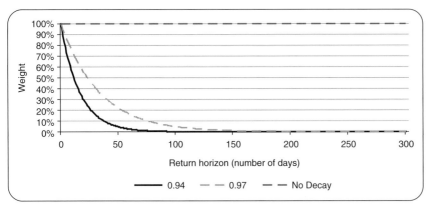

Figure 12.5 Decay factor

- *Parametric simulation*: estimates VaR directly from the *standard deviation* of the portfolio returns.
- *Historical simulation*: estimates VaR by using actual historical rates of return to revalue the entire portfolio for several changes in market rates (i.e. each trial) according to user-specified start and end dates.
- *Monte Carlo simulation*: estimates VaR by simulating random scenarios to revalue all positions in the portfolio for each trial.

One of the first factors a pension scheme should consider when deciding on the calibration of the VaR model is the confidence level, which should depend wholly on the needs and preferences of the pension scheme. For example, a 99.5 per cent confidence level (commonly used by banks and insurance companies) indicates that there is a 1 in 200 probability of a given loss in a one-year period. A popular metric among pension schemes is a 95 per cent confidence level, meaning there is a 1 in 20 probability of a given loss in a one-year period. In terms of time horizons, depending on the number of days, weeks and years of data used, different variance/co-variance matrices result. Where the data is available, it is prudent to use at least two years and, if possible, five years of historic data.

A decay factor is another important ingredient in the modelling of VaR. This is used to apply importance weightings by time to the data in order to generate the variance/co-variance matrix; the pension scheme can determine what weightings to apply. A decay factor of 1 means that all data analysed carries an equal weighting. A 'return horizon' indicates the time period over which data is captured and compared, and can be a day, a week, a quarter or otherwise specified by the pension scheme. For example, a decay factor of 0.94 with a return horizon of a week (five days) will apply a 100 per cent weighting to the most recent data set, a 94 per cent weighting to the second data set (the preceding five days) and so on (see Figure 12.5).

As indicated by the graph, a lower decay factor allows a scheme to place a greater emphasis on more recent data.

Asset and liability breakdown report

When a VaR analysis is completed, the output can often take the form of an asset and liability breakdown report. Firstly, this report shows the VaR and duration of the scheme's assets by asset class (equity, bonds, cash, property and alternative assets), making visible which assets are generating the greatest proportion of risk in the portfolio.

Secondly, this report shows the VaR and duration of the scheme's liabilities, and can be tailored to fit the particular scheme's needs. For example, the liability cash flows can be subdivided into buckets of ten-year periods, or can be broken out by actives, deferred and pensioners and/or by nominal-, RPI- and LPI-type liabilities. The purpose of this report is to display clearly where exactly the principal risk sits in the scheme; for example, it will reveal if the majority of the risk in a scheme is stemming from the 40-year 'bucket' or that, for example, pensioners comprise 17 per cent of a scheme but account for less than 7 per cent of the risk (see Table 12.1, which breaks down the VaR stemming from each component of the scheme's assets and liabilities).

Deficit risk analysis (assets/liabilities)

VaR can take more forms than just a minimum amount that a pension scheme might lose over a given time horizon. A comprehensive VaR risk analysis will analyse the scheme's entire ALM position, and will also show the different forms of VaR (see Table 12.2). Incremental VaR, for example, measures the impact of minute changes in each of the positions within the portfolio on the total portfolio VaR. In the same vein, marginal VaR is a measure of how the overall risk in the portfolio would change if a position or set of positions were to be removed from the portfolio and replaced with cash. Again, this gives the pension scheme an idea of how certain activities would change and affect the overall risk of their scheme. And in order to target that long-held criticism of VaR – that it tells the scheme nothing about the 'expected loss' if the worst were to happen – conditional VaR can be measured. Conditional VaR is a measure of the expected *maximum* loss on a portfolio, within a specific confidence level.

Table 12.2 is an example of an asset liability breakdown report displaying the different types of VaR within a pension scheme's portfolio; the key benefit of a robust risk report like this one is that it acts as a common framework for trustees and sponsor to work together in establishing and implementing a risk budget.

Risk attribution

Overall, VaR is a useful number that seeks to represent the total value 'at risk' within the portfolio as a whole. The vital next step is to break that figure down

Table 12.1 Sample asset and liability breakdown report (analysis of VaR stemming from each area of the scheme's assets and liabilities)

	Present value	Modified duration	VaR 95%
Surplus	419,574,409	–13	339,677,216
Assets	2,836,123,289	8	129,325,254
Bond	1,956,925,069	9	120,979,020
Conventional gilts	657,980,603	8	32,845,172
iBoxx sterling gilts	476,468,713	9	21,936,348
Index-linked gilts	822,475,754	25	68,405,657
Cash	28,361,233	0	0
Cash – no risk	28,361,233	0	0
Equity	567,224,658	0	74,175,163
FTSE All share	394,221,137	0	58,812,594
Overseas equity	173,003,521	0	20,569,507
Property	283,612,329	0	12,808,006
UK property	283,612,329	0	12,808,006
Liabilities	**–2,416,548,880**	**–23**	**431,806,507**
Actives	–297,554,020	–29	66,565,390
Nominal	–93,313,582	–27	18,474,469
RPI	–204,240,438	–30	50,623,134
Deferreds	–1,446,293,714	–27	312,429,497
Nominal	–274,733,617	–26	50,657,227
RPI	–1,171,560,097	–28	267,876,466
Pensioners	–672,701,146	–11	47,877,799
Nominal	–488,754,009	–9	30,972,282
RPI	–183,947,137	–14	19,648,246

to understand the various roots of that aggregate risk number. A risk attribution chart is a vital output of a thorough risk analysis, and shows how the scheme's various assets and liabilities contribute to the overall VaR, i.e. where the risk is stemming from. Figure 12.6 reveals that the scheme's total VaR is less than the sum of the individual VaRs, which is a beneficial consequence of portfolio diversification.

Once a trustee board has considered its scheme's *sensitivity* to particular events (i.e. micro factor analysis has been completed) and the VaR or aggregate value of risk in the scheme has been calculated and analysed in terms of its origin, a clear picture of the scheme's overall risk will begin to appear. But

Table 12.2 Sample asset and liability breakdown report (different types of VaR within a pension scheme's portfolio)

	Incremental VaR	Marginal VaR	Conditional VaR	Worst case	Best case
Gap	100.0%	339,677,216	439,729,784	689,119,310	−443,324,020
Assets	−26.1%	−92,129,291	154,292,563	205,540,573	−313,465,916
Bond	−38.5%	−112,078,576	149,617,449	261,681,842	−312,374,173
Conventional gilts	−10.1%	−28,006,241	41,798,075	73,349,252	−91,218,478
iBoxx sterling gilts	−5.5%	−16,503,095	27,730,337	45,591,187	−52,585,353
Index linked gilts	−22.9%	−63,935,975	85,535,744	142,741,404	−168,570,342
Cash	0.0%	0	0	0	0
Cash – no risk	0.0%	0	0	0	0
Equity	11.9%	16,566,833	95,932,130	136,301,056	−231,044,779
FTSE All share	8.6%	19,874,726	74,094,839	109,352,489	−178,049,933
Overseas equity	3.3%	7,431,181	26,700,620	41,160,108	−63,360,886
Property	0.4%	−52,587	15,275,761	27,158,637	−26,873,855
UK property	0.4%	−52,587	15,275,761	27,158,637	−26,873,855
Liabilities	**126.1%**	**210,351,963**	**556,627,331**	**893,112,577**	**−622,402,662**
Actives	20.0%	66,483,132	88,089,595	140,519,458	−94,201,310
Nominal	5.4%	15,268,199	23,353,074	43,327,774	−28,393,515
RPI	14.6%	47,581,650	66,416,111	101,245,279	−65,807,794
Deferreds	92.6%	248,454,986	411,145,424	640,317,693	−437,710,689
Nominal	14.8%	49,002,537	64,569,732	120,029,616	−81,004,670
RPI	77.8%	233,822,252	351,934,343	533,827,350	−356,706,018
Pensioners	13.5%	45,837,671	62,004,332	112,275,426	−90,490,664
Nominal	7.9%	27,676,080	38,534,968	71,252,724	−57,318,734
RPI	5.6%	18,932,845	25,554,244	41,022,702	−33,171,929

one more perspective from which to regard the scheme's risks can be used to clarify that picture further: a kaleidoscope of large-scale market moves.

Stress testing is a measure of how well equipped (or not) a scheme is to withstand sudden and severe jolts or sustained market dislocations. A number

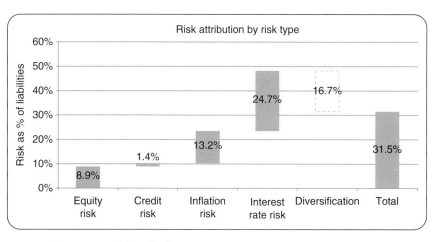

Figure 12.6 Risk attribution report

of simulated bleak and dismal market events are used in this type of analysis, which is designed to give trustee boards an idea of how their scheme would react in extreme market conditions.

Financial regulators have always advocated the importance of stress testing, but one of the lessons from the current global crisis is that the tests were insufficiently severe. Trustees can and should simulate their own bespoke kaleidoscope of rising inflation, falling interest rates, plunging equities, falling property and weakening credit – in other words, a brutally tough obstacle course to test the real-time robustness of the scheme and its current investment strategy.

Trustees could find out from these kinds of tests, for example, how the portfolio would perform if the yield curve were to move down by 100 basis points, or what would happen if the yield curve were to twist or kink. In addition, one can add the scenario of extreme volatility in the equity markets. For unusual but more realistic scenarios, stress tests can be run based on historic market events; a portfolio can be put to the test, for example, in the 9/11 environment in 2001, Black Monday (1987), the Russian Crisis (1998) or the 2008 Lehman collapse. It is possible to analyse how capital markets reacted in those real events, and apply those behaviours and results to the analysis of the assets and liabilities of the scheme.

A chart such as the one in Figure 12.7 below is the output of a stress test; it shows the effects of the events on the portfolio and, for illustration, what the effect would be if the scheme were hedged.

LDI – managing risk

The introduction of tighter regulatory and accounting approaches to measuring and reporting defined benefit pension liabilities resulted in highly volatile

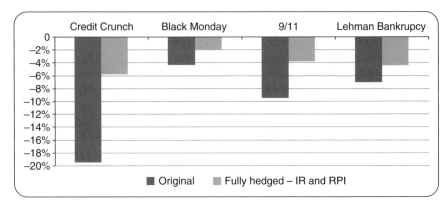

Figure 12.7 Portfolio stress test

pension scheme deficits as, broadly, assets have fallen and liabilities have risen over the last ten years. The risk lenses described above help to categorise and measure the various risks, but, ultimately, defined benefit pension schemes require a means of controlling and managing risk.

The wide spectrum of instruments and techniques used to contain or *hedge* risk is now known universally as 'Liability Driven Investing' or 'LDI'. The essence of LDI is the recognition that asset performance must be measured with reference to the liabilities. In other words, the key question is no longer whether the assets have risen or fallen per se, but rather whether they have risen or fallen relative to the liabilities. Historically, the main determinant of positive performance would have been, for example, the fact that the benchmark equity index fell 10 per cent and the plan's equities fell 9 per cent over the same time period. That is no longer the case. An LDI approach is far more concerned with how the scheme's assets, separately and together, have performed relative to the discounted (or mark-to-market) value of the liabilities.

'Managing the liabilities' is key to the process of LDI. This is because, as we saw earlier, the discounted value of the liabilities can change quickly and significantly with certain market movements such as interest rates and inflation expectations. In fact, in the last ten years, a large part of the increase in pension scheme deficits has been attributable to rising liabilities without an offsetting rise in assets.

Once the liabilities are recognised as a key source of the volatility in pension funding, it becomes obvious that the liabilities need to be 'matched', i.e. they need to be arranged in such a way that as the liabilities rise, the assets rise in lock step. An LDI strategy properly implemented will ensure that if the liabilities rise by £50 million, there will be an element of the assets that will do the same.

Most LDI strategies utilise conventional, long-dated instruments to neutralise or hedge the liabilities. I use the term 'conventional' because other industries have successfully used some of these instruments for the past 20 years or more.

As we saw in the sections above, defined benefit pension scheme liabilities are highly sensitive to changes in interest rates. The reason for this is, primarily, that they are very long dated. It is not uncommon for a pension scheme to have contractual liabilities payable up to 60 years from now. Statistically, there is a chance that an active member currently aged 18, for example, will marry a 25 year old in 50 years' time and then die. That spouse might be entitled to a defined pension benefit for many years after that. Secondly, the scheme's liabilities tend to be 'zero coupon' in nature. This means that the 'weight' of the scheme's liabilities tend to be cash flows payable far in the future.

The result is that most defined benefit pension schemes in effect have large, long-dated, zero-coupon liabilities, the present (or fair market) value of which is highly sensitive to movements in long-term interest rates. For example, a typical pension scheme with, say, £500 million of liabilities today probably has an interest rate sensitivity of more than £1 million per basis point. That is to say, if the yield curve shifts down one basis point, the liabilities will increase by £1 million – all other factors remaining constant. To put it another way, they have very high duration. For an illustration of the impact of high duration, consider the following example. On 18 September 2003, shortly before the first LDI transaction was implemented, the long end of the Sterling yield curve opened at 4.99 per cent. By close of business on the same day, it had fallen to 4.825 per cent. That 16.5 basis point move increased the fair market value of the liabilities of our (£1 billion) sample pension scheme by 16.5 x £1 million, i.e. £16.5 million.

Almost certainly, few participants were focusing on that particular market factor. In all probability, most were watching FTSE – which opened at 4,260 and closed down at 4,238 that day, providing no relief.

Long-dated, zero-coupon liabilities are also very 'negatively convex'. This is a particularly unfortunate property and it is one of the principal reasons why pension schemes have discovered that their deficits have not improved despite a moderately decent recovery in the equity markets. By way of explanation, it helps to think of interest rate risk as comprising two additive properties – duration and convexity. Duration risk is directional – if interest rates rise, the liabilities fall linearly. If interest rates fall, the liabilities rise linearly.

Negative convexity does not care about the direction of the interest rate movement. It has an additive effect that becomes increasingly pronounced the further the interest rate moves, irrespective of the direction of that movement. So, as interest rates rise, the beneficial effect upon the size of the liabilities gets smaller and smaller. And as interest rates fall, the adverse effect upon the size of the liabilities gets greater and greater.

When a pension scheme is thinking about hedging its liability risk, it is vital that it undergoes rigorous asset/liability analysis which breaks down the

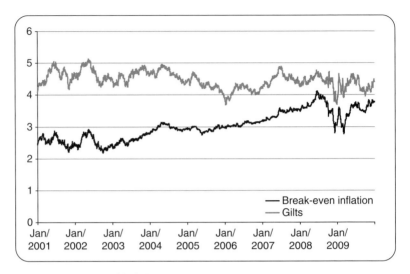

Figure 12.8 Rates and inflation – 2001–10

liabilities into their basic risk components. In order to do so, it is essential to model the pension scheme's accrued liabilities in detail and then to stress test them extensively. The results are often surprisingly counter-intuitive. For example, it is not immediately obvious that liabilities due to middle-aged, active members (40 to 49 years old) are often much more sensitive to adverse market movements than those due to pensioners aged 60 and over.

A rigorous and comprehensive ALM exercise will not only serve to highlight pockets of serious risk (see, for example, the risk attribution chart, Figure 12.6), but should suggest appropriate hedging strategies to mitigate that risk.

Here are some basic, but nonetheless key, questions that will illustrate the real level of familiarity with a scheme's assets and liabilities:

- If the yield curve moves by 0.01 per cent, how will this affect the total scheme liabilities, all other factors remaining constant?
- If the yield curve moves by 1 per cent, the liabilities will not move by 100 times the answer to the point above, since they are negatively convex. How much will they move?
- To the nearest £1 million, how much will the liabilities move, if long-term inflation expectations rise or fall by 1 per cent?
- Which class of scheme member (active, deferred or pensioner) and which age group is currently most sensitive to adverse movements in interest rates and inflation expectations, and by how much?
- Does the scheme's current asset allocation mitigate the risks outlined above, and if so by how much?

- Given a 50bp fall in interest rates and an accompanying 50bp rise in inflation expectations over the next eighteen months, roughly how much will the scheme's surplus/deficit change?

It is the answers to these questions that will begin to reveal just how much risk the pension scheme is running, and will allow an experienced adviser to determine the extent of the required LDI hedge.

Before we come to the actual process of implementing LDI, it would be useful to set out some background. LDI developed out of awareness that pension schemes needed to match their liabilities with long-dated, inflation-linked assets. In July 2001, the Boots pension scheme converted all of its equity and short-term bond holdings into highly rated (AAA), long-dated sterling bonds. The bond portfolio had an average maturity of 30 years and a 25 per cent exposure to inflation, attempting to match the underlying scheme liabilities.

The strategy was partly successful and, for its time, represented a credible attempt to match assets to liabilities. In summary, it matched the scheme's long, inflation-linked liabilities with very long, somewhat inflation-linked bond coupons and, to that extent, it succeeded. But there was one significant problem with the Boots approach. It forced the pension scheme to sell its equities and buy the bonds. And in the end, it was simply unable to buy sufficient physical assets to match the liabilities properly. Add to that the difficulty of sourcing assets of high credit quality, and the task became impossible. In 2006, Boots Pension Scheme reported a £56 million deficit despite having received a contribution from the company of £85 million.

Pension schemes actually needed something different. They needed, firstly, to match accurately the liabilities' sensitivities to interest rates and inflation and, secondly, crucially, to allow the scheme simultaneously to invest in 'growth assets'.

By late 2003, it had become obvious that volatile and burgeoning liabilities were an increasing threat to the long-term viability of pension schemes. In December 2003, Friends Provident Pension Scheme transacted a long-dated hedge with an investment bank. The pension scheme had liabilities at that time of around £600 million and, in recognition of the scheme's significant exposure to interest rates and inflation, it hedged those risks in their entirety.

As an observation, it should be noted that the hedging exercise arose principally out of sound risk management principles. It was clear to the trustees that *if* (and it was a 'big if') interest rates fell and/or inflation expectations rose, then the liabilities would soar. At the time, it was far from obvious that these market moves would in fact happen. The vast majority of informed opinion said otherwise. Interest rates were already very low and inflation was not considered (at the time) to be at risk of rising. The collective body of opinion was that the greatest threat to pension schemes was from the equity allocation. Given that the markets were still in a fragile recovery after the trauma

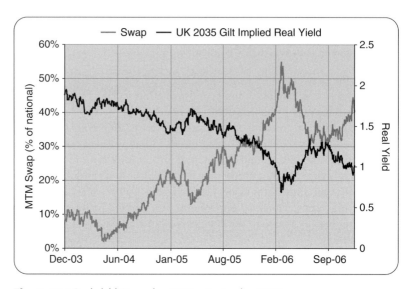

Figure 12.9 Real yield December 2003 – September 2006

of 9/11 and the Enron, WorldCom gigantic financial disasters, this view was understandable.

In the event, interest rates did fall and inflation did rise. Every pension scheme experienced major increases in its liability valuations and none (not even the Boots Pension Scheme) was properly matched. The assets simply could not keep pace with the inexorable rise of the liabilities. None, that is, except the Friends Provident Pensions Scheme, which found that its hedge worked. As its liabilities rose, so did its hedge.

Since the Friends Provident transaction in December 2003, LDI has become firmly ensconced in the lexicon of pensions risk management.

The bedrock of LDI is the interest rate swap, the inflation swap, and the gilt market. These instruments, properly structured, will rise and fall with the value of the liabilities. However, there is a degree of complexity associated with swaps instruments and it is important to understand the framework within which they work.

All swaps are executed under an umbrella agreement called an ISDA Master Agreement. This has a set of detailed generic terms that govern swaps transactions. In addition, there is a schedule, which modifies and clarifies specific provisions for the particular swap counterparties. For example, this may include spelling out the conditions under which either party may terminate the swap(s). There is also a swap confirmation. This details the precise terms of the swap itself – its start and end date, the coupon, the way in which inflation will be calculated, the dates on which any coupons will be paid and so on.

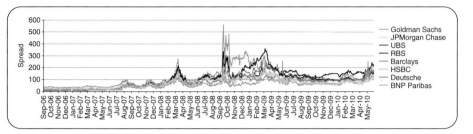

Figure 12.10 Credit default swaps through the credit crunch

In addition to the ISDA, there is a Credit Support Annex (CSA), which sets out the framework within which collateral will be posted between the parties.

Collateral works in the following way. Suppose two parties (Party A and Party B) enter into a swap transaction. Interest rates fall and, from the perspective of Party A, the value of the swap rises to, say, £10 million. In effect, it will cost Party A £10 million to replace the swap in the event that Party B becomes insolvent (per Lehmans).

In order to protect Party A, Party B posts (or transfers) £10 million of eligible collateral to Party A. In the event that Party B does become insolvent, Party A is able to realise the £10 million and pay the replacement cost of the swap in the market. This process is repeated daily (or weekly) and collateral passes in both directions depending upon the value of the swap at that point in time.

In the event that the swap subsequently swings in value to the benefit of Party B, the roles are reversed and Party A now makes collateral payments to Party B instead. This process continues throughout the life of the swap.

Collateral does not always take the form of cash. More often, collateral takes the form of highly rated bonds such as gilts or investment grade credit. The lower the quality of the collateral itself, the more the party has to post in order to cover its obligation. For example, a bank may post £10.5 million of corporate bonds in order to cover a £10 million swap value. This difference is known as the 'haircut' and its precise terms are set out in the CSA.

A swap is executed between the pension scheme and a counterparty, typically an investment bank. The creditworthiness of that investment bank is a key concern to its counterparties as this will affect its ability to make payments under the swap and the likelihood that it may find itself in difficulties in the event of a financial crisis. The posting of collateral goes some way towards alleviating these concerns, but it is still extremely important to transact swaps (which can be very long dated) with highly creditworthy financial institutions.

At times of extreme pressure in the financial system, the markets express concern through the pricing of credit protection on various institutions and these levels can indicate acute stress – see Figure 12.10.

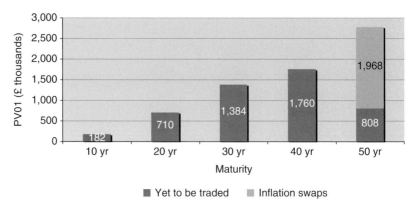

Figure 12.11 Inflation risk hedged

It is imperative that the pension scheme is fully aware of the value of its swaps portfolio and this information will typically be provided by its custodian. The custodian is a large financial institution which collates and manages assets and derivatives for its clients, making swap payments on behalf of its clients. Custodians include JP Morgan, Bank of New York Mellon and State Street Global Advisors.

As we have seen, a basic part of pension risk management is the control of interest rate and inflation risk. However, timing and tactics are extremely important when it comes to the actual process of reducing (hedging) these risks.

Pension schemes often struggle to decide on the appropriate framework in which to implement a large hedging programme, not least because it is (rightly) emphasised by asset managers, banks and investment consultants that secrecy and discretion is paramount. Even a hint of impending hedging activity can result in the market moving sharply against the pension scheme.

One point worth making at this point is that the hedging process can be broken down into components. Two basic segments are 'risk type' (inflation and interest rates) and 'time bucket'.

For example, it makes sense to break the aggregated risk into *two* core types: interest rates and inflation. Next, in respect of each type, the pension scheme should allocate risk across the ten-year bucket, the 20-year bucket, the 30-year bucket and so on out to 50 years. This is the way in which the market trades risk and it is very helpful to approach the hedging process using the same template. The pension scheme ends up with ten separate components (five for interest rates and five for inflation). Each segment is hedged as opportunities present themselves. The graph in Figure 12.11 is a snapshot of the inflation risk hedged as one pension scheme took advantage of some highly attractive opportunities to enter into 50-year inflation swaps.

Over time (eight months in this case), this pension scheme filled the ten risk buckets (five inflation and five interest rates) and achieved excellent pricing across a volatile period. It was also highly flexible in its approach to the markets, indifferent in a sense to whether today's opportunity was in respect of 20-year interest rates or 40-year inflation. They were simply buckets to be filled as efficiently as possible over time.

In practice, there are a few more sub-categories (such as LPI and RPI) that may be utilised, but the approach above serves as a very good illustration.

This point about process is important because too many pension schemes have historically failed to implement hedges due to poor implementation frameworks. A poor framework is one that insists on treating the buckets as a single parameter and in effect requiring hedging trigger levels to be reached across all buckets simultaneously. This, unsurprisingly, rarely happens. There are several examples of pension schemes unnecessarily missing opportunities to hedge risk at certain points because other trigger conditions were not reached at the same time.

LDI has developed to provide increasingly sophisticated protection to pension schemes, and new and efficient ways of hedging are evolving all the time in reaction to changing market conditions. For example, the extreme volatility and liquidity problems of the last 18 months threw up some counterintuitive challenges. It became progressively more expensive for investors such as banks to hold gilts of any type. This is because, simply put, banks have to borrow the money to pay for the gilts and the cost of borrowing rose prohibitively. So the price of gilts fell to a level where it made sense for pension schemes to own gilts instead of swaps. This 'anomaly' has persisted, although arguably this now has more to do with increasing worries over the state of the UK's long-term creditworthiness.

However, it is not just about using swaps and/or gilts to match long-dated assets. For those pension schemes able to undertake the complex analysis required, there are alternatives to holding swaps and/or gilts. A major advantage that pension schemes have over other investors is their long-term investment horizon – this translates into an ability to invest in less liquid assets which may not be appropriate for investors with shorter-term liabilities. Pension schemes also need assets which give them protection against inflation.

Increasingly, we are seeing brand new initiatives like the creation of the new asset class of social housing cash flows to help pension schemes hedge; these are long-dated, inflation-linked and relatively safe cash flows and, effectively, are widely being viewed as 'LDI 2.0'.

Risk management, for pension schemes, is paramount. The accuracy with which it is measured and the output of that risk analysis will form the bedrock of the pension scheme's risk budget and underpin any subsequent decisions taken by the scheme about managing that risk. It is vital that any pension scheme running risk analysis ensures that the output is clear, understandable and directional – i.e. that it gives the trustees of the board a clear idea of where the risk is within the portfolio, and provides some practical idea of what needs to be done as a result. Advisers should be providing pension schemes with this kind of analysis, and providing them with a workable game-plan through which they can target unacceptable risk within the scheme, with the stakeholders' risk budget in mind. Ultimately, the measurement of risk and the prudent management of it are the two factors that a pension scheme cannot afford to ignore.

13

Managing longevity risk

CHINU PATEL

Introduction

Defined benefit pension schemes face a wide range of risks which can broadly be classified under the headings of market risk, operational risk and insurance risk. The latter comprises a whole host of risks affecting the demography of the scheme, arising from human contingencies and member options. Amongst them is the risk of scheme members outliving expectations – longevity risk. As pension schemes have grown and matured, so has their longevity risk, and as schemes have taken steps to reduce their financial risk, their longevity risk has become proportionately greater. In many schemes it now represents a significant proportion of the total risk. At the end of 2008, the pension schemes of the FTSE 100 companies were in aggregate taking half as much risk from longevity as they were from exposure to equity markets (see Figure 13.1). Compared with inflation and interest rate risk, the proportion was even higher – nearer two-thirds. While these proportions do vary from scheme to scheme, there is little doubt that for many schemes their exposure to longevity risk is significant, and perhaps takes up a disproportionate share of the risk budget.

While longevity risk has increased, its measurement has also become more uncertain, thus requiring a more proactive approach to its management. For years, actuaries had the longevity risk pretty well buttoned down and the view around trustee boards was that this was one esoteric risk which changed slowly and predictably and was best left to the actuary's professional judgment. But that is no longer the case due to significant changes in the forces underlying mortality, as well as new options available for managing the risk. Any successful attempt at managing longevity risk requires an understanding of principal causes of mortality, their recent trends and an appreciation of the uncertainty surrounding any projections into the future.

This chapter begins with such an analysis, including a review of some of the new tools and techniques being employed to gain a better understanding of the drivers of longevity risk. It then considers the options currently employed by trustees to manage longevity risk, including some of the newer options to transfer risk to third parties, either in isolation or as part of a package of risks

207

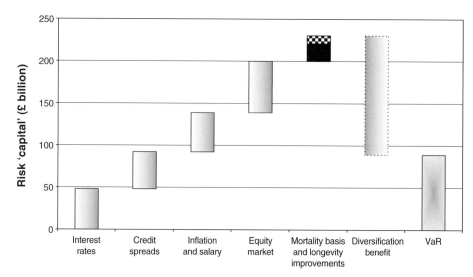

Figure 13.1 FTSE 100: attribution of pension risk

under LDI strategies. The chapter concludes by commenting on areas in which we can expect further innovation going forward as all stakeholders become more comfortable with the emerging market in longevity risk.

Given the intended readership, there may be a slight bias towards trustees in what follows. In practice, risk-management initiatives could originate from trustees or sponsors, and although the perspective of each will be different, decisions are best taken jointly, preceded by a careful analysis of the options and issues involving a number of other parties and usually a lengthy gestation period.

Death: an uncertain certainty

While death is still a certainty, the length of the average lifespan and our confidence in predicting it have become more uncertain, with huge implications for the funding, reserving and risk strategies of pension schemes and their consequential implications for the commercial activity of the sponsoring companies.

The pace of improvement in recent years has been unprecedented. For men aged 65 to 74 in England and Wales, the reduction in mortality rates over the 15 years to 2005 was similar to that achieved over the whole of the previous 150 years. In the United Kingdom, actuaries' estimates of life expectancy for males reaching retirement age have probably changed more in the last ten years than in the previous 100 years. But, as ever, the headline statements can mask many of the underlying trends important to individual schemes. So a closer examination of the trends and their relevance to the characteristics of each scheme is important.

The statistics show that the rate of improvement in longevity in England and Wales has applied across the board and the pace of change has accelerated in recent years. However, the emergence of a particularly healthy cohort of men and women born between 1925 and 1945 has added to the uncertainty of planning for the future. This cohort, now largely retired, has experienced more rapid improvements in mortality than generations born either side of it. However, the reasons for this particular observation are not known (or are at best speculative) and there is no sign of abatement in the improvements, thus begging questions about the uncertainty surrounding any quantification of longevity risk for this particular group.

Apart from the mystery of the 'healthy' cohort, much is known about the pattern of deaths and the reasons for the unprecedented improvement in mortality. In young people, violence and accidents are the most significant causes of death, whereas for people aged 40 and above the dominant causes are heart disease (men) and cancer (women). For people in their 40s and 50s, death rates due to cancer are broadly the same for men and women. However, death rates from heart disease for men are four to five times those of women. In old age (age 80 and above), deaths from cancer and heart disease are relatively less significant, with strokes and respiratory disorders more prevalent. Clearly, the make-up of each scheme between men and women as well as young and old matters.

The data also shows that the reduction in death rates from circulatory diseases (which include heart disorders and stroke) has dominated the downward trend in mortality. Many of the reasons are familiar: better standards of living, increased nutrition and the reduction in smoking. But preventative management in medicine, particularly the significantly increased use by the NHS of drugs to fight cholesterol (statins) and the increased number of surgical interventions on heart attack victims (angioplasties), have also been an important contributor to the improved health of the nation. Analyses of the causes of circulatory diseases and their trends suggest that there may be scope for further significant improvements in longevity from this cause. However, improvements from other causes may be slowing down and the risks from new diseases may be increasing, so the overall picture is far from clear.

The difference between the mortality of men and women and blue and white collar workers is well known. Recent analysis has also shown that the life expectancy gap between the rich and the poor is increasing and at a faster pace. This may seem counter-intuitive since the lower socio-economic groups, who should have the most scope to benefit from medical advances and better nutrition, are in fact enjoying lower longevity improvements than the higher socio-economic groups. There are clearly some selective forces and complex interactions at play which can only be understood by considering a number of the driving forces together.

An examination of international statistics shows that citizens of other countries (notably Japan and France) have longer life expectancies than their counterparts in England and Wales. It could be argued that in a global economy which encourages easy exchange of information, technology and research, and where political and financial stability are linked to a harmonisation of value structures and living standards, there might eventually be convergence to a global norm, thus leading to the conclusion that in the United Kingdom there is yet scope for further improvements. On the other hand, cultural and other factors which are endemic to the lifestyles of different nations are not easy to change in practice and could remain as selective forces for generations to come. One lesson from international comparisons is that the future of longevity is probably more uncertain than that shown by analyses of domestic data.

So, amidst all this uncertainty, which makes it difficult to plan ahead and could cost dearly if not managed sensibly, what are trustees to do? They could start by looking behind the headline statistics to understand the trends and their reasons. They should consider the characteristics of their own membership (now and in the future) to place the general information in the context of their own scheme. Quantification of longevity risk inevitably involves subjective judgments, so trustees also need to be clear that they are comfortable with the models and assumptions used and make sure that if they (or their sponsors) have any particularly strong views about the future of longevity, they have been properly addressed. As uncertainty increases, so the role of sensitivity testing becomes more important and testing outcomes against a range of carefully constructed scenarios should help to put longevity risk in perspective with other risks with which trustees are more comfortable, or against specific risk thresholds and risk budgets which may have to be addressed in conversations with sponsors, and possibly with regulators in the future. Finally, it is vital to make sure that their governance framework is comprehensive enough to manage longevity risk as part of a more comprehensive and dynamic strategy for managing all of their risks.

Risk management

In general, there are four main approaches to managing longevity risk:

- The first is to refuse or avoid the risk altogether, which may still be an option for some (sponsors rather than trustees) with regard to future accruals, but not for past accruals.
- The second is to reduce the risk, which can be done through various actions within the scheme to change the liability cash flows. These may include tightening up of discretionary practices, which might otherwise have increased longevity risk or, where possible, changing the terms of certain member options to induce risk reduction (for example, improving terms for cash commutation and transfer values to encourage decisions by members which have the effect of removing risk).

- The third is to retain the risk and hold sufficient capital, which is what has been done traditionally through the actuarial valuation process.
- The fourth is to remove some or all of the longevity risk by transferring it to a third party, either in isolation or as part of a package of risks.

These options are not of course mutually exclusive. In practice, they should all be part of a coherent risk-management strategy and trustees and sponsors will generally seek to employ all of them in varying combinations over time. The recent emergence of what appears to be a sustainable market in longevity risk transfer makes the dynamics of any risk-management strategy more challenging, but at the same time opens up new opportunities that were previously unavailable.

Any attempt to reduce or transfer risk generally requires active involvement of trustees and sponsors, with a significant role for lawyers and other third-party advisers. More than ever, the silent role of scheme members should not be underestimated – after all, they might view each exercise to reduce or transfer risk as taking something away from them. Sponsors will often be the instigators of risk reduction and risk transfer exercises, but where the initiative is being driven by trustees, sounding out the sponsor at an early stage is vital since, amongst other things, sponsors will have a different perspective requiring independent advice to understand the cash flow, accounting and regulatory implications better before they can engage seriously. The interplay with new options, triggered by a rapidly evolving market for new solutions and products for risk transfer, now adds a further dimension to sound risk management of pension liabilities. While introducing more options, the market for third-party risk transfer also adds considerable complexity to coherent decision-making and underlines the need to consider carefully the interactions of any potential action with the principal strategies of the scheme: funding, risk and investment.

Managing longevity risk within the scheme

Once schemes are past the stage of 'picking the low-hanging fruit' (tightening the discretionary practices, cutting down on unnecessary benefits and options, offering inducements for individual risk transfers, etc.), the choice is really between deciding how much of the longevity risk trustees (and sponsors) feel comfortable carrying within the scheme, how much to transfer to external parties and by what route. The amount retained should depend on how confident trustees are that they understand the underlying nature of the longevity risk in the scheme and its potential implications for them and the sponsor. This is essential to enable them to make the judgments that will be required later when asked to sign off the funding and investment strategies, implicit within which will be informed choices about the level of risk that is affordable, the capital required to manage the retained risk and the value offered by external transfer options.

It is best to think of the longevity risk in two parts: the current underlying longevity as reflected by the mortality experience of the scheme and the expected future improvements. If sufficient data is available, looking at past history can be a valuable source of information for establishing the current position, and this provides a good starting point for the purposes of future projections. Past experience is perhaps most helpful in highlighting features of membership that may be indicative of why the mortality experience of a particular scheme is different from the aggregate data on which the standard mortality tables are based.

Improving the calibration of a scheme's underlying risk

Pension actuaries usually quantify the reserves required to cover longevity risk using a standard mortality table, with suitable adjustments for particular features of the scheme in question that might be indicative of a different underlying experience. Since the adjustments can only be approximate, the closer the standard table fits the underlying experience of the scheme the better, otherwise trustees could be running significant residual risks which are not being managed. Until recently, standard mortality tables used by pension actuaries generally reflected the experience, on a pooled basis, of the smaller pension schemes which choose to insure their pensioner portfolios. But now standard tables reflecting the experience of large, self-administered pension schemes (SAPS) are available. There are some stark differences between the two, with the SAPS data exhibiting heavier mortality. In other words, the life expectancy of pensioners in self-administered schemes may be lower than that implicit in the insured pensioner tables hitherto used in actuarial valuations. It is worth knowing on which side of prudence the trustees stand and whether the SAPS tables provide a better fit to the experience of their own scheme.

Life expectancy is of course just one short-hand measure of longevity. In practice, longevity risk depends on a number of factors such as age, sex, geography, occupation, pension amount, etc. Traditional analysis of past data has focused on a single factor at a time (usually age or sex and sometimes amount) with correlations (or dependencies) between the factors ignored for simplicity or on grounds of immateriality. Much of the recent research has focused on incorporating other factors in the models for measuring risk. These range from a better examination of isolated factors using proxies for factors such as wealth or social status, to more comprehensive and complex models such as generalised linear models (GLMs). The latter work on a number of risk factors simultaneously and identify those that have a statistically significant 'predictive power'. Depending on availability of the more comprehensive data required by these models, the significance of a host of other longevity risk factors can also be investigated, such as the amount of pension, marital status, occupation, socio-economic group, geographic location, etc. Analyses such as these may help to improve the quantification of longevity risk – what gets measured stands a better chance of being managed better.

The future: measuring the immeasurable?

It is said that the current rate of improvement in longevity is equivalent to adding five hours to our lifespan each day, and more recent studies might even indicate six hours! Will this trend continue indefinitely? How can it? Will it continue at a reduced pace or even reverse, and if so why? Alternatively, will it be replaced by something entirely new based on new technologies and new medical treatments? What will they be? Today, this is the dilemma facing anyone trying to crystallise a future set of pension cash flows into a capital value, and the longer the time-frame of the cash flows, the more critical the impact of any judgment made.

Understanding the factors that have shaped the past is helpful, but assuming that the same factors will dominate the future, and with the same intensity, can be dangerous. For example, in the eighteenth and nineteenth centuries, there was a large reduction in communicable diseases such as smallpox and typhoid, and in the late nineteenth and early twentieth centuries there was a decline in respiratory diseases and tuberculosis. Today, cardiovascular diseases have taken centre stage. As the treatments for these improve, what will take their place in the future as the United Kingdom's biggest killers, and at what age will it strike and over what period? Answering this question would go a long way towards predicting the future course of longevity, but of course it may be an impossible question to answer.

There is considerable debate within the academic community as to the level of longevity improvements that can be sustained in the future. At one end there are powerful arguments from demographers such as Olshansky,[1] who believe that other forces such as obesity, diabetes and spread of disease will cause life expectancy improvements to level off or even decline, and that in any case the existence of a practical biomechanical limit on our lifespan means that longevity improvements cannot continue forever, despite medical advances. At the other end, there are equally credible arguments from other demographers such as Vaupel,[2] who believe that there is no conclusive evidence that life expectancy is approaching a limit, but that ageing is plastic and survival can be extended by various genetic changes and non-genetic interactions. At the extreme, Dr Aubrey de Grey,[3] a professor of gerontology at Cambridge, believes that ageing is a curable disease, that there are seven factors which lead to ageing and that regenerative medicine has the potential to defeat each of these entirely within a few decades; indeed, he has even provocatively suggested that the first person to live to 1,000 might already be a pensioner!

To put some of this debate in the context of risk management, the difference between assuming that there will be no future improvements and assuming

1 J. W. Vaupel and S. J. Olshansky, 'The Uncertain Future of Longevity', Public lectures on longevity at Cass Business School (2005).

2 Ibid.

3 D. J. Brown, 'The seven lively SENS: An interview with Dr Aubrey de Grey', *Smart Publications* (2005–06), www.smart-publications.com/interviews/mavericks-of-medicine/dr-aubrey-de-grey.

that there will be a continued acceleration of the recent trends could add about 30 per cent to the aggregate UK pension scheme liabilities. This level of uncertainty can be alarming for pension scheme trustees and sponsors, given the potential for unpredictable calls to divert significant amounts of capital from businesses to support pension schemes.

Traditionally, when considering funding and investment strategies, longevity risk has been quantified on a deterministic basis and then treated as a constant when considering strategies for managing the other risks. Given the uncertainty surrounding longevity trends, there is no reason why in future its measurement should not be based on stochastic models. This should appeal to those who see the merit of managing the longevity risk consistently with, say, investment risk within a wider risk-management framework. Many stochastic models of longevity have been developed to supplement the lead given by the actuarial profession, so trustees should expect a healthy dialogue with their scheme actuary on the pros and cons of each and their variants, as well as the relevance of each within the particular strategy trustees are minded to follow. Like all stochastic models, it is important to understand the key beliefs and assumptions which drive each, and whether they are consistent with trustees' view of the future. For example, most models, despite their apparent sophistication, project forward some element of the past, so trustees need to understand what and why and challenge their actuary to describe it in simpler language so that they may engage better (not just with the actuary, but also with the sponsor) by putting it in the right context alongside their own views.

While most stochastic models in current use merely project an element of the past into the future, new research on 'predictive' models takes a fundamentally different approach. These go beyond a consideration of the past data and, with the help of other experts such as demographers, epidemiologists and medical practitioners, model the incidence and intensity of the key causes of longevity which are then used to predict future aggregate mortality levels through scenario setting aligned with expert medical opinion. While more complex in their application and interpretation, and not yet in common use, they provide refreshing new avenues to test the impact of any strong beliefs on particular causes of longevity or developments that promise to have an impact on the future course of longevity. Considerable effort is being applied in this area by different domestic and international groups, with the promise of some well-needed and multi-disciplined thought leadership; it is worth keeping track of progress.

Managing longevity risk by transfer to emerging markets

The difficulty of predicting the future course of longevity makes the consequences for the financial position of pension schemes highly uncertain. Longevity is a gradual, long-term trend risk with the possibility of huge discontinuities, for example, from a flu pandemic or, at the other extreme, following significant medical breakthroughs such as a cure for cancer. This makes it more difficult to quantify and plan for. In addition, longevity risk is generally considered to be uncorrelated with the other risks to which a pension scheme is exposed. In other words, there is no mitigation from other compensating risks and if trustees take the view that the forces of change will continue to operate in the direction of increasing their longevity risk, they might conclude that for them this is a one-way risk for no apparent reward and, if the terms are right, this is best transferred to third parties who feel they can make a business from it.

Who are these third parties and why should they be interested? Very simply, these are parties who can use some of the features of longevity risk in their business or who feel that they have access to superior tools and techniques or investors and distribution networks to exploit opportunities for buying and selling longevity risk.

Insurance companies of course have a natural appetite for risks related to life contingencies. For example, life insurers are generally concerned about policy-holders dying too early, so investment in longevity risk gives them some protection in the other direction. Life reinsurers, given their experience, expertise and deeper research, may consider themselves better capable than others of understanding the risk and hence its pricing. They should also be better at distributing it in the markets in which they operate – something which pension trustees neither do, nor have the capability to do.

The gradual nature of longevity risk and its lack of correlation with traditional equity and bond markets are features which make it attractive to asset managers. For example, in multi-strategy hedge funds, longevity risk could be a source of diversification which would help to reduce the overall volatility of their portfolios.

Other capital market investors have also shown interest, whether looking for new investment opportunities or to take advantage of skills acquired in other markets. Such investors usually rely on gearing up risks, re-packaging them and distributing them efficiently to other investors to enhance returns. Therefore, they should also be attracted by the diversification opportunities and additional returns uncorrelated with the equity and bond markets. The sub-prime crisis may have dented investor interest for the time being, but longer term, this category of investors is thought to provide the best potential for the significant increase in capacity required to absorb the volume of longevity risk pension schemes have to offer, and to create a liquid market for trading it.

Other parties who should have a natural appetite for longevity risk and may in due course become interested are companies whose revenue streams benefit from increased longevity, for example, utility companies, drug companies and nursing homes. Governments, who should also have a natural appetite for such risks, have to date shown little interest.

Traditionally, there was only one way of removing mortality risk – to buy out the scheme's benefits with an insurance company. This market had evolved to serve the needs of pension schemes that had to transfer their liabilities to a third party as part of winding up the scheme. As a result, the products on offer had many limiting features which did not make similar transfers viable for solvent schemes. In recent years, however, there has been an increasing amount of innovation to promote a spectrum of solutions to the wider market, principally from the risk-management angle. Risk-management menus have been growing rapidly, from full and partial buy-outs to buy-ins to hedging solutions such as longevity swaps. Some of these are reviewed below.

Buy-outs and buy-ins

Buy-outs and buy-ins bundle a number of risks, including longevity, to be passed to a third party (usually an insurance company). They potentially involve a significant initial cash payment, but at the same time come closest to providing the ideal matching investment. These transactions are generally with FSA-authorised insurers.

The biggest difficulty for trustees and sponsors is in finding what might be a substantial additional amount of cash (or other assets) above the level at which the pension scheme has been funded. The loss of investment flexibility associated with locking up a large part of the fund's assets with a third party may also be of concern to pension trustees and sponsors, whose funding and investment strategies depend on a sizeable element of risk taking (although it is quite likely that for such schemes reducing longevity risk may not be such a high priority).

Buy-outs and buy-ins usually involve all or some of the pensioner portfolio only. In practice, this gives rise to a gearing up of the longevity risk, since it is the non-pensioners in any scheme who pose the greatest risk from the uncertainty regarding future longevity improvements. The implications of this for future de-risking strategies and funding are rarely given sufficient consideration. For example, superficially it might seem attractive to have removed, say, £400 million of pensioner liability in a £500 million scheme, but if the remaining liabilities are largely in respect of non-retired members, the resulting portfolio may no longer be very attractive to buy-out firms and other providers of risk-management products (who are generally selective in the risks they take on). Consequently, the trustee's options with regard to future de-risking strategies may become limited, or their negotiating power reduced. Further, the proportion of risk removed is likely to be rather less than the proportion of liability transferred. This is because the risk actually removed was more predictable (both on the asset and liability side) due to its shorter time horizon, and was consequently more manageable. The remaining portfolio should have greater risk per unit of cash flow and therefore future funding and investment strategies might end up being more volatile.

The convenience of transferring a whole package of risks also needs to be weighed against the price of so doing. Small schemes, because of their greater exposure to idiosyncratic risks (a small number of individuals representing a large proportion of the total liability) and random variation in mortality due to the smaller number of members, may find the price worth paying since other risk-transfer options might be limited. Larger schemes that have the expertise to manage separately each of the risks in the bundle need to consider whether buy-ins and buy-outs are indeed cost effective; often there are other considerations which help to swing the balance.

A buy-in is the same as buying a perfectly matched investment from a single provider. It is an investment of the whole scheme, even though it is apparently identified with particular beneficiaries (usually pensioners). The risk of paying the pensions remains with the trustees and the support of the sponsoring employer also remains. Buy-outs involve a complete transfer to the provider of all of the risks associated with the particular tranche of liability insured, with a proportionately heavier demand on data quality and governance, as well as lengthy considerations of the 'before' and 'after' situation for the transferred members. Among these is the issue of security. Quite often, the transfer is to an insurer whose financial strength is stronger than that of the sponsor. Additionally, in the event of failure of the insurer, there is protection provided by a compensation scheme under the insurance regulatory regime (although detailed coverage may not precisely match that of the Pension Protection Fund (PPF)). It could be argued that this combination provides a better level of protection for the transferring members. However, the practice has evolved of ring-fencing the transferred assets to provide additional security over and above that provided by the regulatory regime for insurers. Gold-plated luxury at a price that is rarely transparent?

Longevity hedges

Longevity hedges are contracts which reduce a pension scheme's exposure to longevity risk by transferring some or all of it to a third party. Although there may not be a large initial payment involved, there is a price paid over the duration of the contract and in return the trustees get the comfort of a much more predictable stream of net cash outflows and the prospect of freeing up some of the risk budget for more efficient allocation elsewhere.

The most common form of hedging product on offer is a 'longevity swap', although in practice this generic description covers many variants and different structures. As illustrated below, this involves a pension scheme undertaking to make payments fixed in advance for the duration of the contract ('fixed leg') in return for receiving from the provider payments that reflect the pensions payable to actual surviving pensioners ('floating leg'). If actual longevity improvements are better than assumed in the fixed leg (i.e. more people are living longer), the pension scheme receives payments representing the difference from the provider and vice versa. These exchanges happen on a periodic basis. At the outset of the contract, the difference between the fixed and floating legs will usually be the margin that the provider wants to retain to cover

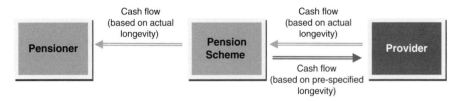

Figure 13.2 Longevity swap

their capital costs, profit and a risk premium. During the term of the contract, as actual mortality experience develops and if it proves to be different from that assumed in the fixed leg, the swap acquires a value which might become quite significant (see Figure 13.2).

Longevity swaps are currently the preferred format for longevity-only transactions due to their apparent simplicity, familiarity and ease of transaction for pension schemes and capital market investors. A key advantage, compared with buy-outs and buy-ins, is that trustees retain control of the assets. However, pricing structures are not uniform and lack transparency, and despite a small number of investors, there are many variations in product features which make the structuring of suitable hedges more complex. Due diligence and negotiation can therefore be time consuming. Apart from affordability considerations, pension schemes also need to consider carefully the value considerations on a consistent footing, including knock-on implications for funding and investment strategies. Some of these features are discussed in greater detail below.

Contract structure

Longevity swaps can be written as either insurance contracts or capital market instruments. The former are issued as insurance policies by FSA-regulated insurance companies and the latter as capital market instruments under standard terms which are commonly used for inflation and interest swaps (so-called 'ISDA' agreements as promoted by the International Swaps and Derivatives Association). Each type of contract has its merits and its suitability will depend on a number of factors which will differ from one pension scheme to another. Pricing differences can flow from the different regulatory requirements, but there are many other considerations.

Coverage

Whilst all providers will accept existing pensioners, the same is not true of deferred pensioners and active members, and practice regarding acceptance of future retirees can vary. Providers do not generally like options embedded in liabilities and therefore the more complicated the plan design, the greater the likelihood of further exclusions or price loadings. Similarly, providers do not like open-ended liabilities due to incomplete data or legislative uncertainty (for example, Guaranteed Minimum Pension (GMP) equalisation) and will either exclude these or price them on a safe basis. Data-cleaning exercises prior to the transaction should make the risk more saleable, and might attract better terms.

Basis risk

Longevity swaps can either be based on the actual mortality exhibited in the particular pension scheme or on the experience of a wider population as captured in an index. In the latter case, the pension scheme carries the residual risk of their actual experience differing from the index (known as 'basis' risk). Products which reflect the scheme's liabilities closest have the obvious merit of being a better hedge, but are more complicated to administer and less attractive to capital market investors. Index-based swaps on the other hand are simpler to 'standardise', which makes them more tradable in the capital markets and hence more liquid and perhaps even 'cheaper'. For pension trustees, the basis risk associated with indexed swaps can be reduced – but not entirely eliminated – by using other techniques.

Tail risk

Some providers offer 'whole of life' contracts where the swap payments continue until the very last member (or dependant) dies. Others will only write swap contracts for limited terms, leaving the pension scheme to assume the residual tail risk. Longevity risk at the longer durations is of course more risky in view of the uncertainty regarding future improvements. Therefore, retaining too much of the tail risk raises questions about the effectiveness of the hedge. Pension schemes therefore need to strike a balance between the level of indemnity they would ideally like (which will govern the complexity of the swap) and the residual risk they can afford to carry. The extent of this residual risk varies significantly between providers and periods of between 10 and 50 years are not uncommon. Limited-term swap contracts also raise questions about the exit terms at the end of the contract. Usually, this will need to be negotiated at the point of striking the deal.

Price structure

The price paid for longevity swaps may take the form of a single, up-front premium or a number of premiums over the life of the contract. In some cases, the premium may be implicitly built into the fixed cash flows paid by the scheme and so will effectively be spread over the term of the contract.

Providers of longevity solutions will structure their premiums in different ways, often to suit the needs of their investors or to ease their capital burden. As such, the margins that are built into their structure are often difficult to identify and so pension schemes must employ a range of techniques to reverse-engineer these.

Collateral

As the life of a swap unfolds and information about actual longevity levels becomes available, the expected value of the future commitments from each party will change. In theory, this can be mitigated by regularly calculating the difference and requiring the party that owes the positive amount to post it as collateral. However, illiquid trades such as those based on longevity can introduce significant incremental complexity. Amongst other things, the calculation details in a longevity swap can be more complex than in, say, an interest rate or inflation swap because of the lack of verifiable market information about mortality rates. The time taken to resolve irregularities or solve disputes can itself become a significant source of credit risk just when the protection is needed most (consider, for example, the recent Lehmann and AIG sagas, which showed how collateral mechanisms can fail even for liquid derivative instruments, the market price of which is unambiguous). Therefore, contract terms need to be negotiated carefully at the outset to reduce the potential exposure to credit risk over the life of a contract that may last for over 50 years.

Future proofing

It is worth considering how the existence of a swap contract might affect future events, for example, mergers and acquisitions (M&A) activity or a full buy-out, possibly with someone other than the swap counterparty. Is there an option to unwind the swap in such circumstances, and if so then at what price? Most providers offer such options either by way of novation to another party or by surrender, although the exact terms need to be negotiated and are typically not fully guaranteed at the outset.

Longevity plus

The actual cash flows for a pension liability will be affected not only by the number of deaths in the scheme, but also, in most cases, by the level of inflation. A further consideration for pension schemes is therefore whether to combine protection against inflation and mortality risks. This should provide a better hedge for the pension scheme, including removal of second-order risks, and in theory there should also be efficiency gains in bundling some risks. For pension schemes following LDI strategies, this may be a natural way of bringing longevity risk into the equation. Others who manage longevity risk in isolation, or not at all, might find that their basis risk is rather more than they first thought; amongst other things they need to consider how a longevity swap would affect the validity of inflation swaps previously put in place.

Managing longevity risk: looking ahead

Longevity swaps have emerged as the natural product for the early stages of the developing market in longevity risk. However, despite the conceptual simplicity of longevity swaps, many pension executives still regard the lack of transparency of transactions and the practical complexities of establishing and monitoring swaps and managing collateral as significant barriers to their use. The first longevity swap by a pension scheme was only executed in 2009, setting the scene for this to be the 'must have' in risk management toolkits for the next few years until knowledge and understanding grows to accommodate more innovative and perhaps better but more complex solutions. At the time of writing, only a handful of longevity swap deals have taken place, but the expectations are that the momentum in this market will be considerably greater than that of its predecessor markets in interest rate and currency swaps (where it took two decades for pension schemes to catch on and for investment managers to create suitable products). Indeed, this appears to be the motivation behind the recently created Life and Longevity Markets Association, a trade body set up by a group of banks, insurers and reinsurers to spur the development of a liquid longevity market. Its initial tasks of developing consistent standards of documentation, indices and standardised valuation models, if successful, should go a long way towards removing the mystique, complexity and unnecessarily long time scales for executing longevity swaps.

Other solutions involving at least a partial transfer of longevity risk include:

- *Longevity bonds*: These are bonds where the coupons are linked to a longevity index. They provide some longevity protection for schemes, but not a full hedge against the scheme's actual longevity risk. They also suffer from much heavier funding requirements.
- *Mortality-linked investments*: These are typically investment products with an underlying link to some form of mortality or longevity risk. For example, funds linked to pools of life assurance policies or to portfolios of high net worth annuities are common in the United States. Apart from potential diversification benefits, these funds have some component of return increasing when people live longer (hence providing some longevity protection to pension schemes, albeit with potentially significant basis risk).
- *Derivatives*: These are standardised contracts which exchange realised longevity for fixed longevity. In other words, the terms are set such that the party seeking protection from longevity risk is able to fix its commitment by reference to a specified assumption regarding future longevity; and the party providing the protection undertakes to settle the commitment based on actual longevity experienced. Derivatives provide building blocks for more complex structures, and are designed to provide liquidity (and hence tradability). Longevity swaps can be synthesised from these, but can add complexity and leave residual risks that need to be managed separately.

- *Futures and options*: These are flexible building blocks allowing, amongst other things, investors to leverage and issuing banks to repackage longevity risk more efficiently. There is no active market in these at present, but one wonders how long it will be before longevity futures become as commonly traded in the capital markets as commodity and energy futures.
- *Composite hedges*: These enable some of the upside from other assets to be traded against the downside from longevity risk: for example, a product that covers longevity risk, but only when equity markets have fallen. The concept behind this is that if equity markets rise, the additional investment returns will soften the blow from increased longevity. In the present stage of development of this market, these may be considered a little complicated, but they may have a role in pension funds which have the governance to address the management of investment and longevity risks in an integrated way.

Conclusion

Longevity risk is firmly on the risk maps of most pension schemes, and as schemes mature and exposures to other risks are actively managed, the significance of longevity risk is bound to increase. For trustees, the first step is to understand the risk better. There are many new tools and techniques available for this purpose, but the biggest component of longevity risk – the rate of future improvements in longevity – is still very uncertain and trustees need to challenge any models or assumptions purporting to give the right answer. The traditional way of managing longevity risk was to retain it within the pension scheme, principally because the risk was considered to be predictable and hence controllable, and also because options for more active management were limited and uneconomic. More recently, there has been an increased interest from investment banks, insurance companies and others to invest in businesses and products linked to longevity risk and all the signs are that this will continue. The products currently available to trustees range from those which allow them to manage longevity risk on a stand-alone basis to others with varying degrees of bundling longevity with other risks of the scheme. With continued interest from risk takers who have access to large amounts of capital, as well as superior innovation skills, the range of options for trustees is bound to grow, particularly if attempts to create a liquid market in longevity risk succeed. From a risk-management viewpoint, pension scheme trustees need to understand the merits of the products and solutions on offer and how, if at all, any of them can help to improve their funding, investment and risk strategies. Given the complexity of the available products, the learning curve is steep and it is necessary for trustees to develop the right governance, if it does not already exist, so that the processes for reaching decisions, implementation of agreed strategies and follow-up are robust and comprehensive, as well as smooth and efficient.

Bibliography and further reading

D. Blake, A. J. G. Cairns and K. Dowd, 'Birth of the Life Market' (2008) 3(1) *Asia-Pacific Journal of Risk and Insurance* 6–36

D. Blake, A. J. G. Cairns and K. Dowd, 'Living with Mortality: Longevity Bonds and Other Mortality-Linked Securities', (2006) 12 *British Actuarial Journal* 153–97

E. Dimitriou, 'On the Wrong Track?', *Actuary Magazine*, November 2009

K. Dowd, D. Blake and A. J. G. Cairns, 'The Myth of Methuselah and the Uncertainty of Death: The Mortality Fan Charts', Pensions Institute Discussion Paper PI-0704 (November 2007)

R. Willets, 'Can the capital markets deliver appropriate solutions to longevity risk?', City and Westminster Conference (2007)

14

The role of insurance in the occupational pensions market

DAVID COLLINSON

Background and development of the insurance market

Insurance is used in wider context for the purpose of pooling risks with other policyholders in order to protect the individual policyholder from extreme outcomes. In essence, the policyholder pays a premium to the insurance company in exchange for a promise that a potential future claim will be met. In order to ensure that the insurance company is in a position to meet that claim as it falls due, the insurer has to hold reserves and capital and be subject to a strict regulatory regime. In effect, the policyholder is purchasing access to the regulatory regime and the capital resources of the insurer.

The insurance market in the context of occupational pension schemes has changed dramatically since 2006. There has been an increase in the number of insurance companies competing in the market, the volume of transactions has increased, the type of products offered has changed and the pricing of those products has reduced.

The reasons why pension schemes (and indirectly their sponsors) use insurance products fall into two main categories:

- risk management – insurance is used as a means of hedging or matching specific risks of the pension scheme, or as a protection against an extreme outcome; and
- settlement – insurance is used as a means of settling a liability, thereby relieving the pension scheme (and hence the employer) of responsibility for meeting the liability, i.e. it is the insurer that becomes directly responsible to the scheme member for meeting the cost of the benefits that have been promised.

Prior to 2006, the insurance market consisted primarily of two lines of insurance:

- insurance of the liabilities of pension schemes that were winding up, typically due to the insolvency of the employer that sponsored the scheme (pension 'buy-outs'); and

- insurance of mortality risk for pension plans that offered lump-sum, death-in-service benefits.

The buy-out market largely consisted of a steady stream of smaller transactions, although there were cases of larger deals (for example, Ferranti). Two players – Legal and General and Prudential – dominated the market.

Other insurers who were not competing in the insurance buy-out market were actively looking to reduce their exposure to annuity liabilities and longevity risk. Indeed, in 2005 and 2006, there were numerous multi-billion-pound transactions involving insurance companies transferring blocks of annuity liabilities between one another.

A buy-out of a pension scheme's liabilities was typically not viewed as an attractive option for a solvent employer of an ongoing pension scheme, primarily due to the significant premium that would need to be paid to the insurer in addition to the assets required to fund the pension scheme on an ongoing basis. This reflected the fact that pension schemes typically included allowance for future investment outperformance above risk-free in their funding calculations and future mortality improvements were allowed for by pension schemes at a lower rate than by insurance companies. This meant that the cost of insurance was significantly in excess of the value placed on the corresponding liabilities by the pension scheme.

In 2006, all of this changed. At least four new insurance companies were established (Pension Insurance Corporation, Paternoster, Rothesay Life and Synesis Life), a number of established insurance companies entered the market (Aegon, Swiss Re, AIG and Met Life) and a range of banks and financial institutions explored whether they could enter the market directly or indirectly (for example, Lehman Brothers and Citicorp). New capital in the order of £5 billion was made available to finance insurance buy-outs and similar transactions.

Why did all of this capital become available? In reality, there was a combination of factors that affected demand for, pricing of and supply of insurance products:

- *Demand*: Occupational pension benefits have been transformed over the past 30 years from a 'best endeavours intention' made by the employer, with pension increases that were discretionary, to a debt-like obligation of the employer carrying mandatory pension increases. Pension liabilities rank ahead of equity investors and the introduction of the Pensions Act 2004 reinforced this position and introduced strict measures to ensure that pension liabilities were not disadvantaged in corporate transactions and restructurings. A pension deficit is now crystallised as a debt-like obligation of the employer. The value of the deficit is volatile, and from the perspective of the employer moves in an extremely unfavourable manner, i.e. it tends to increase during an economic downturn, just when the employer is least able to deal with increased liabilities. Employers engaged in transactions and restructurings are increasingly having to negotiate with the trustees of the relevant pension schemes, and are faced with significant demands for funding and security if it is felt that proposed transactions would negatively affect the pension scheme. At the same time, increasing numbers of pension schemes are being closed to new members and frozen with regard to the accrual of new benefits, meaning that the pension scheme benefits are no longer a central plank of the employee benefit package. In summary, employers with pension schemes find that they have a significant and volatile obligation, which is increasingly time consuming to deal with and which represents an obligation mainly to former (rather than current) employees. Employers find that they are responsible for making good the consequences of investment underperformance without having a direct control of the investment policy, i.e. they are responsible for the liability, but the trust owns and directs the investments.

In this light it was felt that employers would seek to settle voluntarily their pension obligations with insurance companies, and be prepared to pay the cost of doing so. Given the vast size of the potential market (estimated at over £1 trillion), even if only 5 per cent of funds elected to insure their liabilities, this would be more than sufficient to use up all of the capital being allocated to the sector. The new insurance companies being established were effectively projecting that the buy-out market would shift from its historical focus of catering for pension schemes of insolvent employers to an entirely new phenomenon of solvent employers choosing voluntarily to settle their pension obligations through insurance. Indeed, a large element of the historical market of insolvent pension scheme wind-ups was to effectively be taken over by the Pension Protection Fund (PPF).

- *Pricing*: The new insurers coming to the market felt that the effective duopoly that existed in the insurance buy-out market meant that there was a lack of full-price competition and that attractive returns on capital could be achieved. In addition, the use of the swap markets for hedging interest rate and inflation risk allowed for more efficient hedging of these risks, which could be passed on in the form of lower prices, without reducing returns on capital. Increased competition and the use of the latest financial techniques would therefore bring pricing down from the levels that existed hitherto. In combination with this development, pension schemes themselves were strengthening their funding approaches. Many schemes were reducing the allowance for future investment performance in determining a prudent target for the funding level and adopting more stringent assumptions with regard to longevity improvements. The funding levels requested by trustees were therefore increasing at the same time that insurance pricing was decreasing. This narrowed significantly the additional cost of buying out the pension scheme liabilities when compared to the funding benchmark of the pension scheme.
- *Supply*: the supply of capital to the market increased significantly the capacity of the insurance sector to insure pension schemes' liabilities. This

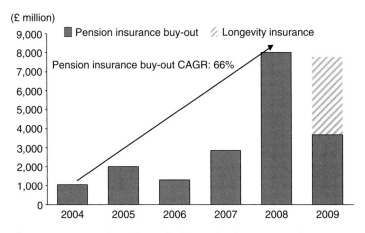

Figure 14.1 Transaction volumes in the pension insurance market

resulted in increased competition, leading to the lower prices noted above. In addition, the new capital encouraged innovation in the type and nature of the insurance products that were offered. Insurance of pension liabilities is a capital-intensive activity, which requires significant up-front capital to be deployed on commencement of the insurance policy and be tied up for many years thereafter. For a long-term investor, the risk/reward equation is attractive, provided that longevity risk can be adequately assessed and managed.

During the course of 2007 and 2008, the insurance market grew dramatically, as set out in Figure 14.1.

This development, a fivefold increase in transaction volume from 2006 to 2008, was seen as justifying the confidence that a significant market in pension buy-outs would develop. Behind this growth in actual transactions, there was also a significant increase in the number of pension schemes and their employers that were actively considering insurance of their liabilities. The total volume of quotations requested during 2008 easily exceeded £100 billion. Although some of these quotation requests were speculative, the underlying trend was that insurance was now seen by many funds to be a key part of their future strategy to honour their obligations to pension scheme members.

Pricing of insurance relative to pension scheme reserving approaches continued to improve, through a combination of increased competition and a significant increase in the returns available on corporate bonds. In many cases, the cost of insuring in payment pensioner liabilities fell below the technical provisions for the same liabilities as set by the pension scheme. This meant that an insurance transaction could create surplus relative to technical provisions, rather than requiring additional contributions. In 2008, we also saw the first billion pound transactions: Prudential's insurance of the pensioner

227

liabilities of the Cable and Wireless fund and Pension Insurance Corporation's insurance of the Thorn pension scheme.

The market turbulence following the collapse of Lehman Brothers in September 2008 did, however, slow insurance activity. Insurance companies needed to bolster reserves following the fall in the value of corporate bond holdings and some pension schemes saw the affordability of insurance move away from them as their holdings in equities diminished in value. The market picked up again in the latter part of 2009.

For many trustees and employers, an insurance transaction will be a one-off event, resulting in the closure and winding up of the fund. It is therefore inevitable that trustees in particular may have no prior experience in how to go about choosing an insurer and negotiating terms. In this context, trustees (and the employer) tend to place significant reliance on consultants to guide them through the insurance process. In most cases, insurance processes are run on behalf of trustees/employers by an actuarial consulting firm. Most of these firms have developed specialist teams who focus on this area of activity. In addition to the actuarial consultants, new consultancies have emerged to advise in this area, often seeking to bring in individuals with a wider corporate finance background and broader experience in advising on transactions in general.

In addition to traditional insurance products, the new entrants to the market brought alternative approaches to transferring risk. These new approaches met with varying degrees of success. Some offered credit insurance to pension funds, others developed the idea of effectively creating multi-employer pension funds and/or taking over from the current employer the responsibility of being the sponsor of the pension scheme.

Risk management – buy-ins and longevity insurance

There are two main insurance products that are purchased by pension schemes for the purpose of risk management: buy-ins and longevity insurance.

A 'buy-in' is an insurance policy purchased by a pension scheme where the scheme is both the policyholder and the beneficiary of the policy. The insurance policy will typically be an annuity (or deferred annuity) product covering a subsection of the pension scheme's membership. The typical form of the annuity product is that in exchange for a single, up-front premium payment, the insurer will pay to the pension scheme the benefits due to the members of the scheme covered by the policy for the lifetime of those individuals. The policy will also typically cover the increases due on the pensions in payment and any attaching spouses' or dependants' pensions. A deferred annuity product is identical, except that it is in respect of pension scheme members who have not yet retired, and the payments due from the insurer under the insurance policy are deferred until the members retire.

Typically, the pension scheme rules regarding pension increases/spouses and dependant benefits/guarantees will be replicated in the insurance policy

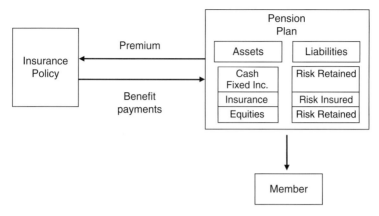

Figure 14.2 What is a buy-in?

to ensure an exact match between the income received from the insurance company and the pension scheme's obligation to the member. In certain circumstances, this exact match may not be possible or desirable. For example, there may be discretionary benefits payable to dependants which involve the trustees making a decision as to whether a benefit should be paid to a dependant – such discretion is not something that could realistically be passed on to an insurance company.

A pictorial representation of a buy-in transaction is set out in Figure 14.2. The buy-in insurance policy is an asset of the pension plan that insures specific liabilities.

Longevity insurance (covered in more detail in Chapter 13) is focused solely on the longevity risk that is carried by the fund. In principle, the concept is straightforward; the pension scheme fixes its exposure to longevity risk by locking it into a specified, 'expected' rate of longevity, whereas the insurer takes the 'actual' longevity risk. For example, if the expected position is that someone will live to the age of 82, the fund will be liable to pay benefits until the member is 82 years old, irrespective of whether he or she dies before age 82, or survives beyond age 82. The insurer will make a profit if the member dies before age 82 and a loss if the member survives beyond age 82. This description is a simplification of the actual workings of longevity insurance, but sets out the principles of what is involved.

Different product types fall under the 'buy-in' heading. As indicated above, the most straightforward approach is to insure all of the benefits promised by the fund for a particular subset of the pension scheme's membership. In this context, the most popular approach in the market to date has been to insure the liabilities for current pensioners of the scheme. This construction is referred to as a 'pensioner buy-in'. The attractions of insuring the liabilities for this subset of pension scheme members are as follows:

- *Perceived cost*: When a pension scheme assesses its required technical provisions, the pensioner liabilities are typically valued using a conservative discount rate (the technical provisions amount is the pension scheme's calculated target for the level of assets needed to fund fully the liability). This means that the gap between the pension scheme's own assessment of its liability and the cost of insuring those liabilities is usually small; therefore, the perceived additional cost of insuring the liabilities is also small.
- *Actual cost*: Pension schemes have tended to match in payment pensioner liabilities with corporate bonds and gilts, thus locking in to an investment return that is close to the risk-free rate and carries lower risk and lower return expectations than the assets typically used to back deferred and active member liabilities. The pricing of insurance contracts typically results in a policy that delivers something close to a risk-free level of return. If the pension scheme was expecting close to a risk-free level of return under the investment policy pursued prior to the insurance buy-in, then the return sacrificed by purchasing an insurance policy may be minimal or even negative.
- *Options*: Once a pension plan benefit has come into payment, there are typically no further options for the pension scheme member to select. Prior to retirement, the member has a number of options, i.e. the age at which he or she wishes to retire and how much of his or her benefit will be taken as a lump sum rather than as a pension. An insurance company will need to be prudent when considering and pricing these options, which will increase the cost of insurance relative to a 'best estimate' expected outcome. This fact makes pensioner liabilities more straightforward and cost effective to insure than deferred pensioner liabilities.

A pension scheme may not wish to insure all of its pensioner members and could seek to ensure a subset of its pensioners, for example, those above a certain age (for example, over 70), or those related to a particular employer.

A number of variations to the straightforward buy-in insurance have been promoted by the insurance sector with varying degrees of success. Some of the variations that have been made available are commented on below:

- *Tail risk exclusion*: The insurance policy covers the majority of the risks associated with the group of members insured, but excludes certain tail risks, i.e. those that are deemed to lie at the extreme end of the distribution of possible outcomes. The most common example is excluding longevity tail risk. This can be achieved by setting a maximum age up to which the insurer will pay benefits, say, 95 years old. If the pension scheme members die before age 95, the insurance policy will cover the liabilities in full. If the member lives beyond age 95, the cost of pensions paid after that age will not be covered by the insurance policy and is retained by the pension scheme.
- *Longevity profit sharing*: The policyholder shares in the longevity experience of the membership after the date of the insurance contract. For example, after five years the actual versus expected longevity experience is analysed

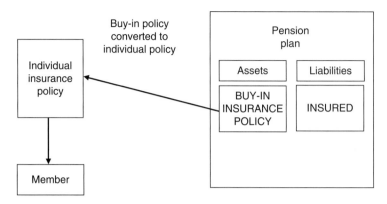

Figure 14.3 What is a buy-out?

and if actual rates of mortality have been higher than expected, some of the savings will be paid back to the pension scheme/employer.

- *Deferred premium payment*: Part of the premium required for the insurance contract is deferred into the future. This could be achieved either through the insurance company taking counterparty risk on the pension scheme/ employer, or the insurance company taking no counterparty risk, with the contract being surrendered if the deferred premiums are not paid.

Settlement of liabilities – insurance buy-out

A pension scheme (and hence the employer) can settle the pension liabilities via an insurance buy-out. Under a buy-out, the insurance company is instructed by the trustees to issue individual insurance policies to the members of the scheme. The pension scheme member is the policyholder and has a direct contractual relationship with the insurance company. Provided that the trustees can judge that the insurance policy adequately replaces the claim of the members against the scheme, they can then wind up the pension scheme (as following the issuance of individual policies the pension scheme has no further liabilities to it members).

Typically, a buy-out is preceded by a buy-in, i.e. the pension scheme buys a single insurance contract to cover all of its liabilities on a buy-in basis (the policy is held as an asset of the scheme) and then starts the process of winding up the scheme. The trustee can then go through the steps needed to complete the buy-out (in particular, data cleansing and verification), safe in the knowledge that it has secured the insurance terms via the buy-in at the start of the process. This is shown in Figure 14.3.

The completion of the pension buy-out means that both the employer and the trustees can consider that they have settled their obligations to the pension scheme members in full and the scheme can be wound up. This is obviously a very attractive solution for those employers who have seen their business activity and profitability severely impacted by pension scheme risks and regulation. The employer can move forward without the cost, time, resource, risk and regulatory burden associated with a pension scheme.

Insurance regulation and pricing

Regulation

Insurance policies issued by insurers regulated by the UK Financial Services Authority (FSA) can rightly be viewed as a very secure home for pension liabilities. Although no financial product is completely without risk (even a government bond!), the risk of an insurance company defaulting on its pension annuity liabilities is very low (to date, I am not aware of any UK insurer defaulting on its annuity policies). The key reasons for this are described briefly below, but this is only a very high level overview of the relevant factors:

- *Full funding requirement*: Pension liabilities held by insurance companies are required to be fully funded at all times; unlike a pension scheme, an insurance company is not allowed to operate with a deficit.
- *Prudent reserves plus a statutory margin*: Under the so-called 'Pillar 1' regulatory requirements, insurance company reserves must be calculated with prudential margins in the assumptions, such that there is no significant foreseeable risk that the liabilities will not be met as they fall due. In addition, the insurer must maintain a minimum level of solvency on top of its prudent reserves (currently at 4 per cent). A breach of the requirement to hold the statutory solvency margin (which should be monitored continuously) would be a trigger for regulatory intervention, which may involve closure to new business or de-risking of the investment portfolio. In addition, there are strict limits on the valuation of investments held to back the liabilities to avoid over concentration in any one asset. For example, if an insurance company has lent 10 per cent of its assets to a non-listed institution, it can only recognise up to 5 per cent of its fund value in respect of that loan when determining its solvency level according to Pillar 1. The insurance company will also have a management target for a solvency level in excess of the Pillar 1 minimum, to be disclosed to the FSA, who will be notified if this target is breached. In summary, the protection under the Pillar 1 regime can be described as:
  - reserving, which includes substantial margins above the best estimate expected outcomes;
  - additional minimum solvency margin requirements;
  - a prudent basis for valuation of assets, including non-recognition of assets concentrated with single counterparties;
  - full funding requirement at all times of the reserves and solvency margins;
  - management targets in excess of the minimum, with FSA notification if these targets are breached; and

- regulatory action possible before a deficit appears.
- *Risk-based capital assessment*: Under the so-called 'Pillar 2' requirements, insurance companies are required to calculate reserves on a best-estimate basis, but with a discount rate equal to a risk-adjusted rate (essentially the liquid, risk-free rate plus a small margin for the captured, illiquid, risk-free rate). They are then required to calculate the exposure of the insurance company to stresses/shocks that would be consistent with a 1-in-200-year event (VaR 99.5 per cent), i.e. the worst one-year event to occur in a 200-year period. The insurance company must hold sufficient assets to remain fully funded when measured against its best-estimate reserves if such a 1-in-200-year event occurs over the following year. In 2012/13, new solvency rules for insurers in the European Union will be introduced ('Solvency II'). At the time of writing, the detailed rules for Solvency II have not been finalised. However, it is expected that Solvency II will introduce higher minimum capital requirements for annuity business, which may in turn place upwards pressure on the pricing of pension buy-outs and buy-ins.
- *Stringent reporting and monitoring requirements*: As indicated above, insurers need to manage themselves to be fully funded at all times and must notify the FSA of a breach of those requirements, well before the assets have fallen below the level of the reserves needed to ensure that benefits are paid in full.
- *Compensation scheme*: The Financial Services Compensation Scheme (FSCS) covers buy-in and buy-out insurance contracts and provides a safety net which underwrites 90 per cent of the policyholders' benefits in the event of insurance company default.

The combined effect of these and other requirements means that insurers are penalised for taking excessive risks, by having to fund fully the risks they do take on. This leads to an investment policy focused on 'low risk' investments such as gilts, corporate bonds and secured lending, and avoids 'high risk' investments such as equities.

The risks faced by a typical insurance company can be contrasted with those faced by a typical pension scheme. The charts in Figures 14.4 and 14.5 result from a simplified risk model (calculating the impact of various market and other stress events) applied to a pension scheme that is 70 per cent funded, and invests 50 per cent of its assets in equities, and a sample insurance company.

The first percentage shown is the sum of the impacts of each 'stress' event, for example, a 40 per cent fall in equity values. The second percentage shown ('net risk') is the impact of these events after making allowance for the fact that some of the stresses modelled would not be expected to happen simultaneously.

Pricing

Insurance pricing is influenced by a number of factors. These factors do not necessarily move in line with the value of a pension scheme's investments and

233

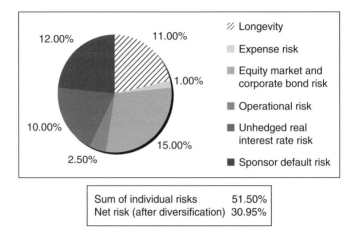

Sum of individual risks	51.50%
Net risk (after diversification)	30.95%

Figure 14.4 Pension fund: risk breakdown

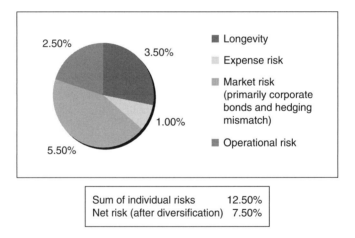

Sum of individual risks	12.50%
Net risk (after diversification)	7.50%

Figure 14.5 Insurance company: risk breakdown

so the affordability of insurance may vary considerably over time. This fact means that pension schemes that have insurance of their liabilities as a strategic objective would be well advised to monitor regularly their asset position versus market pricing of insurance contracts, as windows of opportunity for tactical purchase of insurance policies will arise. Speed of transaction is also important. If a pension scheme is able to afford insurance, but takes too long to transact, the movement of insurance pricing versus the pension scheme's asset values in the meantime may put the transaction out of reach.

The key factors affecting insurance pricing are as follows:

- *Real and nominal risk-free rates*: Insurance companies do not generally take interest rate or inflation rate exposure and will typically seek to hedge fully their exposure to these risks via the swap and gilt markets. This means that insurance pricing will move directly in line with the cost of hedging these risks. For example, a 1 per cent movement in long-term interest rates will typically lead to a 15 per cent change in the price of an insurance buy-in/-out. If a pension scheme is not hedged against interest and inflation rate movement, rising interest rates and falling inflation rates will make insurance pricing more attractive.
- *Returns above risk free available on long-term corporate bonds ('credit spreads')*: Insurance companies that write pensions annuity business will typically invest a substantial amount of their assets in corporate bonds. The credit spreads available on those bonds, minus allowance for possible defaults, will influence the underlying returns that the insurer projects when pricing the contract. When credit spreads are low, insurance pricing is higher, and when credit spreads are higher, insurance pricing is lower. If a pension scheme's assets are not invested in corporate bonds, increasing bond spreads should make insurance deals more affordable, although over the last year we have seen the beneficial impact of increasing corporate bond spreads offset by falling equity values.
- *Target return on capital*: The return on capital required/targeted by insurance companies will impact on insurance pricing. If capital is scarce, and/or the insurance is deemed to be higher risk, then targeted returns may be pushed up. If the proposed transaction has special features (for example, entry into a new market), insurers may be willing to accept a lower return for a specific transaction, taking into account the potential franchise value created by the deal.
- *Longevity level and improvement*: Most insurers adopt relatively sophisticated approaches to assessing longevity risk, often rating mortality on a member-by-member basis. The socio-economic profile of the pension scheme's membership will therefore influence insurance pricing. For example, a higher price will be charged for a pension scheme membership that consists of office workers in the south-east of England when compared to industrial workers in Glasgow. In addition, the insurance company will look at concentration risk, i.e. how much of the liability is concentrated in a few members with high pensions.

Other factors that will affect pricing include definition of spouse, pension increase definition, complexity of benefits, options and guarantees and other risks insured. The extent to which the premium will be paid in cash or through an in-specie transfer of assets will affect the price.

Considerations when purchasing a buy-out or buy-in

Considerations on a buy-out

Typically, the power to initiate a wind-up of a pension scheme in normal ongoing circumstances rests with the employer. In addition, most pension schemes are less than 100 per cent funded when measured against the cost of an insurance buy-out. This means that a buy-out will only be possible if the employer makes an additional contribution to the scheme. A full buy-out is therefore usually the decision of the employer, although the choice of the buy-out provider rests with the trustees.

In deciding whether or not to buy out the scheme, the employer will need to consider the costs and benefits of the transaction, the key items being as follows:

Benefits:

- the employer will no longer carry the risks associated with the pension scheme, thus will no longer be subject to volatile accounting liabilities and contribution requirements that go up following an economic downturn, at the very time when the employer needs to cut costs;
- without a pension liability, the employer's cost of unsecured borrowing should reduce;
- the company will be able to attract more and different investors, given that many investors/potential acquirers will not invest in businesses with large pension liabilities, no matter how well funded;
- a pension scheme reduces/slows the employer's freedom of action with regard to corporate restructuring and M&A; this impediment will be removed;
- a potentially significant saving of management time currently spent on pension matters; and
- removal of the risk of being subject to additional even more onerous pensions legislation and regulation in the future.

Costs:

- triggering a buy-out will incur some one-off costs associated with the wind-up (typically less than 1 to 2 per cent of the pension scheme liabilities);
- the buy-out will involve locking in to the insurance regime for the pension liabilities, which means that the price paid will be somewhat greater than the best estimate of the expected cost of meeting the benefits in the pension scheme environment; and
- the insurance company will be paid a risk premium for accepting the pension scheme risks.

The decision fundamentally boils down to whether the employer feels that the price paid is justified given the risks that are removed.

In a buy-out situation, the trustees' main concern will be with the choice of the insurer. Further comments on this subject are covered at the end of this chapter.

Considerations on a buy-in

Despite the fact that a buy-in is typically for a subset of the pension scheme's liabilities, the considerations are somewhat more involved than for a straight-forward, full buy-out. Given that a buy-in is essentially a decision to invest a proportion of the scheme's assets in an insurance contract, the party in the driving seat for the transaction is typically the trustee. Where the employer is voluntarily making additional contributions in order to facilitate the transaction, it may have more influence on the transaction.

The prime considerations to be looked at from the perspective of the trustee are as follows:

- *Impact on funding level and recovery plan*: A buy-in will crystallise a tranche of the pension liabilities at a specific cost, which may be greater or less than the scheme's corresponding technical provisions for those liabilities. To the extent that the cost of the insurance is greater than the technical provisions, the scheme should consider whether it could be afforded from the scheme assets as they stand (given the risk reduction and covenant enhancement that is achieved), or whether additional contributions or changes to the recovery plan should be considered.
- *Risk reduction and relative covenant strength*: An insurance contract will typically involve a significant reduction in the overall risks faced by the pension plan, since longevity, investment, interest rate, inflation and proportion-married risks are typically insured. Following this risk reduction, the ratio of employer covenant strength to pension scheme risks should be improved considerably, which should be considered in the context of the price paid for the insurance.
- *Impact on expected returns*: Given that buy-ins typically get written at an effective discount rate of risk-free plus a small margin, this level of implied return can be compared with the investment returns expected on the assets being sold or transferred as part of the deal. If gilts are being sold or transferred, the buy-in transaction will be expected to enhance the return expectations of the fund (with the added bonus of longevity and other risks being covered!). If corporate bonds or other assets are being sold or transferred, the insurance buy-in may result in a reduction in the expected overall returns for the fund – this needs to be considered in the context of the risk reduction that has been achieved. Consideration should be given to increasing the return targets on the pension scheme's remaining assets on the basis that some of the risk reduction achieved via the insurance could be 're-spent' on taking investment risk on the remaining assets.

- *Fairness between different groups of policyholders*: This consideration arises where the trustee is concerned that in holding an insurance policy in respect of a particular sub-group of members, they have not treated the insured members and non-insured members fairly in the context of both the allocation of the fund's assets and in the level of security and covenant protection afforded to the different groups of members (for example, have the members whose liabilities have been insured been treated more favourably because they now have the high level of security associated with insurance policy and/or the fund's assets used to purchase the insurance are greater than the share of the fund's assets that would otherwise be deemed to be backing their liabilities?). For a buy-in transacted in the normal course of business, this should not be a consideration since the buy-in policy is an asset of the scheme as a whole and its proceeds are not explicitly assigned to a particular group of members, i.e. there would be no restriction on the fund using the income from the insurance policy to pay benefits due to non-insured members. In addition, the covenant of the employer is still available to support all of the fund's liabilities, including both the liabilities that are matched by the insurance policy and those that are not. This consideration does arise, however, in circumstances where there is a crystallisation event which will formally allocate the assets of the fund to different groups of members, for example:
  - *A future wind up of the fund*: If a fund that holds a buy-in policy for a sub-group of members (for example, pensioners) is subsequently to be wound up and all of the fund's liabilities are insured, then ideally the buy-in contract would simply be assigned to the individual members covered by the buy-in policy and the remaining assets would be used to purchase insurance policies for the members not covered by the buy-in policy. The concern arises in the case where the wind up of the fund results in the situation where the available assets are insufficient to secure the members' benefits in full, and some reductions in benefits are required. This may result in the need to reduce benefits to the members covered by the buy-in policy below the level that is insured, with a view to 'reallocating' some of the insured benefits to members who were not covered by the buy-in policy. Provided such an eventuality is allowed for in the original buy-in policy, this should not be a problem.
  - *A buy-in followed by a partial buy-out*: Under this deal structure, a buy-in policy is purchased by the trustees for a sub-group of the plan's membership and this policy is then immediately converted into individual policies that are assigned to the insured members, who exit the fund. This construction is very attractive to the employer, as it means that it has no further direct or indirect obligations to the insured members and the insured liabilities are removed from the liabilities that are reported in the employer's financial statements. (Under a normal buy-in, the full liabilities are still reported and the insurance policy is reported as a plan asset.) From the

trustee's perspective, it is a definitive allocation of the scheme's resources between the insured and non-insured members, and a definitive allocation of the employer's covenant, i.e. the insured members enjoy insurance security following the deal and the non-insured members enjoy the whole of the employer covenant (after deduction of any incremental contributions needed from the employer) rather than sharing such covenant with the insured members. The trustee in this context will need to decide whether both groups of members are being treated fairly in the transaction.

- *Covenant strength of the insurer*: The trustee will wish to understand the current and prospective financial strength of the insurance company. Given that under a buy-in the employer will still be liable to cover the cost of any default by the insurer, this will also be of interest to the employer. Given that in theory any insurance company could be managed down to the minimum regulatory requirements, the employer and trustee should be comfortable that this minimum requirement is sufficient security. However, the current and intended strength of the insurer is relevant, and the key features of a review of the financial strength should include:
  - latest solvency position on Pillar 1 and Pillar 2 (and in due course Solvency II);
  - sources of additional capital;
  - current level of risk in the portfolio and the insurer's approach to risk management;
  - operational and administrative capabilities;
  - recent financial performance;
  - exposure to losses (and profits) from other lines of business; and
  - business plans.
- *Administrative arrangements*: The procedures to be adopted for the administration of the buy-in need to be considered as well as whether the payment of members will continue to be made by the trustee's incumbent administrators or by the insurance company acting as agents of the trustee.
- *Benefits insured*: In principle, the trustee will seek to insure the actual benefits promised to the members, to ensure that its actual liabilities are exactly matched by the insurance policy. This will also more easily facilitate a subsequent buy-out. In some cases, however, the trustee may not seek to insure the benefits on a one-to-one basis, either because it judges a particular benefit is best left uninsured (for example, on price grounds) or is discretionary and not insurable. In such cases, the trustee needs to make sure that it will not face issues if at a future date it wishes to convert the buy-in policy to a buy-out one.

The insurance process

In a typical situation, the trustees, the employer or both will have received initial advice and input from their consultants as to typical insurance pricing and the options available prior to deciding whether to run a formal quotation process with a view to concluding an insurance transaction. This advice may be supplemented by initial indicative quotations received from one or more insurers.

Prior to embarking on a formal quotation process, the trustee and/or employer would be advised to take a number of actions designed to make the quotation process as smooth and efficient as possible:

- *Appoint an adviser*: For the trustee and the employer, this may well be the first time insurance of pension liabilities has been considered. It is therefore advisable to appoint an adviser with experience in running insurance quotation processes that can bring both expertise and resource to the project.

- *Determine the scope*: There are many possible variations on how insurance might be implemented. It is very useful for the trustee/employer to have a clear idea on what it is seeking to achieve, and obtain advice on which structure might be best suited to those aims. A part of the process may also usefully include asking the insurance company whether it has any suggestions for possible solutions in addition to those specifically being requested in the process. It may be helpful to request quotations for different tranches of the total transaction, such as older/younger members, pensioners/deferreds and higher/lower pension amounts. This will enable an assessment of whether better pricing can be obtained by insuring different tranches with different insurers.

- *Be ready to manage the transaction*: Trustee bodies in general are not in a position to devote the day-to-day resources that would be typically applied to running a material financial transaction. It is advisable to set up a subcommittee with delegated authority to run the quotation process and negotiate with the chosen insurer. In many cases it is helpful for both the employer and the trustee to be engaged in the process, for example, by way of a joint working party. This will help to ensure that last-minute obstacles are not put in the way of completing a transaction.

- *Prepare the data*: In general, the greater the quality and scope of the information provided to the insurer, the greater the probability of obtaining the best price for the transaction that will reflect the ultimate cost of insuring the benefits, free from later adjustments due to data errors or new information. Key points include:
  - data verification – the trustees can carry out a data audit to ensure that the scheme membership data is free from material errors. The data supplied to the insurers should ideally include sufficient information to enable a detailed analysis of the socio-economic profile of the membership;
  - mortality information – if the scheme is sufficiently large, provision of detailed data regarding the deaths experienced over historical periods will be of relevance; and

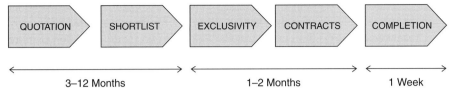

Figure 14.6 Typical insurance quotation process

- asset information – a detailed breakdown of the scheme assets will enable the costs associated with transitioning the assets to the insurer's proposed asset portfolio to be considered.
- *Agree the benefits to be insured*: As noted previously, the trustee should review its position on discretionary benefits and determine the extent to which it wishes to crystallise the discretionary benefits in any insurance contract. The most common issues to consider here are the definitions of dependant, and ill-health retirement. In addition, there may be options available other than insurance, for example, when a scheme is wound up members with small pensions can have their entitlements settled via the payment of a wind-up lump sum. The pension scheme benefits may also include options for members, such as date of retirement and commutation of benefits at retirement. The actuarial factors to be applied in these circumstances under the insurance contract need to be considered, i.e. will the insurance company apply its own factors (typically more generous than those adopted by the pension scheme) or will the scheme's own actuarial factors be written into the contract?

A typical quotation process is shown in Figure 14.6.

Clearly, it should be possible to get from a quotation request to a preferred insurance provider in a shorter timescale than 3 to 12 months; however, that timescale is what is typically being experienced in the insurance market.

The length of process is a key risk for the trustee. If the trustee has made a decision in principle to insure and has sufficient assets to do so, it should move rapidly to secure a transaction. Delays in the process only lead to risks that insurance pricing will drift apart from the value of the assets earmarked to finance the transaction.

Price and terms comparability

A critical part of the quotation process is ensuring that the quotations received from different insurers are directly comparable. In this context, it should be ensured that the insurance proposals from different insurers are based on the same basic assumptions in the context of the membership

241

data used, the benefits to be insured, the date assumed for the transaction, the date when responsibility for benefit payments commences, the treatment of increases due on the benefits, the actuarial factors used for member options, the approach to dealing with data errors and omissions and other factors.

It should also be clarified whether the insurance price is based on receiving the premium in cash or an in-specie transfer of assets, and whether such assets are valued at mid or bid price.

Certainty versus best price

As indicated above, the best approach to achieving certainty in an insurance process is to move quickly. Given that an insurance policy is only formally effective following the signing of an insurance contract, there remains a risk that the insurance price will change up until this point. Clearly, there is a need to run a process whereby the various insurers are given an opportunity to improve on their initial offers and give a best and final price, but this process should not be dragged out for too long as the price improvement that may be obtained may be far outweighed by the negative impact of market movements in the intervening weeks.

Insurance companies will typically quote a price based on market conditions on a specific date, and indicate the approach for adjusting the price for a transaction that occurs at a later date. Given that the quotation needs to be based on known market conditions, the quotation price will always be for a date in the past; therefore, the price adjustment mechanism will need to be considered carefully as there is typically a four- to six-week period between the final quotation being received and the signing of the insurance contract. The price adjustment mechanism used by the insurer will typically be time limited (as it will not be a perfect match for the actual movement in the insurance price and therefore exposes the insurer to risk). The adjustment formula will usually be based on the cash-flow profile of the liabilities and the interest rate, inflation and corporate credit markets.

Clearly, there is a risk that the value of the pension scheme assets moves out of line with the premium adjustment formula, thus making the insurance deal either impossible or requiring an additional contribution from the employer in excess of that originally envisaged. There are two key ways to mitigate this risk:

- adjust the assets to match closely the price adjustment formula proposed by the insurer; and
- negotiate with the insurer that the transaction price is locked into the value of an agreed pot of assets, and follows exactly the movement in those assets.

In either case, this will typically involve the pension scheme switching its investments to predominantly gilts and corporate bonds.

Additional security

Under a buy-in contract, the pension scheme retains the ultimate liability to pay the pension benefits to insured members and hence the employer retains responsibility for making good any shortfall. In this case, both the trustee and the employer are exposed to counterparty risk against the insurer, in so far as a default by the insurance company on the buy-in contract will need to be made good by the trustee/employer. Given that a buy-in contract may represent a significant proportion of the pension scheme's investments, there is a question of whether additional security should be sought, over and above that provided by the insurance regulatory regime.

Additional security typically takes the following forms:

- *Surrender right*: The trustee is given the right to surrender the contract if the insurance company solvency position falls below certain minimum thresholds.
- *Ring-fenced assets*: In order to ensure that sufficient assets are available to meet the surrender payment noted above, assets at an agreed level may be held in a ring-fenced account either within the insurer or held separately. On the occurrence of a trigger event, the trustee has the right to claim the assets held in the ring-fenced account. Under certain structures, these assets are deposited back with the trustee at the policy outset.
- *Guarantees*: Guarantees are given by entities outside of the insurance company issuing the policy (for example, other members of the insurance group or a bank).

In essence, the additional security gives the policyholder an advance claim over the insurer's assets in preference to the other policyholders who do not have this additional security. In order to comply with the principle of treating customers fairly, any additional security granted from within the insurer's resources should in normal circumstances be reflected by an additional premium for granting this benefit. In addition, if a policyholder is given an advance claim on certain assets, and these assets are insufficient to meet the policyholder's full rights on insolvency, its remaining claim may be subordinated to those of ordinary policyholders.

There are variations on the ways of granting additional security and the above does not necessarily capture all of the possible alternatives.

Additional security measures may in principle be attractive to a trustee, but it needs to be considered carefully whether the additional costs involved justify the additional security obtained in practice. These include not only the additional premium charged for this feature, but also the possibility that the insurer with the most competitive quote is not selected because it is unwilling to offer additional security. In addition, the trustee may incur considerable ongoing costs in monitoring the security arrangements. It should also be noted

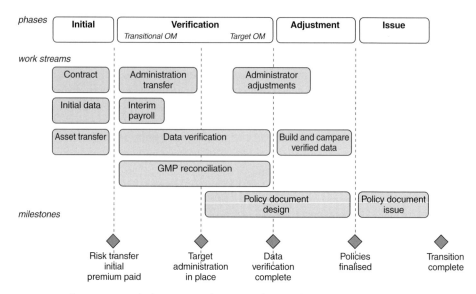

Figure 14.7 Typical sequence of events: policy signing to issuing individual policies

that the insurance regime already provides an extremely high level of security without these arrangements.

After the deal

Under both a buy-in and a buy-out, there will typically be a period of data verification after the policy has been signed, with the objective of ensuring that the membership data upon which the insurance policy is based is fully up to date and accurate. Typically, the insurance policy will include the terms on which the data corrections will be translated into adjustments to the premium paid. In some cases, the insurer may take on the risk of data errors (i.e. there is no change to the premium in respect of correcting data errors).

Under a buy-out policy, further actions will be taken which will progress through to the issuing of individual policies to the scheme members followed by the winding up of the pension scheme.

A typical sequence of events, focusing on administration and verification actions, from policy signing through to issuing individual policies, is shown in Figure 14.7.

Summary

Insurance provides both risk management and liability settlement products to pension schemes. The insurance sector has attracted new players, capital and products in recent years, which has led to increased competition, lower pricing and greater choice for pension schemes and their corporate sponsors. Trustees who are looking to de-risk their liabilities and purchase insurance should review insurance pricing on a regular basis to take advantage of windows of opportunity when insurance pricing moves favourably compared to pension fund asset movements.

15

Pensions – a corporate perspective

DAVID BLACKWOOD

Most corporate owners of DB liabilities now recognise that pension risk management is a core issue in managing their corporation's balance sheet – and, absent some buy-out or fully-hedged and funded solution, will continue to be so for a very long time.

Economically, a DB scheme is the company's problem – not the trustees'. However, as we know, the company does not manage it per se, and the governance structure of the trustee framework supported by the actuarial and legal profession when combined with the changing legislative and regulative framework make the influencing of scheme direction far more difficult.

The trustee issues are touched on towards the end of this chapter, but it is important to say at this juncture that generally – unless the trustees have a firm plan to exit the corporate balance sheet – they will likely recognise that the company and the fund are in it together for the long haul and a well-developed, sensible company proposition for pension operational and financial risk management is likely to get appropriate traction.

Pensions in context

The starting point for a corporation and its approach to pensions should be the group balance sheet. The diagram in Figure 15.1 is a simple representation of the 'economic' balance sheet (not the accounting one). Think of it as the sum of the parts analysis an equity analyst would attribute to the stock.

Long term, the equity market value of a company is a function of:

- the enterprise value of the operating businesses, valued by various means, but often referenced to an EBITDA (Earnings Before Interest, Tax, Depreciation and Amortisation) multiple as a short cut;
- the nominal value of the debt that has to be repaid to lenders; and
- the deficit in the pension fund (the difference between two potentially big numbers).

I have also put in other assets and liabilities. Often, a company will have other issues of financial value, to do with the past or unrelated to future

246

EV (=enterprise value) operating assets	Other assets	Pension investments	Total assets
Net external debt	Other liab's	Pension liabilities	Total liabilities
Enterprise value (EV) less debt (A)	Net at fair value (B)	Net deficit or surplus (C)	*Market cap (A)-(B)-(C)*

Figure 15.1 Representation of the 'economic' balance sheet (I)

trading – loosely, contingent assets and liabilities. These might be a surplus plot of land, a legal case where you are claiming – or a legal case where you are being claimed against. They have nothing to do with the cash generation, and therefore the EV (enterprise value) of the operating businesses – but could result in a cash inflow or outflow, so affect the market capitalisation. They need to be considered if significant.

All of the parts of the pictogram are subject to risk. It is the role of a corporation to deliver value to its shareholders – and this involves understanding and managing risk. If corporations do not understand all of the group's material risks, bankruptcy will be more likely – and a bit of a surprise, no doubt. Pensions must be seen as part of all of the risks run by a corporation. There are people who argue that a corporation should hedge all of its pension risk and concentrate on what it is good at; some the opposite. The company must take its own position – from a corporate perspective, there is ultimately nothing substantially wrong with taking risk in a pension fund – it is just part of the company's balance sheet: the important thing is to have understood the risks, weighed them against all of the other risks of the corporation and taken the decision deliberately.

This 'helicopter' view of balance sheet risk management is the first step for a company in managing pension schemes – understanding its scale in the context of all of the other moving parts of the balance sheet. Clearly, the larger it is relative to the other parts, the more attention it should get.

The next financial step is to understand the risk inherent in the assets and liabilities of the scheme, alongside the risks of the other parts of the balance sheet (including currency) and determine the approach to risk in the pension scheme itself. For example, with a big pension scheme and a big deficit, would it be wise to run the company with a lot of debt? Clearly, this would increase the risk for the company.

This last point is relevant to working with trustees. A well-run balance sheet, with a sensible approach to all risks, is a sound basis for getting a 'working together' outcome with trustees – one that has very excessive leverage is typically not. Corporations that substantially increase their risk profile should expect an aggressive response from trustees.

However, before moving on to financial risk considerations, there is an important aspect of pension risk management that is often ignored, namely, the management of the liabilities themselves.

Liabilities – the operational side

Say 'liability management' to someone in the pensions industry and they start talking about clever LDI strategies and matching assets with liabilities. The first thing to do before leaping into any complex (possibly unnecessarily complex) financial risk management associated with liabilities is to take a look at what could be done about the liabilities themselves. The following is a simple checklist of issues to contemplate, drawn up from a perspective that these schemes are going to be shut (eventually) and the end game is a long-term, financial issue, possibly terminated by a straight buy-out.

Liability management checklist

- closure to new entrants;
- benefit modification;
- closure to new accrual;
- audit of liabilities;
- transfer of liabilities;
  - enhanced transfer values;
  - selective annuitisation;
- reshaping existing benefits; and
- administration costs.

The first three of these clearly limit the rate of accrual of new liabilities into the pension scheme, and therefore the increase in balance sheet economic liabilities and associated risk.

The vast majority of private-sector UK schemes have already closed their defined benefit pension schemes to new entrants. Companies that make widgets should not be accruing liabilities that are more appropriate for a life insurer. Step one, therefore, on any rational approach to managing pensions from a corporate perspective is to close the scheme to all new accrual. Alongside this, one would provide some element of compensation designated as specifically associated with pensions – a DC scheme. Care should be taken here as well. Many DC schemes are set up as trust-based; in my view, this is to be avoided as they have their own governance burden, and any such arrangements should similarly be closed, with DC delivered by a group personal pension arrangement where each employee has their own fund with a regulated provider.

Benefit modification for existing members is a half-way house to which some corporations have gone. It is understandable – taking away some, but not all, of the defined benefit is likely to be easier – although it brings further benefit structure complexities. However, 'the biggest enemy of better is best' – so if management's view is that full closure to future accrual is not achievable or desirable for HR or other considerations, then benefit modification is the way to go – but with a view to coming back to full closure when the environment might permit it. (In my current company, the benefit modification was implemented in 2006/07, and final closure to future accrual was implemented in 2009/10.)

Benefit modification usually involves capping future accrual, so one short-term upside of benefit modification is an immediate reduction in the accounting liabilities. IAS 19 allows for future salary increases ahead of inflation to be built into the current liability – one of its shortcomings. Capping inflation for future accrual (as an example) could take some 5 per cent off the liabilities. However, it is an accounting anomaly: real accrued liabilities are rarely affected. In equity market terms this is a positive, and in economic terms significant, step in reducing future accrual.

The role of trustees in modification and closure to future accrual will vary according to the terms of the trust deed, and situations vary. Advice which trustees will receive may also vary depending on the leanings of the advisers. However, a reasonable starting position for a corporate is that it is the trustee's role to protect accrued benefits – and it is not particularly their role to focus on future accrual – although this may vary depending on the trust deed itself. It is also an emotive issue, so there may well be a desire for the trustee board to do something to keep the scheme open in some way, shape or form, although this will ultimately wane over time.

The corporate message to the trustees should be clear: closure to new accrual (or benefit modification) is positive in terms of protecting accrued benefit. The sponsor will not attract future risk, and the covenant is improved as a result. Many trustees would support this.

Auditing the liabilities has two purposes. Firstly, it is not unusual to find payment errors in pension liabilities. At ICI, we found over £150 million net present value (NPV) in favour of the company from one identified payment practice. The second reason to audit liabilities and do some work on the data, of course, is to try and tidy the data up such that, if at a future time one looks at buy-outs (either partial or full), the data is in good shape.

Enhanced Transfer Value (EHTV) arrangements appear to have had some success over the last few years. EHTVs involve offering an additional payment to deferred members to supplement the transfer value out of the scheme. There are clearly going to be various scenarios where it is possible to strike an appropriate economic compromise where it is in the company's interest to contribute extra money. The history of these is quite interesting. When they started, a number of advisers to the pension industry saw these as the next great mis-selling scandal and wanted to ban them. Personally, I struggle with this. The current regulatory framework envisages transfers – so why should there be an objection to a larger transfer value? The downside of the EHTV scheme is that there is a fair amount of fixed cost to make them work (such as the actuaries' fees for the transfer value calculations), and often a relatively low take up.

The objective of the corporation here may vary. At one level, it might want to simply make a gain against IAS 19 – not necessarily a sound economic rationale – but likely a positive for the equity market. On a very qualitative basis, just to have the assets and liabilities reduce a little may be helpful in its dealings with the outside world. It should certainly be considered carefully as a serious opportunity to reduce risk and long-term cost.

Recently, other ways of limiting the liabilities have emerged. One of the interesting ones is to reshape the liabilities, for example, offering, based on current life expectancy, a higher fixed pension or a pension with fixed increases rather than variable, inflation-linked increases. These approaches can reduce some risk (obviously inflation) and more extreme mortality if the pension has been adjusted to a level basis. Again, these are not straightforward exercises, but may warrant some consideration. As ever, the cost/benefit needs to be considered up front: it remains easy to spend large amounts of money developing ideas, only to do nothing.

Lastly, administration costs are ultimately the liability of the sponsor, just as all of the other economic issues are. The industry, on balance, is driven by rules, and therefore I have not found it to be particularly commercial: if something is supposed to be done, cost-benefit concerns are often not factored in. With advisers accountable to trustees and the corporate picking up the bill, the situation is not ideal. The corporate should get involved in the administration costs and should not be shy of challenging inefficiency and a non-commercial approach to charging, as it would do in its business activities.

Financial assets and financial liabilities – measurement and risk

As the liability management issues areas above are developed and implemented, the scheme tends towards a financial black box of liabilities (with no new liabilities being created) and assets. From here onwards, a corporation will look to develop a 'run off' plan, addressing these risks and funding.

The end point may of course be quite short term if buy-out is the plan, but if long-term run-off is the plan, you may well be looking at holding this position for some several decades – a long time indeed in the life of corporations that prepare strategic plans with maybe a five-year time horizon!

I would surmise that, as the world moves forward, any plans to hold for the long term will be tested periodically against buy-out, and there will be a gradual move off sponsor balance sheets (the ultimate end), but until then it is likely that the plan will be to reduce gradually risk within the scheme over time.

Table 15.1 Basic facts – closed scheme (m = million)	
EBITDA	£125m
EBIT	£110m
Implied EV	£1,000m (assumes the sector trades on 8 x EBITDA)
Net debt	£250m

EV (=enterprise value) operating assets	Other assets	**Pension investments**	Total assets
Net external debt	Other liab's	**Pension liabilities**	Total liabilities

Enterprise value (EV) less debt (A)	Net at fair value (B)	Net deficit or surplus (C)	*Market cap (A)-(B)-(C)*

Figure 15.2 Representation of the 'economic' balance sheet (II)

Therefore, let us return to the balance sheet schematic in Figure 15.2. The sum of the parts defines the equity value of the company. As EBITDA and economic prospects move, so the enterprise value changes over time in the eyes of investors. The scheme assets and liabilities are undoubtedly moving in value and since the corporation is accountable to make sure everyone gets paid, that is effectively a gain or loss to the market capitalisation of the company.

For future use, let us put some numbers to this – for a company of some substance, with a pension scheme well worth worrying about. Currency risk and contingent assets are ignored.

- pension scheme IAS 19 liabilities £600 million (discounted at 5.5 per cent);
- pension scheme assets £475 million;
- liability duration around 16 years;
- 'risk free' valuation of liabilities, say, £720 million (say a discount rate of about gilts plus 30 bps – assume gilts at 4.1 per cent, so 4.4 per cent);
- mortality – current table at medium cohort + 1 per cent (best estimate); and
- current funding deficit £135 million (technical provision basis) – being proposed to be funded over ten years at £18 million per annum.

This scheme fits the introduction that it is certainly big enough to warrant careful attention in managing the balance sheet and risks of the corporation. The basic equity valuation of this company would be:

EV	£1,000
Net debt	–£250
Pension accounting deficit	–£125
Implied market value	£625m

To consider risk, one needs a perspective on the liabilities – so how does one measure liabilities?

The accounting standards say high grade bonds. The accountants interpret this as AA bonds. The actuaries use the funding valuation and 'technical provisions'. The buy-out market has a more conservative valuation, but it needs to allow for mortality being worse than expected, amongst other things, and make a return on risk capital. The PPF has its own basis, but then it varies the benefits slightly.

The interesting development over recent years has been the use of structured products using cash pools and swaps (effectively synthetic bonds) that can be structured to pay liabilities on a matched or hedged basis. A valuation can be done using the 'swaps curve', which is relevant to risk management and will be touched upon later. Before the 2008 financial crisis, they would yield about 30 bps over gilts (and I would have seen this as a 'risk free' basis), but this moved to a discount to gilts post the crisis. I have kept the 30 bps premium in the 'risk free' calculation, although to deliver it long term one would now need to get it with reasonable certainty from somewhere other than swaps (at the moment).

In the above example, the 'risk-free'-based valuation is probably not a bad surrogate for the buy-out market. At this level, the company could buy the liabilities out (perhaps with a small top up), but it would need to fund the accounting deficit and also find an extra £120 million. It would currently be perceived as having a net debt to EBITDA ratio of 2, which would be re-financeable. If it bought the scheme out, it would rise to a net debt to EBITDA ratio of almost 4 – considerably more risky to re-finance. It is doubtful whether this company would want to buy the scheme out, but with a scheme of this size, it would want a carefully controlled plan with regard to risk inside the scheme.

It is important to grasp that the liabilities are a series of cash flows, not an NPV. Since the assumption now is that the scheme is shut, the liabilities are mainly a function of:

● deferred pension entitlement/pension in receipt;
● inflation, on some of the amount, probably with constraints; and
● projected life expectancy, including surviving spouse assumptions and their entitlement.

These have to be paid, and they are at this juncture only a forecast: we do not know when people will die or what inflation will be. They are to be paid out of scheme assets, company contributions and investment returns from these.

Before looking at risk, hedging and all of the clever stuff, it is worth considering simplistically how a corporate (in this case, a UK corporate) might deal with any other financial liability.

Example 1: $10,000 to pay in six months? Typically, this would be hedged into sterling by a swap, no cash required. Currency can move significantly in short periods of time. The hedge would simply be a swap.

Example 2: money (a loan) raised in dollars, repayable in ten years – say, $500 million. Assuming this is not part of a larger hedging strategy, a corporate would hedge using a swap. Typically, these days, because the banks understand that the longer the time, the more likely the swap could accrete substantial value, there would be collateralisation arrangements, so liquidity issues would have to be considered.

The point here is that hedging is put in to make things certain.

Example 3: if a fixed sterling liability exists in ten years of, say, £500 million – say a deferred payment for something – with no need to monetise it, what then? The accounting standards would require it to be discounted, with the annual unwind on the debt going to interest, so it will feel like a debt – with a current value of less than £500 million. The discount rate would probably be gilts, but might be at the company's cost of debt.

Here, accounting is creating the economic reality: it is a debt, or is it not? Normally, loans would have covenants and constraints about borrowing and the deployment of capital. If someone agrees to a fixed nominal deferred payment in ten years with no conditions, are they a lender or some form of quasi equity investor?

Example 4: the last one – the same as example 3 – but it has to be collateralised? This is the pension-equivalent example. The only certain way to make sure there is exactly the right amount of money is to put £500 million discounted at the ten-year gilt yield into ten-year gilts. Even then, there is a small amount of re-investment risk on the interest.

However, given a free hand, would a corporate do this? Many would, but some, given a free hand, may choose to invest in riskier assets to keep the overall cash flow call down, even if it is just a little credit risk. Remember: if they could avoid monetising the liability, they would deploy the cash elsewhere in the business, looking to make higher rates of return. Do most people in commerce not believe in superior returns on equities to gilts? What is the point in them doing otherwise then?

This is at the heart of the risk issue. Its equivalence in personal pensions is if you are saving to have cash for your retirement in 30 or 40 years, the advice is to invest in equities, but better returns than gilts are not guaranteed! Returning to the liabilities of the pension fund, Figure 15.3 shows the cash-flow profile of the pension scheme above. While the NPV at the 'risk-free' rate

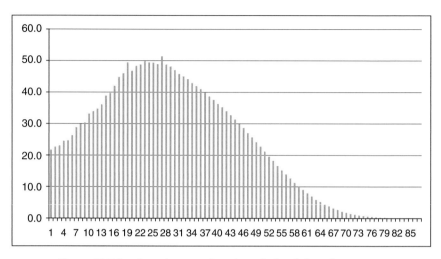

Figure 15.3 Pension scheme projected nominal cash flows by year

is, say, £720 million, the sum of all of the bars is £2 billion – the total nominal value of the liabilities as forecast.

Each of the bars (based on the mortality and inflation assumptions) is an amount of money to find in each year. Coming back to Example 4: if you were required to monetise the promise for each year (i.e. fund it), would you put it in gilts or a higher-yielding asset class? Which bars would one aim to fund with equities or other risky assets? For those who say ten years is too short for risky asset classes, what about the bar in year 20, or year 30, etc.?

There are effectively two extremes of investing: low risk (matching these cash flows with 'risk–free' assets (gilts, or, in our example, gilts plus a small risk premia such as that previously available in LDI structures); to high risk – basically equities (or perhaps something racier).

Reconciling the two extremes requires that the company take a clear position on the risks, as it will have to make good any downside – assuming it can.

Cash flow comes into the equation in two respects:

- *Liquidity*: risky assets cannot deliver superior returns over ten years if you have to sell them to pay current liabilities in year 1 – a point often over-looked in valuations which use a discount rate embracing these returns.
- *Investment period*: the theory is, the longer risky assets are held, the more likely they are to deliver superior returns (or the more likely it is that it will look like a good decision not to have invested in risk-free assets). It is the same principle as in personal retirement savings.

Personally, I believe that the 'risk-free' way is the right approach to measuring the issue: it is consistent with the idea of hedging and allows measurement of risk for alternate asset strategies compared to this benchmark. I also personally tend towards the lower risk approach to investing and leave the company to direct the bulk of its risk capacity elsewhere.

Each corporate must determine its own approach and the position should reflect the balance sheet. If it is leveraged up to, say, three times net debt to EBITDA excluding the scheme, would it want all of its pension assets in equities with a bond-like pension liability? This increases the risk enormously. If it wants to take investment risk, then the issue is how (there are other sections of this book that cover investment risk, albeit from a trustee perspective – see Chapters 11 and 12). The issue is also one of pragmatism. For a company with a significant fund, switching to an investment strategy based on risk free will crystallise a large deficit, which could damage the equity of the company and make it difficult to fund. Rightly or wrongly, pragmatism often drives risk decisions.

What should be obvious is that for a closed scheme, the longer it runs, the less appropriate it is to hold risky assets: at the extreme, one year before the end of the scheme, you would not have the remaining investments in equities – you would have it matched. In practice, good risk management would have you matched a long time before that.

Coming back to the idea of hedging and risk, the most appropriate reference point is, in my view, the 'risk-free' valuation. It is a liability number that, simplistically, for a given view of mortality one can hedge. Basically, for that amount of money, a portfolio can be constructed which more or less should pay the liabilities as they fall due, as long as people die to forecast. Inflation is a factor, but this can be addressed in the portfolio. It is not perfect, but it is normal to measure risk compared to a fixable (hedged) outcome, and this would broadly do just that – fix the outcome. What is 'risk free' needs some thought. One could plump for gilts, but as mentioned above, prior to the 2008 financial crisis, I would have taken swaps – delivering gilts plus 30 bps – so even the measurement reference for hedging can be dynamic. Perhaps the accountants were not a long way off when they settled on the AA rate (if one interpreted its intent as gilts plus the 'normal' AA credit spread). Somewhere in this region is an appropriate benchmark that should be the basis, which is broadly hedgeable and is likely within a manageable additional payment to a buy-out number. A reference framework that is not too detached from buy-out has the advantage that, at some point in time, if the run-off plan reaches fully funded against that measure and de-risked to match, the extra payment to reach buy-out should be manageable – especially as all administration and governance costs would disappear at the same time.

I have set out later how a corporate might approach risk taking in a scheme in run-off – as ever though, subject to agreement with the trustees!

Pension fund risk measurement and limitations

When looking at pension funds in isolation, the measure used by consultants is VaR (Value at Risk). It is basically a cut-off point on a statistical bell curve.

The 95 per cent VaR point is typically used, meaning that there is a 5 per cent chance that the answer will be this or worse. It is useful tool for articulating outcomes, and as there is little else available for doing this it should be used.

The run-off plan shown later on in this chapter shows some VaR calculations.

VaR is used in financial markets for many things, such as short-term currency movements in measuring financial risk – the emphasis being short-term (a few months if that). The VaR statistics for pension schemes are based on annual movements and the statistical validity of the data is questionable. It is based on past movements: a reference point of how assets have moved in the past, how liability discount rates have moved in the past and how they have moved relative to each other.

However, it is a lifeline for lay people looking for a reference point for their risks, but it is ultimately potentially very misleading. The analysis has no memory. From the current point the upwards and downwards movements have equal weighting: an equity market that has just halved is equally likely to halve again or move up 50 per cent. The data points are insufficient. However, it has substantial traction. It is clearly helpful in showing how things can move, but it needs to be tempered with judgment. Furthermore, under VaR analysis, there have probably been two (possibly three) one in twenty downside events on annual equity movements in the last decade: possible, but very unlikely. In addition, it is well recognised in downside risk measurement that 'bad' events happen more often and are more severe than typically predicted by the measurement framework.

From a corporate perspective, VaR provides one approach to measuring risk. It is increasingly well embedded with trustees, who do not generally grasp its limitations. As such, a corporate will want to ensure that trustees are not 'seduced' by the simple solution that VaR-based analysis often seems to offer. Stress testing and scenario testing are other tools, which basically measure how bad it can get and what we can survive.

Again, to be repetitive, the corporate must consider all of the above and determine its preferred strategy for pension asset and liability risk management as a subset of the management of its total balance sheet.

Longer term – an example

Let us go back to our example company. It has closed its scheme and is planning to run with the scheme for the foreseeable future: it cannot and does not want to raise the funding for a buy-out.

Let us assume that its members' pension increases are essentially nominal, so ignore inflation.

Deficit funding – the company will fund the pension payroll – that way it can separate the assets from re-balancing and avoid liquidity issues in the plan, and focus on growing them to a target level.

The target is to get the assets to a level where a return of gilts plus 0.5 per cent will fund the remaining liabilities. This would probably be considered a

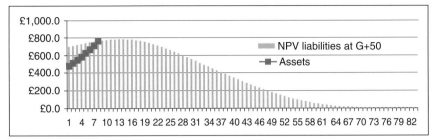

Figure 15.4 Asset/liability planned migration

very low risk return strategy – 20 bps more than their 'risk-free' benchmark. At the start of the plan, gilts plus 50 bps would have NPV liabilities of £700 million compared to £720 million on the 'risk-free' basis.

The maths shows that it will have to grow the assets at 6.8 per cent per annum for eight years to get to that level. It changes its governance framework with the trustees to modify asset strategy quickly as required, and includes a method for reducing investment risk if short-term excess returns are delivered.

The plan has an implied forward yield for gilts eight years out at 4.3 per cent: it needs to devise a way to lock in those yields going forward. This is another aspect of the risk: if the yields rise and they can be locked in, the assets will have to work less hard, or funding can be stopped earlier.

It determines a net debt to EBITDA ratio that reflects the underlying debt in the pension fund and the risk of it opening up significantly using VaR or scenario assessments. This limits the company's acquisition strategy out of debt-only acquisitions, and therefore acquisitions are more likely to need an equity-raising element.

It sets its dividend cover to reflect the substantial call on free cash flow to pay the deficit payments.

The chart in Figure 15.4 shows the journey path of its plan.

The chart shows the NPV of liabilities discounted at gilts plus the 0.5 per cent. The assets are planned to deliver 6.8 per cent per annum to catch up the liability line in eight years, during which time the pension payroll equals the deficit remediation payments.

Nominal payments into the plan during this timeframe (being the pension payroll) will be £200 million.

When the asset line catches up with the liability line, the asset strategy should be fully migrated to a gilts plus 50 bps target.

This is simplistic and clearly regular actions would be taken along the way. It would not be a two-step plan – buy the assets and in eight years switch! However, the two primary risks are now easy to see:

● Will the assets deliver their expected return over the eight years?

● Will gilts be available for purchase on a 4.3 per cent yield in eight years?

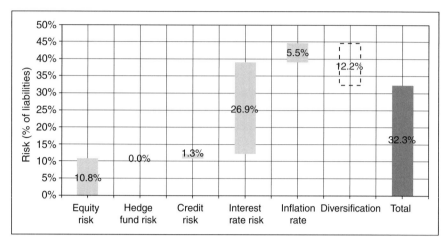

Figure 15.5 Example VaR analysis

The plan would deal with the assets and techniques to secure the gilt yield now or in the future. The probabilities of the movements in these can be articulated using the VaR analysis referred to above. See Figure 15.5.

Stability and higher certainty can be introduced by diversifying the assets, and hedging out some of the interest rate risk implied by a desire to move to gilts at current rates over time. Inflation is illustrative: it has been left out of the example above for ease.

It is worth bringing out the use of VaR on the above. If long-dated gilt rates were at an all time low, the liability VaR would be similar, but many would find it difficult to accept locking in low rates and the plan might simply embrace preparing to lock in the interest rates at some future target level (although, as we have seen in interest rates in Japan, this plan could fail).

Of course, there are many variants and issues to flesh out for the above, and it does not answer the question of what happens if the asset values crash and long-dated yields fall at the start – a 'double whammy'. If one takes a risk, it does not always work out, but having set its financial policies to deal with liquidity risk and manage its full balance sheet, the corporation is still in good shape for the next eight years – better than most – a position the trustees should be pleased with. The corporation that leverages up, pays away a huge dividend cover and pushes for extreme risk strategies in the fund (deliberately or in ignorance) to limit funding will 'crash and burn' if things go against it.

Two key risks left out of the above are inflation and mortality. Inflation can be looked at as a financial issue and it should be weighed with the investment return and gilt rate issue for the liabilities. Mortality is a difficult one: forecasts have moved along significantly in the last five years. Who knows how accurate they are. A corporate can measure the cost of people living a couple of years longer than forecast and determine whether the risk is worth eliminating. If buy-out is a long-term goal, then buy-in of annuities might be an option along the journey. However, in the early stages of a run-off plan for a fund with a reasonable deficit, it is unlikely that mortality risk will be a key focus compared to the asset-return and interest-rate risk issues, but it will become more relevant as things develop. Mortality swaps are a recent product that allow even this risk to be addressed without moving to buy-out.

There are too many variants to go into huge detail on a company's approach to pension asset liability risk and many sophisticated approaches to modifying and managing the risks. I would just repeat that it needs to be seen as part of the total balance sheet and planned accordingly.

Actuarial valuations limitations

None of the above uses an actuarial valuation – the source of the funding plan for trustees. From a corporate perspective, an actuarial valuation is not a valuation. It is a plan – a forecast of how much money is required, at certain rates of return – which to some extent is what a corporate should have as articulated above, but:

- The assumptions sometimes have embedded margins for 'prudence' built in, so it can be a poor starting point for a proper cash-flow-based plan.
- The NPV approach often splits the risk assets as focused on deferred members and low-risk investments as focused on the retired. Annual cash flows do not differentiate – and why should they – it is all cash; the important issue is the period holding risk assets and the migration to low risk assets.
- Liquidity is not considered.

Basically, a well-structured plan addressing annual cash flows, funding and the investment strategy over time is a far superior way of assessing and managing the problem. So coming back to the theme of a corporate perspective on this, a corporate should have a detailed run-off plan for the scheme that captures these dynamics.

Looking back to our example company, if it had a £30 million capital investment proposal, it would have annual cash-flow projections, NPV calculations, sensitivities and a whole lot more to go with it: after all, it would be investing nearly 5 per cent of its net worth. How is it that, for £2 billion of nominal liabilities, a cash-flow profile stretching 80 years and risk measures that say there is a 5 per cent chance the deficit could widen by over £100 million in any one year, its planning could possibly be based on the limited analysis of a deficit-only valuation of the trustee's actuary?

Accounting

The introduction of FRS 17 in the United Kingdom was clearly ground breaking in forcing deficits onto company balance sheets, and more importantly focusing financial managers of companies onto the risk and cost issues. However, they had to wrestle with the thorny issue yet again of how to value these liabilities (the assets are easy). Assuming the best view of mortality and inflation is factored into the cash-flow projections, the two major issues in bringing in it onto the balance sheet is ABO versus PBO (Accrued Benefit Obligation versus Projected Benefit Obligation) and the discount rate (the latter being the more significant of course). PBO was the chosen route: this causes UK schemes effectively to reflect the anticipated increases in salary in excess of inflation (typically 1 to 1.5 per cent) projected into the future to be brought back into the liability as an NPV. However, if the scheme is closed to future accrual with the link to salary increases taken away, ABO and PBO become the same and this particular problem is solved, which I think demonstrates that ABO would have been the proper choice for valuing liabilities. The discount rate that was picked was the AA discount rate. Many people are critical of this, but some decision had to be made. It did in fact put a degree of stability into deficits over the period of recent market collapses around the end of 2008 through to early 2009. Whatever the rights and wrongs of the discount rate, we do currently live in a world where, broadly, the corporate's equity valuation factors in the accounting deficit. While the finance director obviously needs to focus on economic issues, it is perfectly reasonable to want to put your best foot forward externally when it comes to the accounting deficit. Therefore, eliminating unnecessary prudence in the valuation, particularly in margins for mortality, etc., is something that is very sensible. Perhaps more importantly in the real world, given this is the way in which equity is valued and boards are generally accountable for equity value, financial risk-management plans do need to consider accounting deficit volatility. This is clearly another drive towards lower risk investment portfolios with higher gilt/synthetic bond and actual bond structures and swap overlays and the like to reduce accounting deficit volatility.

Rationally, it is the economic problem that needs to be managed, but equity markets do use the accounting deficit in a classic sum of the parts valuation of a company's equity. Managers are accountable for this, so it is the old adage of what gets measured gets managed. I have seen in my time a whole series of 'risk-management solutions' that get 'the right accounting answer': these need careful consideration though – the right accounting answer is potentially a poor basis on which to make a long-term economic decision.

Taxation

Never forget that a pension deficit, although it is often treated as debt in a sum of the parts valuation, is tax deductible. It is the only debt I know of that is tax deductible. If there is £500 million of market cap after reflecting a £200 million deficit, then with taxation at around 30 per cent, the tax deduction is worth over 10 per cent of the market cap: not something to miss out on. This may be reflected in the deferred tax asset, but not netted off the deficit. It is important for corporates to display the net effect: it is more representative of the economic cost of settling the deficit over time.

There may also be tax-planning opportunities linked to financial support. The contingent asset provided by the Marks & Spencer property transaction was an excellent example of this.

Working with trustees and their advisers

The bulk of the commentary to date has been based on the sponsor developing their own plan – a rational thing to do. Ultimately, it has to be agreed with the trustees.

Having worked with a number of pension funds, it is easy to get depressed about the advisory and governance framework and the way in which it has developed. It has to be there: everyone should understand that. However, it is full of opportunity to deliver form over substance and eliminate commercial judgment. Processes and change can be slow at best (the word 'glacial' is bandied about). It is all a bit harsh really. The bottom line is that it is important to understand that the framework can be slow, some parts can be improved and some will always be limited.

A few years ago, with the formulation of the regulator, it felt like advice was becoming increasingly focused on a simple idea that getting as much money over the wall into the fund as quickly as possible was a good idea, possibly to the exclusion of all else. I think there has been some moderation of this: perversely, the financial crisis may have helped. It can be detrimental to both trust and corporation to fund too quickly.

The best approach in dealing with trustees and advisers involves honesty and integrity. A good-reasoned plan, where the sponsor is behaving rationally (for example, in the outline run-off plan above, balancing dividend policy with funding), should get traction and create flexibility. Whatever a corporate may want to do with the plan, you are not always going to get what you want; but if it is sensible and beneficial (improves the covenant, moves forward funding, reduces risk or whatever), you have a good chance. Besides, what is the alternative?

To help trustees move along where, for example, they are advised that the plan does not fund sufficiently quickly or involves too much investment risk, then simplistically there are broadly two solutions: change the plan or give them something else!

Giving them 'something else' in the form of a contingent asset or the like is covered in the next section. Suffice to say that some form of extra security or entitlement may help to get the trustees on board, but it should be granted with considerable caution.

In dealing with trustee boards, independence can vary. They are required to be independent and there are penalties for individuals who behave improperly in the management of the fund (individuals and trustees). However, people are different, and the ability of the company to influence the trustee's plans will vary depending on who the trustees and advisers are. If the corporate puts forward a well-thought-out plan, it should get traction, but it might not. The advisers might not 'get it', or it sits outside the 'policies' they have adopted as a firm in their own right. The trustees may decline because they do not understand it, or simply because they can. I would stick to my thesis, though, that a sensible plan has the best chance.

Independent trustees have been a recent trend. Corporates may or may not be able to influence a decision to appoint, and such influence may or may not be appropriate. To the extent that a corporate is part of the decision, the decision from a corporate perspective ought to be earthed in whether it will be helpful or prejudicial in getting the job done. If it is likely to be unhelpful, it should be opposed. It is likely to be a permanent decision and that needs to be considered.

Advisers play a key role. One of the ironies about the situation is that they are executive and trustees are non-executive. So much of the governance environment requires advice, and once advice is given to a board of primarily lay people, it is difficult to go against it. Advisers are likely to be conservative because of their own liability risk.

Asset-backed security, etc.

The pension fund ranks as an unsecured creditor. You can improve matters by either giving the fund some non-cash assets or some sort of contingent assets. As mentioned above, this could be a technique to support adoption of the corporate's plans.

By way of example, in 2003, when I was Group Treasurer of ICI, the company provided asset-backed support to the pension scheme. The background was a prior-year rights issue to stop the company going to sub-investment grade, a rating agency environment that looked at pension issues as a cash-flow issue (which has subsequently changed) and a draft deficit that would, had the prevailing practice of remediation over six years been applied, have caused the annual cash flow to rise to £110 million compared to the then current £30 million – a result that would have caused a downgrade – a bit of a disaster having just carried out an £800 million rights issue.

We put together a contingent asset that would make the scheme a priority creditor for £250 million on insolvency of the group. Receivables were sold from across the European subsidiaries into a special purpose vehicle (SPV). This was funded by intergroup loans, so it was all a paper exercise, but legally effective. The SPV issued a guarantee to the pension fund that only triggered in the event of insolvency, and was senior to the intergroup funding. If the group went insolvent, basically a liquidator would come along, sell the receivables and pay the fund. Any balance would go back to the holding company for other creditors.

It was not particularly clever: it was basically a structure for raising money for a receivables securitisation programme, but instead of borrowing money the assets backed the guarantee. It did not cross existing financing arrangements, since there was no money-borrowed limit to breach in loan documents: it was basically structural subordination of other lenders. The banks were not pleased, but it caused little issue at the next re-financing. It was probably marginal enough and ultimately only an issue on insolvency.

We got a weaker valuation basis (lower prudence) and agreed on funding over nine years, which worked out at £60 million per annum. Both credit ratings held, although one went to negative outlook, so the mission was accomplished.

I would argue that the trustees should have flexed the arrangement anyway to nine (or more) years' funding, since it was in their interest to support the credit rating, but that never got traction (not all rational approaches do).

Much work has gone into identifying various contingent assets in the pensions industry subsequently: the PPF even allowed them for levy purposes (although ICI's arrangement did not qualify).

Schemes are often structurally subordinated to other lenders. Banks use upstream guarantees to mitigate this. Schemes could do likewise, or corporates could offer this.

I have seen quite a bit in this area, and on balance I think most of it is generally to be avoided absent real value to the sponsor. The ICI arrangement dug the company out of a hole, but it was novel, and the trustees ended up with a pension lawyer addressing what was a securitisation arrangement. The fees ended up substantially greater than they needed to be – the main driver being attention to detail, no matter the size of the economic issue – rather than the commercial trade-offs one would get in a real securitisation process. It took two years to document.

Subsequent offerings discussed in the pensions world include cash deposits, letters of credit, pledging of physical assets (such as land – low book value, high economic value) and more creative structures, such as the Marks & Spencer deal referred to above, which had real tax-cash-flow value to the sponsor.

If this is the route a corporate wants, or is forced by the trustees, to follow, perhaps then the issue is to make sure that it has appropriate economic value, consider how it might impair operational flexibility and how it interacts with current and future financing issues. It is something to do after very careful consideration – many arrangements cannot be reversed easily – or it may require funding at a difficult time (for example, a letter of credit which could get called).

Conclusion

It seems to me that planning a long-term de-risking of the scheme, so that it is substantially 'hedged' over an appropriate time frame (which could be more than a decade), is a 'must-do' for corporates. Beyond that, how to do it, and whether or not to buy out along the way or at the end is a matter of choice and risk preferences. How to do it, though, is something that is substantially in the hands of the trustees and their advisers, but it is an outcome the sponsor must seek to optimise.

16

A note on the investment management of defined contribution schemes

PAUL THORNTON

The following chapter addresses the meaning of good governance for defined contribution (DC) schemes. The issues arising are somewhat different from those for defined benefit (DB) schemes and this note is intended to explain the difference in context.

DC is different from DB

There is a fundamental difference in who carries the risk between a DC scheme, in which the benefits are determined by the contributions paid, the investment return achieved and the terms on which the capital accumulated at the point of retirement is converted into a series of future payments by purchase of an annuity, and a DB scheme, where the benefits are determined by the rules of the scheme in terms of salary and years of service. In each case, the member contributions are normally fixed as a percentage of pensionable salary. The uncertainty of future investment returns thus represents a risk to the member in a DC scheme, whereas in a DB scheme it creates uncertainty in the amount of future contribution and funding requirements, and hence represents a risk to the employer.

DC schemes may be trust based or contract based, but this does not affect these fundamentals.

Design of suitable investment choices for members

It follows from this that good governance in a DC scheme is concerned with the design of suitable investment solutions for the members, the efficient delivery of the administration involved and ensuring that the investment outcomes for members are acceptable.

Much of the present focus of those charged with the management of DC schemes is on the design questions rather than on the outcomes. Such questions include how large a range to offer members, which asset classes should be included, whether the funds offered should be actively or passively managed and which asset managers to include.

Default options

A further focus is on the design of the default options offered. In practice, few scheme members have the financial knowledge or aptitude to make investment choices themselves and prefer to make a simpler choice based on what they are advised would be suitable. Thus, they choose or allow their choices to be determined by what is known as a default option. The question then arises whether provision of a default option constitutes advice, and what is optimal for different profiles of member. For example, what is suitable for a younger member would be regarded as different from what is suitable for a member approaching retirement, while level of income and the extent of non-pension savings and other assets could also affect the level of investment risk that a member should be expected to run.

Responsibility

An important issue which tends to be swept under the carpet is where the responsibility for overall success lies. Should the investment performance delivered turn out to be poor, for whatever reason, a member may experience some considerable disappointment with the employer for having failed to provide a more successful scheme. However, the current state of reporting is largely focused on the returns of the individual funds offered rather than the overall outcome at the member or scheme level, and usually fails to factor in the asset allocation decisions taken. Thus, the analysis of investment performance in most DC schemes is currently some way behind the sophistication of investment performance monitoring in a typical DB scheme.

17

Effective investment governance in defined contribution schemes

DIETRICH HAUPTMEIER AND GRAHAM MANNION

DC pensions are guided consumer products

Effective investment governance in defined contribution (DC) schemes needs to start with a clear understanding of the members' role and responsibilities within the investment process.

When DC pension plans were first introduced, there may have been an expectation (or at least a hope) that employees would act as the rational consumers of classical economic theory, making optimal saving and investment decisions in accordance with their personal preferences, and thereby doing effectively everything that the professionals had previously done for them in defined benefit (DB) pension schemes.

If consumers would indeed conform to this model, investment governance could legitimately be limited to making a large menu of investment options available to members as cost-effectively as possible, while exercising some limited oversight to ensure that investment managers actually remain within their specific fund mandate.

Experience has clearly demonstrated, however, that people are mostly not behaving like the 'homo oeconomicus' envisaged by traditional economists. Instead, as summarised by the Pensions Regulator:

> ... a range of evidence which may loosely be termed 'behavioural eco-
> nomics' suggests that even when people do fully understand the decisions
> they need to make, they do not always take the decision that is best for
> them. A growing literature suggests, for example, that inertia is powerful,
> that the 'framing' of decisions affects outcomes, that people procrastin-
> ate and that too much choice can put people off ... Partly as a result of
> some of these features, many people do not save in pensions at all. This
> may be appropriate in some cases, but for most people it is something that
> they may later regret.[1]

Furthermore, pension scheme members may simply not know what a 'good' investment option looks like: in the words of the Financial Services Consumer

---

1 TPR, 'Our Corporate Strategy 2008–2012' (2008), www.thepensionsregulator.gov.uk/docs/
corporate-strategy-2008-2012.pdf.

Panel, 'the complexity of many financial products and the difficulty of finding an acceptable way to describe risk means that most consumers are ill-equipped to judge how a product will perform in future, and whether it meets their needs'.[2]

Current DC investment governance practice is unfortunately still often focused on the investment fund or fund choices offered in the DC scheme, rather than on the members. Yet, a menu of best-of-class funds does not equal a best-of-class DC plan, if the outcomes achieved by members are not aligned with their needs and expectations.

These observations have led to the current trend towards designing 'auto-plans'. Members are auto-enrolled, their savings rates are auto-escalated over the years and their funds are auto-invested into a professionally managed default strategy. While members can usually opt out and make choices, it is expected and accepted that most people will rely on the respective defaults.

Under this paradigm, DC plans start to look almost like DB plans again, and all of the parties involved are falling back into their old roles: sponsors and trustees negotiate about contribution rates, actuaries and investment consultants advise on appropriate de-risking glide-paths and asset allocations, and asset managers are working to adapt the 'liability-driven-investment' techniques from DB to DC to create 'smarter' default funds.

Employees might therefore be forgiven should they also fall back into their old role and expect a safe pension income. That is, of course, where the similarities break down. No longer will the employer pick up the bill if the experts get it wrong. It is now the employee who has to pay the price. And even where no one got it wrong, and where the default truly matches members' needs, employees may still form inappropriate expectations about risks and returns and potentially face disappointment with the results.

By sponsoring a DC pension plan, employers, however, are effectively perceived by their employees to endorse the plan and by implication any default investment strategy. Simply because the legal plumbing changed when DB turned to DC, this does not mean that employees have actually taken responsibility for their retirement planning. While the legal responsibility within the DC framework lies with the individual to save and invest for their retirement, if they have not recognised this responsibility and have not understood what it is that their employer does or does not provide, the employer faces a significant reputational risk in the long term. This may especially be the case if members find that the investment strategy that their money has been put into has not performed as well as the strategies pursued by others.

DC is a consumer product; this makes it fundamentally different from DB. Allowing the consumer to remain entirely absent from the DC decision-making process is wasteful and risky for two reasons. Firstly, if employees are

2 Financial Services Consumer Panel, 'FSA is Unrealistic on Consumer Responsibility', press release, 16 June 2009, www.fs-cp.org.uk/newsroom/2009/133.shtml.

not involved in DC, they will attribute much less value to this benefit, which certainly does not maximise the shareholder value of all of the money spent on pension contributions. Secondly, by sponsoring a DC pension plan, employers are effectively seen to endorse the plan and by implication its investment strategies. If employee expectations are not met, then what was meant to be a benefit may turn instead into an employee-relations issue.

DC pensions need to appeal to their target group, like any consumer product; however, members need guidance to use the product appropriately and form realistic expectations. Finding ways to break through the inertia and help employees to accept that DC is their product and their responsibility remains the most important task facing the industry today.

Therefore, members need to be put firmly at the centre of DC investment governance: either, to the extent possible, by empowering each member to get involved as ultimate 'governor' of his or her DC pension investments; or at least by building governance processes and systems that align investment outcomes with consumer needs and expectations.

In summary, a member-centric approach to investment governance needs to be built on an understanding that DC pension plan members are consumers in need of guidance.

Understanding member needs and expectations

Understanding the characteristics of the target audience of any DC pension scheme is crucial for the design of the scheme's investment objectives and investment governance processes. As part of ongoing governance, it is important to review regularly members' profiles and, where necessary, to make adjustments to the investment approach to ensure that it remains in the members' best interests.

Based on their profession's in-built belief that 'everyone is different', Independent Financial Advisers regularly see an opportunity to offer advice to individuals within DC pension plans. However, take-up rates tend to be disappointing. The same behavioural factors (especially inertia) that prevent people from planning themselves also prevent them from investing the time and effort to seek independent advice, even where employers offer to pick up some of the bill.

However, designing a single investment strategy (typically in the form of a default investment option) based on a theoretical 'average member' is clearly also a dangerous over-simplification. Within a typical DC pension scheme, there will be significant dispersion among the membership in terms of their circumstances, attitudes and needs – a young couple saving to buy a house and planning for children have very different needs compared to people close to retirement.

In current market practice, implementation of default options is therefore typically informed by one variable: the customer's time horizon to retirement. This is true of both traditional lifestyle arrangements and target-date strategies.

Ideally, however, it would be possible to know much more about the customer besides their time horizon, enabling more sophisticated matching of investment options to customer needs. A more robust approach would therefore be to establish ongoing processes to identify and track segments within the membership showing relatively uniform characteristics, wants and needs.

This may then enable the design of investment defaults that are more closely tailored to the specific characteristics of different membership segments, replacing 'one size fits all' defaults aimed at the median member. Also, investment-related communications could be more closely targeted to the needs and attitudes of members within different segments. As with any segmentation exercise, it would be important to optimise the trade-offs between complexity, ease of implementation, costs and benefits for members.

Broadly, there are four categories of target consumer characteristics relevant for DC investment governance (see Table 17.1). Two of these categories are more difficult to ascertain, but are directly relevant with regard to DC pension scheme design generally and investment governance specifically: (i) knowledge and skills; and (ii) attitudinal and behavioural characteristics. The two other categories are easier to observe, but are less directly relevant: (iii) observed behaviour; and (iv) socio-demographic characteristics. The latter two categories may, however, be used on an ongoing basis as 'proxies', relating the respective attitudinal and behavioural characteristics of members within specific segments to their (easier to observe) socio-demographic profile and actual behaviour.

Knowledge and skills

Level of financial understanding and familiarity with investment

Higher levels of financial understanding tend to be 'strongly associated with greater investment portfolio diversification, investment risk tolerance, financial wealth, participation in pension schemes and ability to make clear investment choices' as stated by the Personal Accounts Delivery Authority.[3]

Insights into members' level of financial understanding should primarily impact investment choice architecture and investment-related communication.

With regard to the most common DC investment choice design, offering a default investment option as well as alternative choices for active investment decision-makers, it may be expected that self-selection will occur (absent

3 Personal Accounts Delivery Authority, 'Building Personal Accounts: Designing an Investment Approach' (2009), www.nestpensions.org.uk/documents/Investment_Consultation_Nov2009. pdf.

Table 17.1 Categories of target consumer characteristics relevant for DC investment governance

Characteristics	*Comments*
Knowledge and skills	
• Level of financial understanding and familiarity with investment	• More relevant for communication and design of investment choices • Less relevant for default investment design
Attitudinal/behavioural characteristics	
• Risk appetite • Attitude towards planning • Mental accounting • Inertia and other behavioural biases	• Most relevant for default investment design and communication • Also relevant with regard to design of investment choices
Observed behaviour	
• Contribution persistency • Contribution levels • Total amount invested • Default investment, and actual risk taking	• Relevant from a 'classical' economics perspective as 'revealed preference' • Relevant from a behavioural perspective to indicate biases and unaddressed needs
Socio-demographic characteristics	
• Age/years to retirement • Income • Postcode area • Employment and education characteristics • Personal circumstances (house-owner, married, dependent children)	• Relevant as objectively observable 'proxies' enabling segmentation and inferences regarding knowledge/ skills, attitudinal/behavioural characteristics, as well as needs

factors such as inertia), i.e. those members with a higher level of financial understanding are more likely to exercise choice and take control of their own investments, whereas those members with a lower level of financial understanding are more likely to remain in the default. Therefore, it may be appropriate to assume (by definition) a lower level of financial understanding with regard to default options.

Attitudinal/behavioural characteristics

Risk appetite

If reliably diagnosed, members' appetite for investment risk should be the most relevant indicator of the type of investment options expected by members. Also, with regard to investment-related communication, this characteristic is highly relevant where it is judged that what members want may not be what members need, so that expectations can be set.

The level of risk appetite among the membership should be least relevant when deciding which investment options to offer (as long as the choices offered cater to all risk preferences), as members who make investment choices would be expected to make their choices in accordance with their risk appetite.

However, it is important to bear in mind certain related research findings. Firstly, Benartzi and Thaler[4] question to what degree individuals actually have well-defined preferences. They describe how investors who picked their own portfolios afterwards actually preferred the median portfolio across investors rather than the portfolio they had chosen. Furthermore, they observed that a number of investors who preferred to pick their own portfolio rather than take investment advice afterwards actually felt more comfortable with the portfolio recommended to them by an adviser than with the portfolio they chose themselves.

Furthermore, Benartzi and Thaler[5] showed that the menu of investment options offered to employees affects their risk-taking behaviour, in light of 'naïve' diversification strategies, such as equally spreading their investments across all choices on offer. On a side note, in PensionDCisions' work with UK pension plans, we have found naïve diversification to be less prevalent, as described in Byrne, Blake and Mannion, who find that 'very few plan members appear to follow the naïve 1/n diversification approach documented by Benartzi and Thaler ... However, there is evidence of members following a conditional 1/n diversification strategy (Huberman and Jiang, 2006) whereby contributions are invested equally across the subset of funds chosen by the member.'[6]

Rather than asking investors to pick directly their own investments, 'automated' guidance may be a more robust approach to aligning members' investments with risk preferences where members' risk preferences are deduced through carefully calibrated risk questionnaires, and members are then pointed towards suitable investments based on the questionnaire results. However, this could prove expensive and operationally intensive depending on the approach taken, and it is difficult to enforce compliance across a large membership.

Attitude towards planning

Survey research by Vanguard suggests a continuum between 'Live-for-Today Avoiders' and 'Successful Planners', with very different attitudes to financial

4 S. Benartzi and R. Thaler, 'How Much Is Investor Autonomy Worth?', (2002) 57(4) *Journal of Finance* 1593.
5 S. Benartzi and R. Thaler, 'Naïve Diversification Strategies in Retirement Savings Plans', (2001) 91(1) *American Economic Review* 79.
6 'Pension Plan Decisions', *Review of Behavioural Finance*, June 2010.

planning. MacFarland, Marconi and Utkus[7] segmented workers participating in or eligible for an employer-sponsored DC plan into five 'money attitude' clusters: groupings of similar attitudes and expectations regarding various aspects of financial and retirement management. The research finds that 'about one half of the plan population does not conform to a "planner" set of attitudes and expectation', and that 'attitudes do matter and are linked to specific behavioural differences'. The authors therefore conclude that 'one size does not fit all' when it comes to pension scheme design.

Mental accounting

There is evidence that DC plan members show a desire for safety with regard to their own contributions, yet have appetite to seek higher risk with regard to employer contributions as found in surveys conducted on behalf of the Personal Accounts Delivery Authority.[8] It may be assumed that the desire for safety extends only to the principal amounts of employee contributions, whereas any tax relief by the government as well as investment gains could also be directed towards higher-risk investments.

If framed correctly in terms of member communication, this could prove a very effective instrument to bridge any gap between members' desire for lower risk and the general perception that higher risk is appropriate for younger members further away from retirement.

Inertia

As shown by a large and growing body of research, inertia is a key behavioural trait that needs to be taken into account with regard to all aspects of DC pension scheme design. Inertia can be beneficial in terms of 'nudging' people towards what they need (using the phrase of Sunstein and Thaler[9]), but it can also be highly problematic as people, for example, remain in defaults that are clearly not right for them.

As Choi, Laibson, Madrian and Metrick explain:

> ... in light of this inertia, defaults are socially desirable when agents have a shared optimum and the default leads them to it (e.g., a low-fee index fund). But even a well-chosen default may be undesirable if agents have heterogeneous needs. For example, in a plan whose workforce includes young, cash-strapped single parents and older employees who need to

7 D. M. MacFarland, C. D. Marconi and S. P. Utkus, '"Money Attitudes" and Retirement Plan Design: One Size Does Not Fit All' in O. S. Mitchell and S. P. Utkus (eds.), *Pension Design and Structure: New Lessons from Behavioural Finance* (Oxford: Oxford University Press, 2002).

8 Personal Accounts Delivery Authority, 'Building Personal Accounts', cited above fn. 3.

9 R. H. Thaler and C. R. Sunstein, *Nudge: Improving Decisions about Health, Wealth, and Happiness* (New Haven, CT: Yale University Press, 2008).

quickly build a retirement nest egg, one savings rate is not right for everyone.[10]

Observed behaviour

Certain characteristics of actual member behaviour may be directly determined from administration data, including;

- *contribution persistency*, i.e. whether members are persistently contributing while employed, and also the degree to which their employment history shows gaps;
- *contribution levels*, both in absolute amounts and possibly also relative to their income;
- *total amount invested* in the pension scheme; and
- *default investing, and actual risk taking* – whether or not a member is defaulting, and the level of investment risk non-defaulting members are actually taking.

This information could be complemented by occasional surveys to update information regarding savings and wealth outside of the DC pension scheme for different membership segments.

Socio-demographic characteristics

Characteristics such as *age/years to retirement, postcode area* and *income* are relatively straightforward to observe on an ongoing basis from administration data, and – particularly by cross-referencing with periodic deeper surveys and studies of attitudinal and behavioural data – may provide relatively robust, ongoing proxies for the characteristics of distinct membership segments, which may allow the scheme design to evolve and better serve the interests of different membership segments, rather than being targeted at the characteristics of a hypothetical average member. Additional socio-economic factors such as employment characteristics and personal circumstances (house-owner, married, dependent children) could be cross-referenced through occasional surveys.

Setting an investment objective

In the absence of the individual member reliably expressing their own preference, it is left to those in charge of investment governance (some combination of the plan sponsor, trustee, consultant, and/or provider) to determine what investment objective is suitable.

10 J. Choi, D. Laibson, B. C. Madrian and A. Metrick, 'Optimal Defaults and Active Decisions' (2003) 93 *American Economic Review Papers and Proceedings* 180–85.

An investment objective should be set for the long term, and should ideally stay in place unchanged for many decades. Therefore, the investment objective best defines a clear framework, yet provides sufficient room to adapt execution to changing social realities and investment practices over such long periods of time.

Investment objectives are typically framed in one of the following ways:

- a specific asset allocation is embedded into a performance benchmark (blending asset-class specific indices), and the investment objective is to track or outperform this asset-allocation-specific benchmark;
- a performance benchmark is set in terms of absolute return, or return relative to inflation or interest rates;
- a specific replacement income level might be targeted; or
- an explicit 'investment risk budget' might be set, judged to be appropriate for defaulters, targeting them to achieve appropriate performance from the investments compared to other investments of similar risk.

Adopting a benchmark that embeds a specific asset allocation and then setting an investment objective to *track or outperform this benchmark* has serious drawbacks. Most importantly, this focuses attention away from the most critical decision – the level of risk to take, and the asset allocation chosen to express this level of risk – and instead promotes fund-manager selection as the primary area of concern.

Absolute return targets (including relative to interest rates or inflation) have the attraction of providing clear guidance in terms of the results to expect from money invested in an investment option, while requiring fewer assumptions than would be the case for a replacement income ratio. Concerns with target returns are primarily driven by doubts about whether the expectations raised can be met with acceptable levels of reliability over the long term. The non-normally distributed character of market prices continues to change conventional views on investment returns, and may present a significant hurdle to the setting of well-founded expectations for investment performance. In any event, the more elusive concept of 'risk' will need to be communicated as clearly as return, where a return is being targeted.

Where target returns are adopted, it may be better to frame the target in terms of money multiples over longer periods of time, rather than stating annualised returns. As an example, rather than adopting a target of, say, 7 per cent per annum (nominally), it may be better to talk about doubling each invested pound over ten years. This better illustrates the effects of compounding, is easier to understand intuitively and focuses on long-term performance rather than potentially causing concerns over volatility, as returns in any single year will invariably be different from the target.

While it will be important to analyse regularly expected target *replacement income ratios* for different segments of the membership, and use this as a tool to assess whether the default design is addressing members' needs, it may be inappropriate to set an income replacement ratio as the overarching investment objective for a scheme, given the inherent difficulties (if not impossibility) in making any reliable, long-term forecasts of replacement income. This applies in particular where there are significant variations in contribution profiles between members, which compounds the difficulties involved in forecasting investment returns and annuity rates. An explicit target income replacement ratio could also set inappropriate expectations with members and thereby do more damage than good.

On balance, however, the prudent approach may therefore be to set (and regularly review) *explicit 'risk budgets'* deemed appropriate for different membership segments, based on their characteristics, and adopt as the investment objective to ensure that members are well rewarded compared to other investment alternatives with a similar level of risk.

This approach requires careful thought about two issues: (i) how to measure risk, with regard to setting and monitoring investment options, and separately with regard to member communication; and (ii) how to set levels of risk deemed appropriate for different membership segments. However, at least a large market of advisory and modelling services is available to support such risk-based investment governance, allowing also separate external calibration.

Looking at current practice, the investment objective set for default strategies in large UK DC plans almost all currently follow a benchmark that embeds a chosen asset allocation, according to a survey by PensionDCisions.[11]

However, the default funds advocated by fund managers are less likely to anchor on an asset-allocation-specific benchmark to define the objective of the investment strategy. Less than 50 per cent of managers surveyed cited an asset-allocation-specific benchmark as the investment objective. A significant minority (29 per cent) cited either an absolute level of return or a return relative to either inflation or interest rates as the primary objective.

Monitoring member behaviour and results

When designing member-centric investment governance processes, monitoring the outcomes and behaviour of members against perceived needs and expectations should take centre-stage, rather than a misplaced focus on the investment performance of specific funds.

The exact design of reporting and monitoring processes will, of course, be determined by the usual trade-off between what is desirable and what is practicable, taking into account factors such as the time and resources available for governance, the type of data available from scheme administrators, as well as

---

11 PensionDCisions, '2009 PensionDCisions Sponsor Default Investment Strategy Survey' (London: PensionDCisions Ltd, 2009).

the level of diversity among scheme membership and the resulting degree of complexity in their investment needs.

Ideally, ongoing, member-centric investment governance would be built around the following processes (with varying frequency):

- regular monitoring of member confidence, satisfaction and expectations;
- regular review of membership characteristics and membership segmentation, as discussed in the earlier section on member needs and expectations;
- ongoing review of observed member behaviour, investment risk and performance for each relevant membership segment, and comparison against investment objectives as well as member needs and expectations;
- monitoring of outliers among the membership (particularly in terms of risk, and risk-adjusted performance); and
- tracking of the effectiveness of communication campaigns and of changes in scheme architecture: are observed investment behaviour and outcomes in line with objectives?

Using robust monitoring processes of member behaviours and results will, over time provide a firm evidence base for what actually works for different membership segments, and allow for iterative improvements in investment practices.

Monitoring investment performance

Good investment performance in DC schemes means that members are rewarded over appropriate time horizons for the risk they take, relative to other options with similar risk levels.

When designing performance-monitoring processes, a clear focus should be set on asset allocation.

There is a rather narrow exposure to different asset classes within the default funds currently used by large UK DC pension funds, according to a survey by PensionDCisions, prior to any de-risking:[12]

- 71 per cent of plans invest default assets entirely in equities. None of these uses a simple global equity index such as MSCI World or FTSE Global. The majority of plans combine a UK index and world ex-UK index in some proportion to reflect the degree of home bias deemed appropriate. This UK home bias ranges from 34 to 100 per cent.
- 27 per cent of plans invest default assets in a multi-asset strategy. In this category, the allocation to equities ranges from 48 to 90 per cent and again there are significant variations in geographic allocations within this equity component.
- One plan invests default assets entirely in cash.

12 PensionDCisions, '2009 Survey', cited above fn. 11.

Fund managers, on the other hand, believe that far more diversification is required, and that strategies should rely less heavily on equities.[13] Plan sponsors today on average allocate 91 per cent of default assets to equities (prior to de-risking). In contrast, fund managers on average advocate an allocation of 71 per cent.

Those in charge of investment governance may face the danger of getting trapped by asset allocations embedded within the specific benchmarks they adopted, and it is important to design processes that monitor performance against a broader risk-return spectrum across different asset class allocations.

Fund performance versus benchmark is easiest to track, but – arguably – is the least important measure. This is a measure to monitor the quality of any manager selection decisions – a secondary issue compared to asset allocation. Yet, quarterly performance reviews of funds against their benchmarks tend to attract far too much attention within DC schemes' approach to investment governance. Perhaps this misguided focus on manager selection is a case of the available information determining the process.

For illustration, among the plans participating in the PensionDCisions survey, there was significant dispersion in absolute performance, due to differences in asset allocation:

- five-year annualised benchmark returns are available for 32 out of 45 plans surveyed. Within this group, the minimum annualised return was 1.8 per cent and the maximum was 5.8 per cent.
- Looking solely at default strategies invested entirely in equities, over the same period, the range was from 1.8 to 5 per cent. Looking solely at multi-asset strategies, the range was from 3 to 5.8 per cent.

In contrast, the range of benchmark-relative performance is much narrower, at between 0 per cent (relative to benchmark) and −0.2 per cent annualised over five years. This clearly suggests that setting the investment objective and prescribing the benchmark has a much more substantial impact on member outcomes than manager selection decisions.

Decisions regarding objective setting, risk levels and asset allocation, as well as benchmark selection, are far more critical than the performance of a fund versus its benchmark.

Investment architecture and governance

The previous sections already discussed implicitly some of the governance consequences of investment options and default funds. Given the prevalence in current DC plans of certain key investment design elements, specifically (i) a limited set of investment choices, (ii) a default investment option for members who make no choices and (iii) automatic de-risking as members

13 PensionDCisions, '2009 DC Default Provider Survey' (London: PensionDCisions Ltd, 2009).

approach retirement, this section further considers the relationship between these key architecture elements and investment governance.

There continues to be significant variation in the number of options offered to members in large UK pension schemes. According to a PensionDCisions survey,[14] the median number of fund choices offered to members is 12, with a maximum of 329 fund choices for one contract scheme.

There is strong behavioural evidence that some choice is desirable and motivating (regardless of whether it is exercised), whereas too much choice may be counter-productive.

Furthermore, some researchers concluded that, when limiting investment options, members may in fact not suffer any significant 'efficiency loss' – i.e. adding further investment choices would not significantly improve theoretically 'optimal' portfolios. Specifically, Ning Tang observes that 'when a plan has more than nine funds [...] adding more funds does not improve the Sharpe ratio much'.[15] Interestingly, she further observes that while 'some plans with fewer than six investment funds have a relatively high loss ... some plans with only two or three funds perform very well', leading her to conclude that 'most important to plan efficiency and performance is the particular set of investment funds offered, rather than the number of options'.

Accordingly, there appear to be two different approaches to ensuring an efficient set of investment choices for members – either offering a range of single asset classes as portfolio choices, or offering pre-packed asset allocations.

When opting for the first approach, offering a range of funds which each represent a particular asset class, this yields the typical 12 or so fund choices, depending on which asset classes are offered and with what degree of granularity (and to what extent ethical or religious options are also offered). However, the specific menu presented to members is likely to influence their level of risk-taking (to the degree that they make active choices), in light of findings on naïve diversification strategies, as well as research into menu composition (where investors confronted with larger menus are more likely to pick choices from categories including many options, rather than from categories including fewer options[16]).

The alternative approach to offering asset class building blocks may allow an even more restricted choice set, possibly even just two or three options, while still allowing 'efficient' portfolios. In this case, each investment option needs to be in itself a carefully constructed portfolio representing an 'efficient' point on the risk-return spectrum. This is clearly more difficult to do well for

14 PensionDCisions, '2009 Survey', cited above fn. 11.
15 Ning Tang, 'The More the Better?' (University of Pennsylvania, PARC Working Papers, WPS 08-02, 2008).
16 See, e.g. A. Karlsson, M. Massa and A. Simonov, 'Pension Portfolio Choice and Menu Exposure' (EFA 2006 Zurich Meetings, 7 February 2006), http://ssrn.com/abstract=888661.

those designing and monitoring the investment funds, and increases the degree of responsibility and governance challenges taken on by them explicitly.

The alternative approach of constructing a range of diversified portfolios is also not without its challenges in terms of member behaviour and expectations.

Specifically with regard to risk-graded funds, the challenge becomes how to translate labels into asset allocations (and vice versa). This is illustrated by the wide variations among different providers. For example, SuperRatings observed that the descriptor of a 'balanced' investment option in Australia could contain as low as 40 per cent in growth assets up to a high of 80 per cent in growth-style assets.[17] Byrne, Harrison and Blake similarly report a quote from an insurance company that 'the ABI definitions are misleading. They imply a particular risk profile, which may not be accurate'.[18]

Additionally, Byrne, Harrison and Blake discuss whether it may be better to offer an even number of choices, when grading investment options, to avoid clustering on the middle choice.

A further consideration regarding choice is whether members are allowed to mix investment options, or whether choices are exclusive of each other. The advantage of allowing only a single choice would be that labels, investor preferences and needs, and investment styles can be more closely aligned. In the United States, some authors have commented that asset-allocation funds (whether risk-labelled or target-dated) are often held by investors as part of a portfolio of several funds, which defeats their purpose of offering a one-stop shop for asset allocation.

On the other hand, forcing members into making a single choice may run counter to their tendencies of mental accounting, and the apparent human tendency to disaggregate portfolios into a 'safe' layer representing downside protection and a 'risky' layer offering a shot at high returns,[19] and may therefore be unpopular with members.

A possible solution to avoid some of the pitfalls of attaching labels to pre-packaged asset allocations while encouraging sensible and transparent combinations of the options on offer might be to limit the choice to just two funds: one option labelled 'safety' and one option labelled 'growth'; the default strategy might then represent a particular approach to combining these two funds, but members could also choose to blend safety and growth differently, if they wish to do so.

The growth fund could follow a broadly diversified growth strategy. The safety fund could, for example, include allocations to long duration, index-linked

---

17 See www.superratings.com.au.

18 A. Byrne, D. Harrison and D. P. Blake, 'Dealing with the Reluctant Investor: Innovation and Governance in DC Pension Investment' (April 2007), http://ssrn.com/abstract=1012862.

19 See, e.g. H. M. Shefrin and M. Statman, 'Behavioural Portfolio Theory' (1997), http://ssrn.com/abstract=5947.

gilts, and high-grade corporate bonds while members are younger, switching to an asset mix more in line with annuities (long duration corporate bonds and some allocation to conventional gilts) and cash (with regard to any draw-down) as members get closer to retirement. Alternatively, the safety option for members further away from retirement might instead include some allocation to growth assets, but with downside protection.

It remains important that whatever 'safety' means is carefully communicated to members. However, this should be a somewhat less difficult challenge than trying to explain what exactly is meant by a 'balanced' risk attitude. As a side note, particularly where 'safety' includes significant elements of inflation protection (for example, index-linked bonds), it might be beneficial to avoid mark-to-market reporting for this fund (to the degree possible), as volatility of the value of this fund may send misleading signals to members.

Of course, it needs to be carefully considered how to present such a two-choice menu to members without encouraging 'reckless conservatism'. This approach might, however, work well for constructing and communicating a 'rules-based' default as described earlier in this chapter, where, for example, member contributions are invested differently from employer contributions and investment gains.

Alternatively, this approach would offer the potential for pre-set combinations to be 'packaged' for the purposes of administration and communication, while leaving those who desire it the opportunity to make active decisions, while still working with the same underlying components.

Among the members who do make active fund choices, it is most likely that they will make an active choice when joining the scheme, or at a similar event when they are being forced to pay attention to the scheme for other 'external' reasons (this is, for example, confirmed by administration data from UK pension schemes that we have analysed, where most choices take place within the initial months after members join).

Many members in pension schemes who at some point made an active choice with regard to their investments fail to re-balance at later points in time, which seems likely to be due to inertia rather than considered preference.

Therefore, it may make sense to implement a general 'de-risking overlay' even for those members who made active choices. This mechanism could require members to opt out proactively shortly before de-risking commences, if they want to continue holding a more risky asset allocation as they approach retirement: this would preserve their choice to do so, yet protect them from inertia.

In the context of the two-fund model described above, where only a growth fund and safety fund are offered to members, this overlay might be based on, say, a 15-year glide path, with increasing allocations to safety rather than growth. Portfolios of members who do not proactively opt out of the glide path, and who have allocations to the growth fund above the respective level implied by their point on the glide path, would then gradually see their growth holdings switched automatically into the safety fund.

To summarise, whichever model is chosen to deliver investment exposure to DC scheme members, care should be taken to tailor investment options towards the needs of specific segments of the target audience. Where appropriate, it may be worthwhile to consider sacrificing some long-term return potential for a greater level of stability, to ensure continuing trust in the scheme.

Investment governance in context

Investment outcomes, and therefore the design of investment governance processes, are closely linked to many other DC pension design decisions, and also to broader benefit arrangements and objectives, and inter-dependencies need to be analysed and monitored.

Contribution levels and persistency

It is clearly the combination of contributions and investment results that deliver whatever outcome a member can achieve from their pension plan at retirement. Therefore, the contribution rates but also the expected persistency of contributions (taking into account career breaks or the possibility of opting out of pension plans) need to be considered when designing a governance framework focused on member needs, expectations and outcomes.

Of course, these dependencies cannot be limited to a naïve calculation along the lines that higher investment risk means higher expected returns, therefore allowing a reduction in contribution rates. Rather, the inter-dependencies are clearly much more complex. On the one hand, the level of investment risk needs to provide an adequate level of certainty to address members' needs. At the same time, the level of risk also needs to be aligned with members' expectations in the shorter term, to avoid members losing trust in their pension and reducing contributions or opting out from saving into their pension at all, after, for example, experiencing a loss of value in their pension account.

Differing contribution profiles of members are an important factor with regard to setting the investment objective.

Firstly (even ignoring the difficulties surrounding any attempt to predict long-term investment returns and annuity rates far in the future), any great variation in contribution consistency will mean that it may be difficult to communicate to members (other than those close to retirement) any information related to their likely income replacement, without the risk of setting the wrong expectations.

Secondly, investment results may impact contribution profiles. Choi, Laibson, Madrian and Metrick describe evidence that:

> ... an investor's 401(k) contribution rate increases more if she has recently experienced a higher 401(k) portfolio return and/or a lower 401(k) return variance. ... These results are explained by a naïve reinforcement learning heuristic: investors expect that investments in which they experienced

past success will be successful in the future, whether or not such a belief is logically justified. Consistent with reinforcement learning's Power Law of Practice, return chasing and variance avoidance diminish with age.[20]

Observations such as this may be particularly relevant when ensuring that younger members and members who recently joined the scheme are not soon after confronted with negative return experiences, and thereby prematurely biased against the scheme and – in the worst case – prompted to opt out. One relatively simple way to achieve this within a default context might be to invest initial contributions up to a certain total amount per member into a low-risk investment option, and only start investing members' contributions above this threshold into more risky funds.

Thirdly, inconsistent contribution profiles make it more difficult to design 'smart' defaults addressing members' needs. Following on from the example in the previous paragraph, for members who still have the large majority of their contributions ahead of them, investment return is a secondary issue, and lower risk in their personal accounts may be acceptable in order to encourage them to continue to contribute rather than risk these members losing confidence because of a period of negative returns, per the previous paragraph. Over time, however, as the account size grows, expected investment returns will start to dominate contributions as a source of value creation. Any interruption in an individual's contribution history creates additional complexity around such considerations, as it becomes more difficult to make assumptions about the amount of further contributions that can be expected to be paid into their pension account by the member – i.e. if no further contributions are to be expected in any event, a more aggressive investment approach might be chosen as the default, as the danger of 'scaring away' the member from contributing through short-term negative return experience is no longer a factor.

Switching

Broad evidence suggests that active trading by individuals is not to their benefit. For example, Barber, Lee, Liu and Odean conclude that:

> ... using a complete trading history of all investors in Taiwan, we document that the aggregate portfolio of individual investors suffers an annual performance penalty of 3.8 percentage points. Individual investor losses are equivalent to 2.2 percent of Taiwan's GDP or 2.8 percent of total personal income – nearly as much as the total private expenditure on clothing and footwear in Taiwan.[21]

20 J. J. Choi, D. Laibson, B. C. Madrian and A. Metrick, 'Reinforcement Learning and Investor Behavior' (2007), www.economics.harvard.edu/files/faculty/37_reinforcementlearning.pdf.
21 B. M. Barber, Y.-T. Lee, Y.-J. Liu and T. Odean, 'Just How Much do Individual Investors Lose By Active Trading?', AFA 2006 Boston Meetings Paper; EFA 2005 Moscow Meetings Paper (May 2007), http://ssrn.com/abstract=529062.

Specifically with regard to investments in pension schemes, rather than active trading in securities generally, research in the United States by Yamaguchi, Mitchell, Mottola and Utkus concluded that: 'as a group, traders outperform non-traders when returns are not risk-adjusted. But because traders assume higher portfolio risk, the difference in returns between the two broad groups disappears after adjusting for risk.'[22] Furthermore, the research presents evidence that 'certain types of trading such as periodic rebalancing are beneficial, while high-turnover trading is costly. Interestingly, those who hold only balanced or lifecycle funds, whom we call passive re-balancers, earn the highest risk-adjusted returns'.[23]

However, it may be questioned whether high levels of active trading are in fact even observable among a small number of members, and whether US findings, where reasonably frequent active trading by a minority of pension scheme members has been reported, are fully applicable to the United Kingdom. It is suspected that pension scheme members in the United Kingdom may be even less active with regard to their pension investments than those in the United States. As an example, PensionDCisions has worked with a UK pension plan that exhibits a relatively high degree of 'active' behaviour (with a low default rate of approximately 40 per cent, a primarily higher-earning, well-educated and white-collar workforce, a very low-risk default fund, and a communication strategy designed to encourage members to make their own active choices). For this pension scheme (where no restrictions on switching apply), over a three-year period, 86.3 per cent of the membership (including only those members who participated in the scheme across the entire three-year period) made no switching decisions, 99.6 per cent of the membership switched once a year or less, and only the remaining 0.4 per cent of members switched more frequently. The highest frequency that could be observed among the membership was making switching decisions in 14 out of 36 months (i.e. on average every 2.5 months).

Where excessive switching does pose an issue to any significant extent within UK DC pension plans, should such behaviour be observed, it might be reasonable to impose some limit on the number of fund switches, or to introduce charges on 'excessive' switching, in light of the additional explicit and implicit costs caused by switching and the lack of evidence that frequent switching benefits members.

An alternative method that is employed by some pension schemes (usually driven by the practicalities of their administration systems, rather than any behavioural considerations) is to limit switching to specific time windows

---

22 T. Yamaguchi, O. S. Mitchell, G. R. Mottola and S. P. Utkus, 'Winners and Losers: 401(k) Trading and Portfolio Performance', Pension Research Council Working Paper No. 2006-26; Michigan Retirement Research Center Research Paper No. WP 2007-154 (1 June 2007), http://ssrn.com/abstract=942378.

23 Ibid.

during the year. However, this may be less popular with members than simply imposing a maximum number of switches, or charging for excessive switching, as we suspect that people will value their 'right to switch at any time' as opposed to being locked into their investments for fixed periods, even if in practice they never exercise it.

Apart from looking at 'switching' (i.e. redirecting existing funds within a pension account), it is also important to explore the interaction between 'switching' on the one hand and changing investment choices with regard to future contributions on the other hand.

Where members make choices, the two distinct processes of switching existing assets and changing the allocation of future contributions can lead to confusion; members who switched their existing assets may be surprised to find that future contributions continue to be invested as before, and vice versa. The design of choice architecture and investment communication needs to take account of this potential issue.

As an example, while for a more experienced investor it may be beneficial to re-balance a portfolio through changing the allocation of additional contributions in order to minimise trading costs, it may be more intuitive for members simply to opt for one allocation across choices (if they actively make any choices) which then applies equally to existing investments as well as future contributions, and periodically holdings may even be automatically re-balanced to the chosen allocation.

Communication and engagement

In a member-centric governance system, where – ideally – the member is the ultimate governor of his or her pension account, and where in any event member needs and expectations are taken as the basis for investment governance, communication becomes the most important risk-management tool available.

While communication is a topic so broad and important that it deserves its own book, we would like briefly to point out a few key aspects of good communication practices as they relate to investment governance:

- communication should ideally be personalised and targeted, and adapted to different segments of the population in terms of circumstances, attitudes and financial knowledge;
- communication always needs to be simple, and ideally focus on a single message;
- information needs to be easy to consume, and the mode and time of delivery as well as the 'packaging' can impact significantly whether the message is received;
- all information should, as much as feasible, steer members away from short-term returns;

- communication needs to be carefully reviewed so as never to promise too much or raise inappropriate expectations;
- communications should ideally demonstrate in simple terms that good value has been generated from the level of risk taken, relative to the investments that members might otherwise have been exposed to; and
- behavioural and attitudinal biases can be used to reinforce messages and make them more interesting; for example, concepts of 'mental accounting' and framing, as well as peer comparison.

As a specific example illustrating the last point, while investment professionals will look at each member's pension account as a portfolio, and consider the risk/return characteristics of the overall portfolio (reflecting diversification and co-variances), it may be better to communicate to members by disaggregating their portfolio into sensible 'sub-accounts'. For example, members might be shown, in amounts, how much of their investments are 'safe', and how much are 'risky', setting expectations around capital preservation and potential for upside. This approach would be related to 'behavioural portfolios' as described by Shefrin and Statman.[24]

Labelling

Where members are provided with investment options, a key question with clear investment governance implications is how to label these options.

Fund managers, not surprisingly, have a preference for labelling their funds with their particular brand. Some pension schemes have already adopted 'white labelling', however, where generic names are used to describe each investment option, which do not refer to the underlying fund manager(s).

'White labelled' funds are more likely to focus members' attention on what matters, risk profiles and asset allocation, rather than effectively asking investors to choose between fund managers' brands. Additionally, 'white labelling' eliminates different naming conventions between different asset managers as another potential source of confusion for members. Finally, it also becomes much easier to change fund managers behind the scenes, reducing the need for potentially confusing and complex communication exercises.

There is a large body of research on clearly 'spurious' information influencing decision-making. In the context of pension investments generally, where consumers have difficulty judging what 'good' means, and particularly in the context of a scheme where those in charge of investment governance have already carefully screened the options on offer, there seems to be little value in offering branded funds.

That said, 'white labelling' will still not eliminate other potential sources of spurious information, such as, in particular, short-term performance, but

---

24 Shefrin and Statman, 'Behavioural Portfolio Theory', cited above fn. 19.

also any unintended consequences from labelling, order of choices on the menu, specific examples used in communications and so on.

Broader benefit design and objectives

Investment governance within a DC scheme may also need to take account of the broader benefits available to employees, and the 'human resources' agenda behind benefit delivery.

Pensions are typically the second largest element of remuneration, after salaries and far ahead of any other benefit. Where DC pension schemes do not perform, shareholder assets are wasted and the consequences of unmet employee expectations may come back to haunt employers for many years.

However, particularly within flexible benefit arrangements, other benefits with a more immediate element of gratification may endanger sufficient DC pension participation.

On the other hand, if employees are also offered other savings options, such as ISAs, apart from a DC pension scheme, this may be a more appropriate vehicle for some segments among the employee population. In any event, any member-centric governance approach should extend across the whole portfolio of savings options.

Responsibilities and accountability

For sound governance of default investment practices, it is important that all parties are clear on who is taking prime responsibility for each aspect of delivering investment solutions. Otherwise accountability is not properly established and/or outcomes achieved in due course are not attributed to the appropriate party. It is clearly very important to ensure that where an agent's influence over a particular matter is high, the agent's accountability in relation to that same matter is also high.

Outlined in Table 17.2 are some of the key activities and parties that may be involved in each, for trust-based and contract-based plans. Plan sponsors or trustees should ensure that a clear primary responsibility is established in each of these areas, together with measures of success and methods of monitoring against these measures.

Conclusion

DC schemes are about members, not investment products. The triangulation between members' needs, expectations and actual investment outcomes has to be at the core of any investment governance process. The unifying element is risk, and the key measure of service quality in this arena can only be to look at how well members have been rewarded for the risk taken with their money. The most difficult question is to determine how much risk should be taken on

Table 17.2 Key activities and parties involved in trust-based and contract-based plans

	Trust-based	*Contract-based*
Understand member needs and expectations Determine membership characteristics, expectations and behaviour, inc. risk appetite, levels and persistency of contributions	Sponsor, trustees	Sponsor, provider
Investment objective setting Determining the appropriate level of investment risk for different membership segments Selecting appropriate methods for monitoring performance	Sponsor, trustees, investment consultant	Sponsor, provider, investment consultant
Investment architecture Choice architecture and defaults Strategic and tactical asset allocation (growth phase and glide path) Automatic de-risking prior to retirement, when (if at all) it commences and how it is managed	Sponsor, trustees, investment consultant, fund manager	Sponsor, provider, investment consultant, fund manager
Fund management Investment approach for each component of the respective asset allocation, i.e. active versus passive, and target setting for each component piece	Sponsor, trustees, investment consultant, fund manager	Sponsor, provider, investment consultant, fund manager
Execution Glide-path execution Investment management	Fund manager, administrator Fund manager	Provider, fund manager Provider, fund manager
Monitoring Member confidence, satisfaction and expectations Member characteristics/segmentation Member behaviour and results Outliers Impact of communication/design changes Quality of investment execution	Sponsor, trustees, investment consultant, administrator	Sponsor, provider, investment consultant, administrator

behalf of disengaged members, and this will remain a subjective issue that requires careful thought by plan sponsors, trustees (where applicable) and their advisers, as well as clear accountability for who is responsible for taking these decisions and the outcomes that result.

18

Inside pension scheme governance

SIMON DEAKIN

Pension scheme governance is a subject that defies straightforward categorisations. From a legal point of view, it is a hybrid of trust law, company law, fiscal law and employment law, with a dense and detailed statutory overlay. For financial economists, the focus is on pension schemes as capital market actors with a distinctive approach to investment strategy, which has wider macroeconomic implications. Management studies would see pension funds as institutional shareholders with the potential to shape the governance structures and managerial practices of their investee companies. For historians of social policy, occupational pension schemes are understood as mostly complementing, but in some contexts as competing with, the various forms of direct state provision for retirement. Few of these disciplines have seen pension scheme governance as a subject of study in its own right, but that is changing as the enormous practical significance of the issues at stake becomes clear. Pension scheme governance directly affects the savings plans and income security of millions of workers and beneficiaries, with consequences for the efficiency and sustainability of the corporate sector, macroeconomic stability and the capacity of government to deliver on social policy goals.

Yet, while there can be few more pressingly important issues for contemporary economic and social research, a dearth of analysis on these questions, a few foundational studies aside,[1] is also apparent. A principal reason for this has been the difficulty researchers have had in gaining access to and understanding the workings of pension schemes 'from the inside'. It is not just a question of the complexity of the subject matter. A legal knowledge of the legislative texts and judicial decisions relating to pension fund governance,

---

1 These include, from a business history perspective, L. Hannah, *Inventing Retirement: The Development of Occupational Pensions in Britain* (Cambridge: Cambridge University Press, 1986); from a legal perspective, R. Nobles, *Pensions, Employment and the Law* (Oxford: Oxford University Press, 1990); from a management perspective, J. Hawley and A. Williams, *The Rise of Fiduciary Capitalism: How Institutional Investors Can Make America More Democratic* (Philadelphia: University of Pennsylvania Press, 2000) (referring mainly to the US case); and from a historical perspective, H. Pemberton, P. Thane and N. Whiteside (eds.), *Britain's Pensions Crisis: History and Policy* (Oxford: Oxford University Press, 2006).

for example, provides only a small part of what is needed to grasp the juridical nature of the pension fund. The critical detail is to be found in the terms of pension scheme trusts and employment contracts as they have been drafted and redrafted over many years, even decades, the content of which is often concealed from the legal observer.[2] In a similar way, models of governance based on the economist's concept of the accountability of 'agents' to 'principals' have limited traction in the face of the multiple and overlapping forms of ownership and control which can be found within pension schemes. The structure of the defined benefit pension scheme poses the question of who exactly are the 'principals' in whose interests the managers of listed companies are supposed to be acting. The realisation that, in addition to the manager-shareholder relationship, there is an additional agency chain linking fund managers through pension fund trustees to the ultimate beneficiaries of schemes, and that these may include not just current and former employees, but the sponsor company itself, is just the first step in understanding that there is more to the good governance of pension funds than the simple application of standard corporate governance ideas.

Against this background, the present volume will make a fundamental contribution not just to good governance in pension schemes, which is its immediate goal, but to the study of a social and economic institution which urgently needs to be better understood. The chapters are written by practitioners with the kind of internal knowledge, derived from experience, which theory in this area has tended to neglect. The chapters reveal how history has shaped the practice of pension scheme governance, and also how the field has been very rapidly changing over the past decade or even just the last five years. Stepping back from the detailed picture they present, it may be useful to reflect on some of the main features of private sector pension schemes, as they have evolved over the course of the last century and the first decade of the current one, and to consider the implications of the transformation they are currently undergoing.

The origins of the defined benefit pension scheme in the early and middle decades of the twentieth century lie in a mixture of employer paternalism, which combined self-interest with benevolence, and state regulation, which saw occupational pensions as a cost-effective alternative to direct governmental provision for income protection in retirement. The legal form of the pension scheme, the trust, was intended to combine security for the assets of the fund with fiscal efficiency.[3] The tax treatment of pension funds made possible their rapid growth in this early period.[4] The principle of fiscal support initially established in the inter-war years was extended, in the context of social security law, in the post-war period; employers earned partial exemption from participation in the government-run national insurance system, in the form

2 See Chapters 7 and 8, above.
3 See Nobles, *Pensions, Employment and the Law*, cited above fn. 1.
4 Hannah, *Inventing Retirement*, cited above fn. 1.

of national insurance contribution rebates, if they provided a defined benefit scheme which met certain conditions.[5] The state thereby used tax and social security law to regulate, in general terms, the types of provision which employers could feasibly make. Defined contribution schemes only became possible on a significant scale once the contracting-out rules for national insurance contributions were modified in the mid-1980s.[6] Yet, beyond setting these general parameters, the law did not intervene to dictate the way in which scheme rules were drafted. As a result, trust deeds and rules played a critical role in determining the scale of employer (as well as employee) contributions. Similarly, employment contracts were mostly drafted in such a way as to give the sponsor the power, within limits set by the common law of contract, to change the extent of its commitment to fund the scheme. Until the advent of 'stakeholder pensions' in the late 1990s, the law imposed no obligation on an employer to provide an occupational pension of any kind (and even then the stakeholder pension option did not require the employer to contribute to a scheme). Nor were employers legally required to keep their schemes running once they had begun, beyond the obligations they had to respect the rights of scheme members which had already vested.[7] Thus, the regulatory framework combined fiscal subsidy and indirect control with an essentially voluntarist approach to the constitution and operation of schemes.

Within this supportive framework, pension schemes became significant capital market actors in their own right. In the immediate post-1945 period, it was unusual for funds to hold more than 20 per cent of their assets in the form of shares. By the early 1990s, fully 80 per cent of all UK defined benefit pension scheme assets were invested in equities, the vast part of which consisted of the shares of other UK companies.[8] As institutional share ownership rose and personal and family investments steadily declined as a proportion of the whole, the characteristic post-war form of ownership of the UK corporate sector began to take shape. Ownership was increasingly dispersed in the sense of being spread across a significant number of institutional shareholders, mostly insurance companies and pension funds.[9] On the whole, pension fund trustees delegated investment decisions to specialist asset managers and rarely dealt directly with the managements of their investee companies. Their influence was more tangible at the level of the market as a whole. Pension fund demand

---

5 N. Wikeley, *Wikeley, Ogus and Barendt's The Law of Social Security*, 5th edn (London: Butterworths, 2002), ch. 17; and D. Williams, *Social Security Taxation* (London: Sweet & Maxwell, 1982).

6 Wikeley, *Law of Social Security*, cited above fn. 5. On the distinctive features of governance in defined contribution schemes, see Chapters 16 and 17, above.

7 In some countries, such as Australia, external legal regulation of employer provision in the context of occupational pension schemes is considerably tighter: see Chapter 2, above.

8 See Chapter 3, above.

9 B. Cheffins, *Corporate Ownership and Control: British Business Transformed* (Oxford: Oxford University Press, 2008).

for equities helped to create the conditions for sustained stock market growth, in particular in the period between the early 1980s and early 2000s.[10] Pension funds also played a significant role, together with other institutional investors, in pressing for market-wide standards on issues such as takeover bids, share issues and board structure, thereby influencing the content of the regulatory mechanisms which helped to shape UK corporate governance during this period.[11]

The 1990s saw the emergence of pension fund governance as an area of interest for legislative policy. The security of fund assets was the major concern following the depletion of the Mirror Group pension schemes, but other matters addressed by the legislature at this time included the inflation-proofing of pension benefits and protection of the rights of early leavers.[12] Litigation began over the use of pension fund surpluses to reduce employer contributions and finance takeover bids. The courts resolved these issues by mostly confirming the wide discretionary powers for employers and trustees set out in trust deeds and rules.[13] Case law and legislation gradually strengthened the requirements for trustee autonomy from the sponsor,[14] and over time there was increased regulation of scheme administration.[15] The basic aspects of the model nevertheless seemed to enjoy wide acceptance. In retrospect, however, the steady state of the late 1990s and early 2000s gave a misleading impression of stability.

The alterations made to the advance corporation tax regime after the election of a Labour Government in 1997 were a first sign of change.[16] They were in part opportunistic, but also represented the beginning of a shift in sentiment against occupational pension schemes. The fiscal subsidy enjoyed by pension funds was seen in some quarters as excessive and unfair. Pension schemes were also viewed as putting their investee companies under undue pressure for high and immediate financial returns, at the expense of investment in research and development. The removal of the corporation tax reliefs was intended to make dividend payments less advantageous in fiscal terms. There is no evidence, however, that it encouraged companies to invest for the longer term, and

---

10 See Chapter 3, above.
11 On the genesis of the City Code on Takeovers and Mergers, see J. Armour and D. Skeel, 'Who Writes the Rules for Hostile Takeovers, and Why? The Peculiar Divergence of US and UK Takeover Regulation' (2007) 95 *Georgetown Law Journal* 1727–974; on institutional investor influence in relation to pre-emption rules and corporate governance codes, see J. Armour and J. Gordon, 'The Berle-Means Corporation in the Twenty-First Century', paper presented to 3CL conference on *Corporate Ownership and Control*, University of Cambridge, January 2009.
12 See Wikeley, *Law of Social Security*, cited above fn. 5.
13 See R. Nobles, 'Pension scheme surpluses: *National Grid* in the House of Lords' (2001) 30 *Industrial Law Journal* 318–24.
14 See Chapter 6, above.
15 See Chapter 8, above.
16 See Chapter 3, above.

the practice of returning 'free cash flow' to shareholders through dividends and share buy-backs continued much as before.[17] However, after the end of the stock market bubble in 2000, the investment climate generally was far less favourable to the pension funds. As a result, scheme surpluses began to give way to deficits.

Accounting changes made around this time made the process of dealing with scheme deficits more problematic. Accounting standards for pension schemes had first been introduced in the late 1980s in order to give share-holders of sponsor companies a clearer view of the potential liabilities arising from the operation of their funds. The accounting treatment of schemes was tightened under FRS 17, which came into force in 2001. Now, pension scheme assets were valued on a mark-to-market basis, that is, by reference to their current market value. Liabilities, conversely, were calculated using a discount rate based on the returns available from high-quality corporate bonds. The resulting difference was expressed as a surplus or, more frequently, a deficit on the balance sheet of the sponsor. Deficits were thereby crystallised in a new form which reduced the possibilities for 'smoothing' gains and losses over the longer term which earlier valuation models, developed by the actuarial profession for the purposes of determining scheme solvency, had provided.[18]

The trend was reinforced by changes in pension legislation. Employer insolvency came to be seen as a significant threat to the stability of schemes during the 1990s thanks to a number of high-profile corporate failures which left pension schemes exposed. Parliament's response was to set up the Pension Protection Fund (PPF) to provide a (limited) safeguard for members in insolvent schemes. Legislation also tightened the rules on employer liabilities in respect of scheme deficits. The Pensions Act 1995 established the principle that a deficit present in a scheme on a winding-up was a debt due from the sponsor employer. The 2004 Act gave the Pensions Regulator (TPR) new powers to ensure that deficits were made up in the case of solvent schemes. For these purposes, scheme deficits were to be calculated by reference to the cost of buying an annuity to make up the gap, an alternative and mostly more stringent measure than even that set out in FRS 17.[19]

These changes formed the backdrop against which employers increasingly began to withdraw from defined benefit scheme provision in the course of the 2000s, first by closing schemes to new entrants, and then by closing them to future contributions from existing members. There has also been a small but significant move towards pension scheme 'buy-outs', or the transfer of funds to insurance companies. This practice is no longer confined, as it was once was, to cases of employer insolvency. From the mid-2000s, a growing segment of the market has been occupied by newly established pension buy-out firms,

---

17 Cheffins, *Corporate Ownership and Control*, cited above fn. 9.
18 See Chapters 9 and 12, above.
19 See Chapters 8 and 9, above.

which aim to take advantage of hedging techniques to realise greater value from fund assets.[20]

Buy-out is still generally regarded as an option of last resort. The buy-out market remains small in the context of the wider occupational pension scheme system, and is likely to remain so in conditions of financial uncertainty. The closure of defined benefit schemes to new members and/or contributions by no means makes pension fund governance more straightforward. Such schemes may face reduced investment risk once new members are excluded and long-term liabilities are thereby confined, but the sponsor's continuing commitment to the fund may in practice be called into question.[21] In such a situation, the trustees' task of monitoring the strength of the employer covenant is greatly complicated.[22]

The recent and rapid decline of the defined benefit pension scheme is at least partially attributable to the pressure for shareholder returns faced by UK listed companies. When a pension fund deficit appears on the corporate balance sheet, it can affect the company's credit rating and share price, and increase its vulnerability to takeover. Thus, a shareholder rights regime which the pension funds helped to create through their support for corporate governance codes and an active market for corporate control in the different market conditions of the 1980s and 1990s has now become one of the factors destabilising defined benefit funds. It is difficult to predict where this process will end. In the short term, the interaction of pension fund governance with wider trends in the corporate governance system continues to create novel pressures on trustees. In the 1990s, hostile bidders sought to access scheme surpluses in order to finance acquisitions, a course of action that was sometimes resisted by trustees, with mixed success.[23] In the 2000s, the situation has been reversed, and scheme deficits can deter bids which might otherwise be financially viable. Pension fund trustees are required to act in the best interests of the beneficiaries of the scheme, and cannot simply defend the sponsor company from what they might, as current or former employees, see as an external threat. In practice, however, the view they take of a bid's merits from the fund's point of view may influence its outcome.[24]

---

20 See Chapter 14, above.
21 See Chapters 12 and 14, above.
22 See Chapters 5 and 8, above.
23 Most notably in the Imperial Tobacco litigation, which arose from Hanson's takeover of Imperial Tobacco in the mid-1980s. The litigation established the principle that a decision to cut employer contributions had to be made in good faith and according to the principle of mutual trust and confidence between the parties to the employment relationship: *Imperial Group Pension Trust Ltd* v. *Imperial Tobacco Ltd* [1991] IRLR 66, discussed by S. Deakin and G. Morris, *Labour Law*, 5th edn (Oxford: Hart Publishing, 2009), pp. 343–4. On the significance of the Imperial Tobacco pension fund as a leader in investment practice in the 1950s and 1960s, see Chapter 3, above.
24 See P. Davies, *Gower and Davies: Principles of Modern Company Law*, 8th edn (London: Sweet & Maxwell, 2008), p. 1040.

TPR can in extremis call for contributions from parties to bid transactions and can appoint an independent trustee in a case where there is concern that the context of a takeover may have undermined the employer covenant.[25] Thus, pension fund governance has come to play a significant role in shaping one of the critical mechanisms of the wider corporate governance system. Whether this development has the potential to mitigate some of the pressures for short-term shareholder returns which are putting defined benefit schemes in general under pressure remains to be seen; its impact is so far confined to a few cases.

Pension fund governance is having an impact on investment practice of a kind that might similarly have an effect in countering the emphasis on short-term shareholder value. There is a widely held view that the fiduciary duty owed by pension fund trustees to the beneficiaries of the fund encompasses an obligation to at least consider the role of social, ethical and governance factors in shaping investment decisions. Funds already have a statutory duty to disclose how far they take these factors into account when formulating their statement of investment principles, and a growing number of them have subscribed to the UN Principles of Responsible Investment. It is possible to go further and argue that ethical investment principles should guide the construction of an investment portfolio on risk-reduction grounds, and that pension fund trustees are failing in their fiduciary duties if they do not engage more directly with their investee companies on social and environmental issues.[26] For the time being, this scenario remains an emerging practice rather than one which is generally followed.

Good pension fund governance should in principle produce improved returns for scheme beneficiaries and should help trustees to strike a balance between the interests of active members and those receiving benefits, taking relevant account of investment and longevity risks.[27] For employers, a well-run scheme is part of a package for remunerating and retaining core employees, while the reduction of deficits helps to maintain shareholder confidence. The government has an interest in seeing that occupational schemes continue to have a wide coverage, thereby reducing the cost of direct state provision. It is calling on pension fund trustees to take on a more active governance role as investors in listed companies, and to address the agenda developing around socially responsible investment practices. For all of these reasons, there is a strong policy case for strengthening private-sector, employer-based pension schemes. Yet, this is happening at a time when the defined benefit option is in retreat as a result of a combination of regulatory and financial constraints, coupled with a less hospitable investment climate. The effectiveness of pension fund governance can be enhanced in ways which help trustees to deal with these

25 See Chapters 5 and 7, above.
26 See Chapter 4, above.
27 See Chapters 11, 12 and 13 above.

multiple and often conflicting pressures, but the wider context will continue to put pressure on pension schemes and the future for this important institution remains unclear. A critical first step towards improved policy would be an up-to-date understanding of the internal workings of the pension scheme system, which this volume provides.

Index

accountability
  governance measures as to 15
  guidelines 15–16
  of trustees 72
accounting
  corporate perspective 259–60
  for deficit 293
  fair value approach 38
  solvency measurement 38–9
accounting objective of valuation 135
accounting valuations, legislative framework
  136
accrued rights, form of 104
act prudently, fiduciary duty of trustees to
  55–6
active ownership of assets, fiduciary duties of
  trustees 62–3
actuarial valuation
  accounting objective 135
  accounting valuations 136
  allowance for additional investment return
    148–9
  allowance for uncertainty 149
  chapter summary 134
  corporate perspective 259
  deficit correction 148
  discount rates as factor
    funding valuations 146–8
    generally 145
  documentation 150
  financial assumptions 144–8
  funding objective 134–5
  funding valuations
    discount rates as factor 146–8
    legislative framework 135–6

Guidance Notes 136
  investment return, allowance for additional
    148–9
  legislative framework 135–6
  meaning 134
  objectives 134–5
  price inflation as factor 144–5
  recovery period 148–9
  recovery plan 148
  return on investment, allowance for
    additional 148–9
  solvency objective 135
  solvency valuations see solvency valuations
  statutory objective 135
  summary of issues 150
  uncertainty, allowance for 149
actuaries, regulatory requirements as to
    appointment 22
administration
  administration team
    accountability 170, 172
    conflicts of interests 172
    culture and values 171
    effectiveness 170
    organisation and management 171
    responsibilities 155
    staff level requirement 170–1
    staff turnover management 170
    and stakeholders 172
    training 171
    and trustees 172
  complaints log, example (Table 10.2) 168
  data management
    audits 165
    DC unit prices 165

administration (*cont.*)
  electronic data management (EDM)
    161–2
  external agency data 166
  interface data, payroll and human
    resources 165
  online services for members 165
  quality 164
  security 164–5
general remarks 151
good practice, features 151–2
and human resources 165
insourcing
  advantages/disadvantages (Table 10.1)
    156
  use 156
operational risk management
  see operational risk management
outsourcing
  advantages/disadvantages (Table 10.1) 156
  contract review 160
  due diligence 160
  implementation 161
  invitation to tender (ITT) 159–60
  market 158
  oversight 158
  process 158
  project planning 158
  request for information (RFI) 159–60
  selection of provider 158
  shortlisting of suppliers 159
  strategy 156
  tendering process 160
and payroll 165
pensions management team's
  responsibilities 155
performance 153, 166–7
performance measures 167–8
processes 161–2
and regulatory bodies 165
reporting process 163
responsibilities 153
risks relevant to (Table) 169–70
service levels
  service level agreement (SLA) 167
  setting 166–7
sponsoring employer's responsibilities 154
straight through processing (STP) 166

strategy
  insourcing v outsourcing 156
  reasons for review 156
  review, issues 156
trustees' responsibilities
  generally 153
  interaction with administration team 172
workflow 161–2
agents, alignment of goals with investment
  governance 181
annual report and accounts, regulatory
  requirements 22
asset allocation (Table 3.5) 44
asset and liability breakdown report
  (Tables 12.1 and 12.2) 194–7
  use 194
asset-backed securities, corporate perspective
  262–3
asset classes, investment in alternative 42–4
asset returns (Table 3.4) 43
assets
  deficit risk analysis 194
  measurement and risk, corporate
    perspective 250–5
associations
  governance structure 8–9
  legal form 3
attribution of risk
  longevity risk (Figure) 207–8
  risk management 194–7
  Value-at-Risk (VaR) measure 194–7
auditors, regulatory requirements as to
  appointment 22
Australia
  governance structures 9
  mandatory provision 4
  trustees, licensing of 14
Austria, governance structures 8–9

balance sheet, company (Figures 15.1 and
  15.2) 246, 251
basis risk, use 219
beneficial ownership of equity investment
  (Table 3.1) 30
best interests of beneficiaries, trustees' duty
  towards 53–5
best practice, investment governance 181
bonds *see* investment

buy-ins
  advantages 229–30
  description (Figure 14.2) 229
  post-purchase procedures 244
  purchase of 237–9
  risk management 228–31
  use, longevity risk 216–17
  variations 230–1
buy-outs
  defined benefit (DB) schemes 294
  description (Figure 14.3) 231
  post-purchase procedures 244
  purchase of 236–7
  settlement of liabilities 232
  use, longevity risk 216–17

capital markets see investment
chapter summaries 1–2
closed funds, fiduciary role of trustees 7
closure of schemes 45–6
codes of practice see also guidelines
  good trusteeship 83–4
  operational risk management 168
Committee for European Insurance and
    Occupational Pensions Supervisors
    (CEIOPS) 6
common law as to conflicts of
    interests 85
communication practices, defined contribution
    schemes 285–6
commutation, solvency valuations 143
company law, regulation via 3
compensation practices in investment
    governance 184
competence and expertise see also trustee
    knowledge and understanding (TKU)
  assessment requirement 14
  investment governance 270–1
  regulatory requirements, strengthening 14
competitive advantage
  from best practice 185
  and risk budgeting 179
complaints log, example (Table 10.2) 168
confidential information and conflicts of
    interests 98–9, 102
confidentiality, and conflicts of interests 87
confidentiality agreements 99–100
conflicted trustee

excusal from relevant discussions/decisions
    93
  resignation 93
conflicts of interests
  administration team 172
  adviser perspective see professional
    advisers
  avoidance, statutory obligation 88–9
  common law as to 85
  confidentiality 87
  conflicted trustee see conflicted trustee
  duty/duty conflict
    exceptions to principle 87
    legal framework 87
  employer perspective see employers
  general remarks 85
  guidelines on handling 10–11, 24
  legal challenges and remedies 87
  legal framework 85
  management of
    conflicted trustee see conflicted trustee
    general remarks 91
    guidelines 91–2
    independent trustee, appointment 94
    policies for 92–3
    regulatory principles 91–2
    steps to 92–3
    by sub-committees 93
  professional adviser perspective
    see professional advisers
  self-interest conflict
    exceptions to principle 86
    legal framework 86
  summary of issues 103
  trustee perspective see trustees
consultations as to pension rights variation
    109–11
consumers
  of defined contribution (DC) schemes,
    characteristics 270
  members as 267–9
contract law, regulation via 3
contract review, outsourcing contracts 160
contractual provision
  governance structures 9
  occupational provision distinguished 6
  open funds, fiduciary role of trustees 7
  responsibilities and accountability 287

corporate perspective
    accounting 259–60
    actuarial valuation 259
    asset-backed securities 262–3
    assets, measurement and risk 250–5
    balance sheet (Figures 15.1 and 15.2) 246,
        251
    EBITDA, use 250–5
    general remarks 246
    liabilities (Figure) 254
        management checklist 248–50
        management generally 248
        measurement and risk 250–5
    main areas 246
    pension fund risk
        example 256–9
        management plan (Figure) 257
        measurement 255–6
        Value-at-Risk analysis (Figure) 258
    professional advisers, working with 260–1
    summary of issues 263–4
    taxation 260–1
    trustees, working with 260–1
corporate sponsor see employer sponsorship
corporation tax policy 292
corporations (providers), governance structure
    8–9
covenant risk analysis 132–3
credit default swaps, use (Figure 12.10) 204

data management see administration
data requirements as to solvency valuations
    137–8
death, longevity risk 208–10
decision-making
    factors for effective 180
    in real time 185
deficit accounting 293
deficit correction, actuarial valuation 148
deficit risk analysis, use 194
defined benefit (DB) schemes
    buy-outs 294
    corporate perspective see corporate
        perspective
    data quality 164
    disappearing surpluses, reasons for 38
    investment governance see investment
        governance

investment management, defined
    contribution schemes distinguished
        265
    origins 290
    regulation, strengthening 21
    risk-management approach generally 7
    shareholder perspective 294
    withdrawal of provision 293
defined contribution (DC) schemes
    consumer characteristics 270
    guidelines 13
    investment governance
        accountability 287
        behaviour monitoring 277
        behavioural and attitudinal characteristics
            271–2
        benefit design and objectives 287
        communication 285–6
        consumer-driven approach 267–9
        context 282–3
        engagement 285–6
        financial understanding, level of 270–1
        and investment architecture 278–82
        knowledge and skills 270–1
        labelling of options 286–7
        membership perspective 269–70
        nature of schemes 267–9
        objective setting 274–6
        performance monitoring 277–8
        processes 277
        responsibilities 287
        summary of issues 287–8
        switching 283–5
    investment management
        chapter summary 265
        default options 265–6
        defined benefit schemes distinguished
            265
        design 265–6
        responsibilities 266
    mandatory provision 5
    membership
        behaviour monitoring 277
        inertia 273–4
        mental accounting 272–3
        observed behaviour 274
        pinning, attitude towards 272–3
        risk appetite 271–2

socio-demographic characteristics 274
risk management approach generally 7
unit prices, data management 165
delta ladder (Figure 12.1) 189
use 188
Denmark, governance structures 8–9
Department of Work and Pensions
(DWP) as regulator 20
dependant's benefits, solvency
valuations 143
deterministic liability rate analysis
(Figures 12.2 and 12.3) 189, 190–1
director as trustee
conflicts of interest 89–90, 95
nomination 69–71
statutory duty 54
disclosure duty
and conflicts of interests 100
regulatory requirements 22
discount rates *see* actuarial valuation
dismissal and re-hire route for pension rights
variation 109
dispute resolution, regulatory requirements
23
distressed company, trustees' responsibilities
122, 130–1
due diligence, outsourcing contracts 160
duty/duty conflict
exceptions to principle 87
legal framework 87

Eastern Europe, mandatory provision 5
EBITDA, use 250–5
emerging markets *see* longevity risk
employees
consent to pension rights variation 108
termination of employment
see employment, termination
wrongful dismissal, pension rights variation
117
employer covenant
assessment
analytical framework 124
key factors 125–6
risk management 132
business environment as assessment factor
127
capital structure as assessment factor 126

corporate structure as assessment factor
125–6
financial performance as assessment factor
126
guidelines 24
insolvency position as assessment factor
126–7
monitoring, proactive approach 131–2
strategic issues as assessment factor 127
employer default risk, approach generally 7
employer sponsorship
administration responsibilities 154
corporate events, responses to 129–31
covenant *see* employer covenant
detriment, mitigation for 130
distressed company 122, 130–1
general remarks 119
and insolvency 126–7, 293
miscellaneous issues 131–2
mitigation for detriment due to corporate
event 130
and pension scheme
relationship 120
relationship (Figure) 119–33
scheme as creditor 120–1
and professional advisers 123–4, 133
questions asked 122
restructuring company 130–1
risk analysis 132–3
sponsor's relationships with owners and
lenders 119–20
summary of issues 133
support for trustees 80
trustee involvement *see* trustees
employers
and conflicts of interests
background 94
confidential information 98–9
confidentiality agreements 99–100
director as trustee 95
disclosure duty 100
fiduciary duties as trustee 95–6
finance director's role 97
key events 100
negotiations, conduct generally 97
statutory authorisation of conflict 95–6
trust deed and rules, authorisation
clauses 96

employers' interests, trustees' duty towards
75
employment, termination, pension rights
variation
general remarks 113–15
simplified loss approach 115–16
substantial loss approach 117
wrongful dismissal 117
employment consultation as to rights variation
111
employment law, regulation via 3
equities *see* investment
equity beneficial ownership (Table 3.1) 30
European Union (EU)
CEIOPS 6
IORP Directive 5
Three-pillar model *see* three-pillar model of
pension provision
executive function, separation in investment
governance 183–4
expenses of scheme, solvency valuations 144
Express Variation Clause, use 107–8
external agency data, management of 166

fair value accounting 38
fiduciary duties of trustees
act prudently, duty to 55–6
acting for proper purpose of trust 53
acting in best interests of beneficiaries
53–5
active ownership of assets 62–3
conflicts of interests, director as trustee
95–6
duties generally 50–2
general remarks 48–9
governance structures 9–10
historical origins 48–9
organic nature 56
recent developments 56
reform proposals 64–5
as to regulation and supervision 7
report on 53, 58–9
responsible investment principles
see Principles of Responsible
Investment (PRI)
summary of issues 63–6
weaknesses 10–11
finance directors and conflicts of interest 97

financial products used in longevity risk
transfer 221–2
Financial Services Authority (FSA)
CEIOPS representation 6
as regulator 21
Finland, governance structures 8–9
fit and proper requirements *see* competence
and expertise
foundations
governance structure 8–9
legal form 3
Freshfields Report on fiduciary duties of
trustees 53, 58–9
FTSE 100, pension risk attribution
(Figure 13.1) 207–8
funding *see* actuarial valuation
funding valuations
discount rates as factor 146–8
legislative changes 135–6
legislative framework 135–6
trust deed requirements 136

Germany
corporate schemes development 31
governance structures 8–9
governing body/board, accountability 15
governance *see also* investment governance
basic goal 7
body *see* governing body/board
categorisation 289
general remarks 26–7
good governance
aims 8
defined 7
focus 10
general application 67
research on 173–4
results 295
guidelines 10–13
and investment practice 295
problems 10
regulation 10, 17–20, 292
research on
contribution to 290
level of 289–90
structures 8, 17–20
supervision generally 13
of trustees, improvements 67

governance budget
  development challenge areas 180
  principles 180
  resources 180
governing body/board
  accountability 15
  assessment requirement 14
  competence and expertise 13, 184
  composition 69–71
  corporate and individual structures
    distinguished 68–9
  degree of delegation by, factors 78
  guidelines 10–11, 12
  operation 69–71
  role 8
  selection 184
  status 8–9
  structure 68
  weaknesses 11
guidelines *see also* codes of practice
  actuarial valuation 136
  adviser conflicts 102
  conflicts of interests 91–2
  governance 10–13, 24
  internal controls 15–16

hedging
  investment risk *see* investment risk
  longevity risk 217–18
Her Majesty's Revenue & Customs (HMRC)
  as regulator 20
Hong Kong, governing body/board
  accountability 15
human resources and scheme administration
  165
Hungary, governance structures 8–9

Iceland, mandatory provision 4
implied consent for pension rights variation
  108–9
independent trustees
  appointment 94
  generally 80–1
inflation rate (Figure 12.8) 200
inflation risk hedging (Figure 12.11) 204
innovation issues as to investment governance
  181, 185
insolvency

and employer sponsorship 126–7, 293
and investment 38–9
insourcing of scheme administration 156
institutional funds, governance structure 8–9
insurance
  additional security 243–4
  administration timeline (Figure 14.7) 244
  best price 242
  buy-ins *see* buy-ins
  buy-outs *see* buy-outs
  capital supply 226–7
  certainty, achievement 242
  comparison 241–2
  demand 225–6
  development of market 224
  growth factors 225–6
  lines 224–5
  market growth (Figure) 227
  post-purchase procedures 244
  price comparison 241–2
  pricing 226, 233, 242
  pricing factors 235
  process 239–41
  quotation process (Figure 14.6) 241
  reasons for use 224
  regulation 232–3
  and risk management 228–31
  risk model (Figure 14.5) 234
  summary of issues 244–5
  supply of capital 226–7
  terms of comparison 241–2
interest rates (Figure) 199
internal controls
  guidelines 12–13, 16, 24–5, 169–70
  regulation and supervision 15–16
  regulatory requirements 22
International Organisation of Pension
    Supervisors (IOPS), role and work 13
investment
  alternative asset classes 42–4
  asset allocation (Table 3.5) 44
  asset returns (Table 3.4) 43
  bonds 34–7
  during bull market 31–4
  equity beneficial ownership (Table 3.1) 30
  equity net investment (Table 3.3) 40
  financial provision for 31
  gap in markets 46–7

investment (*cont.*)
  governance *see* investment governance
  and insolvency 38–9
  during instability 37
  knowledge and skills 270–1
  liabilities 34–7
  long-term investment 28–9
  and pension scheme closures 45–6
  pension schemes as actors 291–2
  post-war environment 29
  Principles *see* Principles of Responsible
    Investment (PRI); Statement of
    Investment Principles (SIP)
  reassessment of equities 39–41
  return on assets (Table 3.4) 43
  risk *see* investment risk
  risk capital 41–2
  statistics (Tables) 30
  strategy (Table) 35–6
investment beliefs, importance of strong 179,
  183
investment governance
  accountability 287
  agents, alignment of goals with 181
  as basis of good decision-making 180
  behaviour monitoring 277
  behavioural and attitudinal characteristics
    271–2
  benefit design and objectives 287
  best practice 181
  board selection and competence 184
  chapter summary 174
  communication 285–6
  compensation practices 184
  competitive advantage 179, 185
  consumer-driven approach 267–9
  context 282–3
  decision-making in real time 185
  defined contribution schemes *see* defined
    contribution (DC) schemes
  engagement 285–6
  executive function, separation 183–4
  financial understanding, level of 270–1
  governance budget *see* governance budget
  innovation issues 181, 185
  and investment architecture 278–82
  investment beliefs 179, 183
  knowledge and skills 270–1

  labelling of options 286–7
  leadership issues 182
  managers, quality of 183–4
  membership perspective 269–70
  mission clarity 181, 182
  Myners Principles 176
  objective setting 274–6
  performance monitoring 277–8
  processes 277
  responsibilities 287
  risk budgeting 176–80, 183
  risk-budgeting method (Figure 11.2)
    177
  risk-management issues as to governance
    budget 180
  risk sharing 179
  summary of issues 185
  switching 283–5
  time issues 181, 183
  trustees' responsibilities 174
  value creation drivers 179
investment practice, governance influence
  295
investment return, allowance for additional
  148–9
investment risk
  analysis *see* risk analysis
  focus 7
  general remarks 187–8
  management 44–5
  reasons for taking 178–9
  value creation drivers 179
IORP Directive
  compliance 21
  standards 5
Ireland
  governance structures 9
  mandatory provision 4
Italy, governance structures 8–9

Japan, governance structures 8–9

Kite chart
  (Figures 12.2 and 12.3) 189, 190–1
  use 189
knowledge *see* competence and expertise;
    trustee knowledge and understanding
    (TKU)

Latin America, mandatory provision 5
leadership issues as to investment governance 182
leaving service rates, solvency valuations 142
liabilities
    corporate perspective *see* corporate perspective
    deficit risk analysis 194
    measurement and risk (Figure) 254
    settlement, buy-outs 232
liability, trustees' 81–3
liability breakdown report
    (Tables 12.1 and 12.2) 194–7
    use 194
liability driven investing (LDI)
    risk management 197–206
    swaps, use (Figure) 204
liability profile
    decay factor (Figure 12.5) 194
    (Figures) 191, 194
    use 190–1
liability rate analysis (Figures 12.2 and 12.3) 189, 190–1
licensing, regulatory requirements 14
longevity insurance, risk management 228–31
longevity risk
    approach generally 7, 210–11
    attribution of risk (Figure 13.2) 207–8
    and death 208–10
    forecasting 213–14
    future developments 221–2
    general remarks 207–8
    scheme management 211
    summary of issues 222
    swaps (Figure 13.2) 218
    transfer solutions 221–2
    transfer to emerging markets
        basis risk 219
        buy-outs and buy-ins 216–17
        collateral 219–20
        contract structure 218
        coverage 218–19
        further protection 220
        future proofing 220
        general remarks 214–16
        hedging 217–18
        price structure 219–20
        tail risk 219

underlying risk 212
Luxembourg, governing body/board
    accountability 15

management team, administration responsibilities 155
managers, quality of 183–4
mandatory provision
    national policies 4, 5
    stringency of regulation 5
members *see also* consumers
    assumptions, solvency valuations 140
    behaviour monitoring 277
    behavioural and attitudinal characteristics 271–2
    as consumers 267–9
    online data services 165
    relationship with scheme 120
    trustees as, conflicts of interests 89
    trustees' duty towards 74–5
Mexico, internal controls supervision 16
Micro Factor Analysis (MFA) *see* risk analysis
mission clarity and investment governance 181, 182
mortality assumptions as to solvency valuations
    post-retirement 141
    pre-retirement 141
Myners Principles of investment governance 176

national policies on mandatory provision 4, 5
Netherlands
    alternative asset classes, investment in 45
    governance structures 8–9
    governing body/board
        accountability 15
        assessment requirement 14
New Zealand, mandatory provision 4
Norway
    fiduciary role of trustees 62
    governance structures 8–9
    mandatory provision 4

occupational pensions
    accrued rights, form of 104
    closed funds, fiduciary role of trustees 7
    deficit accounting 293

occupational pensions (*cont.*)
governance *see* governance
and insurance *see* insurance
provision
book reserves 3
contractual provision distinguished 6
regulation, approaches to 3
taxation 292
OECD
guidelines 10–13, 15–16, 51
Recommendation 10
taxonomy 3
three-pillar model *see* three-pillar model of
pension provision
online data services for members 165
open funds, fiduciary role of trustees 7
operational risk management
actions 169–70
code of practice 168
focus 7
identifying risk 168
internal controls guidance 169–70
statutory requirement 168–9
outsourcing *see* administration

payroll and scheme administration 165
pension consultation as to rights variation
109–11
pension fund governance *see* governance
pension funds
administration, guidelines on quality and
standards 24
assets, meaning distinguished from
provider 3
associations *see* associations
bank account, regulatory requirements 22
corporations (providers), governance
structure 8–9
disclosure *see* disclosure duty
dispute resolution, regulatory requirements
23
foundations *see* foundations
institutional funds, governance structure 8–9
internal controls *see* internal controls
investment *see* investment
legal form, types 3
professional advisers *see* professional
advisers

provider, meaning distinguished from assets
3
as risk capital providers 41–2
trust *see* trust-based provision
pension increases, solvency valuations 143
pension plan, meaning 3
Pension Protection Fund (PPF)
levy, solvency valuations 144
as regulator 20
pension provider, meaning 3
pension rights, variation
consultation obligations
employment consultation 111
general remarks 109
other potential obligations 111
overlap 111
pension consultation 109–11
dismissal and re-hire 109
employees' consent 108
Express Variation Clause 107–8
general remarks 106
implied consent 108–9
methods 107
miscellaneous commercial matters 113
termination of employment
see employment, termination
pension schemes
actuarial valuation *see* actuarial valuation
administration *see* administration
as capital market actors 291–2
closure 45–6
corporate perspective *see* corporate
perspective
as creditors
characteristics 120–1
overview 120–1
employer sponsorship *see* employer
sponsorship
in employment package
general remarks 104
termination of employment
see employment, termination
variation of rights *see* pension rights,
variation
expenses, solvency valuations 144
funding *see* actuarial valuation
insolvency 293
key relationships (Figure 8.1) 119

meaning 3
members, relationship with 120
real yield, example (Figure 12.9) 202
risk model (Figure) 233 *see also* risk
    management
sponsor *see* employer sponsorship
valuation *see* actuarial valuation
winding-up, governance during, regulatory
    requirements 25
pensions
    defined benefit *see* defined benefit (DB)
        schemes
    defined contribution *see* defined
        contribution (DC) schemes
    occupational pensions *see* occupational
        pensions
    private pensions *see* private pensions
    public pensions *see* public pensions
    three-pillar model *see* three-pillar model of
        pension provision
Pensions Advisory Service (TPAS) as
    regulator 21
pensions management team, administration
    responsibilities 155
Pensions Ombudsman
    as regulator 21
    remit 72
Pensions Regulator (TPR) 91
    CEIOPS representation 6
    Code of Practice 83–4
    guidelines
        adviser conflicts 102
        conflicts of interest 91–2
    as regulator 20–1
    supervision by 23
    trustee knowledge and understanding,
        guidance as to 72
performance *see* administration
Poland, governance structures 8–9
portfolio stress test (Figure 12.7) 197–206
Principles of Responsible Investment (PRI)
    adoption 56
    overview 59–62
private pensions
    development 3
    mandatory provision, national policies 4, 5
    provision types distinguished 6
professional advisers

appointment, regulatory requirements 22
and conflicts of interests
    acting for employees and trustees,
        practice 103
    confidential information 102
    general remarks 100
    identifying conflicts 101–2
    regulator's guidance 102
    corporate perspective 260–1
    and employer sponsorship 123–4, 133
    relations with, guidelines 24
    support for trustees 78
proper purpose of trust, trustees' duty towards
    53
prudence, trustees' duty to act with 55–6
prudent person principle
    definition 55–6
    introduction 7
    and trustees' duties 71
public pensions reform 5
public policy
    mandatory provision 4
    regulation *see* regulation

real-time decision-making 185
recovery period, actuarial valuation
    148–9
Recovery Plan requirement 150
regulation *see also* supervision
    approaches to 3
    chapter summary 3
    conceptual framework 3
    development of 3
    focus 6
    of governance 10, 17–20
    risk based *see* risk management
    and scheme administration 165
    self-regulation *see* fiduciary duties of
        trustees
    solutions 10–11
    standards 5
    stringency 5
reporting process 163
resignation of conflicted trustee 93
responsible investment principles, fiduciary
    duties of trustees 59–62
retail price index (RPI), use 144–5
retirement rates, solvency valuations 142

return on investment, allowance for additional
148–9
risk analysis
delta ladder *see* delta ladder
general remarks 188
Kite chart *see* Kite chart
liability profile *see* liability profile
risk budgeting
framework, best practice 183
issues 176–80
method (Figure 11.2) 177
tolerance factors 178
risk capital, pension funds as providers 41–2
risk management
approach generally 7
asset and liability breakdown report
see asset and liability breakdown
report
attribution of risk 194–7
attribution report (Figure 12.6) 194–7
basis risk 219
corporate perspective 255–6
deficit risk analysis *see* deficit risk analysis
delta ladder *see* delta ladder
employer default risk *see* employer default
risk
employer sponsorship 132–3
and governance budget 180
hedging *see* hedging
inflation risk hedging (Figure 12.11) 205
and insurance 228–31
internal controls *see* internal controls
investment *see* investment risk
investment risk *see* investment risk
Kite chart *see* Kite chart
liability driven investing (LDI) *see* liability
driven investing (LDI)
liability profile *see* liability profile
liability rate analysis *see* liability rate
analysis
longevity risk *see* longevity risk
operational risk *see* operational risk
plan progression (Figure 15.4) 257
portfolio stress test (Figure 12.7) 197–206
prudent person principle *see* prudent person
principle
and scheme administration 168
sharing of risk 179

solvency risk *see* solvency risk
swaps, use (Figure 13.2) 204, 218
tail risk 219
and trustee knowledge and understanding
(TKU) 8

salary increases, solvency valuations 142
Schedule of Contributions, requirement
150
securities, asset-backed, corporate perspective
262–3
self-interest conflict
exceptions to principle 86
legal framework 86
self regulation/supervision *see* fiduciary duties
of trustees
senior employees as trustees, conflicts of
interests 90–1
service levels *see* administration
shareholder perspective on defined benefit
schemes 294
simplified loss approach to pension rights
variation 115–16
skills *see* competence and expertise
solvency objective of valuation 135
solvency risk, focus on 7
solvency valuations
accounting approaches 38–9
assumptions 139
commutation 143
data requirements 137–8
dependant's benefits 143
expenses of scheme 144
leaving service rates 142
legislative framework 136
members' assumptions 140
method 138–9
mortality assumptions
generally 140–1
post-retirement 141
pre-retirement 141
pension increases 143
Pension Protection Fund levy 144
process 138
responsibilities 136
retirement rates 142
salary increases 142
Spain, governance structures 9

sponsoring employer *see* employer
    sponsorship
stakeholders
    and administration team 172
    fragmentation of stakeholder constituencies
        125
    relationships within employer sponsorship
        119–20
    trustees as representatives, conflicts of
        interests 91
    trustees' duty towards 74
Statement of Funding Principles, requirement
    150
Statement of Investment Principles (SIP)
    content 175
    regulatory requirements 22
statistics on investment (Tables) 30
straight through processing (STP), use 166
sub-committees, management of conflicts of
    interests by 93
substantial loss approach to pension rights
    variation 117
supervision *see also* regulation
    authorities *see* supervisory authorities
    chapter summary 3
    conceptual framework 3
    development of 3
    focus 6
    of governance 13, 17–20
    risk based *see* risk management
    self-supervision *see* fiduciary duties of
        trustees
supervisory authorities
    categories of governance 17
    establishment 5
    governance of 16
    UK *see* Financial Services Authority (FSA);
        Pensions Regulator (TPR)
swaps, use (Figures) 204, 218
Sweden, mandatory provision 4
Switzerland
    governance structures 8–9
    mandatory provision 4

tail risk, use 219
taxation
    corporate perspective 260–1
    policy 292

taxonomy 3
tendering for outsourcing *see* administration
termination of employment *see* employment,
    termination
three-pillar model of pension provision
    components 3–4
    recommendations 4
time issues as to investment governance 181,
    183, 185
tolerance factors for risk budgeting 178
trust-based provision
    governance structure 9
    responsibilities and accountability 287
    weaknesses 10–11
trust deed and rules
    authorisation clauses 96
    statutory requirements 136
trust law, regulation via 3
trustee knowledge and understanding (TKU)
    as to duties and responsibilities generally
        71
    regulation, strengthening 22
    regulatory requirements 23
    risk management and 8
    weaknesses 10–11
trustees *see also* conflicted trustee;
        independent trustees
    accountability 72
    and administration *see* administration
    boards *see* governing body/board
    Code of Practice 83–4
    composition, regulatory requirements 21
    conflicts of interests
        duty/duty conflict 89–90
        general remarks 88–9
        self-interest conflict 89
    corporate perspective 260–1
    detriment, mitigation for 130
    directors as, conflicts of interests 89–90
    and distressed company 122, 130–1
    duties generally 71 *see also* fiduciary duties
        of trustees
    and employer sponsorship
        corporate events, responses to 129–31
        financial distress responsibilities 122
        need for engagement 122
        new model 127–9
        support for trustees' position 131

trustees (*cont.*)
  employers' interests, duty towards 75
  fiduciary role *see* fiduciary duties of
    trustees
  governance, improvements 67
  independence 80–1
  investment governance responsibilities 174
  key issues 76–8
  liability 81–3
  licensing of, regulatory requirements 14
  meeting minutes, regulatory requirements 22
  as members, conflicts of interests 89
  members' interests, duty towards 74–5
  mitigation for detriment due to corporate
    event 130
  of other schemes, conflicts of interests 91
  persons barred, regulatory requirements 22
  professional advisers
    proactive relationship 133
    support from 78
  and prudent person principle 71
  questions to sponsors 122
  resources 175, 180
  and restructuring company 130–1
  senior employees as, conflicts of interests
    90–1
  sponsoring employer, support from 80
  as stakeholder representatives, conflicts of
    interests 91
  stakeholders' interests, duty towards 74
  summary of issues 83
  support for 78, 131
  voting, regulatory requirements 22

unit prices for defined contribution schemes,
  data management 165
United Kingdom (UK)
  advisory service *see* Pensions Advisory
    Service (TPAS)
  CEIOPS representation 6
  equity beneficial ownership (Table 3.1) 30
  governance
    general remarks 27
    regulation and supervision of 17–20

regulatory bodies 20
  regulatory context 17–20
  structures 9
  investment strategy (Table 3.2) 35–6
  IORP Directive compliance 21
  mandatory provision 4
  occupational pensions governance 21
  Ombudsman *see* Pensions Ombudsman
  regulatory and supervisory bodies
    see Department of Work and Pensions
    (DWP); Financial Services Authority
    (FSA); Her Majesty's Revenue &
    Customs (HMRC); Pensions Regulator
    (TPR)
United States (US)
  alternative asset classes, investment in 42–4
  fiduciary role of trustees 50–2
  fund investment value 48–9
  governance structures 9–10
  safe-harbour rules 27

valuation *see* actuarial valuation
Value-at-Risk (VaR) measure
  asset and liability breakdown report
    see asset and liability breakdown
    report
  attribution of risk 194–7
  calibration 192
  confidence level 193
  critiques 192
  decay factor (Figure 12.5) 193
    use 193
  deficit risk analysis 194
  models 192
  pension fund risk (Figure 15.5) 258
  use 190–1, 255–6, 258
value creation drivers 179

winding-up, governance during, regulatory
  requirements 25
workflow process, use 161–2
World Bank recommendations 5
wrongful dismissal, pension rights variation
  117